THE BESHT

THE BESHT

Magician, Mystic, and Leader

Immanuel Etkes

TRANSLATED BY SAADYA STERNBERG

Brandeis University Press

WALTHAM, MASSACHUSETTS

Published by University Press of New England

HANOVER AND LONDON

BRANDEIS UNIVERSITY PRESS

Published by University Press of New England,
One Court Street, Lebanon, NH 03766
www.upne.com

Originally published in Hebrew as *Baal Hashem: HaBesht—
Magyah, Mistikah, Hanhagah* by The Zalman Shazar Center for
Jewish History, Jerusalem, 2000

This book was published with the generous support of the Lucius
N. Littauer Foundation, Inc.

Library of Congress Cataloging-in-Publication Data

Etkes, I.
    [Baal hashem : haBesht—magyah, mistikah, hanhagah. English]
    The Besht : magician, mystic, and leader / Immanuel Etkes ;
translated by Saadya Sternberg.—1st ed.
        p.   cm.—(Tauber Institute for the Study of European Jewry
series)
    Includes bibliographical references and index.
    ISBN 1-58465-422-8 (cloth : alk. paper)
    1. Ba'al Shem UTov, ca. 1700-1760. 2. Magic, Jewish. 3. Mysti-
cism—Judaism. 4. Leadership—Religious aspects—Judaism. I.
Title. II. Series.
    BM755.18E8413 2004
    296.8'332'092—dc22   2004019243

THE TAUBER INSTITUTE FOR THE STUDY OF EUROPEAN JEWRY SERIES

Jehuda Reinharz, General Editor
Sylvia Fuks Fried, Associate Editor

The Tauber Institute for the Study of European Jewry, established by a gift to Brandeis University from Dr. Laszlo N. Tauber, is dedicated to the memory of the victims of Nazi persecutions between 1933 and 1945. The Institute seeks to study the history and culture of European Jewry in the modern period. The Institute has a special interest in studying the causes, nature, and consequences of the European Jewish catastrophe within the contexts of modern European diplomatic, intellectual, political, and social history.

Gerhard L. Weinberg, 1981
World in the Balance: Behind the Scenes of World War II

Richard Cobb, 1983
French and Germans, Germans and French: A Personal Interpretation of France under Two Occupations, 1914–1918/1940–1944

Eberhard Jäckel, 1984
Hitler in History

Frances Malino and Bernard Wasserstein, editors, 1985
The Jews in Modern France

Jehuda Reinharz and Walter Schatzberg, editors, 1985
The Jewish Response to German Culture: From the Enlightenment to the Second World War

Jacob Katz, 1986
The Darker Side of Genius: Richard Wagner's Anti-Semitism

Jehuda Reinharz, editor, 1987
Living with Antisemitism: Modern Jewish Responses

Michael R. Marrus, 1987
The Holocaust in History

Paul Mendes-Flohr, editor, 1987
The Philosophy of Franz Rosenzweig

Joan G. Roland, 1989
Jews in British India: Identity in a Colonial Era

Yisrael Gutman, Ezra Mendelsohn, Jehuda Reinharz, and Chone Shmeruk, editors, 1989
The Jews of Poland Between Two World Wars

Shmuel Almog, Jehuda Reinharz, and Anita Shapira, editors, 1998
Zionism and Religion

Ben Halpern and Jehuda Reinharz, 2000
Zionism and the Creation of a New Society

Walter Laqueur, 2001
Generation Exodus: The Fate of Young Jewish Refugees from Nazi Germany

Yigal Schwartz, 2001
Aharon Appelfeld: From Individual Lament to Tribal Eternity

Renée Poznanski, 2001
Jews in France during World War II

Jehuda Reinharz, 2001
Chaim Weizmann: The Making of a Zionist Leader

Jehuda Reinharz, 2001
Chaim Weizmann: The Making of a Statesman

ChaeRan Y. Freeze, 2002
Jewish Marriage and Divorce in Imperial Russia

Mark A. Raider and Miriam B. Raider-Roth, editors, 2002
The Plough Woman: Records of the Pioneer Women of Palestine

Ezra Mendelsohn, 2002
Painting a People: Maurycy Gottlieb and Jewish Art

Alan Mintz, editor, 2002
Reading Hebrew Literature: Critical Discussions of Six Modern Texts

Haim Be'er 2002
The Pure Element of Time

Yehudit Hendel, 2002
Small Change: A Collection of Stories

Thomas C. Hubka, 2003
Resplendent Synagogue: Architecture and Worship in an Eighteenth-Century Polish Community

Uzi Rebhun and Chaim I. Waxman, editors, 2003
Jews in Israel: Contemporary Social and Cultural Patterns

Gideon Shimoni, 2003
Community and Conscience: The Jews in Apartheid South Africa

Haim Be'er, 2004
Feathers

Iris Parush, 2004
Reading Jewish Women: Marginality and Modernization in Nineteenth-Century Eastern European Jewish Society

Avraham Grossman, 2004
Pious and Rebellious: Jewish Women in Medieval Europe

Immanuel Etkes, 2004
The Besht: Magician, Mystic, and Leader

Ivan Davidson Kalmar and Derek J. Penslar, editors, 2004
Orientalism and the Jews

To Rabbi Ben-Zion Gold

Contents

ACKNOWLEDGMENTS

This book was originally published in Hebrew by the Zalman Shazar Center for Jewish History in 2000. The work on the various chapters took several years, during which I had the generous support of institutions and individuals. I wish to express the gratitude I feel toward them. The initial stages of the research were conducted within the framework of the Institute for Advanced Studies of Hebrew University in 1994. I was at Harvard University during the academic year 1994–1995, and the warm welcome shown me there by the Center for Jewish Studies and the Center for the Study of World Religions permitted me to work steadily on this text and to make substantial progress with it. An important institution without which it is hard to imagine writing a book of this kind is the National Library in Jerusalem, and in particular its Gershom Scholem Library, whose storehouse of treasures and efficient staff deserve every praise.

Ada Rapoport-Albert and Israel Yuval read the manuscript and made acute and intelligent remarks that allowed me to improve it. David Assaf added important comments as well. My deepest thanks go to them.

While conducting research I was aided, at different times, by three of my students at Hebrew University who served as research assistants: Ronny Beer-Marks Rivka Feintoch, and Tamar Perl. Two other students helped me adjust the footnotes and bibliography for the English edition: Hanan Harif and Uriel Gelman. Hanan Harif also prepared the English index. I thank each of them for the dedication and responsibility they showed.

Special thanks go to Sylvia Fuks Fried, Director of Brandeis University's Tauber Institute, who accompanied the preparation of the English edition from its inception through all stages and contributed much of her experience and sensitivity to it.

Finally I wish to express my deep appreciation to Dr. Saadya Sternberg, who toiled over the English translation with great intelligence and grace.

The English edition of this book is dedicated to Rabbi Ben-Zion Gold in appreciation of many years of friendship and support.

Jerusalem, August 2004   Immanuel Etkes

THE BESHT

Introduction

W hy another book on the Besht, Rabbi Israel Baal Shem Tov? What does this book seek to add to all that has already been written and published on this topic? In response, I would like to point to certain developments in the scholarship of Hasidism that form the background and point of departure for the work presented here.

The historical treatment of the Besht has always been quite closely linked to the question of the origins of Hasidism. The prominent place that the Hasidic movement occupies in the history of the Jewish people in the modern period, and the fact that from its beginnings up to the present, Hasidism has named the Besht as its founding father, have made obvious the connection between the man and the movement. The question that has preoccupied the majority of scholars has thus been, What role did the Besht play in the emergence of Hasidism? This question was an issue both for those who believed that the Besht played a decisive part and for those who denied him any influence in this regard. The former sought to explain what it was about the Besht's personality, religious approach, and teachings that held so great a fascination for his followers; the latter sought to explain how the legend about the Besht as founder of Hasidism arose *ex nihilo*. The question of the link between the Besht and the emergence of Hasidism is at the heart of the present book as well.

In studies published in the first half of the twentieth century, Hasidism is described as a movement that from its earliest stages was manifestly populist in nature. Furthermore, Hasidism's populism was associated with dissent and rebellion against the religious and social elites. Hasidism purportedly gave vent to the distress of the simple Jew, who was suffering under the onus of strictures imposed upon him by the rabbinic establishment. Hasidism, for its part, supposedly championed the aspirations of the masses, those who were subject to the oppression and exploitation of a corrupt community leadership.

A long line of studies published since the late 1950s, however, has challenged the image of Hasidism as a popular movement that arose in revolt against the religious and communal establishment.[1] Today, scholars are in agreement that during its initial stages, the phenomenon of Hasidism was narrow in scope, centering around a new approach toward religion and spirituality. The transformation of Hasidism into a broad movement, embracing many from the popular classes as well, was thus a gradual process that occured over an extended period of time. Accordingly, a scholar wishing to tell the story of the emergence and spread of Hasidism must explore each and every stage in this

1

process independently. This book restricts its focus to the first stage of this process, the stage that relates to the figure of the Besht.

A further development of the scholarship, which is likewise part of the background of this book, has to do with the phenomenon of magic and its master practitioners, the *baalei shem*. The early scholarship of Hasidism took the point of view that magic is a debased attribute of society associated with the popular and uneducated social classes. The *baalei shem,* meanwhile, were seen as deceivers who preyed upon the ignorant masses. A few of the scholars who held this point of view had difficulty reconciling themselves to the fact that Rabbi Israel Baal Shem Tov, the man considered to be the founder of Hasidism, was by profession a *baal shem.* Hoping to overcome their difficulty, these scholars tended to downplay the element of the magical in the figure of the Besht or to deny its existence altogether.

Gershom Scholem came out strongly against this apologetic trend, declaring that not only did the Besht practice as a *baal shem* throughout his life, but that he was proud of his profession. Meanwhile, a major transformation has occurred in the appraisal of the place occupied by magic and *baalei shem* in the period in question. It has become clear that magic and its practitioners were phenomena accepted and respected by all classes of society. Moreover, because magic was identified with practical Kabbalah, and *baalei shem* with Kabbalic mastery, considerable prestige accrued to those who served as *baalei shem.* Accordingly, what is called for now is a thorough reassessment of the place of the magical in the figure of the Besht.

A discernible trend in scholarship of early Hasidism has been the attempt to identify this movement's innovations in the domains of religion and spirituality. Gershom Scholem had a substantial influence on this trend through his perspective on *dvekut* (literally, *communion*) a concept that in Kabbalist and Hasidic literature denotes a mystical experience. Scholem asserted that the key to understanding the innovation of Hasidism rests in how it revolutionized the concept of *dvekut.* Although Hasidism was not new in regarding *dvekut* as a religious ideal of paramount importance (in this, the Hasidim merely followed their predecessors, the Kabbalists) nevertheless, where the Kabbalists had treated *dvekut* as an ideal attainable only by the virtuous few, Hasidism came out and declared it to be a path available to each and every Jew. This radical shift regarding the "place" of *dvekut,* Scholem went on to argue, accounts for the transformation of Hasidism into a popular movement. The new movement appealed to the masses because it offered them spiritual opportunities that had previously been denied. This perspective on the place of *dvekut* in early Hasidism was adopted by several of Scholem's students, and it earned substantial currency within the scholarly literature.

Over the past three decades, however, certain of the scholars who arrived on the scene have challenged Scholem on this point. Yeshayah Tishbi, Gedaliah Nigal, Mendel Piekarz, Ada Rapoport-Albert, and others—all for their own reasons have rejected the notion that Hasidism transformed *dvekut* into a spiritual path that each and every Jew could access. This, however, takes us back to the question, What was the innovation in spirituality and religion that Hasidism made at its outset? Or more exactly, What was the Besht's contribution on the subject of *dvekut*? What was the novel approach that allowed the Besht to regard himself, and his followers and associates to treat him, as a pioneer in divine worship?

A further question in study of the emergence of Hasidism is that of sources. The Besht did not leave behind doctrinal writings of his own, and our knowledge of his ideas is drawn almost entirely from the works of his students. Much of our information about the Besht and the members of his circle derives from the collection of tales known as *Shivhei Habesht*, first published in 1814, some fifty-five years after the Besht's death. Yet the hagiographical nature of this collection (its association with the genre of stories told about holy men) and its saturation with miracles and marvels, have raised serious doubts about its credibility. The doubts about the credibility of the tales have only been added to by the circumstances of their collection and publication in book form, circumstances that suggest modifications may have been made to their content. Matters reached the point where some scholars even argued that the Besht never existed, but was entirely a figure of legend. In other words, the presentation of the Besht as the person who founded Hasidism has no basis in reality, and is merely a retrospective invention made by the movement's true founders and leaders in the 1760s and 1770s. Even those who would not go so far came to the conclusion that the sources available to us permit painting only the faintest and dimmest representation of the figure of the Besht.

Nevertheless, over recent decades, substantial developments have taken place on the question of the sources pertaining to the Besht in general and *Shivhei Habesht* in particular. An important milestone was the article by Gershom Scholem, "The Historical Figure of Rabbi Israel Baal Shem Tov." Scholem assembled all the independent sources about the Besht that he knew of, and drew inferences from them about certain tales in *Shivhei Habesht*. Using this compilation of materials he was able to sketch several of the Besht's salient characteristics. Other scholars, including Avraham Yaari, Khone Shmeruk, Avraham Rubinstein, Joseph Dan, Yehoshua Mondshine, Moshe Rosman, and Elhanan Reiner, carried forward with the scholarship of *Shivhei Habesht* and satisfactorily clarified questions pertaining to its composition, editing, and printing. Likewise elucidated was the link between the Hebrew original of *Shivhei Habesht* and its translation into Yiddish. An important development in this context was the discovery and identification of a manuscript version of *Shivhei Habesht,* a text whose accuracy is superior to that of the print edition. A facsimile of this manuscript version was published by Yehoshua Mondshine; while the manuscript encompasses not the entire book but only its substantial majority, it nevertheless suffices for resolving certain obscurities posed by the print edition. A further development has been Avraham Rubinstein's publication of a critical edition of *Shivhei Habesht.* This edition contains comparisons of the print to the manuscript version and numerous references elucidating the persons, places, and events mentioned in the book. Besides the studies focusing on *Shivhei Habesht* itself, some of the recently published scholarship has corroborated tales found in the book on the basis of external sources. Given all the above, I am persuaded that the historian who seeks to rely on *Shivhei Habesht* for a reconstruction of the life and character of the Besht can today tread upon firm ground.

An extremely valuable source of information about the Besht is the letter he wrote to his brother-in-law, R. Gershon of Kotov, in which the Besht gives a detailed report of an "ascent of the soul" he had experienced. This letter, known as the "Besht's Epistle," was first printed in the early 1780s and has been considered authentic ever since. Doubts about its authenticity were raised only after the discovery and publication of two manuscript versions of this Epistle, each of which has substantially different textual content. And, as if that were not enough, it turns out that both of the manuscript versions differ from the print edition. The presence of all these variant versions has made scholars wonder which, if any, represents the true version of the original Epistle. Now, Yehoshua Mondshine, who published one of the two manuscript versions, offered an elegant and persuasive solution to this conundrum. Mondshine proposed that the existence of two manuscript versions can be explained by the hypothesis that the Besht actually sent two different letters to his brother-in-law, while the print edition is a later amalgam of the two letters. Mondshine's reconstruction suggests that what has actually come down to us are two "Besht's Epistles" and that both are authentic. It is hard to understate the importance of the contribution these two letters make for our understanding of the internal world of the Besht.[2]

In this context, one must also mention the important discoveries made by Moshe Rosman during his research in the archives of the Czartoryski family, the family of Polish magnates on whose estates the town of Miedzybóz was situated. These findings shed light on the life of the Jews in the town of Miedzybóz, where the Besht resided between the years 1740 and 1760. Moreover, Rosman found archival records that mention the Besht himself and several of his associates. These documents complement and corroborate what we know about the Besht from other sources.[3]

In sum, if we combine the independent sources concerning the Besht, his letters (especially the two epistles he wrote to his brother-in-law), the numerous testimonies about him in *Shivhei Habesht,* and the numerous sermons attributed to him in the writings of his students, then we have a quite rich and diverse array of sources at hand, one that permits a detailed historical reconstruction of the figure of the Besht.

A milestone in scholarship of the Besht and of early Hasidism is Moshe Rosman's *Founder of Hasidism: A Quest for the Historical Ba'al Shem Tov* (1996). Certain chapters of Rosman's work contribute toward our understanding of the background of the Besht's life and work. Other chapters incisively and systematically examine the sources on which a biography of the Besht may be built. Based on all of these, Rosman offers a reconstruction of the Besht and his work, presenting him as a "person of his times." Although my research on the Besht commenced before Rosman's book was published, I freely admit that reading this book gave me an important incentive to complete and publish my own study. While there was much that I learned from the chapters dealing with the background of the life of the Besht, I found myself in considerable disagreement with Rosman's conclusions about the credibility of the source materials—*Shivhei Habesht* in particular. As a result, my own reconstruction of the Besht, as presented in this book, differs substantially from the one put forward by Rosman.[4] One hopes that the appearance, within so relatively short a time, of two books offering different points of view on the Besht may only inspire and enrich discussions of this topic.

As noted, the historical question that forms the basis of this book is that of the relation between the Besht and the beginnings of Hasidism. May—and how may—the Besht be regarded as the founder of Hasidism? This formulation must immediately be qualified; clearly the Besht did not found a movement in the organizational sense of the term, nor did the idea of doing such even occur to him. In fact, the Hasidic movement did not come into existence before the 1760s and 1770s; that is, well after the Besht's death in 1760. Accordingly, the question of whether the Besht was the "founder of Hasidism" must be formulated as follows: Can one point to aspects of the figure of the Besht— to his spiritual path, to his personality, and to his relations with his contemporaries—that sufficiently accounts for the phenomenon of Hasidism? May one discover, in retrospect, that the Besht set in motion a process that ultimately resulted in the launching of Hasidism as a movement?

To reveal the secret of the Baal Shem Tov's influence on his contemporaries (and through them on people in subsequent generations), I have distinguished among three of the Besht's roles, which may be regarded as three separate aspects of his figure or three different spheres of his activity. These are *baal shem*, public leader, and mystic. Accordingly the main questions discussed in this book are, What was special about the Besht as a *baal shem*, and how did this vocation play a role in the subsequent emergence of Hasidism? How did the Besht conceive of his mission as a public leader, and in what ways was this sense of public mission realized? What innovations in mysticism and spirituality are attributable to the Besht, and who were the people to whom he transmitted his new path in divine worship? What sort of entity was the "Besht's circle" of associates, and what role did this circle play in the emergence of Hasidism? I maintain that discussion of these questions throughout the book will lead to the conclusion that the Besht indeed deserves the title "Founder of Hasidism."

CHAPTER ONE

Magic and Miracle Workers in the Days of the Baal Shem Tov

Blocking the way forward for the historian who seeks to examine the place and role played by magic in the figure of the Baal Shem Tov, is the distorted picture of the *baalei shem* (the sorcerers or miracle workers) that has taken root within Hasidic historiography.[1] According to this conception, magic and its practitioners are contemptible phenomena inherently associated with the broad masses, the ignorant and superstitious public. This picture has its origins in the literature of the Jewish enlightenment movement—the Haskalah—which set itself the goal of banishing from Judaism's domains any semblance of belief or behavior it regarded as expressing superstition and ignorance. Pride of place in this campaign was assigned to the phenomena of magic and the *baalei shem*.[2]

Characteristic of the Haskalah literature's battles against magic and *baalei shem* was its identification of these with Hasidism and Hasidic leaders. This identification did much to serve the Haskalah's aims in its confrontation with Hasidism. To the maskilim of eastern Europe, Hasidism represented the very incarnation of all that was degraded and atrophied about traditional Jewish existence. Hasidism, furthermore, was seen as the chief obstacle in the path of the "proper reformation" of Jewish society. Given this perspective, the maskilim found it convenient to have Hasidism be associated with the ignorant masses, who wallowed in beliefs about demons and spirits and the powers of incantations and amulets. The maskilim found it equally convenient to have the leaders of Hasidism be closely associated with the *baalei shem,* who deceived and preyed upon the simple people for their private gain.[3]

Under the influence of the Haskalah literature, the conception of the *baalei shem* as inferior and contemptible beings made its way into Hasidic historiography as well. It thus comes as no surprise that even those scholars who were sympathetic to the Hasidic movement (at least in its early stages) felt themselves obliged to clear the Besht of the disgraceful stain of having been a *baal shem.*[4] This trend in the scholarship was sharply condemned by Gershom Scholem. Scholem cited evidence that left no room for doubt that the Besht indeed plied his clients and supplicants with amulets, and in this respect was no different from the other *baalei shem.*[5] Yet with the Besht now liberated from the chains of rationalistic apologetics—which had struggled to decouple the founder of Hasidism from the remainder of the *baalei shem*—the time has come to liberate these other *baalei shem* as well from the loathsome reputation imposed upon them by the authors of the Haskalah and the historians who followed their lead.[6]

It is not my purpose here to discuss the evolution and status of magic in Jewish society in earlier generations.[7] I do not, consequently, intend to compare the salient characteristics of Jewish magic to those that were to be found in the surrounding society. These issues deserve treatment by themselves. The purpose of this chapter is, as said, to present a more balanced picture of the status and role of magic and *baalei shem* in Jewish society in and around the time of the Besht. This picture will then serve as a background and framework for my examination of the magical underpinnings of the world of the Besht and the origins of Hasidism.

Magic in the Lives and Perspectives of Contemporaries

The phenomenon of the *baalei shem* in seventeenth- and eighteenth-century central and eastern Europe must be understood, first and foremost, against the background of the beliefs and ideas then prevailing as regards the demonic powers and their ability to affect the fates of mortals. This general background was universal: it was unlimited by the bounds of geography, religion, and nationality. Naturally there were discernible differences between the demonologies of Jews and Christians, just as there were differences in texture and emphasis between the different regions and across the different periods. The common factor linking all these systems of belief, whatever their differences of degree or kind, was the supposition that demonic powers have a vast potential for impairing the health and welfare of human beings. As if that did not suffice, it was further believed that magical means could be used to mobilize these demonic powers and press them into the service of humans.[8]

What were the demonological beliefs and opinions that prevailed among central and eastern European Jews in the seventeenth and eighteenth centuries? What sort of afflictions led the common people to turn to magical measures in general and *baalei shem* in particular for relief? In order to respond to these questions, at least in part, we shall first consider the *sifrei segulot,* the books of "spells" or "charms" that were printed and circulated in the period in question.[9]

The world of the people of those times was saturated with demons and specters, evil spirits, and acts of witchcraft. That demons were invisible to mere mortals, and had a deep-seated propensity to wander about and injure

human beings, made them horrifying. This hazard intensified in those periods, places, and circumstances in which demons grew especially active. Thus,
for example, the night hours were thought to be a time when demons left their
hiding places and set out to attack human beings. Evil spirits too were especially active at night. Accordingly, it was best not to travel the highways by
night, and anyone who could not avoid such travel had best take precautions
and prophylactic measures:

> If a man should take to the road at night and see what appears to be
> a candle jumping from side to side what is called in Yiddish *Farfir
> Lichter,*[10] these are spirits and their nature is to lead [the traveler]
> astray and one must thrice recite the verse "And the Lord spoke unto
> Satan" [Job 2:2].[11]

The most important events in the cycle of human existence—birth, death,
and marriage—were also thought to be occasions on which the demonic
powers posed grave dangers. In their quest to attack humans at their weak-
est, demons would prey upon newborn infants or upon the corpses of the
recently deceased. Worst was their assault upon the tender newborn: demons,
typically Mahlat and Lilith, as well as witches, were liable to carry out "body-
replacement."[12] The concept of "replacing" (*banemen* in Yiddish) refers to the
snatching of an infant's body: in place of the infant the snatchers leave a sort
of doll in the cradle made of straw and grist. A picturesque story indicative
of contemporary perspectives on this topic is cited in *Toldot Adam.* The tale
is as follows:

> This happened in the days of the Kabbalist rabbi the master (etc.)
> R. Eliyahu of righteous memory, rabbi of the holy community of
> Chelm. In the adjacent hamlet there was a man by the name of R.
> Gabriel whose wife gave him birth to a son. And he sent word to the
> holy community of Chelm to have the *baal shem* come to perform a
> circumcision on the boy, for the rabbi there was a recognized circum-
> ciser. And the name of the hamlet was Galinck. And the event
> occurred in the month of Sivan on a Thursday. And R. Eliyahu set out
> from his town before nightfall toward the town of Galinck and arrived
> during the night at the town center of Galinck. And he beheld sorcer-
> esses and male witches more than a hundred thousand, and from the
> mouths of all spouted fire and flames, and around them too a blaze
> raged, while they played with a newborn infant. And when the rabbi
> saw these goings on he told his boy valet to pass him water from his
> pitcher. And he cleansed himself with the water and uttered the Great
> and Almighty Name. . . . And he spoke as follows: I hereby break the
> spell cast upon these women and men without injury to the infant by

the worthy and powerful mercy of the Holy Name and worthy *Tal-macha Hishapam Aamashba Zzi Hon Abzug.* . . . Blessed be the Name of His Holiness for ever and ever. . . . This great and courageous and powerful and capable Name can even break a spell made a thousand years ago for its secret is fathomless. . . . And with this Name our master and rabbi R. Eliyahu Baal Shem slew all the witches and came and retrieved the boy and brought him to his father and mother. And when he brought him to them he uttered the Holy Name *Shimshiyahu* and immediately all who were present beheld that the object which had been laying by the mother was merely straw and grist and had only seemed to take human form and he handed the boy delivered from the fire of the *qlipot* back to his mother.[13]

R. Eliyahu Baal Shem, the rabbi of Chelm, "performed marvelously" by recovering the stolen infant for his father and mother. Yet more commonly the parents of a tender newborn would do everything in their power to prevent such a disaster from befalling them in the first place. Indeed, they had various means at their disposal to accomplish this, including amulets, charms, and incantations, each of which was designed to protect the baby from the depradations of demons and witches.[14]

Nuptial relations and childbirth were further occasions for calamity. Phenomenon such as male impotence and female infertility were interpreted as the effects of witchcraft. The prevalent term for someone who was impotent was "one who is blocked from *tashmish*"; that is, someone whose ability to perform conjugal relations has been obstructed by witchcraft. Often this was a bridegroom fresh from his wedding, who had already been set upon by the witches. The wide variety of magical means available to husbands suffering from such spells is an indication of how common and serious this affliction was. And here is one example of a charm to break a spell of this kind: "For one to whom *tashmish* is blocked, take a sword which had slain a man in the same year, and take a red apple and cut it in two with said sword and give one half to him and one to her at dawn on Tuesday and on Friday let the deed be done."[15]

The phenomenon of infertility, considered by the concepts of the time to be a functional failure on the woman's part, also secured for itself a wide range of antidotes, mostly charms and some amulets as well. The common factor linking all these antidotes was their power to break the spell suppressing the fecundity of the woman.[16] Besides barrenness, the demonic forces were to blame for a long line of malfunctions and mishaps associated with childbirth and the health of the mother during labor. Accordingly, a wide range of magical means were contrived to assist the mother through a difficult labor, to secure her health in childbirth, to prevent miscarriage, and so forth.[17]

Generally speaking, demons tend to inhabit remote or abandoned areas, minimizing their contact with mortals. Travelers on the highways, however, who find themselves in remote regions, risk confrontations with them. Thus, passage through forests known to be possessed by demons is presumed to be perilous. At times demons even enter homes and play havoc with their inhabitants. Especially grave perils are associated with newly built residences. Consequently,

> whosoever builds a new house and yard, lest he come to any bodily harm he must write the great name *Adiriron Adiron* on a deerskin and place it on the door of each and every room. And it is best to write this on a Sunday or a Thursday or a Friday. And he must drill a hole and place the same in the doorway both from above and from the side.[18]

As noted, the threat of demons invading the home is particularly severe when the house is of recent construction. Yet demons may at times gain a foothold in older houses as well. A case in point is the story cited in *Kav Hayashar*.

> In the year 1681 and 1682 [. . .] there was one house built of stone which stood in the main street of the holy community of Poznan, the cellar of which was sealed shut so that no one could enter the cellar. One day, a youth broke into the cellar and some quarter of an hour later the household's inhabitants found this youth laying on the sill of the cellar dead and the cause of death was unknown. And some two years after the death of said youth, Outsiders [demons] came in to the hallway of the homeowner and when those in the house were preparing food to cook on the stove they found in the pots, mixed in with the food, so much ashes and dust that the food was inedible. And afterward the hand of the Outsiders greatly strengthened to the point where they began to enter even the area of the house where the people were living and would take the household implements and the lamps hanging in the rooms for decoration and throw the implements and the lamps on the floor. But they injured no one and only baffled the people living there. And a great outcry ensued in the holy community of Poznan. And the community gathered to take counsel and debate what and how to act and they sought the aid of two Jesuit priests yet these could do nothing to banish the Outsiders. And afterward they sent a special messenger to find the most famous *baal shem* of the era called our master [etc.] Yoel Baal Shem of the holy community of Zamosc. And behold, no sooner did the rabbi our master Yoel of blessed memory arrive that he made [the Outsiders] take oaths by the names of the Holy Ones to tell him the cause for which they had come to this house which is a residence for human

beings, as Outsiders have no right to live in domesticated areas but only in wastelands or in the desert. And they replied that this house was owned by them entirely by law, and the Outsiders agreed to come to the court of Justice in the holy community of Poznan.[19]

In the course of the debate in court, the "Outsiders" sought to present their case that their stake to the house was entirely legitimate. Their claim rested on an event that had occurred a generation beforehand, when the same house had been occupied by a Jewish goldsmith. This goldsmith, although he had a wife and children, had been seduced by a she-demon who had revealed herself to him as a beautiful woman and by whom he had several children. When this bizarre tryst came to light, the wife of the goldsmith appealed to Rabbi Shabtai Sheftel Horowitz, seeking his aid. The rabbi inscribed an amulet that forced the goldsmith to abandon the she-demon. Nevertheless, when the goldsmith was near death the she-demon returned and seduced him into deeding the cellar in the house to her and her offspring as a gift. Consequently, argued the demons, they were the legal occupants of the home. The human tenants made three arguments in rebuttal. First, they had purchased the home from the heirs of the goldsmith making payment in full. Second, the she-demon had forced the goldsmith into having relations with her. Third, demons are not of human seed and hence residential rights do not apply to them. The court found for the human tenants, and R. Yoel Baal Shem swore the demons to an oath that they would never return to the house—the cellar included.[20]

This tale sheds light on contemporary perspectives as regards the mutual relations between demons and mortals. Demons too live and behave within the framework of laws and regulations. Their penetration of a human residence was not an arbitrary, unfounded act. Consequently, a human must beware of granting a demon any sort of grounds or excuse to cause injury to himself or to his family members. In the case at hand, it is entirely clear that the goldsmith was at fault for having allowed himself to be seduced by the she-demon. Indeed, the author of *Kav Hayashar* draws the necessary moral from this tale: "Therefore a man ought to distance himself from promiscuity so as not to attract a she-demon in the image of a woman and hence (heaven forbid) attach to himself or his seed a malevolent factor."[21]

Even when demons do infiltrate a house occupied by mortals, coexistence is possible so long as habitat zones are clearly demarcated. In the case at hand, the Outsiders settled for the cellar given to them by the goldsmith and initially did not stray from it. Only when their zone was trespassed upon by the youth who broke into the cellar did they cause trouble for the residents of the house. It follows that an abandoned and destitute site, even if adjacent to a human domicile, may serve as an abode for ghosts and one is well advised to steer clear of it. Once their zone of jurisdiction has been transgressed upon by mortals, demons are liable to employ a wide variety of techniques to cause fear and mayhem. Indeed, even such relatively slight damage as spoiling food or breaking utensils suffices to cause the inhabitants to flee their residence. These slight assaults serve as indications of the intent and capacity of the demons to escalate their battle.

An assault on one residence causes fears and panic to spread through the entire community. In their quest to exorcise the demons, the inhabitants of Poznan do not shrink from turning to priests for assistance. This fact accords with the prevailing belief that non-Jews too had effective means of magic available. The priests, moreover, are locals who may be summoned without delay. Only once the priests prove ineffective is a special messenger sent to Zamosc to summon R. Yoel Baal Shem. Upon arrival, R. Yoel demonstrates that the means at his disposal (i.e., sacred names drawn from an esoteric Jewish tradition) are superior to the magical methods the priests were able to deploy.

Thus far, I have been addressing the role assigned to magical methods in the battle against the demonic powers. Yet these means were also of potential service in all that concerns hardships and mishaps of human origin. Thus, for example, a house can be protected from thieves through the use of *shmirot;* that is, amulets one places in certain locations around the house. Moreover, there are even charms and incantations with the power to locate thieves and to cause stolen goods to be returned to their rightful owners.[22]

Especially grave dangers, as noted, attend those who travel the highways: chiefly merchants and peddlers, who must frequently pass from place to place and are exposed to attacks by robbers and "haters" of other kinds. It is thus unsurprising that those who travel frequently have a wide variety of amulets, incantations, and charms available for their safety.[23] Here are a few examples: "If a man should encounter a robber, heaven forbid, he must place the fourth finger of his left hand in his mouth and recite at the moment of danger *Isputan Zeira;* so he must say thrice. So that the sword does not overcome him, heaven forbid, he must recite seven times at the moment of danger in a whisper *Tosersof* which is a great thing."[24] And if the majority of charms and amulets were designed to prevent encounters with bandits or to rescue those who do encounter them, the traveler on the highway had a much more potent and astonishing means of defense at his disposal: "Here is a great secret for the highway traveler to see and not be seen by any enemy or hater or ambusher or bandit or robber. It is tried and tested. And I tried it by the aid of God several times in a place where there were mortal dangers and it was effective and a wondrous thing."[25] This charm is attributed to Nachmanides and it is based on the recital of certain verses in a fixed order.

Still another realm in which human limitations could be transcended by magic was the divination of secrets or future events. Typically, the questions divined involved a person's future state: Will this mortally ill person ever rise to his feet again? Will a disappeared husband, who has left his wife an *aguna* (unmarriagable because not definitively widowed) ever reappear? Will a certain business decision turn out for the best? Is the woman's barrenness the fault of the man or the woman? and so forth. And, as if these were not enough, there was also a charm that allowed a man to see paradise while still alive.[26]

As I have noted, magical methods served a critical function in everything having to do with the maintenance of physical and spiritual health. Such methods were used side by side with natural medicaments. Absent a means of determining whether a particular malady had its origins in natural or demonic powers, the people of the period thought it best to apply natural medicines along with the charms and amulets.[27]

The Topic of Magic in *Yesh Manhilin*

The beliefs thus far surveyed about magic and its applications were by no means exclusive to the broad masses. Such opinions were no less prevalent among the scholarly and privileged classes. Indeed, magical knowledge was apparently conserved within the scholarly and rabbinic circles, which transmitted the information from generation to generation and even made use of it as required. A valuable source on this topic, that sheds light on the place of magic in the life of a rabbinical family, is the book *Yesh Manhilin*, by R. Pinchas Katzenelbogen.[28]

R. Pinchas was born in Dubnow, in 1691, to a prestigious family that had held rabbinical office in Poland and Germany for generations. R. Pinchas's father, R. Moshe Katzenelbogen, served in the rabbinate of Podhjce in eastern Galicia. In the year 1699, the blood-libel issued in that town resulted in R. Moshe's arrest. A year later he obtained his release from prison and fled to Fürth; subsequently he served as rabbi in several German communities. R. Pinchas first held rabbinical office in Wallerstein in southern Germany in 1719. Over the years he served as the rabbi of Markbreit, likewise in southern Germany, and as the rabbi of the communities of Leipnik and Boskowitz in Moravia.[29]

R. Pinchas composed *Yesh Manhilin* between 1758 and 1764, as a testament to his sons, taking the book *Yesh Nohalin* by R. Shabtai Sheftel Horowitz as his model.[30] So as to instruct his sons in moral ways, much of the material R. Pinchas included in his book concerned the family's history and especially his own life. The author's predilection for detailed and revelatory accounts make *Yesh Manhilin* a treasure-house of data about the rabbinical elite in Ashkenazi society at the turn of the seventeenth and the first half of the eighteenth centuries. For the purposes of my inquiry, his book is an extremely important resource, providing as it does a contemporary and concrete account of the prevailing stance toward magic among the rabbinical class.

When turning to the topic of Names, R. Pinchas begins by stressing how dangerous they are. To that end, he cites the testament left by his grandfather, R. Shaul Katzenelbogen, who "commanded his sons who succeeded him not to get involved with Holy Names." So as to convey a sense of the extremity of the hazards, R. Pinchas tells of an event he heard about from his uncle when visiting him in Prague. This was one of several "marvels" the author heard from his uncle about the latter's father-in-law, described as "a Kabbalist, a pure man of God," who also dealt in practical Kabbalah. The event he relates is as follows:

> Once, during the night, he told his boy valet: go to my room and bring me the book that lies on the table, but beware and watch with the utmost care that you do not open said book in the slightest and do not glance into it to peruse it in the least. And the valet went off and in his innocence thought the matter amusing. . . . And he said to himself: what is this great warning our Holy Rabbi has warned me of, what could possibly happen if I opened the book. . . . And in his folly he went and opened said book and saw written in it several Names. . . . Instantly he went mad and a spirit of insanity entered him. . . . And all at once that room filled with malevolents, heaven protect us. . . . And only after our Holy Rabbi employed devious strategies and his noble intellect and the Names of the Holy was he able to exorcise said Outsiders from said room and was he able to purify it. . . . All except that boy valet to whom the dybbuk adhered. . . . For the boy valet was so haunted by the malevolents, heaven protect us, that he verily could not find peace in any place.[31]

R. Pinchas does not content himself with merely reporting this frightful event; he cites various texts that prove the dangers of involvement with Names. He quotes a passage from *Sefer Hasidim:* "Malevolents do not adhere except to those who are involved in them, e.g., one who himself or his fathers writes amulets or practices oath-taking." Similarly, the author cites Menahem Azariah of Pano, who in *Asis Rimonim* says that when "knowledge of the interactions of the worlds and how each is derived from the other is lacking, knowledge of the power of Names is lost." Accordingly, invocation of Holy Names, when not grounded in a proper comprehension of the secrets of the worlds, is liable to lead to disastrous consequences.[32]

The evidence from the literary sources is rounded out and confirmed by the experiences of R. Pinchas himself: "And I, minor figure though I be, know and am witness. . . . I am myself acquainted with *baalei shem* who deal in Names in these very times, and know that the vast majority of them do not come away unscathed: some have themselves been injured, others have shortened their days, others still have not been graced with sons." The cases cited by the author as concrete illustrations include two famous *baalei shem* of his day: R. Naftali Katz and R. Yoel Baal Shem (the second).[33]

Given his statements about the dangers inherent in using Holy Names, and given the proof-texts and evidence drawn both from books and current events, one might think R. Pinchas would have avoided the use of Names altogether. Not so! Later on, R. Pinchas builds an elaborate case to justify involvement in Names in spite of it all. In the first stage of this case, he speaks admiringly about his father who had mastered the writings of the ARI (Rabbi Itzchak Ashkenazi Luria [1534–1572], the most prominent Kabbalist of sixteenth-century Safed) including also the Holy Names in those writings. R. Pinchas explains that his father did not shrink from study of the Holy Names as he distinguished between learning Names for the sake of inscribing them and study, the sole aim of which was to "comprehend and instruct."[34]

It would thus seem at first glance that the border the author's father draws on the issue of involvement with Names is that which divides scholarly pursuits (which are permissible) from practical magic (which had best be avoided). Yet later on, R. Pinchas has a surprise for us. He relates that he discovered in a notebook of his father's, in the latter's very own handwriting, a charm for the improvement of memory based on an incantation made out of Holy Names. From this R. Pinchas infers that despite his father's urgings in his will, he himself did not abstain from the use of Names. Moreover, R. Pinchas defends his father with the somewhat opaque clause: "and he had his own motives and reasons."[35] Nor was this the sum total of the father's involvement with Names. R. Pinchas goes on to disclose that in the very same notebook, on the very same page he found the following:

> A wonderful charm for a boy or a girl who has been struck by the falling sickness so long as it had not happened three times. Make yourself a ring of pure silver and write on its inverse side, before it has been rounded, the following names using the cursive style of the Torah scribes: *Agla Agaf Apalon Apimin.* And later round it and dip the ring and hang it on the infant. This is tried and tested. And I heard this from the learned rabbinical master Rabbi Zvi Hirsch son of the Gaon Rabbi Shmuel Kaidanover.[36]

The very fact that the author's father found cause to enter into his notebook details about the charm obtained from R. Zvi Hirsch Kaidanover, makes one suspect that he made use of it, or at least does not rule out the possibility he would do so. Yet on this point I need not rely on conjecture. Later in his book, R. Pinchas tells of an event that occurred in his youth and sheds light on the father's involvement in Names. The gist of the tale is as follows: When the author was about twelve years old, R. Zvi Hirsch Kaidanover, author of *Kav Hayashar,* visited his father's home.[37] Obeying R. Zvi Hirsch's guidelines, the father instructed that two bands of silver be prepared and that Names be inscribed on them. Afterward he ordered that the two bands be bent into rings. One of these two rings, the one that wards off nocturnal emissions, was intended for his son; and indeed as a youth R. Pinchas had worn the ring on his hand.

Many years later, R. Pinchas chanced upon the other ring. Yet meanwhile R. Pinchas' father had passed away and he himself had forgotten the purpose of the second ring. When, in his father's notebook, he discovered the instructions for preparing a ring against epilepsy, he realized that the reference was to the ring he had found among his father's possessions. Once he became aware of this ring's qualities, he made a gift of it to his son, and even showed him the passage mentioning it in his father's notebook. The son copied the lines out for himself.

Now R. Pinchas was baffled. Why didn't his father's notebook contain the instructions for preparing the first ring too, the one that protects against nocturnal emissions? Trying to resolve this mystery, it occurred to him that as the two rings had been prepared to R. Zvi Hirsch Kaidanover's specifications, just possibly the topic of this ring might be mentioned in his book, *Kav Hayashar.* R. Pinchas closely examined the book and indeed discovered a detailed description there of the stage-by-stage preparation of the ring. This, consequently, was the reason his father hadn't taken the trouble to spell everything out in his own notebook. Nevertheless, R. Pinchas copied out the formula for preparing this ring too from *Kav Hayashar.* He explains his behavior as follows: "While the subject is treated in said book *Kav Hayashar,* this is not in reach of everyone, and I said to myself do not withhold the good from its owners with what comes to your hand to provide."[38]

This was not the sum total of the author's discoveries about his father's skills in the Names department. R. Pinchas goes on to quote from his father's notebook a "marvelous charm for nocturnal emissions." The author's father remarks in his notebook that this charm was sent to him by "the excellent justice the learned rabbi Hayim (may his Maker and Redeemer preserve him) of Burgkundstadt [of north Bavaria]." The fact that the same charm appears, with minor modifications, in *Amtahat Binyamin,* a book by the famous *baal shem* R. Binyamin Binush, is cited by R. Pinchas as conclusive evidence of his father's greatness. R. Pinchas also tells as an aside that he hosted this same R. Binyamin

Binush when serving a rabbi in the Wallerstein community, and that he heard "marvels" from R. Binush, that is, tales of his activities as a *baal shem*.[39]

At this stage, R. Pinchas confesses: "And I myself never dealt in practical Kabbalah, and never performed a single deed on the basis of Holy Names." The background to this admission is an event from R. Pinchas's life: In 1720, a *baal shem* from Jerusalem by the name of R. Yosef visited his home. As this event took place just after the death of his first wife, R. Pinchas asked the guest, who was also adept in the arts of palmistry and phrenology, to apply his skills to divine the identity of his future wife. R. Yosef did not disappoint. He presaged that R. Pinchas was destined to earn a "honorable match of the daughter of great ones by whose hand I shall increase (God willing) and shall have plentiful income." On this same occasion, the *baal shem* revealed to R. Pinchas a charm with the power to overpower witches who slay tender newborns:

> As it chances sometimes that female witches slay children, which by
> our sins happens quite often, therefore let the injured child be taken
> and carried to the edges of a fountain of fresh water which is encased
> in surrounding stones, and scrape the injured child's gums against the
> upper lip of the stone casement of the fountain until blood runs from
> them. By doing so the injury will attack the selfsame witch so that she
> will no longer be able to do harm.[40]

R. Pinchas goes on to say that a year later, while serving as a rabbi in Leipnik, several infants perished and he hadn't the slightest doubt that the cause was witchcraft. Accordingly, he invited the "town elders—men learned, God-fearing, and virtuous," told them of the charm received from R. Yosef Baal Shem, suggested that they now were in position to have a "clear demonstration" of the *baal shem*'s powers, and asked: "Which man is it who will choose bravely [or: from among you] to perform a deed such as this done by said *baal shem*?" Unhappily, none of the people present took up his challenge. And as to himself, R. Pinchas explains in an apologetic tone, "it was beyond my honor to take action myself. Furthermore, I had always been fainthearted and had not the heart to drag said child." One gathers from the tone of these statements that R. Pinchas felt genuine regret that no one would fight the witches using the charm received from R. Yosef Baal Shem.[41]

R. Pinchas's assertion that he never employed charms is not the final word on the subject. Later on he qualifies this claim and admits: "except in one matter, which I have from the Kabbalist our master and rabbi R. Binyamin Binush, the author of *Amtahat Binyamin*, some charm for a woman who has a difficult labor, it has been several times tried and tested and has been shown effective by the grace of God." Later in the text the author tells in detail how and why he was able to lay hands on this charm and what uses he made of it. He begins

with the topic of the curse given to biblical Eve, "in sorrow shalt thou bring
forth children," and points out that "not all women are equal in this regard;
there are some who give birth in misery and while others do so in comfort." Is
there a way of knowing in advance which women will have a difficult labor and
which an easy one? Indeed there is: in *Toldot Adam Vehochmat Haparzuf Vesirtutei Yadayim* [The history of man and the arts of phrenology and palmistry],
by R. Moshe Galina,[42] it is explained that the relevant mark is the length of the
wife's palm; the longer the palm, the wider the aperture through which the
newborn must exit. Accordingly, a woman whose palm is shorter is likely to
suffer more during childbirth than one whose palm is longer. The reliability
of this indicator was demonstrated to the author by personal experience. He
checked and discovered that the palm of his late first wife had indeed been
short, and she had indeed suffered greatly during the delivery of her two
daughters. The third child emerged stillborn, and the wife took ill and died
several weeks later. Although this woman's difficult labor was due to natural
causes, R. Pinchas had no doubt as to why she died: "And it was obvious that
the Gentile midwife (cursed be her name) put a spell on her relentlessly attack-
ing her until she died in misery."

After the death of R. Pinchas's wife, R. Binyamin Binush came to visit him
in his home. R. Pinchas told R. Binyamin that during his wife's difficult labor
he had tried to ease the delivery using charms he had found in *Amtahat
Binyamin,* but to no avail. Accordingly, he was in need of a different charm in
this department. R. Binyamin gave him "two things." The first was a set of
Names, which were to be tied to the woman's belly button during childbirth
via a linen sheet. R. Pinchas explains in detail precisely how one must tie the
talisman to the woman's body, and warns that it is to be promptly removed
when the newborn begins to emerge; otherwise there is a danger that the
mother's internal organs too will be drawn from their place.[43]

The second method for easing a difficult childbirth that the author received
from R. Binyamin Binush is "little notes in his very own handwriting written
in Assyriac and they are as follows: *Agla Alfa Ahtza Azha Avik Yekutiel Tutiel
Hutziel Mikael Rahmiel Rahashiel."* The author explains how one must attach
these slips of paper to the forehead of the woman during childbirth. Later he
tells of the use he made of these names:

> And this technique I tested several times when I resided in the com-
> munity of Leipnik as well as in Markbreit on several women and it
> was effective. And when I came here to the community of Boskowitz
> I forgot about it. Once my spouse the *Rabbanit* may she live came and
> told me I know that you have Names which could be effective for a
> difficult labor, and we have here a woman who has been in labor for

one or two days now and she is in danger, hurry go bring the names and give them to me and we'll take them to her, maybe you can help by God's grace. And I labored and hastened and searched and found it, and inscribed it for her, and by the grace of God it aided her. Immediately they took effect and the newborn emerged alive and healthy by God's grace and by His Great Name. And from that day onward all women who are in need of it when they are due come to me and I give it to them and it has been effective each time by God's grace.[44]

R. Pinchas goes on to relate that he went to the trouble of instructing the delivering mothers that they must remove the Names as soon as the baby is out. In addition, he requested that they return the Names to him when they were done. Yet not all of them bothered to return his Names and some of the slips grew crumpled from overuse. He therefore turned to a man who had mastered Assyrian script and instructed him to write these names out on a sheet of foolscap. R. Pinchas contentedly notes that the new Names he prepared "are as effective by God's grace as the originals."[45]

Another episode illustrating the use R. Pinchas and his family members made of magic involved the illness of his daughter. We learn of it from a letter R. Pinchas received from his daughter, a widow living in Prague, that he copied into his book. In her letter, the daughter complains that she has been suffering from fever for fifteen months now. She has tried all sorts of medicines recommended by physicians, including the physician R. Zalman of Prague, to no avail. Even the various charms she tried had no effect. She therefore begs her father to pray on her behalf. Moreover, she asks her brother to go to Vienna and consult with expert doctors there who might have a cure for her ailment.[46]

Consequent to his daughter's entreaties, R. Pinchas conducted research and inquired of his relatives and acquaintances whether they knew of a charm against fever. Sure enough, R. Pinchas's son-in-law discovered in the manuscript of his grandfather—Rabbi Aryeh Yehuda Leib, who in years past had been the rabbi of Boskowitz—a precise description of a charm against fever. As was his custom, the author copied the details of this charm into his book:

> For those who suffer from fever heaven forbid: Purchase a pot with a lid paying the full price demanded by the seller. And pour into the pot seeds of beans and recite the following: *Nit Einz, Nit Zwei*, etc., up to seventy-seven. Afterward the owner of the pot should urinate into the pot onto the beans, and afterward he should coat the pot in soft plaster around it so that the coat adheres to the pot, and afterward bury the pot with the coating and all its contents deep in the ground in a place that no man shall walk over. . . . And this is tried and tested by the grace of God.

R. Pinchas did not rest content with the charm his son-in-law had found. He also prescribed a second charm for her, one he had heard about from "a certain woman" whose husband, suffering from fever, had found as an effective remedy. Yet the story does not end here either. R. Pinchas went on to copy a charm for remedying toothache from the manuscript his son-in-law discovered, explaining: "and as this comes from my son-in-law's grandfather, the rabbi our master Aryeh Yehuda Leib, blessed be the memory of the righteous, [these charms] are deemed by me to be a heritage received from his Holy and great ancestors who dwell in the land; I therefore will not refrain from writing down something I saw and found there besides."[47]

Thus far I have been surveying the various manifestations of the attitude toward magic and *baalei shem* that appear in *Yesh Manhilin*. I now list several of the conclusions that may be drawn from this survey.

The worldview expressed in the book is consistent with the beliefs and ideas on the subject of magic described in the first section of this chapter. Generations of the Katzenelbogen family were convinced that demons and witches were behind many of the mishaps and maladies afflicting human existence. It is thus unsurprising that R. Moshe, the father of R. Pinchas Katzenelbogen, should have noted various charms in his notebook to be used as needed. Others of the family behaved likewise. R. Pinchas was to be commended for taking the trouble of transcribing into his notebook and testament every charm that he came across. By so doing he was able to conserve his accumulated magical information for the benefit of his surviving offspring. This was not an unusual pattern of behavior. In other rabbinical families too, magical knowledge was accumulated and transmitted from generation to generation. Thus, for example, we saw that R. Pinhas's son-in-law too discovered charms in the manuscript written by his scholarly grandfather.

The sources that R. Pinhas drew upon for his collection of Names and charms were rather diverse: they included members of the family, the books of charms in his possession[48] and the *baalei shem* who were his household guests. At times the magical information turned up by accident, as occurred when he found the entries in his father's notebook; and at times it was located on demand, the result of intensive research carried out for an urgent need. The fact that certain spells found in a charms book proved inefficacious did not deter R. Pinchas from requesting some other charm from the same *baal shem* who had authored the book.

The unquestioned faith in the powers of charms does not come with the corollary of a skepticism toward doctors and natural medications. R. Pinchas' daughter tried to treat her illness both by using "expert doctors" and by applying charms. Similarly, when the author's grandfather was on his deathbed, the family members sought to bring him to health using natural medicines. At the same time, however, the prevailing opinion in the family was that he took ill and died because of a demon.[49]

The charms that R. Pinhas and his father noted down were meant for "internal" use, that is, for use by the family. However, once a charm received from R. Binyamin Binush proved its efficacy, R. Pinhas began to offer it to every woman in his community who was experiencing difficulties in labor. This by itself did not suffice to render R. Pinhas a "*baal shem.*" R. Pinhas did not deem himself an authority on matters of charms and his activities in this field were limited. Nevertheless, one may perhaps characterize him as an intermediate figure, somewhere between a private user of charms and a *baal shem* who plies his spells to the public at large. R. Pinhas was not the only rabbi to put his knowledge from the realm of magic at the disposal of his community. In the story cited earlier about the goldsmith from Poznan, we found that R. Shabtai Sheftel Horowitz, the community rabbi, wrote a talisman to force the goldsmith to abandon the she-demon. Even if we suppose that this tale is legendary in one form or another, it is hard to imagine that the writing of an amulet would have been attributed to so dignified a personage if there was no factual basis to behavior of this kind. We have also found that R. Zvi Hirsch Kaidanover, the author of *Kav Hayashar,* practiced the art of amulet writing. R. Zvi Hirsch may not have served on the rabbinate, but he was a *talmid haham* (an erudite talmudic scholar) and a member of a prestigious rabbinical family.[50] In light of these examples, one may venture the assessment that rabbis with access to "tried and tested" magical information found it proper to apply such knowledge so as to assist people in distress. To be sure, rabbis were not the only sources of magical knowledge: doubtless common people too accumulated and transmitted information having to do with charms. It stands to reason, however, that the people of the period would have placed greater faith in charms deriving from authorized rabbinical figures.

R. Pinhas evidently came to be involved with Names chiefly on account of their practical utility. Yet other factors too seem to have motivated this involvement, such as a sense of self-worth and public prestige. The fact that R. Pinhas prided himself on his father's proficiency with Names suggests that he considered magical knowledge of this kind to be esoteric in nature. This attitude is plausible, given that R. Pinhas, like most of his contemporaries, considered magical knowledge to be a department of the Kabbalah. Indeed, R. Pinhas links his father's knowledge of the art of Names to his mastery of the tradition of the ARI. And if a scholar who has acquired a certain familiarity with Holy Names is to be lauded on that basis, how much more so are the *baalei shem,* whose knowledge and practical use of Names is unsurpassed. It was only natural, accordingly, for R. Pinchas to have hosted in his home the *baalei shem* who chanced upon the community where he served as rabbi, treating them with the utmost respect.

People in the Katzenelbogen family liked to hear tell of the deeds of demons and the battle against them. When describing the visits of the *baalei shem* in his home, R. Pinchas remarks that they related "marvelous things" to him. These were tales of the "marvels" and "performances" carried out in the course of combating the demonic forces. R. Pinchas himself cites at length the story his uncle told him about the boy who had been possessed by a dybbuk for having peeked in a book containing Holy Names. Elsewhere, R. Pinchas cites a story about a "malefactor" who took up residence near the *sukkah* in his grandfather's yard. This malefactor, so related R. Moshe Katzenelbogen to his son Pinchas, resided inside a chimney that was next to the *sukkah*. On the first night of Sukkoth, when R. Pinchas's grandmother made her way to the *sukkah,* she fell down and was severely injured. The grandmother accounted for her tumble as follows: "She felt as though someone had firmly grabbed her and pushed her off the stairs." This event caused considerable anxiety and apprehension among members of the family. The explanation of the grandmother's peculiar tumble came to light only years later, when R. Moshe Katzenelbogen learned and reported to the family about the "malefactor" living beside the *sukkah.* So as to remove all doubt that what had attacked the grandmother was indeed a malefactor, R. Moshe goes on to tell his son about several others who encountered the same spirit:

> And he said to me that the same servant Zekharia Katzav had told him, that he saw that malefactor residing in said place in the yard. And also I was told by my master father and rabbi, that the rabbi Gaon our master (etc.) Baruch Katz of blessed memory . . . used to sit in that same *sukkah* . . . and said malefactor revealed himself to him and came to him in the *sukkah* dressed in the customary Polish style and laughed at him saying: Hello there, rabbi. And said rabbi replied: Depart, unclean.[51]

What is the secret of the fascination such stories held for the Katzenelbogen family in particular and for the people of the period more generally? Two answers to this question suggest themselves. First, these tales and their like contain evidence for and confirmation of the beliefs and ideas that people of the time held about demons and spells. Second, the amazing and bizarre nature of these phenomena, the terrors associated with them, and the hope that despite everything the demonic powers can be bested—all perhaps account for why people were fascinated, their imaginations fired, and their souls sustained by stories of this kind. In addition, the fact that certain stories concerned family ancestors presumably aroused special curiosity amongst the descendants.

In concluding this discussion of the various manifestations of magic in *Yesh Manhilin,* I must comment on the sharp contradiction in R. Pinchas's stance about the use of Names. As mentioned, R. Pinchas begins his remarks on this topic by citing the will of his grandfather, R. Shaul Katzenelbogen, who forbade his sons to practice the art of Names. To that end, he gathered proofs from books and records of events to support the view that grave dangers are associated with the use of Names and consequently this realm is best avoided. How, then, is one to understand the fact that both R. Pinchas and his father did not avoid practicing the art of Names?

The severe reservations about the use of Names were backed by an ancient tradition. R. Pinchas himself quoted, as we noted, from *Sefer Hasidim.* The fact that magical knowledge was identified with Kabbalism presumably intensified the aura of the esoteric that had already long shrouded such knowledge and increased apprehensions about its use. And yet, counteracting these concerns and hesitations was the tremendous attraction of using charms and Names. This attraction was a function of the torment felt by those locked in the firm conviction that witches and demons were seeking to injure them and the equal certainty that the ill effects could be warded off through the correct use of charms and names. The case of R. Pinchas Katzenelbogen and his father R. Moshe illustrates how the attraction overcame the apprehension. It stands to reason that what was true of the Katzenelbogen family was true also for the many others who used Names and charms despite the severe admonitions against them.

This is not to say that in mentioning his grandfather's testament, and citing additional evidence about the hazards associated with Names, R. Pinchas was merely paying lip service to an ancient convention. A close and attentive reading of *Yesh Manhilin* leads to a different conclusion: that R. Pinchas was entirely serious about the hazards involved in applying Names. It is for that very reason that he so firmly insists on following the example of his father, who despite the prohibition prepared amulets and noted down the precise formulas of charms. With his father as model, R. Pinchas also permitted himself to engage in the use of Names. Far from taking the hazards lightly, he took pains to find how they may be circumvented. If this assessment is correct, I may offer one further conclusion: that the hazards attendant on the employment of Names intensified the fascination and mystery associated with them—which was already seen as marvelous in any case.

Baalei Shem and Books of Charms

Who were the carriers of the knowledge of magic? How was this knowledge used to benefit the people who needed it? We have seen that the scholarly elite was the class that conserved and disseminated information about magic. First and foremost, however, it was the *baalei shem* themselves who were acknowledged by the public as authorities on magical knowledge and as the people who could apply it when necessary. Who were the *baalei shem*? What social status did they occupy? Where did they draw their knowledge and authority from?

I lack the means of proposing definitive and exhaustive answers to these questions; the historical scholarship of the phenomena of the *baalei shem* is still in its infancy.[52] Nonetheless, I shall attempt to describe several characteristics of the *baalei shem* who practiced in central and eastern Europe at the end of the seventeenth and in the first half of the eighteenth centuries. This investigation will largely be based on the books of charms that were printed in this period. I begin this discussion by a survey of several figures who earned renown as *baalei shem* from the sixteenth through the eighteenth centuries.

R. Eliyahu b. R. Aharon Yehuda of Chelm

Born circa 1550 in the town of Chelm. Year of death unknown. Studied Torah at the yeshiva of R. Shlomo Luria in Lublin. Upon receiving *smicha* [license as a rabbi], was invited to serve as the rabbi of Chelm. R. Eliyahu earned a reputation for piety and asceticism, and was reported to have performed marvels through the application of practical Kabbalah. Among other things, legend has it that he created a golem through an invocation of the Divine Name. He healed the sick and exorcised dybbuks by means of Names and charms.[53]

R. Eliyahu b. R. Moshe of Luanez

Born in Frankfurt am Main in 1555, died in Worms in 1636. Came from a prestigious lineage and in Kraków was a student of the Maharal of Prague. In addition to his Halachic studies, frequently delved into the Kabbalah. At the start of the sixteenth century began to serve as a rabbi in several German communities. In his final years held rabbinical office in Worms. In each community where he served as rabbi, he also functioned as yeshiva director and had student trainees. Wrote several compositions, especially in the field of Kabbalah. Earned renown as a *baal shem*.[54]

R. Yoel b. R. Yitzhak Ayzik Halpern

Lived in the second half of the seventeenth and in the early eighteenth centuries. Died in Ostra in 1713. Served as rabbi of several Polish communities; from 1692 until his death was rabbi of the Ostra community. In 1691 was appointed as one of the rabbis to

lead the *Vaad Haartzot.* His *haskamot* [ratifications of books]
were printed in several of the texts published during that period.
Worked as a *baal shem* throughout Podolia; accounts of his performances were widely recounted. Was reputed, among other
things, to have saved a ship from capsizing and to have exorcised
a dybbuk. Lists of names and charms in his possession reached
his grandson, R. Yoel II, and became the basis of several books
of charms.[55]

R. Naftali Katz of Poznan

Date of birth unknown. Died in 1719. Served on the rabbinate of
the communities of Ostra, Poznan, and Frankfurt am Main.
Became famous as a master of both theoretical and practical
Kabbalah. Stories spread far and wide about his activities as a
baal shem. Among other things, was reputed to have brought a
man back from the dead so as to free his wife of the status of
aguna. Likewise, was able to discover the incarnation sequence
of his own soul as well as that of many others.[56]

R. Hirsch Fraenkel

This rabbi's biography was only recently brought to light by
Gedaliah Nigal.[57] R. Hirsch Fraenkel lived at the end of the seventeenth century and in the first half of the eighteenth century.
He served as rabbi in several communities in Germany, among
them Heidelberg and Ansbach, dealt in practical Kabbalah, and
consorted with Kabbalist masters. After his brother, a court Jew,
got into trouble with the authorities, R. Hirsch's books were
confiscated. Inspection of his books revealed that they contained
writings critical of the Christian religion along with matters of
"sorcery." For these, he was sentenced in 1713 to an extended
term of imprisonment. In 1737 he was pardoned and released,
but emerged from prison broken in body and spirit. Three years
later he passed away.

Scrutiny of his interrogation report reveals that the basis for R. Hirsch
Fraenkel's conviction as a sorcerer was a single manuscript containing instructions on how to write talismans and oaths. The "operations" these amulets and
oaths were meant to effectuate included: overpowering demons, conversing
with spirits of the dead, "travel hops," an ability to see without being seen,
injury to enemies, restoration of stolen property, assistance for women in
pregnancy and release of the imprisoned from jail. In his interrogation,
R. Hirsch confessed that he took the "book" of oaths with him when he left on

voyages, and that he copied texts from it and gave or sold the lines he transcribed, apparently in the form of amulets, to others.

This was not the sum total of persons who combined rabbinical activities with practice in the arts of Names and talismans. Gedaliah Nigal lists three further such individuals whose lives paralleled, in one way or another, that of the founder of Hasidism. The greatest and most prominent of them was R. Yehonatan Eibenschütz.[58] Among the *baalei shem* who practiced in the eighteenth century, after the death of the Besht, one must note R. Zekil Leib Warmesser, who became famous as "the *baal shem* of Michelsstaadt." R. Zekil (1768–1847) served as rabbi and yeshiva director and his fame spread throughout Germany.[59]

This brief survey definitively demonstrates that the personages who were known in the sixteenth through eighteenth centuries as *baalei shem* were considered members of the scholarly and religious elite. In addition to their erudition in Halachic literature, they were masters also of Kabbalist literature. Apparently, practical Kabbalah was an important source, if not the only one, of their knowledge of magic. The work done by such personages as *baalei shem* was merely one further branch of their main work as rabbis and yeshiva directors. It can thus be viewed as a sort of additional service they put at the disposal of their communal flock.

Were there *baalei shem* who lived and worked at a time and place near to that of the Besht, and thus might be viewed as colleagues of his in this regard? We know of two such persons. One is R. Binyamin Binush of Krotoszyn; the other is R. Yoel b. R. Uri Halpern of Zamosc. An examination of the characters and modus operandi of these two *baalei shem* will be the focus of my discussion here. To this end, I shall examine the books of charms with which these *baalei shem* were associated; these books shed light on how the knowledge of magic was spread as well as on the nature of the practice of *baalei shem*.

R. BINYAMIN BINUSH

We do not possess accurate information about R. Binyamin Binush's dates of birth and death. An approximate estimate is that he was born between 1660 and 1670 and died sometime in the 1730s.[60] The little known to us about R. Binyamin's life is based on fragmentary information found in the prefaces and ratifications to two of his books[61] as well as in *Yesh Manhilin*. R. Binyamin complains about being an itinerant. His roaming life carries him far from his wife and six children. The towns we know of along his itinerary include Fürth, Wallerstein, and Poznan. From his designation, R. Binyamin Binush of Krotoszyn, it appears that he was born and educated in Poland and from there drifted to the communities of central Europe. In the course of his migrations, he often lived in the homes of patrons, who assisted him financially and helped him to publish his writings. Before his nomadic period began, R. Binyamin sat in a *beit midrash* and studied Torah for several years without having to worry about providing for his family.

His contemporaries considered R. Binyamin to be a *talmid hacham.* In the ratifications signed by rabbis to his books he is described using terms such as the *torani rabbani* [the prodigal Torah master] and so forth. Apparently, then, the support he earned from his patrons was granted him by virtue of his being a prodigy. In addition, R. Binyamin Binush was also considered a "Mekubal" or Kabbalist. So far as can be ascertained from his writings and from what is told of him, he was not a mystic of the sort current in the fraternities of Hasidim that predated the Hasidic movement. It thus appears that the designation "Kabbalist" hints at his proficiency in the literature of the Kabbalah and in the ritual customs that developed under its influence. Indeed, R. Binyamin reports that in addition to study of the Halachah he also delved into study of the Zohar and the writings of the ARI. Nevertheless, it appears the designation "Kabbalist" stuck to R. Binyamin also—perhaps chiefly—because of his proficiency with Names and charms. Such too is implied by the ratification written by Rabbi Naftali Katz of Poznan to the book *Amtahat Binyamin:*

> I herewith inform anyone who wishes to know that the exalted master and Torah prodigy the divine Kabbalist our master Rabbi R. Binush Hacohen (may his maker and savior preserve him) of the holy community of Krotoszyn was here with me within my home for a great many weeks and I beheld how vast a talent he has and he is one of the ascendant ones of which there are few. And I examined the pitcher and found it a new pitcher full of old. He has a hand and a name in the art of the Kabbalah. No mystery eludes him, as his own mouth attests. And all who behold him will say he is the seed blessed by God.

It should be recalled that R. Naftali Katz himself became famous as a Kabbalist and a *baal shem.* Hence his pronouncements carry the status of expert testimony. The recommendation that R. Naftali gave for R. Binyamin's book of charms is based on two factors: a direct impression of his "talented actions" (that is, of his practical achievements as a *baal shem*) and recognition of his mastery of the wisdom of the Kabbalah. The conjunction of these two reflects the author's presumption that Kabbalist knowledge is the relevant knowledge substrate on which R. Binyamin's activities as a *baal shem* are to rely.

A further source that sheds light on the status and reputation of R. Binyamin as a *baal shem* is, as noted, *Yesh Manhilin.* Here is what R. Pinchas Katzenelbogen tells his sons about him:

> Do you not know that this author of *Amtahat Binyamin* who was a
> great Kabbalist was our master (etc.) Binyamin Binush of blessed
> righteous memory, who stayed with me in my home, when I resided
> in the community of Wallerstein in the year 1720 and I heard mar-
> velous things from him. He was a great *baal shem* and performed
> wonderful deeds, as can be seen from his said book *Amtahat
> Binyamin*, he had a hand in everything.[62]

I have already commented on the honors that R. Pinchas bestowed upon R.
Binyamin Binush when the latter was a guest in his home. His statements
clearly suggest that he was deeply impressed by R. Binyamin Binush's expertise in the field of Names and charms. This impression was formed both on the
basis of what he heard from him in person and on his reading of *Amtahat
Binyamin*. One may recall that R. Pinchas Katzenelbogen tells that he had
occasion to use R. Binyamin's book of charms and even turned to him directly
for a charm to meet a specific need. And as all of this was incorporated in a
text he wrote as a sort of testament to his children, it seems the moral to be
drawn is that it is worth taking advantage of charms that have R. Binyamin
Binush as their source.

R. Binyamin's two works are not cut from the same cloth. *Shem Tov Katan*,
first published in 1706, can be considered a charms book mainly on account of
its concluding pages. The bulk of the book is devoted to *tikkunei tefila*—special
prayer formulations with ameliorative powers—and practices deriving from the
Kabbalah. A central topic of the book is how to deal with the phenomenon of
nocturnal emissions. The author suggests *tikkunei tefila* that have the power of
blocking nocturnal emissions and others that provide *tikkun* (mending or abso-
lution) for those who have experienced them. In addition, the author proposes
"practical charms for nocturnal emissions to quash appetite," such as: "one
should lay all night on the left side and this is very good for subduing Lillith . . .
and quashing appetite."[63] Also included in the book are "sacred practices" for
the conduct of conjugal life. In addition to the hope that conjugal life will be conducted along pure lines, some of these practices have a utilitarian aspect: "so as
to be graced with kosher sons who will not perish before their time."[64]

A substantial portion of the book is devoted to "practices and laws and holy
and awesome prayers for the month of Ellul and the High Holidays." Among
other things, this portion includes detailed instructions on how the person
blowing the shofar on Rosh Hashanah should intend his thoughts. As in the
sections on prayers and practices to govern nocturnal emissions and conjugal
purity, the sections on High Holidays customs are based on the Kabbalah.

The bulk of the book is thus devoted to *tikkunei tefila* and recommended
practices; only incidentally does it incorporate a few charms. By contrast, the

final section is devoted entirely to charms. Among other things, R. Binyamin offers there various charms for those who travel the roads. These include the charm attributed to Nachmanidies that lets one "see and not be seen." There are also charms to protect the home, charms to protect against fire, and charms to counteract spells and the evil eye.

Amtahat Binyamin, R. Binyamin Binush's second book, published in 1716, differs noticeably from its predecessor. *Amtahat Binyamin* also contains prayers and practices concerned with purification and moral improvement. Yet the bulk of the book is a discussion of various methods for dealing with ailments and maladies of the body and soul, as well as methods of guarding against the hazards that lurk for one in daily life. What is common to nearly all these methods is their magical nature. This may, arguably, be a questionable way of characterizing the book: the presence of a substantial body of prayers, and the use of prayers as a prophylactic against misfortune, does not necessarily signal the presence of magic. Yet closer examination of the prayers reveals that they too are to be classed as magical. The powers or efficacy of these prayers depend upon a close recitation of the formulas as written; these include combinations of verses and Holy Names.

Among the prayers meant to guard against maladies of various sorts, what is striking is how many have to do with childbirth. As we have already seen, the people in this period were greatly concerned with problems of reproduction, and as they lacked effective medical means of confronting such afflictions, R. Binyamin had several special prayer formulas with which to address them. In addition, R. Binyamin included in his book quite a few talismans and incantations designed to assist a woman through her labor. He also offers several charms to help women who are having difficulties in conception.

Among the various other bodily dysfunctions for which *Amtahat Binyamin* proposes a remedy, we find fever, "falling sicknesses" (i.e., epilepsy), stones in the kidney or urinary tract, and postmenstrual bleeding. The vast majority of remedies offered by the author take the form of charms. Only a tiny minority may be categorized as natural medications.

Ze'ev Gries, whose *Sifrut Hahanhagot* [Conduct literature] has a small section devoted to the charms books, lists *Shem Tov Katan* and *Amtahat Binyamin* as examples of books that combine Lurianic customs along with charms.[65] Yet while the content of these works does on the whole confirm Gries's assertion, these two books ought to be distinguished from each other. If *Shem Tov Katan,* R. Binyamin's first book, consists in the main of conduct and customs, with only a small amount of charms included, *Amtahat Binyamin* is to be categorized primarily as a book of charms, with only a small portion that may be classed as conduct literature. It seems to me, then, that in the case of R.

Binyamin Binush we are witnessing a gradual shift from the literature of the Kabbalist-conduct type to the literature of the charms books.

How does R. Binyamin explain the purpose of his texts to his readers? A partial answer to this question appears in the frontispiece to *Amtahat Binyamin:* "Just as it is a very great *mitzvah* to arouse all of Israel in the ways of awe and repentance . . . so is a man obligated to deliver souls in Israel by application of charms and medicines, as our rabbis of Blessed Memory have said: He who knows medicine and does not tell, to him applies the verse 'Thou shalt not stand on thy neighbor's blood.'" R. Binyamin Binush thus is not content merely to note the benefits of the remedies offered in his book. By characterizing publication of the charms as a *mitzvah*, he seeks to attract to his own work a share of the prestige and authority traditionally ascribed to sacred literature. Drawing a parallel between soul-saving in the moral sense and healing bodily ills is a way of tightening the association between the conduct literature and the books of charms.

A more detailed explanation of the expected utility of R. Binush's book may be found in the preface he wrote to *Amtahat Binyamin:*

> And our rabbis of blessed memory said: He who saves a single soul in Israel is as if he had saved an entire world, and especially as one does not commonly find expert doctors or peddlers except in the big cities. And indeed the small localities and villages are not frequented by the physicians, and where they are frequent there is no money to pay them with.

The "expert physicians" mentioned here are not certified doctors but rather popular healers, who relied on the accumulation of medical knowledge passed down from master physician to his apprentice. It thus would appear that even physicians of this type practiced only in the large population centers. The same applies to the "peddlers"; that is, those who plied the public with the medicinal herbs and materials used for the preparation of charms. It thus seems at first that R. Binyamin's book was designed to serve the Jewish population of the small settlements who were beyond the reach of physicians or peddlers. Yet further on the author points out an additional and important component of his book:

> Moreover, I have listed charms and medications and prayers against witchcraft and insanity and evil eye and falling sickness and all manner of Externals which cannot be cured even by expert physicians. Verily the majority of the charms I listed have been examined and tried and tested by the grace of God and these charms can protect a man in advance so that no ill shall ever befall him.

Evidently the book's unique contribution can be said to be its exposing readers to esoteric knowledge from the realm of magic; that is, a range of techniques that has the power to protect against the demonic forces. For that very reason one may speculate that *Amtahat Binyamin* and similar books of charms might have functioned as substitutes not only for doctors, but also for *baalei shem*. I shall later reexamine this conjecture. Meanwhile, I summarize my findings about R. Binyamin Binush.

Unlike the other *baalei shem* from the survey above, R. Binyamin Binush did not hold rabbinical office or office of any other sort. It appears that he chiefly earned his income through his practice as a *baal shem*. This conclusion is consistent with the fact that he traveled a great deal, and thus was able to offer his services as *baal shem* to the various communities through which he passed. We have seen that R. Binyamin was a guest in the home of R. Pinchas Katzenelbogen, at a time when the latter served as rabbi of Wallerstein; and that R. Binyamin plied him with charms and told him of the wonders he had performed. We have also found that Rabbi Katzenelbogen had his own copy of *Amtahat Binyamin* and used some of the charms it describes even before R. Binyamin became a guest in his home. It follows R. Binyamin gained some of his reputation through his book and that this may have encouraged people to seek his services.

What were the sources for the charms R. Binyamin included in his books? A partial answer to this question emerges from the following remarks he makes: "For the Lord Blessed Be He chanced to my hands sayings of comfort and sayings of wisdom . . . by the sacred candle Nachmanides of eternal memory and by the ARI of eternal memory. . . . Ancient matters from the apex of the universe are collected side by side with writs from the earliest Kabbalists, men of renown, men of deeds."[66] These lines suggest that R. Binyamin's book is an amalgam of knowledge gathered from various sources. This feature is typical of all the books of charms. Two qualities bestow authority and reliability upon a charm: a derivation from an ancient source and an association with the Kabbalah. Knowledge of magic was considered something based on the received tradition; consequently a charm's value increased to the extent that it had a more antiquated origin. It thus comes as no surprise that there are charms attributed to figures from the Talmud and Mishnah and even to biblical personages. For all that, what chiefly invests magical knowledge with its aura of sanctity, prestige, and authority is its ties to the Kabbalah. There is no doubt that a considerable portion of R. Binyamin's charms and talismans had Kabbalist origins. The same is true of the other charms books. Clearly, however, the magical tradition this literature reflects also had foundations in earlier sources as well as non-Jewish influences. What gave this tradition, in all its components, the stamp of *kashrut* and authority was the presumption of a Kabbalist origin. One of the clear indications of this presumption was the practice, referred to above, of designating the masters of magical knowledge as Kabbalists.

The question of the mutual relations between the *baalei shem* and the charms books will be discussed later. For the present, I turn my attention to a different *baal shem,* who also lived and practiced at a time and place near to that the Besht: R. Yoel Baal Shem.

R. YOEL BAAL SHEM

R. Yoel b. Uri Halpern was born in Zamosc, circa 1690, and died there circa 1755.[67] He was also known as Rabbi Yoel II, as he was the grandson of R. Yoel b. Yitzhak Ayzik Baal Shem, who lived in the second half of the seventeenth century and earned wide renown for his marvels and "performances."[68] As will become clear later on, this pedigree was of great significance for R. Yoel II's practice as a *baal shem.* Although he did not serve as a rabbi, R. Yoel was considered a *talmid haham* with great competence in matters both Halachic and Kabbalist. In addition, he was famous for having acquired a certain knowledge of the "external arts."[69]

Various sources attest to the great fame that R. Yoel's activities as a *baal shem* earned him in the region of Poland; his fame spread through the Ashkenazi communities and even reached the Holy Land.[70] It is no accident that when Solomon Maimon sought to exemplify the phenomenon of the *baalei shem* for his readers, he selected R. Yoel as his paradigm, describing him as one who "had at that time achieved great fame through individual successful acts of healing, which he carried out aided by his medicinal knowledge and the fabulous tricks of conjury."[71] His phrasing clearly suggests that Maimon never met R. Yoel and only knew of him by reputation. The fact that Maimon struggled to explain R. Yoel's success by rational means indicates that he did not doubt the substance of the assertion about R. Yoel's abilities to heal the sick. This certainty was presumably grounded in the numerous stories that the Jews of Poland told about R. Yoel.

A further indication of R. Yoel's fame as a *baal shem* is suggested by what R. Pinchas Katzenelbogen wrote of him in *Yesh Manhilin.* It may be recalled that R. Pinchas tried to caution his sons of the hazards involved in the art of Names. He therefore points out that several *baalei shem* had done themselves injury through this practice. It is in this context that he writes of R. Yoel:

> And even that *baal shem* who was famous in all the countries I had
> been in, that acute and accomplished rabbi proficient in all the arts,
> our master (etc.) Yoel Baal Shem of the community of Zamosc, who

worked wonders and performed marvels, did not come away
unscathed; some two or three years ago he was struck by a measure
of Divine judgement and lost his reason, Heaven protect us, and perished before his time.[72]

Evidently R. Pinchas considered R. Yoel to be the leading figure among the
baalei shem of his day. That was why he believed that he more than anyone
could serve as an example of the ill-consequences that may affect anyone
engaging in the art of Names. A further mark of the prestige enjoyed by R. Yoel
is that he was asked to write ratifications for several books. We know of five
books that bear R. Yoel's haskamah. They were all published between 1711 and
1756. One of the most prominent of these books is Netzah Israel [Posterity of
Judaism], by Rabbi Israel of Zamosc, who may be considered a herald of the
Haskalah in eastern Europe. In his Netzah Israel, published in 1741, Rabbi Israel
sought to demonstrate the importance of scientific knowledge as an aid to
understanding the Halachah.[73] R. Yoel, in his ratification to this book,[74] attests
that he was the author's close friend and thus could not refuse his request to
write the haskamah. The bonds of friendship between these two figures, as well
as R. Israel of Zamosc's desires to win ratification from someone famous as a
baal shem, teach us that this proto-Haskilic figure did not see anything wrong
with the phenomenon of baalei shem. To put this point in perspective, we
should recall that R. Israel of Zamosc did not refrain from harshly condemn-
ing various aspects of the religion and society of his day.[75]

The other four books that R. Yoel ratified include a book of mussar (morals
or homiletics),[76] a book of Halachah,[77] and two charms books. R. Yoel's signature on the Halachah and mussar books appear with those of the rabbis of
the communities and they reflect his status as a talmid chaham. His ratification of the charm books, by contrast, indicates his status as the supreme
authority on all that concerns applications of magic.

The first of these two charms books is Zevach Pesach [Passover sacrifice]
published in 1722 by Rabbi Yaakov Pesach, a preacher in the Beit Midrash of
the community of Zolkiew. The book is devoted entirely to treatment of the
phenomenon of "ipush," a contagious disease the symptoms of which the
author describes in the beginning of the book. The book includes "natural
medicines" on the one hand and charms and amulets on the other. In his ratification, R. Yoel explains that the author turned to him to verify the manuscript by comparing it against the writings of R. Yoel Baal Shem's grandfather,
whose "reputation has spread to every climate and island [and] all his books
are truthful." As it happens, R. Yoel II attests that the book indeed is a faithful
copy of his grandfather's manuscript. He further certifies that the natural
medicines described in the book are correct. R. Yoel's contribution to this book

of charms was not confined to his ratification of it. In several places the author
presents charms from "the writings of R. Yoel Baal Shem, of blessed memory."
It thus appears that R. Yoel made his grandfather's manuscripts available to
the author, R. Yaakov Pesach.[78]

The second book of charms ratified by R. Yoel was *Menahot Yaakov Solet,*
by R. Yaakov b. R. Moshe Katz of Yanov. This book, published in Wilhelms-
dorf in 1731, has two parts. The first part is an epistular formula written by the
author. The second part is a collection of charms by Rabbi Shlomo b. R. Hayim
of Jerusalem. In his preface to this part, R. Shlomo b. R. Hayim tells that he
had meant to publish these charms in a book of his own. However, after being
rescued from highway robbers by R. Yaakov b. R. Moshe, he gave the latter his
collection of charms in token of his gratitude. In his ratification of this book
of charms, R. Yoel writes: " I come to announce at every gate of the multitude
that these matters leave from under my hand and that I transcribed them word
for word and they are truly and rightly proofread . . . and fit to be relied upon
in the hour of need." It appears, then, that the author of this book passed the
manuscript he received from R. Moshe b. R. Hayim on to R. Yoel, and asked
R. Yoel to produce a proofread version fit for printing. Apparently, in this case
too the author needed R. Yoel's professional authority to publish his book of
charms. Moreover, R. Shlomo b. R. Hayim notes in several places that he
received this or that charm from R. Yoel or that he found it in his writings.[79]

Presumably, R. Yoel's involvement in the publication of the two books
described here contributed to their trustworthiness and circulation. Nevertheless, this involvement was only partial: he did not initiate the publication of
these books and was not exclusively responsible for their contents, even if he
did check the manuscripts and certify their quality. Entirely different was the
involvement R. Yoel had in the other two charms books: *Toldot Adam* [History
of Adam], first printed in Zolkiew in 1720; and *Mifalot Elokim* [God's deeds],
also published in Zlokiew, in 1725. Though it may seem at first that R. Yoel's
association with these books was limited to his ratifications of them, in fact
the connections were much more extensive and complex. This fact is hinted at
both in the "compiler's" preface and in the ratifications penned by R. Yoel.

In his ratification for *Toldot Adam,* R. Yoel wrote the following: "And the
evidence of my pen and the signature of my hand herewith do faithfully attest
that these formulas and charms were gathered and compiled from the ancient
collection of the great Kabbalist our master (etc.) Eliyahu Baal Shem of blessed
memory and from the writings of my father's father, viz., the great Kabbalist
our master (etc.) Yoel Baal Shem the both of whom were men of God." Further on, R. Yoel emphasizes that the book is an exact copy of the writings of
these two *baalei shem* and that its formulas are identical to those he obtained

from his grandfather R. Yoel (the First). Apparently, the manuscript containing the magical information from R. Eliyahu Baal Shem, the above-mentioned Eliyahu of Luanetz, was likewise obtained by R. Yoel through his grandfather. We thus have here an example of the transmission of magical knowledge from generation to generation within a "lineage" of *baalei shem.*

The importance of R. Yoel's *haskamah* is attested to by the "compiler." The "compiler" relates that the sages of his day, whom he first turned to to ratify his book, were reluctant to do so, maintaining that they did not have sufficient qualifications in practical Kabbalah. Yet by contrast, "the entire world knows that our master (etc.) this said Yoel Baal Shem (may the Lord preserve and redeem him) is an authority and expert for many in our generation. And if he alone approves the sons of Jacob will believe." In sum, both *Toldot Adam* and *Mifalot Elokim* are books based on manuscripts that had been in R. Yoel's possession and both were issued thanks to his ratifications. The fact that R. Yoel, considered an important *baal shem* in his own right, was the owner of the manuscripts and the ratifier of their printed version, is what granted these books their trustworthiness and authority.

The suspicion that *Toldot Adam* was in fact composed by R. Yoel himself is hinted at in the "printer's apology," which appears at the end of the book:

> For here I have heard the gossip of many who speak ill of the rabbi the great luminary the universally wise the perfect Kabbalist the famous one this very master (etc.) Yoel Baal Shem (may the Lord preserve and redeem him). . . . And those connivers say that he himself printed the book and estranged himself from it so as to multiply his praises and fill his neck with epithets. And said persons try to justify their accusation by saying there is nowhere in the introduction to said book any man who comes to sign it, instead it simply begins with "the compiler says" etc. and at the end of the introduction no signature appears. And for this reason they cast false aspersions upon the rabbi the luminary the great this very said our master (etc.) Yoel (may the Lord preserve and redeem him), saying that he himself wrote the text of the introduction so as to extol his name as one of the great.

The printer further relates that those same "connivers" charge that because Rabbi Yoel was afraid of jeopardizing his income, his book contains only "untested formulas," that is, charms and medications of dubious efficacy. Hoping to persuade the reading public that there was no substance to these charges, the printer swore "by the honor of the Creator, and by His great and almighty name" that the introduction to the book and all the praises of R. Yoel contained in it were written by himself, the printer, not by R. Yoel. Moreover,

R. Yoel received no financial compensation from publication of the book, excepting several copies which he received as a gift.

The charge that R. Yoel only included charms of doubtful efficacy in his book is rejected through and through by the publisher. R. Yoel has no reason to fear that his income would be jeopardized by the book; surely "any person with the possibility of traveling to [R. Yoel's] place of residence, the holy community of Zamosc, or to wherever he currently is, will do well to spend the costs of traveling as this man is expert and famous as is known." The book is designed to aid those who live in remote hamlets who do not have the means of calling upon him. Likewise, the book contains charms and medicines "for the hour of need," as with a woman having a difficult labor, and in cases of this kind the option of traveling to find a *baal shem* is ruled out. So as to leave no doubt in the minds of readers, the printer ends his "apology" by citing also the testimony of R. Yaakov Pesach, the preacher of the Zolkiew Beit Midrash and author of *Zevach Pesach,* who by his own signature confirms that "these words of said printer are sincere and truthful."

Even if we accept the printer's denials, and there is no apparent reason not to do so, one may not on that account conclude that the charges of the "connivers" are groundless. It may well be true that the "compiler" is the person who brought the book to press, with all that implies in terms of finances and organization. Perhaps the compiler also affected the final editing of the book. Nevertheless, it may be affirmed that in terms of content, *Toldot Adam* is in large measure a book by R. Yoel Baal Shem. This assertion relies upon two fundamental facts. First, the manuscript on which the book is based was in the possession of R. Yoel. Second, R. Yoel is the one who proofread the book, verified it, and gave it his ratification. In addition, the book contains several pages of Torah innovations explicitly attributed to R. Yoel. The same considerations and inferences relating to *Toldot Adam* apply as well to the book *Mifalot Elokim.*

The fact that within a period of five years, two books of charms associated with the name of R. Yoel Baal Shem were brought to press prompts the question, What is different about these two books? Indeed, examination of the contents and the structure of these books reveals that *Mifalot Elokim* is substantially unlike its predecessor. *Toldot Adam* focuses on a relatively small number of maladies for which it offers remedies. Most of the book's sections are concerned with the following topics: women having troubles conceiving; men rendered impotent as a result of witchcraft; women in a difficult labor; women who miscarry; safeguarding the mother during childbirth and the newborn from demons and witches; and falling sickness. Thus, *Toldot Adam* focuses almost exclusively on the topic of nuptial relations and reproduction.

By contrast, the range of topics treated in *Mifalot Elokim* is far broader. A substantial number of the charms and medicines contained in this book are of the sort that one would today consider to be "first aid." Thus, for example, the book offers instructions for how to treat snakebite, scorpion stings, or attacks by a rabid dog. Another class of charms and medications is meant to relieve ailments of various sorts. Among these we find remedies for earache, swellings, stomach pains, and ocular pain or inflammation. The book further proposes remedies for women unable to lactate and for those suffering from kidney stones or urinary tract pains. In the latter case the author does not merely prescribe medications, but also adds explanations to aid in the malady's proper diagnosis.

Alongside relief for medical ailments of the type mentioned and the many others of the same kind, *Mifalot Elokim* suggests "operations" aimed at goals rather different than health: an oath formula that lets one behold paradise, a prayer that prevents reincarnation into another human or into an animal, a charm to improve memory, incantations and amulets that assist in the successful delivery of sermons, and so forth. It is quite clear, then, that besides having contents much richer and more diverse than its predecessor, *Mifalot Elokim* is also broader in scope. Furthermore, the charms and medications offered in *Mifalot Elokim* are arranged alphabetically by subject, to enable easy perusal and location. In sum, the differences we have listed between the two books help explain the justification for publishing *Mifalot Elokim* only a scant five years after bringing out the first edition of *Toldot Adam*. Clearly, a factor in the initiative to print a second book of charms was also the publisher's positive experiences as regards demand for *Toldot Adam,* and his expectation of a handsome profit from sales of *Mifalot Elokim.*[80]

These differences between the two charms books associated with R. Yoel Baal Shem do not mask their common denominator. Both books offer a relatively large number of charms for dealing with the same malady. The underlying presumption is that the assorted charms do not cancel each other out and that simultaneous use of several of them is recommended. Another characteristic of both books is the absence of anything that distinguishes natural medicines from charms, talismans, or oaths. All sorts appear on the same page, as if all were of the same type. Yet it would be a mistake to infer that the authors or readers of these books were unaware of the difference between natural medicines and magical means. If they nevertheless did not find cause to separate the two, that is because they thought it desirable to work on both planes at once. This perspective finds a typical illustration in the compiler's preface to *Zevach Pesach*. The compiler lists four causes for outbreaks of plague, two of which are natural and two supernatural. To counteract these factors, the compiler offers both natural medications and charms. And as one cannot know for certain whether plague is the result of natural or supernatural factors, the compiler advises: "He who craves life shall apply them all."

Above we found that the authors of the charms books attribute the magical knowledge in their books to Kabbalist sources. What, conversely, were the sources for the natural medicines? In the preface to *Mifalot Elokim* the compiler asserts that the medicines listed in the book are recommended by "expert and famous natural healers such as the distinguished and famous rabbinical physician our master (etc.) Simcha of blessed memory and other expert physicians who are still alive." Seeking to stress the trustworthiness of the medical knowledge his book contains, the compiler suggests a surprising distinction between charms and natural medicines. As we have seen, magical knowledge gains in value the more antique the source to which it is attributed. There is no fear that ancient knowledge may lose its worth over time; "charms are not susceptible to deterioration and never lose their quality or potency." By contrast, with natural medications the opposite obtains: it is best to rely on medical knowledge deriving from physicians of a current or recent generation. The presumption on which this assertion is based is that "in these generations on the whole there have been changes in the order of nature of man." Accordingly, medicines originating in ancient books of medicine no longer match the current human constitution and are not to be used. The advantage of *Mifalot Elokim* is that the medical information it contains is drawn from contemporary physicians.

The confession that "expert and famous" physicians are relied upon may seem perplexing in that it suggests that the realm of natural medicines is not the *baalei shem*'s proper area of expertise. Yet this conclusion must be qualified. It is true that *baalei shem* are supposed to be masters of the use of Names and not necessarily of the use of natural medicines. In practice, however, they did apply medicinal herbs and other techniques that were perceived as being natural medicaments. In so doing they answered the expectations of the people of the period, fitting their modus operandi to the contemporary view that ailments are best addressed both on the magical and on the natural planes. It seems that one can distinguish between different *baalei shem* on the basis of the degree of their expertise in natural medicines. This sort of difference is prompted by a comparison between the two books by R. Binyamin Binush and the two associated with R. Yoel Baal Shem. Those by R. Yoel contain vastly more applications of natural medicine than do the books by R. Binyamin Binush. Nevertheless, it is hard to imagine a *baal shem* who would not have been able to offer natural medicines as well as charms to those who turned to him for aid.

The flurry of charms books published in the beginning of the eighteenth century was reacted to with some hostility by those circles that disapproved of the exposure and dissemination of esoteric knowledge. One hears an echo of this reaction in the ratification that R. Yoel Baal Shem wrote for *Mifalot Elokim:*

> And here I know truly that many and fair persons will challenge this publication, and it has happened that I was asked by a wise man, one of the wise of the times, wherefore did I give my *haskamah* to the publication of *Toldot Adam* and the publication of the small book *Zevach Pesach* and he cited evidence that I acted improperly.

Against those making this argument, R. Yoel draws upon precedent:

> However, whosoever refrains from such publication is obligated first to explain why the First Geonim permitted publication of *Shoshan Sodot* by Nachmanides[81] . . . which is a most sacred text full of Torah secrets and practical Kabbalah . . . and likewise the book *Brit Menuha,*[82] which is entirely of this nature . . . as well as the rest of the books of practical Kabbalah of which there are many on many. . . . surely they had their own motives and reasons.

The reliance on precedent and the opaque remark that "they had their own motives and reasons" are reminiscent of the manner in which R. Pinchas Katzenelbogen justified his own involvement with Names. Yet this was not the only justification R. Yoel gave for publication of his charms books. In the preface to *Mifalot Elokim,* the "compiler" relates that he asked R. Yoel about the contradiction in the ARI's position on the use of Names. On the one hand, the ARI forbade involvement with Names, asserting that a necessary prerequisite for such involvement is purification through the ashes of a Red Calf, a requirement known to be unsatisfiable. On the other hand, he permitted application of Names when the issue was a "genuine matter."

To resolve this contradiction in the position of the ARI, R. Yoel proposes two distinctions. The first distinction pertains to a difference among types of Names. The ARI's remarks prohibiting the use of Names in the absence of Red Calf–ash purification refer to "ordinary" Names. However, some Names are of such extreme sanctity that they are effective even without prior purification by the ashes of a Red Calf. The second distinction concerns the type of operation for which the Names are being employed. The prohibition against using Names without Red Calf–ash purification applies only to operations where the deviation from natural law is discernible to the senses. This condition does not obtain with the normal application of Names, which serve merely to subdue or defend against the demonic powers. As the predominant use of Names in the charms books is of this latter sort, there is nothing to prohibit such use.[83]

If this seems like an overarching permission to publish books of charms and to apply the Names cited therein, the authors of the charms books are quick to issue a long list of "principles" restricting such application. These principles concern both the person inscribing the amulet and the manner in which it is to be inscribed. First, the scribe must purify himself prior to the act of inscription. This purification involves several stages:

> During the morning prayers on the day of the writing, he must make repentance and recite "For the sin of . . ." etc. . . . And on the day of the writing he must fast, and he who increases his penance, is granted increased power and illumination and influence from above. . . . And prior to the morning prayers he must dip in the *mikvah* . . . and give alms on behalf of the person for whom he is writing the amulet. . . . And he must wear a white smock and pants and wear clean clothes. And three days prior to writing the amulet he must not approach his wife. . . . And if heaven forbid he sees a nocturnal emission he must not approach the operation for he is in mortal danger and his life comes first.[84]

So much for the purification activities required of the inscriber of an amulet. Meanwhile, the amulet itself needs to be inscribed on a piece of parchment made from the skin of a deer whose *shekhita* (animal slaughter by Jewish ritual law) was kosher. In addition, there are several further requirements concerning the forms of the letters. Still another condition of the amulet's effectiveness is that the writer must be knowledgeable about the identities of the angels whose names he inscribes. Careful adherence to these requirements, and of others of their kind, is essential; else, as *Mifalot Elokim* puts it:

> the principle is that even the smallest matter upsets all fundamentally. For it is acceptable in the case of medications of the natural kind, that possibly a minor adjustment can in any case be effective, for if one doesn't do a thing whole one does it halfway. But with charms and operations based on Names even the slightest matter interferes. It is also known to all men of practical Kabbalah that each malady and condition has a particular amulet appropriate for it and this should be taken as an explicit admonishment for all those who take amulets from authors not adept in these matters, surely all their efforts are for naught and they will achieve nothing.[85]

The requisite conclusion is that in all that concerns amulets one must turn exclusively to the masters of the field, that is, to the *baalei shem*. A typical expression of this assessment can be seen in the remarks by R. Pinchas Katzenel-bogen, when he reports that the amulet for a woman in a difficult labor that he had from R. Binyamin Binush was "in his very own handwriting."[86]

I now summarize my findings about R. Yoel Baal Shem. R. Yoel first earned fame as a *baal shem* in the second decade of the eighteenth century; that is, when he was in his twenties. He continued to work in this field almost until his death, circa 1755, some five years before the death of the Besht. Many people flocked to his hometown of Zamosc to pay him homage, owing to the reputation he acquired throughout Poland. Nevertheless, from time to time he would leave his hometown to visit various communities in response to a summons for aid. R. Yoel's reputation and authority as a *baal shem* were based on his prestigious lineage; that is, on the fact that he was the grand-son of the first R. Yoel, who practiced as a *baal shem* in the second half of the seventeenth century. R. Yoel often prided himself on this pedigree and stressed the fact that his work as a *baal shem* was based on the magical knowl-edge passed down to him from his famous grandfather. It was also his grand-father's manuscripts that formed the basis of the charms books connected with his name. The status R. Yoel earned as a leading authority in the realm of magic was further reflected in his being asked to ratify the charms books of other authors. Concurrent with the reputation he acquired as a *baal shem*, R. Yoel enjoyed the prestige of a *talmid chaham*. Evidence to this effect may be seen in that he was asked to write ratifications for books of *Halachah* and *mussar*.

Unlike the majority of *baalei shem* of previous generations, R. Yoel held no rabbinical office, nor indeed any other kind of office. His work as a *baal shem* was his sole occupation and only source of income. In this he resembled R. Binyamin Binush as well as the Besht. It thus would seem that in the first half of the eighteenth century, one sees the beginnings of a process that might be termed the professionalization of the *baalei shem*. As will be recalled, we found that several *baalei shem* held rabbinical office. For them, their vocation as magicians was a secondary sphere of activity. The new type of *baalei shem* differed from rabbis who practiced as *baalei shem* in another way as well: the latter worked primarily in the communities in which they resided, whereas *baalei shem* such as R. Binyamin Binush, R. Yoel, and the Besht often traveled among the various communities and thus were able to serve a broad and diverse public. It is needless to reemphasize that like the rabbis who also prac-ticed as *baalei shem*, figures of the type of R. Yoel and R. Binyamin belonged to the scholarly elite and enjoyed the prestige characteristic of this class. More-over, through their mastery of Holy Names and methods of applying them, these individuals earned a special honor.

Summary and Conclusions

Contrary to the distorted picture about magic, fashioned and sustained by the Haskalah literature of the nineteenth century, magic was not associated only with the lower and uneducated classes of society. Quite the contrary: demonological beliefs and the application of magic were common to all classes of society—including the scholarly elite. It was the scholarly elite, furthermore, that conserved and transmitted the knowledge of magic from generation to generation.

Although knowledge of magic was widespread among the various sectors of the population, the *baalei shem* were the people thought supremely qualified to transmit such knowledge and to apply it when necessary. The qualifications of the *baalei shem* were a function of the esoteric knowledge they had available. Because such knowledge was considered "practical Kabbalah," mastery of the literature of the Kabbalah came to be an essential prerequisite for the profession of *baal shem*. Hence also the common identification of the *baalei shem* as "Kabbalists." If, besides mastery of Kabbalist literature, the *baal shem* also possessed ancient manuscripts containing "tried and tested" magical knowledge, so much the better. As noted, this was the basis of R. Yoel Baal Shem's authority. A further basis for the authority of a *baal shem* is his public fame. Quite naturally, such fame is nourished by tales of the enchanter's "performances"; that is, his successes in battles against the demonic powers. It is not an accident that *Toldot Adam* includes tales about marvels performed by the *baalei shem* whose manuscripts form the basis of the book.[87] At times, it was the *baalei shem* themselves who were the first to report their achievements. R. Binyamin Binush, as noted, tells R. Pinchas Katzenelbogen "marvelous things." Another *baal shem* who was a guest in R. Pinchas's home is R. Yosef of Jerusalem, and he too tells his host about "several marvelous performances which he happened upon and he was able to carry out by the grace of God."[88]

The majority of the *baalei shem* who practiced between the sixteenth and the eighteenth centuries were trained scholars, who served as rabbis or held other religious offices. Accordingly one may say that their work as *baalei shem* was a side vocation, a sort of added-value service they were able to offer their communal flock. In the first half of the eighteenth century, one sees the first signs of the professionalization of the *baalei shem*. The *baalei shem* of this new type differed from their predecessors both in that magic was their sole (or at least main) source of income, and in their tendency to travel from community to community. Obviously, such travel allowed them to serve a comparatively broad population. What further characterized the professional *baalei shem* was their involvement in the publication of charms books. It should be noted that the first half of the eighteenth century saw a vast increase in the number of charms books brought to press.[89]

It stands to reason that both the professionalization of the *baalei shem* and the impressive growth in the publication of charms books reflected an increase in demand for magical services. It is no less plausible that the proliferation of charms books and the growth in the numbers of *baalei shem* whose sole occupation was magic increased this demand still further. Through the publication of charms books, knowledge that previously had been considered esoteric became openly available to a broad public. There is no doubt that magic played an important role in Jewish society even before the charms books achieved wide circulation. Nevertheless, it seems likely that a society exposed to charms books would have developed greater expectations for curing ailments and afflictions by magical means, as these books proposed a wide variety of remedies for every sort of affliction. Furthermore, unlike magical knowledge that spreads by hearsay and is of uncertain origin and reliability, the charms books allowed the public for the first time to gain access to magical knowledge that was authorized and precise.

The professionalization of the *baalei shem* and the publication of the charms books are mutually and complexly associated events. On the one hand, the *baalei shem* were the people who composed the charms books or lent them their authority. On the other hand, these books helped spread the fame of those same *baalei shem*. By making magical knowledge available to the public, a certain amount of the trade may have been lost to "do-it-yourself" healings; yet the numerous restrictions on how magical methods were to be properly applied, and especially the strictures associated with inscribing amulets, would have emphasized the advantage of turning to qualified professionals. It thus appears that while the charms books may have substituted for the direct services of *baalei shem* to a certain extent, they functioned no less as a potent means of advertising the *baalei shem's* skills and of promoting recognition of their powers.

The sources we have looked at show no traces of conflict or tension between the *baalei shem* and the healers. On the contrary, it seems that the *baalei shem* and the physicians worked in harmony and complemented each other's work. As noted, the people of the period saw no contradiction between the use of natural medicines and the use of charms and amulets. Hence, although the *baalei shem's* primary expertise was in the magical realm, they were expected to offer natural medicines as well to those who sought their services. It is possible, therefore, that the conflict between scientific medicine and magic only arose in the second half of the eighteenth century.[90] At any rate, it was not evident in the first decades of that century.[91]

As said, the end of the seventeenth century and the first half of the eighteenth century saw an increase in the public's interest in magic. This growth was manifested in the plethora of charms books published throughout the period and in the professionalization of the *baalei shem*. How may one account for these phenomena? It seems likely that a basic factor was the growing involvement of the scholarly elite, over the course of the seventeenth and eighteenth centuries, with the literature of the Kabbalah. The increased exposure to Kabbalist literature had the twin effects of strengthening the authority of demonological beliefs and increasing trust in magical powers. As mentioned, the charms books were presented as faithful and authorized articulations of practical Kabbalah, and the *baalei shem* were recognized as Kabbalists. The identification of magic with the Kabbalah, during the period of the Kabbalah's greatest prestige,[92] explains how magic came to be accepted by the public as a respectable phenomenon with solid grounding in Jewish tradition.

The picture presented here of the status of magic and the *baalei shem* will serve as a background and frame of reference for my inquiry into the Besht's activities as a *baal shem*. To what extent did the Besht resemble the other *baalei shem* who practiced in his day, and in what respects was he unique? This subject is to be considered in the next chapter.

CHAPTER TWO

Israel Baal Shem

The professional designation, *baal shem,* does not bring out the special qualities of the Besht's personality or suggest the scope of his activity; still less does it explain the secret of his influence on his contemporaries and on so many in subsequent generations. Nevertheless, there are good grounds for beginning the detailed treatment of the Besht by considering this aspect of his person and activity. Notwithstanding the virtues by which the Besht surpassed the other *baalei shem* of his day, this aspect was substantial to his identity and reputation. Merely recall that "baal shem" is the designation by which the Besht became known to the public, and is the term he himself used in signing his correspondence.[1]

Methods and Areas of Professional Competence

In many respects the Besht was a *baal shem* like the other *baalei shem* who lived and worked in his day and era. The demonological beliefs reflected in the book *Shivhei Habesht,* those that were the background to and framework for his work as an enchanter, are identical to those that prevailed throughout Jewish society in that period. Likewise, the range of services the Besht offered was similar to that of other *baalei shem.* Most of those who turned to him were seeking relief from ailments of the body or of the soul. These were joined by women having trouble bearing children or bearing male offspring. Many turned to the Besht seeking amulets that would safeguard them from diseases and other maladies. Additionally, the Besht's practice included exorcisms, banishing demons from homes, reversing spells, locating lost persons and fortune-telling.

Like other *baalei shem,* the Besht employed amulets, incantations, and oaths in the course of his practice. The common denominator of all these was the invocation of Holy Names, through the power of which the desired "performance" could be effectuated. The Besht also used "charms"; that is, recipes of sorts that were thought to have medicinal effects. Alongside magical methods, the Besht did not shrink from using such accepted medical practices as bloodletting, leech-attaching, or applying medicinal herbs. It will be recalled that the Besht's contemporaries believed that illnesses were the result of either natural or demonic forces. And, as the cause of a disease could not always be ascertained, it was best to operate on both planes at once. In blending magical methods with "natural medicines," the Besht was thus acting in line with the accepted norms and expectations of those who turned to him for relief.

Can one point to features that characterize the Besht in particular and that distinguish him from the other *baalei shem* who worked in or near his day? It seems to me that this question may be answered in the affirmative. In the preceding chapter we found that the principal source of information upon which the activity of the *baalei shem* was based was the esoteric knowledge of magic they had available. We further found that enchanters tended to be valued because of the antiquity and prestige of such knowledge. Not every person was so privileged as to have access to esoteric information, and the mere fact that a particular person did have such access was evidence of his singularity. All the same, the ability of the *baalei shem* to perform marvels was first and foremost a function of their competence with Names and charms. A clear indication of this may be found in the oft-repeated caution that only a person who correctly and carefully employs Names will succeed in activating the powers inherent in them.

Now, what was characteristic of the Besht's working methods, and what set him apart him from the other *baalei shem* whom we know about from the same period, was that side by side with his employment of magical knowledge, the Besht made use of his remarkable spiritual powers. By this we mean powers of a prophetic nature: remote vision, prognostication, ability to hear decrees from on high, and so forth. As the Besht himself and as his admirers and followers saw it, these powers were a gift of divine providence. It is this point of view that explains the special sense of mission that imbued the work of the Besht as a *baal shem*.

Let us turn now to an examination of individual cases that illustrate the ways in which such powers were manifested. We begin with a letter sent by the Besht to R. Hayim, rabbi of the Sdeh Lavan community, that curiously combines prognostication and medical prescription:

> On your return from the road you will find in your home, in your yard, a great tumult of men and women and children and you will faint from terror. And when you are awakened, immediately order that blood be let from two veins. And promptly send a special messenger to inform me of the tumult, even though God be praised I have eyes to see from afar, even so send me letters by messenger. So spoke Israel Baal Shem Tov.[2]

This letter gives a sense of the breadth of the Besht's capacities. On top of his competence with Names, charms, and "natural" medications, he was gifted also with an ability to predict the future and to see from afar. The Besht's style and the tone of his statements express a self-confidence, authority, and determination. He does not qualify his avowals about what will take place with any suggestion that things may not turn out as predicted. The Besht's declaration, "God be praised I have eyes to see from afar," leaves no doubt that he was far from modest about his unusual capacities.

Certain tales dealing with the healing of the sick begin with an account of how the Besht "heard a Decree"[3] that so-and-so was ill, and came to that person's aid. A typical example is given at the outset of the following tale: "I heard this from the rabbi of our community: Once, when the Besht was traveling on the highway and resting someplace he heard: hurry back home as R. Yosef is very weak."[4] The hearing of the decree is thus what prompts the Besht's intercession, without the ailing person or members of his family calling upon him at all. The decree functions as a sort of summons from above that requires the Besht to take action of behalf of a certain patient. A further example of a healing performance that follows the hearing of a decree is this:

> I heard from R. Pesach b. R. Yaakov of Kaminka, that the Besht was traveling and came to a certain town and heard a Decree that he should take up lodging in the house of so-and-so. And he came to said house and they did not wish to take him in to lodge, because the son of the master of the house was severely ill. And he sent the scribe to the house and the wife told him how can anyone lodge here don't you see the sick boy and I am in great distress.[5]

The master of the house also rejected the Besht's request on the same grounds. In the end, the Besht promised the concerned parents that if they let him lodge in their home he would heal the boy. As this story tells it, the Besht did not know in advance that he would find a sick child in the house. The essence of the mission to which he had been assigned became clear only in retrospect.

In certain tales from *Shivhei Habesht,* we find the Besht busy locating missing persons or finding stolen property.[6] By their nature, property losses and certainly the disappearance of a loved one are not the sorts of misfortune to which one readily resigns oneself. In cases such as these, the people of the period in question tended to seek the assistance of miracle workers. Presumably the reputation the Besht had as someone endowed with the power of farsightedness would have put him in great demand in this regard.[7]

A further gift the Besht had was an ability to tell futures. *Shivhei Habesht* tells certain stories in which the Besht cautions a man not to go to a certain place, because of the danger lurking there for him. Here is one such tale:

> I heard from R. Moshe, b. R. Yekil of Miedzybóz, who was at the holy community of Nemirov. And when his father came with him to the Besht to give him his blessing the Besht told him: Take care, do not travel to the city of Winnica. . . . And said R. Moshe took care never

to set foot in the city of Winnica all his life. And when he told me this, it was not many years before he passed away. And he was traveling, and was conspired against in connection with the residence permit for Jews, and they carried him off to the city of Winnica. And he begged them not to take him to Winnica, yet nonetheless they took him there as a captive and he died in captivity. And this was some forty years or more after his marriage.[8]

This story is based on what *Shivhei Habesht*'s compiler had heard from R. Moshe—a hero of the story. R. Yekil of Miedzybóz and his son R. Moshe are mentioned in the compiler's preface to *Shivhei Habesht,*[9] implying that R. Yekil was an admirer of the Besht. R. Yekil's association with the Besht is also implied by the story in which the Besht's soul rises during the *Neilah* service with which Yom Kippur concludes. As is related there, it was R. Yekil who read out the prayer verses at the time the Besht passed before the ark in the Beit Midrash at Miedzybóz.[10] Hence he evidently was a person whom the Besht knew well. Likewise, the two other persons whom the Besht warns of dangers awaiting them in a certain location, are people he knew. We thus have a recurrent pattern of behavior: the Besht foresees a catastrophe that will befall someone whom he knows, if that person should go to a certain location, and makes haste to warn him of the danger in advance.[11]

By contrast with cases in which the Besht takes the initiative and warns an acquaintance of the lurking dangers, there are cases in which people turn to the Besht on their own initiative and ask him to tell their fortunes. A case of this sort involved Tovele, the wife of the famous and wealthy leaseholder, Shmuel of Sluck. In the course of the Besht's stay in her home she asked him:

> How long will my days of fortune last? The Besht irately replied that one does not ask about such things. Yet she greatly beseeched him, and he shut his eyes for a moment and said: they will last two and twenty years.[12]

In addition to the ability to see from afar, the Besht was known for his ability to discover a soul's previous incarnations. Under the influence of the Kabbalah, and especially of Lurianic Kabbalah, belief in the reincarnation of souls had grown widespread over the course of the seventeenth and eighteenth centuries.[13] This was especially true of the spiritual elite, the class that had had exposure to Kabbalist influence in general and to the ethos of the Kabbalists of sixteenth-century Safed in particular. Clearly, those who hold to the belief in reincarnation will highly value any scrap of information they can obtain about the previous incarnations of their own souls or those of their loved ones. Such persons also have a great desire to learn what had become of the souls of people they knew who had passed on. The discovery of one's previous incarnation could very well be paramount, as quite often one could use one's present incarnation to redeem defects incurred in a previous incarnation. Learning about one's previous incarnation could also potentially provide information about the mission of one's soul in its present body. A further ingredient of the doctrine of incarnation had to do with animals. Sinners who were destined to be reincarnated as beasts could spare themselves this punishment only by reforming themselves while in their human state. Hence, the discovery that one is destined to a future life as an animal allowed one to take prophylactic measures in the present life.

Given the importance assigned to reincarnation in the Besht's cultural environment, it is not surprising that he saw fit to discover how he himself had previously been incarnated. We learn about this from the testimony of R. Alexander the *Shochet,* who served as the Besht's "scribe" for several years, as cited by his son-in-law: "I heard from my father-in-law of blessed memory that the Besht said of himself, that he is the reincarnation of R. Saadia Gaon. And I told this to the rabbi of our community. And that rabbi said that he knew that the Besht used to studiously pore over books by said R. Saadia Gaon."[14] It is quite likely that R. Alexander's report is based on something he heard directly from the Besht himself. Apparently, the Besht's associates were familiar with this incarnation of his and knowledge of it spread to others as well. At any rate, the reply of "the rabbi of our community," (that is, R. Gedaliah of Lince) suggests that he was not surprised by this information, and even knew enough to respond that the Besht was an assiduous student of the writings of R. Saadia Gaon. The attribution of such behavior to the Besht ought not to surprise us: it follows almost necessarily from the beliefs that prevailed at that time about the reincarnation of souls.

A rare piece of evidence, stemming from a contemporary of the Besht, describes an appeal made to the Besht in this regard. Dubnow has brought to light portions of a manuscript of a book of responsa titled *Beit Yaakov.* The author of this text was R. Yaakov Halpern, rabbi of the Zwaniecz community. In the introduction to the book, R. Shlomo Yitzhak Halpern, the author's son, writes as follows:

> And this incident of my youth I remember, when the famous rabbi fluent in the divine wisdom [Kabbalah], our teacher Rabbi Israel Baal Shem of blessed righteous memory, prayed for a dream-revelation and was shown that the soul of my father and teacher of blessed memory was [a reincarnation of] the soul of R. Alfasi; and as Rabbi Alfasi had not managed to compose [a commentary on] Seder Kodashim my master and teacher and rabbi had come to remedy this. So he said explicitly.[15]

Apparently, R. Yaakov, whose hometown of Zwaniecz was near Okopy, the Besht's birthplace, heard of the Besht's powers and turned to him to discover the identity of his previous incarnation. R. Yaakov seems to have prized highly the information the Besht revealed to him. Otherwise, it is unlikely that he would have found it proper to speak of it to his son and unlikely the son would have mentioned the affair in the introduction. Incidentally, the description R. Yaakov's son gives of the Besht as "fluent in divine wisdom" corresponds to the reputation the *baalei shem* had in the period in question. It seems safe to assume the Besht's fame as one who could identify people's previous incarnations would have brought him additional clients, and that the case of R. Yaakov Halpern was not unique.

Indeed, we learn about the Besht's powers of discovering incarnations from *Shivhei Habesht* as well. In one instance, the Besht discovers that R. Yudele, a relative of R. Nahman of Kosov, is the reincarnation of the prophet Samuel. In another case the Besht is able to tell that the soul of a certain informer was destined to be reincarnated as a dog, but that he was saved from this punishment thanks to the stern words that the Polonne *Mokhiah* (preacher, chastiser) had uttered during his funeral. A further revelation made by the Besht was that the soul of R. Hayim Tsanzer, one of the Brod Kloyzter sages, was a reincarnation of Rabbi Yohanan ben Zakai.[16]

Certain stories from *Shivhei Habesht* suggest a further characteristic of the Besht, one that may also be added to the list of his unusual powers. I refer to his ability to confront supernatural entities face-to-face and to deal with them on an authoritative basis. The Besht is said to have contended with demons, with the spirits of the dead, with the spirits of the living, and with the Angel of Death himself. A confrontation between the Besht and two demons ("jokers") is at the core of the following tale:

> I heard from the rabbi of our community, and also from the rabbi of
> the holy community of Polonne, that in the holy community Zbaraz
> two jokers were seen in the women's synagogue. And the women were
> so terrified that they had to abandon the synagogue. And R. Hayim
> the *maggid* of our community went and sat in the synagogue and
> studied there and banished the jokers from there. And they went and
> injured two of his children. And he sent for the Besht who slept in his
> reclusion-house with the scribe our teacher Zvi. And he ordered that
> they should bring the children to him where he was lodging and so
> they did. And when they lay down to sleep the resting place of the
> Besht was by the head of the table and the scribe slept on the side
> opposite the Besht. And before they fell asleep the two malefactors
> came to the house and stood by the entrance joking, mimicking the
> way the Besht sings *Lecha Dodi*. And the Besht rose and sat on his bed

and said to the scribe: Did you see that? And the scribe too had seen
it and tucked his head under the Besht's pillow and said: Leave me
alone. And when they ceased speaking the [demons] went to the children. The Besht leaped from where he was lying and shouted at them
saying to them: Where is it you are going? And they were not afraid
and replied: What do you care? And once again they began joking,
singing *Lecha Dodi* in the Besht's tune. And he did what he did and
the two malefactors fell to the ground and could not get up. And they
began to beseech him and he said: Soon you will see that the children
have healed. They said: it is too late, for they had injured the internal
organs and now we have come to finish them off, yet it was their fortune that his eminence was here. He asked them: How and why did
you come to the synagogue? They replied that there was a cantor who
prayed in the synagogue, and his "bass" accompanist was a great for-
nicator. And when he was singing his intention was to please the
women and he fantasized about them and the women too fantasized
about him. And from these two fantasies we were created, two malefactors, a male and a female, and we live in the synagogue. So the
Besht gave them a place by a well somewhere where no people are to
be found.[17]

The present tale reached *Shivhei Habesht*'s compiler from two sources: R.
Yaakov Yosef of Polonne and R. Gedaliah of Lince. It offers us a typical depiction of the nature and mode of operation of demons in the society in which
the Besht lived and worked. The demons' invasion of a home is seen as something that is threatening and that cannot be abided. Demons terrorize people
and drive them out of their homes. In the case at hand, the area affected was
the women's section of the synagogue. Naturally, the presence of the demons
made it impossible for women to be able to pray. R. Hayim, who later served
as the *maggid* (community preacher) of Lince, and apparently at the time lived
in Zbaraz, attempted a tried and tested technique: he sat in the synagogue and
studied Torah, thus forcing the demons to abandon the building. Yet the
demons did not take this lying down and attacked his two children. When matters reached this point, R. Hayim turned to the Besht for assistance. Although
it is not explicitly stated in the passage, apparently the Besht vanquished the
demons by means of Names. Yet the Besht's task was not complete until he had
discovered the cause of the demons' appearance in the synagogue, and until
he had found the demons a place in which they could reside without bothering mortals.

The story is a reflection of the widespread fear of contact with demons. R.
Hayim dared to contend with them up to a certain point. Even R. Zvi, the Besht's
scribe, was seized with panic when the demons appeared, and he preferred to

hide his head under a pillow. The behavior of these two persons is not in the least unusual. It was, rather, the Besht's behavior in confronting the demons face-to-face, without dread or awe, that was remarkable.[18]

A further case illustrating the Besht's methods in the battle against demons involved R. Moshe, the rabbi of Kotov, and R. Yehuda Leib, the Polonne *mokhiah* (preacher, chastizer) both of whom were from the Besht's circle. R. Moshe's home had been infiltrated by a demon, forcing R. Moshe to abandon it. At the time, the *mokhiah* had been looking for a place to live. He received permission from R. Moshe to take up residence in his abandoned house. Yet the *mokhiah*'s bravery was not long-lived. The demon revealed himself to him while threatening to injure his newborn son. After various attempts to deal with the demon on his own, the *mokhiah* was forced to appeal to the Besht for assistance. The story ends as follows: "The Besht said to [the *mokhiah*]: I will go to your place and [the demon] will no longer strike in the house. And I will lay down to sleep and when you hear a scratching at the window or elsewhere say: 'Israel ben Eliezer is in here!' And he will strike no more, and so it was."[19] The conclusion of this story is surprising, in that the Besht elects to combat the demon not through the application of Holy Names but through mention of his very own name. The story thus expresses a considerable degree of self-confidence and boldness on his part.

The Besht's ability to combat supernatural entities was evident also in his efforts to heal the sick. In one story, the Besht cures a child on his deathbed by confronting the soul of the child and commanding it to reenter his body.[20] Another story is associated with R. Liebsh of Mezerich, who came to the Besht in order to spend the High Holidays in his proximity and took ill. At a certain stage the patient's condition deteriorated to the point of mortal danger. As soon as the Besht learned of this he ran to his home and found the Angel of Death standing beside R. Liebsh. The Besht kept shouting at the Angel of Death until the latter took his leave. The Besht himself commented on the unusual nature of his behavior in this case, saying: "That for this deed they wanted to cast him out of both this world and the world to come. And he said that he behaved as he had only because the thing had come upon him all of a sudden, as earlier he had not seen any signs of mortal danger. And when I suddenly beheld the Angel of Death my heart melted for him and I behaved as I did."[21]

A further quality that characterized the Besht specifically by contrast with the other *baalei shem* was his use of ecstatic prayer as a healing technique. Prayer as an element of magical ritual was a familiar phenomenon in that period. Typically a certain verse, or a series of verses recited in a certain order, was deemed to have the virtue of healing or of guarding against some evil. Recall that something of this kind was seen in the books of charms by

R. Binyamin Binush of Krotoszyn. The use of prayer formulas with magical qualities was common in Christian European society as well.[22] Yet the use that the Besht made of prayer was of a different nature. The prayer by means of which he sought to heal the sick was an ecstatic prayer, similar to the prayer he employed to induce his mystical experiences.[23] For example, one story tells that when trying to cure a child who was mortally ill the Besht remained with him through the night: "to the point where the scribe feared lest (heaven forbid) the Besht had endangered himself owing to his great efforts in prayer over the ill, for the matter is hazardous."[24] The scribe's fears are understandible if we consider how exhausting a spiritual effort the Besht's ecstatic prayer was.[25] Another story relates that when the Besht was ill, he healed himself by passing in front of the ark while praying like "a blaze of fire."[26]

Testimony that sheds further light on the use the Besht made of his prayers to aid individuals is attributed to Rabbi Meir Margaliot. In their youth, Rabbi Meir Margaliot and his brothers were close acquaintances of the Besht. Wishing to do them a favor, the Besht told them that he commonly prays out of a handwritten prayer book and that he would be willing, if they so desired it, to inscribe their names in the prayer book alongside any blessing of the *shmoneh-esreh* that they chose. The two young men requested that the Besht write their names beside the blessing "The Hearer of Prayers." Furthermore, Yaakov Margaliot—great-grandchild of the aforementioned R. Meir, and one who heard the tales of the Besht from his father and set them down in writing—goes on to report that on one occasion his father peeked in the Besht's prayerbook and indeed found the names of R. Meir Margaliot and his brothers written there.[27]

The topic of the Besht's prayer book has been recently treated extensively and thoroughly by Yehoshua Mondshine. For our purposes, it suffices to state that examination of the actual prayer book, which today may be found in the library of the Lubavitch Hasidim in New York, confirms the tradition associated with Rabbi Meir Margaliot. The names of people with whom the Besht was affiliated, including those of the brothers Margaliot, are indeed inscribed in the prayer book beside the *shmoneh-esreh* blessings so that the Besht could keep them in mind favorably and make various requests on their behalf while he prayed.[28] What is implied by this episode is that the power of the Besht's prayer to assist others and fill their wishes was not merely something believed in by his followers, but was first and foremost a belief of the Besht himself; it was the Besht who turned to Meir Margaliot and offered to write his name and that of his brother in the prayerbook.

What sort of public came to the Besht for relief? What were the classes of society that drew upon his services as a *baal shem*? The sources we know of suggest that most of these people came from the upper classes of society. Several examples support this general assertion. A certain customs official from a small town came to the Besht because he had "had a spell cast on him, such that out of anything standing in his house or in a vessel or any change in his pocket, after a night's passage only the half would remain." The Besht ordered the scribe to write out *shmirot;* that is, a type of amulet meant to protect possessions from malefactors.[29] Another customs official, who was having severe troubles in his business, appealed to the Besht to seek his blessing. When the Besht saw that "the Angel of Death was chasing after him" he chastised him and implored him to turn his attention away from affairs of this world and to repent.[30] Wealthy leaseholders too were among those who came to the Besht. The most prominent case is, of course, the Besht's stay with the Dzierzawcas, the chief arrendators or leaseholders of the Sluck community.[31]

In addition to customs agents, leaseholders, and merchants,[32] the Besht's clientele also comprised rabbis and *maggidim.* One of these was R. Hayim, the rabbi of the Sdeh Lavan community, whom the Besht attempted to cure and to whom he even sent, as mentioned, a letter with medical instructions.[33] The Besht also was called upon to heal the girl who was the granddaughter of R. David of Zaslav, rabbi of the Ostra community, and the daughter of R. Ayzik the *Gvir* (Jewish noble or peer).[34] We recall that rabbis too used the services of the Besht, as previously seen in the case of Rabbi Yaakov Halpern of Zwaniecz who hoped to identify his soul's previous incarnation. We learn of yet another rabbi whom the Besht assisted from the Besht's letter to R. Moshe, the rabbi of the Kotov community and a member of the Besht's circle. This letter contains, among other things, a medical prescription.[35]

R. Moshe of Kotov was not the only member of the Besht's circle to have enjoyed his services as a *baal shem.* The Besht also displayed concerns for the health of Rabbi Yaakov Yosef of Polonne, and forbade him to fast.[36] The Besht taught R. Yehiel Michal of Zloczow an incantation he was to whisper in his wife's ear when she was on the verge of giving birth, thanks to which the newborn would turn out to be male.[37] Likewise, the Besht's famous brother-in-law, R. Gershon of Kotov, sought his aid. Evidently R. Gershon used to wear an amulet given to him by the Besht so as to maintain his good health. Against this background one may understand R. Gershon's request in the letter he sent to the Besht from the land of Israel: "If it was at all possible for him to send me a general amulet rather than one that needs to be renewed each year, so much the better."[38] R. Gershon's request that the Besht send him an amulet of unlimited duration is understandable given the distance and difficulties in the communication between Poland and the land of Israel. It stands to reason that the case of R. Gershon of Kotov is only an instance of a more general rule; namely, that other relatives of the Besht also enjoyed his skills as a *baal shem*. A tradition that supports this conjecture involves the amulet the Besht gave his grandson R. Ephrayim of Sadilkov.[39]

What is the significance of the fact that most of the information about the Besht as a *baal shem* involves leaseholders and custom agents and merchants on the one hand, and rabbis and *maggidim* on the other? Did his clientele really consist only of the financial and spiritual elite? There is no doubt that members of the less prestigious classes turned to the Besht as well and enjoyed his services. The prominent appearance of members of the upper classes in *Shivhei Habesht* and in the other testimonies available to us may be attributed to two causes. First, most of the traditions and testimonials having to do with the Besht originated from these classes. Second, the storytellers and those who noted down the traditions quite naturally preferred to highlight the cases in which the Besht assisted well-known and leading figures. In any event, the fact that the clientele of the Besht included wealthy merchants, famous leaseholders, rabbis, and *maggidim,* is consistent with the conclusion at which we arrived in the previous chapter: the concept that only the ignorant masses used *baalei shem* lacks basis in fact. Furthermore, in societies that believe in the powers of the *baalei shem,* it is apparently the members of the upper classes who are more likely to enjoy their services.

Reputation, Authority, and Self-Image

How did the Besht come to be a *baal shem?* How did others become *baalei shem?* Anthropological studies of the phenomenon of the shaman in various cultures suggests that new shamen are inducted into their roles only after a extended period of preparation. This induction is a structured and institutionalized process that occurs under the guidance of a veteran shaman and includes fasting periods, trials of various kinds, and rites of passage.[40] Such institutionalized preparation of new shamen, and their ritual induction into their official positions, is entirely understandable in cultures in which shamen are assigned a definite, essential function. In traditional Jewish society, however, such phenomenon are unheard of. Hence, when a person became a *baal shem* it was the result of his individual determination and initiative.

It is safe to assume that certain *baalei shem* were trained and given esoteric knowledge by their predecessors: sons from their fathers and students from their rabbis. As we have seen, R. Yoel Baal Shem, who worked contemporaneously with the Besht, inherited manuscripts containing magical knowledge from his famous grandfather. Naturally, he inherited from his grandfather a certain degree of reputation and authority as well. What about the Besht? So far as we know, the Besht was not the beneficiary of any familial inheritance in this regard. Likewise, one can point to no person as having been the tutor or guide from whom the Besht received an apprenticeship on the subject of magic. The fact that Hasidic legend associates the Besht with R. Adam Baal Shem, who supposedly bequeathed to the Besht the esoteric knowledge at his disposal, only confirms and reinforces the existence of a gap in this respect.[41] It would thus seem that the Besht's transformation into a *baal shem* was the end result of an internal spiritual process, one that was not shaped—at least not directly—by persons beside himself. What do we know of this process?

The primary material from which this question may be answered is evidently the collection of "revelation" stories in *Shivhei Habesht,* in the portion of the text compiled by R. Dov Ber of Lince. The compiler heard these stories orally from his father-in-law R. Alexander, who was the Besht's "scribe" during his first years of employment as a *baal shem.* R. Alexander apparently heard them from the Besht himself, and perhaps from others who were acquainted with the Besht in the early period of his life. What these stories suggest is that the advent of the Besht's "revelation" (that is, the commencement of his practice as a *baal shem* serving the broad public) was preceded by a lengthy period of preparation. Here is how that period is described in *Shivhei Habesht* in Dov Ber of Lince's somewhat terse and dry style:

> For he resided in a small village in an inn and it was his manner that after he brought his wife the liquor he would go live as a recluse across the river called Prut. And there he had on the mountain a rock like a small house hewn from the mountain. And he would take himself for each meal some bread and would eat once a week. Thus was the penance he performed for several years. And he came home on the eves of the Holy Sabbath. His brother-in-law R. Gershon of Kotov thought him a lout and ignoramus. And he used to incite his sister to divorce him and she did not agree as she knew what he was yet did not reveal it to anyone.[42]

Apparently, the Besht's preparation period took place at the time that he and his wife were living in a rural environment near the Carpathian mountains. While his wife ran an inn the Besht lived as a recluse in the mountains. Reclusion and fasting are characteristic marks of Hasidism of the old style.[43] For the Besht, apparently, this period of reclusion was one of reflection and soul-searching. These were fed, presumably, by study of certain texts from which he drew inspiration.[44] Furthermore, it is not inconceivable that during this period the Besht would have had exposure to the miracle workers practicing in the rural environment in which he lived as a recluse. One way or the other, during this period of isolation and training, seeds were planted that were to germinate several years later. The Besht began to discover remarkable powers within himself, and he interpreted these powers as a gift of the divine providence that had conferred a sacred mission upon him.

Indeed, the "revelation" tales, as cited by *Shivhei Habesht*'s compiler in the name of his father-in-law, are little more than a series of episodes, each of which discloses a further aspect of the Besht's unusual powers.[45] Viewed broadly, these episodes may be seen as unfolding the gradual process through which the Besht becomes aware of his own powers, at the same time as the people around him likewise begin to. This process begins when the Besht and his wife are still residents of a town near the Carpathian mountains. Once, the Besht happens by the town of Kotov where a dybbuk had taken possession of a woman. To everyone's surprise, the Besht manages to exorcise the dybbuk. Later, the Besht is invited to serve as a *melamed* (teacher in a traditional elementary school) in the home of a customs official. Yet the house set aside for him to live in by the customs official is considered to be haunted. The Besht does not hesitate to take up residence in the domicile and thus demonstrates his ability to impose his will upon demons. During the period of the Besht's employment as a *melamed* in the customs official's house, there was a drought. The Besht gathered a *minyan,* imposed a penance, passed in front of the ark, and prophesized that it would rain that very same day; so it did. Of the subsequent events we read the following:

> Afterward, several people with ailments chanced his way and he did not wish to meet with them. Finally they once brought an insane man or woman to him, yet he did not wish to receive that person. And at [the same] night he was told he was thirty-six years of age. And in the morning he made the calculation and it was so. He then received that insane person and cured him, and left off the post of *melamed,* and accepted my father-in-law of blessed memory as a scribe, and people began to travel to him from all places.[46]

According to this story, the Besht was of the opinion that it would not be proper for him to employ his powers openly before he had reached the age of thirty-six. It seems to me that this account expresses the awareness of the missionary purpose that was taking shape in the Besht's breast. At any rate, the main disclosure in the tale has to do with the completion of the formative process of the Besht as *baal shem.* After astonishing those around him, and perhaps himself as well, through several demonstrations of his powers, he acquired a reputation as a miracle worker and the ailing and unfortunate began to come to his door. When their numbers increased, he left off employment as a *melamed* and work as a *baal shem* became his stock in trade and source of income. This shift is clearly marked by the fact that he took on R. Alexander of Lince as his scribe, that is, as an inscriber of amulets.

What are the criteria for the success of a *baal shem*? One may say this much: a *baal shem* is one with a reputation (that is to say, has earned a name) for being able to heal the sick, exorcise dybbuks, impose his will on demons, prognosticate, and perform the other "operations" the public requires. Naturally, the large numbers of people who turn to a *baal shem* for assistance is further confirmation of a *baal shem*'s professional authority and success.

How does a *baal shem* acquire reputation and authority? The first answer to come to mind is that the more "operations" the *baal shem* is able to perform (that is, the more he can meet the expectations of those who turn to him), the greater grows his pool of potential clients and the wider his fame as a *baal shem*. This explanation, however, does not seem to me sufficient. The key to the success of a *baal shem* is the trust placed in him by those who used his services; a prerequisite for the development of such trust is the confidence the *baal shem* has in his own person and powers. In other words: a *baal shem*'s self-image, which he projects onto those who turn to him for assistance, is the foundation of the entire process!

As it happens, we do have certain fragments of evidence available about the Besht's self-image and about the manner in which he projected this image on those around him. I begin with a passage from *Shivhei Habesht*: "The rabbi of the holy community of Polonne had in his possession an amulet from the rabbi R. Naftali and he showed said amulet to the Besht and the Besht recognized that it had been written while [R. Naftali] was in a state of purity from ritual bathing and fasting, and he said: I will write an amulet [of equal potency] after a meal and while sitting on a bed."[47] The R. Naftali mentioned here is none other than R. Naftali Hacohen of Poznan, one of the greatest rabbis of his day, who was celebrated as a Kabbalist skilled in both theoretical and applied Kabbalah, and who had gained a reputation as a *baal shem* of wide performance.[48] Quite obviously, an amulet written by such a personage is not to be taken lightly. One may thus suppose that when R. Yaakov Yosef showed this possession of his to the Besht, he was hoping to hear his professional opinion on an amulet that had been inscribed by a famous *baal shem* from the previous generation. Nor is it inconceivable that this display of the amulet was an act of hubris. At any rate, the response of the Besht leaves no doubt as to the high esteem in which he held himself as a *baal shem*: R. Naftali required ritual bathing and fasting so as to inscribe this amulet, whereas he, the Besht, was capable of inscribing such an amulet as a mere afterthought. To be more precise: the need to bathe and fast does not attest to any inferiority of spiritual rank on the part of R. Naftali, as this was the general practice followed by *baalei shem*.[49] The Besht here is the unusual one, for being able to dispense with such matters entirely.

Further evidence as to the Besht's self-image is contained in a letter he wrote to the rabbi of Sdeh Lavan. Though I have cited this letter above, it is worth a second glance:

> Return from the road and you will find in your home, in your yard, a great tumult of men and women and children and you will faint from terror. And when you are awakened immediately order that blood be let from two veins. And promptly send a special messenger to inform me of the tumult, even though God be praised I have eyes to see from afar, even so send me letters by messenger. So spoke Israel Baal Shem Tov.[50]

The final sentence in this short letter—"even though God be praised I have eyes to see from afar"—is somewhat superfluous. It would thus seem that the Besht was not only sure of his powers, but also enjoyed reminding people of them.[51]

What this letter makes clear is a further phenomenon of considerable significance for understanding the formation of the Besht's reputation as a *baal shem:* The Besht often told his close acquaintances about his powers and "performances." It seems to me, accordingly, that it would not be unwarranted to assert that the seed of the myth that sprang up about the powers of the Besht may be found in what the Besht reported of himself. Supporting evidence for this claim may be found in the following statements by Rabbi Yaakov Yosef of Polonne:

> That I heard from my teacher may he be remembered in the world to come an explanation of the Mishnaic verse, "The eye sees and the ear hears" etc. (Tractate Avoth 2:1). In its essence, the eye has the capacity to see from one end of the world to the other and the ear to hear that which is decreed from On High. Only our sins divide us from that essence, for our souls are in the captivity of the evil instinct and three *qlipot* [rinds] of foreskin bind our sight and hearing, and it is necessary for these *qlipot* to be broken for one to see and to hear. And my teacher may he be remembered in the World to Come is proof of this, as he was able to see from afar and to hear Decrees which were demonstrated to be true. And if so, it is indeed possible to hear and to see in said manner.[52]

R. Yaakov Yosef was, as is known, a close student of the Besht. What he quotes from his teacher here gives a good representation of the Besht's tendency to formulate notions of general application on the basis of his own personal experiences. Yet the passage also sheds light on the way in which the Besht regarded himself. If he was favored with the power of sight from afar and an ability to hear decrees, it was thanks to the high spiritual rank he had achieved. We find this as well: R. Yaakov Yosef was not content to transmit the statements the Besht made about himself verbatim, but also added his own testimony, confirming that the Besht was indeed graced with such sight and such hearing. Yet where could R. Yaakov Yosef have learned of these powers of the Besht? One may assume he was informed of them by the Besht himself—just as the Besht had drawn attention to his ability to see from afar in his letter to the rabbi of Sdeh Lavan, and just as he let R. Yaakov Yosef know he was capable of writing amulets without prior cleansing. The fact that a personage endowed with such powers as his should feel a need to share the secret with others is not astonishing. It is also the case that those in the Besht's circle would quite naturally have reported to others the things they had heard from the Besht himself.[53]

Something of the way in which the reputation of the Besht and his powers spread may be found in a passage from a letter that R. Gershon of Kotov sent to the Besht from the land of Israel:

> My beloved brother-in-law, I would like to say that once when I was in your sacred company you told me you had seen in a vision that a *hacham* [Sephardic rabbi] had arrived in Jerusalem from a country to the west [Morocco] and he was the Messiah's spark, only he does not know it himself and he is a great sage in matters of Halachah and Kabbalah and a master of soulful prayer. And afterward you told me that you no longer see him and that it appears to you that he has departed from this world. And when I came here, I investigated the matter and I was told who this man of great wonders was: his name was R. Hayim b. Atar and he was a great Hasid and learned and versant in matters of Halacha and Kabbalah and all the sages of Israel were to him as monkeys are in comparison to human beings. . . . And by our great sins he did not live for long in Jerusalem, but only for a single year. . . . And I told the sages here what you had said of him and they were astounded to hear it. In brief, your name is already known in the gates of Jerusalem and the local sages requested of me that I write you to encourage you to come here to take up residence and to tell you they are hungry for the sight of your countenance.[54]

It seems that R. Gershon had no doubts about the ability of the Besht to see from afar. Accordingly, upon reaching the land of Israel he began to make inquiries so as to ascertain the identity of the figure the Besht had seen in his vision. When he learned of R. Hayim ben Atar, he realized that he was the person in the Besht's vision, and reported his discovery to the sages of Jerusalem. Now according to R. Gershon's letter, the Besht's ability to "see" the Kabbalist R. Hayim ben Atar immigrating to the land of Israel deeply impressed Jerusalem's sages. One may also readily surmise that once having demonstrated the Besht's powers of long-distance vision, R. Gershon went on to regale these sages with further accounts of the Besht's wondrous performances. In any case, the name of the Besht "was already known in the gates of Jerusalem."[55]

The establishment of the Besht's reputation was not something that proceeded unchallenged. The Besht apparently had to deal with skeptics on the one hand and competitors on the other. The doubts that various people express of the Besht's capacities form the nucleus of several stories. Most of these tales follow a fixed plan: such-and-such a person of honorable standing, a wealthy merchant, *gvir,* scholar, and so forth, does not believe in the powers endowing the Besht. In due course, the skeptic himself suffers some mishap and must turn to the Besht for aid. Once the Besht demonstrates his abilities, the skeptic is converted into a believer.[56] At first sight, these tales seem designed to meet the needs of the storytellers and of their audience, people who enjoyed demonstrating to themselves and to others that the Besht was indeed blessed with extraordinary powers. Yet it seems to me that it would not be overbold to surmise that the seed from which these tales sprang was the Besht's own need to protect his reputation as a miracle worker against the doubts that were raised on this score.

This conjecture is strengthened by a story that revolves around a confrontation between the Besht and certain persons who ultimately became associates of his. The story opens with these lines: "It happened that when the Besht came to the community of Miedzybóz he was not well regarded by the Hasidim, that is by R. Ze'ev Kotses and R. David Furkes, on account of his being called the Baal Shem Tov, as such a name does not befit a *Zaddik.*"[57] What follows is a marvelous and meandering tale about a pupil of these two Hasidim who took ill, at which time the Besht is summoned to heal him. The Besht reveals to the student that he is about to die and promises to find him a place in the Garden of Eden. After his death, the student appears to his teachers in a dream and tells them about a Talmudic difficulty and its resolution which the Besht, in the heavens, had raised and resolved. After having the remarkable experience of this revelation, R. Ze'ev and R. David went to eat the Sabbath afternoon meal at the Besht's, and were stunned when they heard the Besht raise precisely the same difficulty they had heard in the dream. When they resolved it for him the Besht told them: "I know that it was the deceased who told it to you; and from that day forward they became his associates."[58]

This tale, presented here only in essentials, is clearly legendary in form. Furthermore, its opening lines have a discernibly anachronistic air. I am referring to the explanation given for R. Zeev's and R. David's poor regard of the Besht for "his being called the Baal Shem Tov, as such a name does not befit a

Zaddik." Nowhere do we find that the Besht's associates refer to him by the designation "*Zaddik.*" Moreover, the employment of the term *Zaddik* in the sense of a Hasidic leader is known to be a later phenomenon. The anachronism in these lines is also evident by their content; during the period in question the *baalei shem* in fact enjoyed great respect. It thus would seem that the present version of this story took form at the hands of persons who did not wish to attribute magical powers to the Hasidic *Zaddik.*[59]

As said, besides its anachronistic air, the story has the characteristics of a legend. One may nevertheless speculate that the factual core on which the story is based was a tension that existed at a certain stage between the Besht and the two Hasidim from Miedzybóz. Let us imagine the following scenario: R. Ze'ev Kotses and R. David Furkes are two Hasidim who live in Miedzybóz and enjoy the prestige, and perhaps also the material advantages, that the community showers upon of such exalted personages.[60] One day, a man arrives in town who is famous not only as a Hasid and Kabbalist, but also as a *baal shem.*[61] The two veteran Hasidim feel threatened by this new arrival, and cast aspersions about his "remarkable powers." The Besht needs recognition of his powers in his new place of residence, and above all needs the recognition of these two Hasidim, as they are the persons closest to him in rank and spirituality. R. Ze'ev and R. David test his mettle; he in turn makes efforts to persuade them that he is indeed graced with unusual powers. After proving his exalted status to them, they are transformed into his followers and associates.

It seems to me that such a scenario follows almost necessarily if one considers the relevant actors and the circumstances of the period. Anyone who maintains that the entire story is a fabrication that can teach us nothing about the Besht's biography, will have to account for why Hasidic legend should have invented, *ex nihilo,* a conflict between the Besht and some of the figures closest to him.

It is entirely natural for a person whose fame as a miracle worker precedes him to be concerned about the potential failures that may cause damage to his good name. Apprehensions of this kind were the lot of the Besht as well. They are illustrated in the following story: "When the Besht was on the way to Chmielnik, he heard a Decree that R. Yosef the *melamed* in said holy community was about to die. And when he arrived in town, the townspeople came to him and wanted to pay for healing him, yet he did not wish to heal him and did not disclose his reasons."[62] Later in the story, the townspeople call in a doctor who seems able to heal R. Yosef. Yet eventually R. Yosef dies, as a result of an ointment given to him by the doctor. "Then the Besht revealed that the reason he had not wished to heal him was on account of the Decree he had heard."[63] The simple moral of this tale is the advantage the Besht had over the doctor, in being able to foresee R. Yosef's death and thus being able to dispense with the attempt at curing him. Yet at second thought the question arises: So what if the patient has been decreed to die? Would it not have been more proper to attempt to cure him, if only to provide him with spiritual comfort? It thus would seem that the Besht acted as he did out of fears that he might appear in public to have failed.

A further example of this phenomenon is contained in the well-known story about the Besht's visit to the home of the wealthy leaseholders of Sluck. In the course of the visit, a sick child of one of the leaders of the community was brought to the Besht. "And he came to the Besht who said he would live and later he saw that he would die and he understood that they were trying to disgrace him and he left that place in the middle of the night."[64] The admission of the Besht's failure and the description of his escape contribute to the trustworthiness of the tale. The Besht's escape "in the middle of the night" reflects the difficulty he had in being publicly exposed as someone who had failed at his job.

A further dimension of the Besht's struggle to maintain his reputation as a *baal shem* involved his tensions with competitors; that is, with doctors on the one hand and with the Jewish and non-Jewish miracle workers on the other. Certain stories in *Shivhei Habesht* describe a conflict between the Besht and the doctors. What significance does this conflict have? What can be learned from it about the Besht's modus operandi as a *baal shem*? I begin my discussion of these questions with two tales:

> I heard from the rabbi of our community: Once the Besht was traveling on the road and lodging in a certain location when he heard: hurry back as R. Yosef is extremely weak. . . . And he came to his home on Friday morning and went to the *mikvah* before prayers, and after prayers summoned a certain doctor and went with him to the patient and beheld that he was very weak. . . . And he told the doctor to perform a bloodletting and the doctor did not want to do so, saying it was quite dangerous to let blood. . . . And the Besht ordered that the bloodletting be performed immediately and there was a great outcry among the people against the Besht for the letting of the blood. . . . And about a half an hour later the patient requested that he be given water to drink and was healed, thank the Lord.[65]
>
> R. Ayzik, the Rabbi's son, had a young daughter thirteen years of age who was married, and she took ill. And when the Besht was in the holy community of Zaslav he was shown the patient. And he ordered that on the morrow the doctor's wife would be summoned for her to attach leeches to her and he said to open some of her anal veins. And the Peer R. Ayzik was wary of relying on the Besht, and sought out the

physician of the Duchess of said holy community, and he said that even for a minor it was common to open anal veins and he came home and sent for the doctor's wife.[66]

In the first of these two stories we are witness to an open conflict between the Besht and the "doctor." Clearly the reference is not to a licensed doctor, but to a popular healer who was competent in such accepted medical practices as bloodletting. Apparently, the Besht himself was not competent in this procedure, or perhaps he considered it beneath his dignity. At any rate, there are no stories or testimony indicating that the Besht preformed bloodlettings by himself. Even when he is of the opinion that bloodletting is the proper prognosis, he directs others to perform the procedure. Something of the sort happened in the story before us except that the doctor defied the decision of the Besht. The conflict described here between the Besht and the doctor may thus be classed as a professional dispute about the degree of benefit and hazard that a bloodletting would yield in this particular case.

In the second story, by contrast, the confrontation between the Besht and the doctor is indirect. The father of the ailing girl has doubts about the Besht's diagnosis and turns to the "physician of the Duchess" as the preferred authority. This time the doctor is presumably a licensed physician, as he is in the service of the duchess. By contrast, the "doctor's wife," who is summoned to apply leeches to the girl, is evidently the wife of a popular healer. Presumably she was given charge of the treatment of the girl for reasons having to do with chastity.

It is worth observing that in the two cases, the Besht elected to apply methods from the realm of "natural medicines" and not from the realm of magic. This feature is also characteristic of all the other stories in which the Besht comes into conflict with doctors. So it is, for example, in the case of the illness of R. Hayim, the rabbi of the Sdeh Lavan community. After the Besht's attempts to heal the patient proved unsuccessful, his sons summoned a doctor from a different town. Of what took place when the doctor arrived, we read the following: "They brought him to their father, and each time the doctor told them to do something they replied: the Besht already did that. And the doctor went away humiliated."[67] The doctor's disappointment is understandable given that the Besht had first recommended the very same medications that he himself prescribed.

What was the nature of the Besht's conflict with the doctors? This was not a conflict between medicine and magic, as the Besht himself employed medicinal means! Moreover, in the society depicted in *Shivhei Habesht*, the decision to employ doctors on the one hand or *baalei shem* on the other was not regarded as a choice between distinct alternatives, one of which was superior to the other. Thus, we see that the sons of the rabbi of Sdeh Lavan summoned a doctor after despairing of the Besht. In another story the Besht was asked to heal a sick person after a famous doctor had given up on him. In the story about R. Yosef, the Besht himself took a doctor along with him when he went to visit the patient. Recall that such summons of a doctor and of a *baal shem,* one after the other or simultaneously, are also to be found in the book *Yesh Manhilin;* their basis is the supposition that it is desirable to combat illnesses on both magical and medical planes. It was for this very reason that *baalei shem* did not confine themselves to magical methods and made use of "natural medicines" as well. Yet it was in just such circumstances that competition was likely to develop between the *baalei shem* and the doctors. This competition is the background for the Besht's conflict with the doctors. The question around which the conflict revolved concerned how extensive an understanding the Besht had specifically of conventional medicine.

A good illustration of this aspect of the conflict may be found in the tale of the illness of the rabbi of Sdeh Lavan. Recall that after the rabbi's sons reached the conclusion that the Besht was not managing to cure him, they summoned a doctor from another town. Of the Besht's reaction to the summons of the doctor and the dialogue between the two, we read as follows:

> And the Besht beheld that the doctor was traveling and he told that rabbi: I will travel away from here for this is the location toward which the doctor of the holy community of Ostra is traveling. And the rabbi did not know of this and beseeched him greatly lest he depart, so he remained there on account of the many entreaties. . . . For this doctor had once threatened the Besht saying: When I see the Besht I will kill him by the rifle that he carries. And in the morning the Besht made haste to depart and the ailing rabbi detained him, by which time the doctor had arrived in town. And the Besht said: Behold, the doctor has arrived in town, and he sat on the cart and rode off. And when he passed by the hotel where the doctor was staying he descended from the cart and entered the house and greeted him. And he asked him: Where did you learn doctoring? And he replied: The blessed Lord taught me.[68]

The story suggests that the Besht was angry or insulted that the sons of his patient believed the doctor could succeed where he had failed. The doctor, in turn, took offense at the Besht for encroaching on his territory. As the person in question was a licensed physician, one can readily understand his question, "Where did you learn doctoring?" as meaning: "Why are you working in a field in which you are unqualified?" The Besht's reply, "The Blessed Lord taught me," is a reflection of the view held of the Besht by the storyteller and presumably also by the Besht himself. In effect, it says: even when employing "natural" healing methods, the Besht's deeds carry a spiritual dimension that the doctors' are lacking.[69] A picturesque expression of the patient's own sentiments on this score may be seen in the reaction that the rabbi of Sdeh Lavan has to his sons' summons of the doctor: "Then the ailing patient scolded his sons: What have you done? Even though I did not receive a cure from the Besht, still when the Besht came in to see me I knew that the *shekhina* [divine presence] arrived with him and when the Doctor came in I felt as though I was being visited by some priest."[70]

What may one learn from the tales describing the conflict between the Besht and the doctors?[71] At first glance, it seems as though they are merely meant to reaffirm the Besht's authority in the minds of the tellers and hearers of the stories. It seems to me, however, that they are just as much reflections of the need the Besht himself felt to shore up his authority in the face of his competitors.

Competitors of a different sort who posed a threat to the Besht's reputation as a *baal shem* were the non-Jewish popular healers. It comes as no surprise that this phenomenon also finds expression in *Shivhei Habesht*. In the continuation of the story cited above about R. Ayzik's young daughter, we read that the girl did not recover, despite the treatment recommended by the Besht—treatment the doctor had supported. Yet the concerned father did not give up hope:

> And R. Ayzik traveled with his daughter to a *kedar* [healer] that was in the community of Constantin and the Besht heard of this and himself traveled to Constantin and berated him and said: Will you too do this to me?! And R. Ayzik promised to go back home, not really meaning it. And when R. Ayzik saw that the *kedar* neither helps nor harms he returned home with his daughter.[72]

When the girl's father sought assistance from the *kedar*, that is, from a popular healer of gypsy or Tatar origin, the Besht was indignant. The idiom the Besht elects to employ, "Will you too do this to me?!" suggests that this was not the only time that persons he was unable to cure sought relief for their ailments from non-Jewish healers.[73] Naturally, behavior such as this would have damaged the Besht's professional standing. It is perhaps needless to add that the injury to his reputation would have been especially distressing in cases in which the non-Jewish healer succeeded where he failed.

When necessary, Jews evidently did not hesitate to turn to the miracle workers or popular healers from the non-Jewish population. These professionals were more widely available, and presumably also less expensive, than the "expert" doctors and certainly than the licensed physicians. And as if all this did not suffice, the non-Jewish healer had a further advantage: he knew

how to deal with witchcraft and demons, matters that were outside the doctors' realms of specialization. Thus it is unsurprising that the educated and
wealthy classes of Jewish society also occasionally employed non-Jewish healers. The tales in *Shivhei Habesht* confirm this: R. Ayzik, the father of the sick
girl mentioned above, was a "nobleman" and the son of a rabbi. Likewise, we
read about a different rabbinic figure as follows: "R. Moshe, the rabbi of the
holy community of Kotov, had a daughter-in-law who was afflicted by barrenness and he hired non-Jewish witches who cast their spells and placed a cas-
trated rooster under the doorsill of the house."[74]

Open condemnation of Jews who turn to popular healers not of the faith
is nowhere to be found: neither in *Shivhei Habesht,* nor in the other Beshtian
sources. This fact is unsurprising: the phenomenon was so widespread that
outright condemnation of it would have been regarded as the issuance of an
unenforceable edict. Yet *Shivhei Habesht* does contain less direct expressions
of disapproval with respect to this phenomenon. Thus, for example, there is
a story about a sick person whom the Besht was summoned to treat. When
he is informed that family members had summoned "non-Jewish witches" as
well, the Besht decides to abandon treatment of the patient.[75] More explicit
expressions of disapproval toward non-Jewish healers appear in the continuation of the story cited above. The assistance the non-Jewish healers extended
to R. Moshe of Kotov lead to a grave misfortune: a demon took possession of
R. Moshe's home, and matters reached the point where R. Moshe was forced
to abandon it. This predicament was no mere mishap: non-Jewish witches
often employed demons in their treatments, making possession of this kind
a real hazard.

The Besht did not contest the contemporary perspective according to
which demons could be used as part of a treatment; he himself, however,
refrained from such employment because demons were untrustworthy. As it
is related in *Shivhei Habesht,* he came to this conclusion on the basis of an event
that occurred to him personally.[76] The Besht expressed his conclusion about
not employing demons in a passage in which he interprets the scriptural verse:
"And Jacob sent forth *malachim* [angels or messengers]" (Gen. 32:2). It runs
as follows:

> And he sent forth *malachim,* these are angels who went before him.
> And he said that before our Patriarch Jacob, angels always went to his
> right and demons to his left. And before the Besht too, angels went to
> his right and demons to his left. Yet he did not wish to employ angels
> because they are holy or demons because they are liars.[77]

By adopting the principle of nonemployment of demons, the Besht clearly
distanced himself from the non-Jewish miracle workers. It seems that this

distinction was important to him, both because Jews commonly called upon non-Jewish healers and because of the seeming similarity in the working methods of the healers and the *baalei shem*. Both types of miracle worker made use of magical formulas, amulets, and charms. Yet from the Besht's point of view, the magical formulas that the non-Jewish healers applied were not the same as the Holy Names he made use of himself. It followed that the competition with the non-Jewish healers was of a moral and not merely a private significance.

Finally, one may not ignore healers of another kind who stood to compete with the Besht, namely the other *baalei shem* who lived and worked in his day. One such *baal shem* was R. Yoel Halpern. R. Yoel, it will be recalled, resided in Zamosc and earned great fame; his services were sought after by many. He passed away only five years before the Besht did. It is hard to imagine that the Besht would not have heard of R. Yoel or of the charms books associated with his name. Indeed, it is not inconceivable that copies of these texts may have found their way to the Besht.[78] Is it truly a coincidence that R. Yoel and his books receive no mention in *Shivhei Habesht* or in the other compositions associated with the Besht's circle? Is this perhaps not an accidental silence but rather a deliberate avoidance? Given our treatment thus far, it would not be too bold to speculate that the Besht's silence as regards the other *baalei shem* who practiced in his day was a reflection of his self-image, as someone greatly superior to all other *baalei shem*.

Exclusivity

The Besht's "performances" as a *baal shem* were based, as we have seen, on both the use of Names and charms and on the remarkable powers with which he was endowed. Where did the Besht acquire his knowledge of Names and charms? Ultimately, knowledge such as this was esoteric, not something available to all and sundry. *Shivhei Habesht* provides an answer to this question through the collection of tales involving R. Adam Baal Shem.[79] As is related in these tales, R. Adam had the powers to perform incredible miracles. Thus, for example, he invited the emperor to a feast in his home, and so as to be able to host him with the appropriate splendor, he magically transported a royal palace in which a magnificent feast was prepared to the site of his meager home.

After the tale about R. Adam and his marvels, there appears a story that links this wondrous *baal shem* to the Besht. Among R. Adam's possessions there were writings that contained Torah secrets. Prior to his death, R. Adam had ordered his son to bequeath these writings to the Besht. R. Adam's son was eager to fill his father's testament, yet he did not find the task an easy one, as this was the period of the Besht's "seclusion." Eventually, R. Adam's son is able to locate the Besht and conveys the writings to him. Astonishing relations develop between the two: R. Adam's son, considered by all to be a scholar of a prestigious lineage, begs the Besht, who at the time was regarded by all as an ignoramus, to teach him from the writings sent on by his father. In the end R. Adam's son receives the fate of an early death for having dared to engage in wonders that were beyond him.[80]

The R. Adam stories have been extensively treated in the scholarly literature. The first scholar to take a special interest in these tales was Gershom Scholem. In Scholem's opinion, the purpose of these fabulous tales was to provide a cover for certain writings that the Besht indeed possessed. The reference here is to *Sefer Hatsoref,* by R. Heschel Tsoref. The transcriber of that book intimates in its preface that the original manuscript had been in the Besht's hands and that the Besht even requested that a copy be drawn up for him. Another source suggests that Rabbi Ephraim Zalman Margaliot found manifestations of the Sabbatean heresy in this book. Scholem combined these two pieces of information and drew the conclusion that the purpose of the R. Adam legends was to blunt charges about writings that were indeed in the Besht's possession. When the Besht possessed these manuscripts their Sabbatean associations had yet to be disclosed; but when the matter was revealed to the Hasidim, following R. Margaliot's discovery, they took pains to invent the R. Adam tales so as to camouflage the fact that the Besht possessed a text that was suspected of heresy.[81]

Scholem's hypothesis was challenged by Khone Shmeruk, who discovered a previous literary incarnation of R. Adam Baal Shem. He found a text in Yiddish that contained the fabulous tales of R. Adam, and established its provenance in Prague in the seventeenth century.[82] It thus would appear that the figure of R. Adam was not an invention of Hasidim who sought to conceal their master's affiliations with Tsoref's suspect text, but had been adopted from a still earlier literary source. Shmeruk is dismissive of the possibility that the Hasidim consciously used the extant R. Adam legends so as to conceal the Besht's links to a work tainted with the odor of Sabbateanism. In his opinion, such an act of concealment would have been inconsistent with the naive literary genre to which *Shivhei Habesht* belongs. Scholem continued to affirm his hypothesis in spite of Shmeruk's discovery.[83] Joseph Dan and Avraham Rubinstein have likewise ventured their opinions that Shmeruk's discovery does not necessarily controvert Scholem's hypothesis.[84]

Yehoshua Mondshine has surveyed the various positions proposed on the R. Adam issue and weighs in himself as regards Scholem's perspective. The gist of his argument is that there is no logic in the supposition that anything about the R. Adam stories lets them "conceal" writings in the Besht's possession that may have been suspected of heresy.[85] To this argument of Mondshine's, which strikes me as on target and convincing, one may add a further argument: Scholem's interpretation ignores the role served by the R. Adam tales in describing the Besht's occupation as a *baal shem*.

This shortcoming is also a feature of the new interpretation to the R. Adam stories proposed recently by Ze'ev Gries. Gries's interpretation is based, in the main, on a passage from *Shivhei Habesht* that tells of the fate of the writings that were in the Besht's possession. This passage relates that the Besht entombed these writings under a stone in the mountain, and goes on to state "that these writings were discovered a fifth time to the Besht, and he said that the writings had been in the possession of the Patriarch Abraham may he rest in peace and in the possession of Yehoshua bin Nun and of the rest I do not know."[86] This sequence of attributions causes Gries to pose the question:

> It is well known that the book of Yetzira was attributed to the Patri-
> arch Abraham; yet if the one receiving these writings from him was
> Yehoshua bin Nun, the successor of our Rabbi Moses, on what basis
> shall we attribute mystical writings to him? For we have no evidence
> or shred of evidence even of the pseudo-epigraphic kind, that
> Yehoshua bin Nun wrote any mystical writings or possessed any such.
> Apparently, the solution to the riddle of the essence of Yehoshua bin
> Nun lies elsewhere, and so *eo ipso* is the solution to the riddle of the
> essence of the writings.[87]

Gries's resolution is based on a reidentification of the Yehoshua bin Nun figure mentioned in the passage cited. Readers of *Shivhei Habesht* may have hitherto been naively assuming that the reference was to the Yehoshua bin Nun of the Bible, but Gries argues that the reference is in fact to a Yehoshua bin Nun who lived in sixteenth-century Safed. This person was an admirer of the ARI who, out of his own pocket, had financed a transcription of the ARI's writings. And as this Yehoshua bin Nun's deed is described in *Shivhei HaAri,* a book that reached the Hasidim, Gries draws the conclusion: "Surely they could not have failed to be cognizant of the part Yehoshua bin Nun played in transcribing the writings of the ARI and preserving them for later generations." Gries further remarks that Lurianic manuscripts were maintained in Hasidic circles. Con-sequently, summarizes Gries:

> The legendary tale of the Besht and Adam Baal Shem serves, if so, to
> establish in the Hasidim's common consciousness and in their mem-
> ories, a chain of inheritance of Lurianic writings which had already
> become sanctified in their day. Nonetheless, stress was laid also on the
> legitimacy of possession of the writings, which was closely linked to
> the line of inheritance of the Besht himself, whose soul, as previously

mentioned, was a reincarnation of the soul of Rabbi Shimon Bar
Yohai and of the ARI, of whom he was the spark.[88]

We are to infer that the Hasidim's links to the Kabbalah and its literature, and
Hasidism's perception of itself as being rooted in the Kabbalah did not suffice
to allow the Hasidim to feel secure in their rights to own Lurianic writings. To
that end they required the additional knowledge that the Besht too had possessed these writings. They were to be informed of this fact by means of the fabulous tales of R. Adam and the writings he bequeathed to the Besht. And how
were the Hasidim to know that these particular writings were Lurianic? This
was to be intimated to them by the mention of the name of Yehoshua bin Nun
of Safed, he who used his funds to finance a transcription of Lurianic writings.

I suspect that Gries's commendable proficiency in the history of the Hebrew
text has led him astray here; it is doubtful that any of those Hasidim who maintained possession of writings from the ARI's heritage was ever aware of the
debt he owed this Yehoshua bin Nun for his role in transcribing them. Moreover, Gries' declaration that the biblical Yehoshua bin Nun is nowhere mentioned in connection with Torah secrets is not well founded. In the *Hekhalot*
literature Yehoshua is indeed mentioned as one who had received secrets of
the Torah from Moses and transmitted them to the elders.[89]

As said above, the common denominator in the interpretations that
Scholem and Gries offer for the R. Adam tales is that they ignore the role played
by this story in the framework of the biography of the Besht as a *baal shem*. The
scholar who does address this aspect of the topic is Joseph Dan. Dan links the
role of the R. Adam stories with the fabulous tales cited in the beginning of *Shivhei Habesht* about the Besht's father. According to Dan, the function of these
two groups of stories is to "extract the Besht from the condition of 'illegitimate
birth,' as someone who has no father and no rabbi." As to the specific function
of the R. Adam stories, Dan explains that they were meant to provide a basis for
"the claim suggested in most of the stories of *Shivhei Habesht* about the Besht's
super-human powers."[90] Dan's approach seems to me correct. The stories about
the Besht's father and about R. Adam are meant to fill a lacuna in the Besht's
biography. What these two groups of stories imply about his history is likewise
similar: the Besht was not born to a prestigious lineage and he had no famous
teacher. If that had not been the case, there would not have been a need to invent
a rabbi for him in the form of the fabulous figure of R. Adam.

Given our earlier treatment of the *baalei shem*, a more concise picture of
the R. Adam tales and their role in *Shivhei Habesht* may be suggested. It will
be recalled that R. Yoel (the Second), a contemporary of the Besht, maintained
possession of manuscripts containing names and charms. Moreover, R. Yoel
repeatedly stressed the lineal inheritance of the writings he owned. According

to him, these writings had been in the possession of R. Eliyahu of Luanz, someone who earned fame as a *baal shem* during the second half of the sixteenth and the early seventeenth centuries, and also in the possession of his famous grandfather, R. Yoel Baal Shem (the First), who lived and worked in the second half of the seventeenth and in the early eighteenth centuries. We also found that Rabbi Hirsch Fraenkel, who worked as a *baal shem* at the close of the seventeenth and in the first half of the eighteenth century, owned a manuscript containing Names and oath formulas. There is no doubt that these cases are instances of a more general rule; namely, ownership of manuscripts containing the esoteric knowledge on which magical performance was based, was typical behavior for *baalei shem*. It will further be recalled that the more ancient the source one could ascribe to these writings (e.g., a famous *baal shem* from a previous generation), the more valuable they were.

We thus find that the R. Adam tales are meant to supply an answer to the question, What is the source of the esoteric knowledge that the Besht drew upon as a *baal shem?* The answer provided by these stories fits a pattern common to the *baalei shem;* namely, the Besht possessed writings that had reached him from a famous *baal shem* from a previous generation. R. Adam's legendary performances surely tell something about the powers of the Besht, who inherited the knowledge that R. Adam had owned. This, it seems to me, is the simple and sole explanation of the R. Adam tales that are embedded within *Shivhei Habesht.* This was also the spirit in which the translator of *Shivhei Habesht* into Yiddish understood these tales. He explicitly writes: "and all the performances and marvels which the Baal Shem carried out, all were drawn from the writings which came to him from the *baal shem tov* R. Adam."[91]

It is perfectly clear that the R. Adam stories are a complete fabrication. Nevertheless, they do correspond to a genuine practice: *baalei shem* did own manuscripts containing Names and charms. The question consequently arises: Did the Besht too own manuscripts of this kind? Or, to rephrase the question slightly: Were manuscripts in the Besht's possession the historical nucleus of the association between the Besht and the "writings" of the legendary R. Adam? One must rest content with the claim that this is a plausible hypothesis. Yet it seems that it finds a certain purchase in a passage from *Shivhei Habesht.* I am referring to a passage earlier cited in part; owing to its importance I shall now cite it in *toto:*

> And those writings the Besht sealed under a certain stone in the mountain, for he swore the stone to an oath and it opened and in it he deposited said writings and it closed again and he set a certain Guard upon it. And the rabbi of our community heard from the *Mokhiah* of the holy community of Polonne who as an old man had

said: I have the ability to take the writings from there as I know its
location, yet because the Besht had sealed them I do not wish to
remove them. And he said that these writings were discovered a fifth
time to the Besht and he said the writings had been in the possession
of the Patriarch Abraham may he rest in peace and in the possession
of Yehoshua bin Nun and of the rest I do not know.[92]

The Polonne *mokhiah* is well known as a member of the Besht's circle. Are
the statements attributed to him about writings in the Besht's possession
entirely baseless? One ought to bear in mind that the *mokhiah* is being quoted
here directly by his student, Gedaliah of Lince. It seems to me that these statements attributed to the *mokhiah* imply that within the Besht's circle of followers, there was some sort of tradition about esoteric writings owned by the
Besht. This was apparently an independent tradition that only later came to
be linked with the R. Adam stories. Support for this conjecture may be seen
in the fact that in the *mokhiah*'s list of the previous owners of these writings,
R. Adam's name does not figure at all. If this impression is correct—that
within the Besht's circle, there was a certain knowledge about the writings in
his possession—it becomes easier to understand why those in a later generation would have put forward the R. Adam stories as a means of accounting
for their origins.[93]

In this context we may remark that the story about the writing repository
is significant in another way: it expresses a view of the Besht's personality as
the Polonne *mokhiah* perceived it. In this tale the Besht is depicted as a *baal
shem* who keeps his professional secrets to himself. He does not bequeath the
"writings" in his possession to the members of his circle, any more than he
transmits his remarkable powers to them. Several other stories from *Shivhei
Habesht* are likewise indicative of the Besht's demands for exclusivity. A common theme in all these stories is that members of the Besht's circle seek to be
favored with powers like those gracing the Besht, and sometimes make so bold
as to claim they have such powers. The Besht's attitude toward the ambitions
and conceits of his followers is one of fundamental disapproval. One of the
figures referred to in these stories is none other than the Polonne *mokhiah*.

The Besht had been summoned to Nemirov so as to exorcise a demon from
a domicile there; he asked the *mokhiah* to accompany him. When reaching the
residence the Besht was able to perceive the "malefactor," yet such vision was
denied to the *mokhiah*, who asked for the Besht's help:

> The Besht said to him: but you will be frightened. He said to him: Nay.
> Said [the Besht]: shut your eyes and open them several times. He did
> so and saw [the demon] standing in the corner of the house. . . . And
> later on the *Mokhiah* began to be frightened. And [the Besht] told

him: Shut and open your eyes as at first and you will no longer see him. So he did, and no longer saw him.[94]

Apparently, the *mokhiah* was incapable of properly confronting demons. At first he can't see them, and when he does see them he is seized with fright. He is thus inferior to the Besht in this respect. However, even when the *mokhiah* is able to act as the Besht does, the latter beats him back. An example may be seen in the following tale. A quarrel broke out between the community of Shargorod and Rabbi Yaakov Yosef, the community's rabbi. Things reached such a pitch that Rabbi Yaakov Yosef was chased out of town just before the Sabbath and had to spend the Sabbath in a village nearby. The Besht asked the members of his circle to accompany him to that village, so as to aid Rabbi Yaakov Yosef in his hour of need. Of the subsequent events, we read the following:

> And the *Mokhiah* too was there with them. And on the Sabbath after the *Mussaf* prayers the *Mokhiah* saw that the Rabbi was chagrined. He said to him: Do not be chagrined, I heard a Decree which was decreed, saying: so-an-so your enemy shall be killed and so-and-so your enemy shall perish on the road and the whole town shall go up in flames. And when the Besht heard his words he shouted at the *Mokhiah* and said: Fool! Do you too hear Decrees? And the *Mokhiah* was silent.[95]

The Besht is not denying that the *mokhiah* was capable of hearing Decrees. In another story relating to the same episode, he even explicitly admits as much.[96] Yet by hearing decrees the *mokhiah* is exceeding the bounds of his territory and encroaching on turf reserved for the Besht. Here is another example: The *mokhiah* had requested that the Besht teach him the language of beasts, birds, and plants. The Besht consented to his request and taught him

> until the *Mokhiah* was thoroughly knowledgeable in the matter . . . [and] could hear how birds converse and how beasts and animals speak. And he expounded all these secrets to him while traveling, until they drew near to the town. And when they drew near to town the Besht told him: Do you have a proper grasp of this wisdom? And he said: Aye. And the Besht passed his hand over the *Mokhiah*'s face and all memory of the details of the secrets of this wisdom were lost to him. . . . And the Besht laughed and said: if knowledge of this wisdom were necessary to you so as to aid you in worshiping the Creator, I myself would hasten to teach it to you. On this occasion, I taught you this wisdom so as to quench your thirst and you have forgotten it as it is not part of your worship.[97]

The lines attributed to the Besht in this story contain an important distinction: the Besht is prepared to teach the members of his circle what they need to know for the worship of the Lord—yet the *mokhiah*'s ambitions to understand the language of beasts and birds exceed these bounds. Secret knowledge such as this must by rights remain in the Besht's exclusive domain.

One may distinguish the tales cited here by the degree of fictionalization they contain. While in the last story the fictional element is prominent, the Besht's rebuke of the *mokhiah*, "Fool! Do you too hear Decrees?" sounds authentic. One way or the other, it seems to me that there is a common historical nucleus at the basis of these stories: the *mokhiah* had ambitions to gain powers similar to those gracing the Besht, while the Besht was inclined to stamp out such ambitions. A hint to this effect may be found also in the *mokhiah*'s assertion that he knew where the Besht had deposited the writings and could have extracted them, yet refrained from so doing as the Besht had asked that they be kept sequestered.

R. Gershon of Kotov too had ambitions of this nature and he too was not favored by any encouragement from the Besht. We learn of this from the following tale: R. Gershom had returned from the land of Israel to Poland so as to find a spouse for his sons, and was staying in the home of the Besht. Late on Friday, the Besht recited the afternoon prayers for a long time, until it grew dark. At the Sabbath meal, R. Gershon asked his brother-in-law why he had taken so long. The Besht explained that when he had reached the prayer "He who revives the dead," he intended a certain *kavvanah* (a mental formula having theurgic power) and then beheld the souls of thousands of dead people. And because he had to speak to each soul individually to find out what its sin was, so that he could redeem and elevate it, his prayer dragged on for some while. Envious of the Besht, R. Gershon asked whether he too could have souls revealed to him during the prayer. The Besht assented, and transmitted the necessary intentions to him, so that he could employ them on the following Sabbath eve. Of what happened at that point, the story tells us:

> The next Holy Sabbath, when the Besht concluded the Kaddish before the prayer, R. Gershon rose to pray as well. The Besht had not yet begun to pray, as he knew that R. Gershon would not be able to bear it and would take fright. And he played with his watch and sniffed tobacco until said R. Gershon would come to the place where intention [was to be inflected]. And when he inflected this intention and beheld the dead people coming to him like a huge flock of sheep he fainted. . . . And that night at the table during the meal the Besht asked him: Why did you faint? And he said: When I directed the intention

dead people came to me in droves. Then the Besht said laughingly to
his people: Beat him so he won't make a mockery of the Besht.[98]

The Besht's treatment of R. Gershon is somewhat abusive. After all, the
Besht knew in advance that R. Gershon was going to fail, and did nothing but
play with his watch and wait for the actual event to transpire. And note especially that in this case R. Gershon's failure was not the result of a lack of esoteric knowledge; the Besht had transmitted the necessary intentions to him. R.
Gershon's failure to imitate the Besht was the effect of differences in their spiritual rank. The Besht had been graced with spiritual powers that enabled him
to engage in the redemption of the souls of the dead; R. Gershon was not similarly blessed.[99]

The fact that certain members of the Besht's circle had ambitions to imitate
him and sought to have him share the esoteric knowledge he had at his disposal ought not to surprise us. The people in question lived in proximity with
the Besht, learned from him of his experiences and were witness to his marvels. Moreover, the members of his circle came from a spiritual background
and had spiritual ambitions similar to those of the Besht. The literature, traditions, and model figures from which the Besht drew his inspiration, would
have been in the minds of the members of his circle as well. Moreover, certain
stories from *Shivhei Habesht* suggest that the ambitions that several of the
Besht's associates had to perform marvels were not entirely baseless. That is to
say, the Besht's exclusivity as a miracle worker, as has been depicted through
the tales presented and discussed here, expresses the Besht's conception of
himself and the image his admirers in subsequent generations held of him,
more than it does the actual state of affairs.[100]

Given all of the above, the question arises: Why did the Besht oppose the
ambitions of some of his followers to emulate him and to work miracles? Why
did he seek to secure his exclusivity as a miracle worker? It becomes all the
more perplexing when one considers that the Besht did indeed share the
import of his personal experiences as a mystic with his followers, intending in
this way to assist them in reaching a mystical experience through their own
powers. Moreover, we have found that the Besht's professional colleagues, the
baalei shem R. Binyamin Binush and R. Yoel, did reveal their secrets, or at least
some of them, by means of the charms books they brought to print.

It seems to me that the answer to this question is to be sought in the conception the Besht held of himself and his destiny. The Besht regarded his
unusual powers as a divine gift, granted to him for an employment that went
well beyond the confines of treatment of individuals and their afflictions. In
effect, the Besht regarded himself as having been charged with the material and
spiritual welfare of the public as a whole. In other words: he saw himself as a

leader of the entire Jewish people. Hence, when certain of his followers showed ambitions or voiced a conceit that they were endowed with powers and esoteric knowledge similar to his, this would to some extent have been taken as challenging his sense of mission and authority as a leader.

The Besht's self-image and his modus operandi as leader of the Jewish people will be the focus of the next chapter. For the time being I would like to add a few remarks as marginal notes to the discussion of the magical component in the character of the Besht.

As a general rule, one may assert that the effectiveness of any *baal shem* is based upon a combination of esoteric knowledge and personal charisma. The relative proportions of these two ingredients varies from case to case. Yet what we find here, in light of the sources available to us, is that in the case of the Besht the ingredient of charisma was decisive. This charisma was expressed through such near-prophetic powers such as the ability to see from afar, to tell futures, to discover a soul's previous incarnations, and so forth. We do not maintain that none of the other *baalei shem* practicing in the Besht's era or in proximate times could boast of being endowed with one or another of the traits that graced the Besht. Nevertheless, we do not know of any *baal shem* to whom so full a range of traits could be attributed.

The unusual powers with which the Besht was endowed had a decisive function in the formation of his self-image and of his relations with those around him. On the one hand, the Besht emerges in our treatment as a person with an extremely high opinion of himself. Self-esteem of this nature can only thrive with the recognition and acknowledgement that the environment provides. This accounts for the Besht's need to inform his followers of his accomplishments. At the same time, the Besht was constantly pursued by a fear of failure and by competitors who threatened his reputation.

What significance does all this have for understanding the role that the Besht played in the emergence of Hasidism? A detailed answer to this question is offered in the final chapter of this book. For the time being, two comments will suffice: First, the Besht's vocation as a *baal shem* helped to prepare him for work as a public leader, as in the course of his occupation he traveled throughout Ukraine, visited different communities, and met individuals from all walks of life. The Besht thus had exposure to the realities of the life of Polish Jewry with all its afflictions and tensions. Such close contact with the public sharply contrasts with the isolationism and seclusion characteristic of Hasidim of the old type. Second, it stands to reason that the Besht's reputation as a miracle worker blessed with unusual powers would have offered him an especially propitious springboard for his efforts to enter the realm of public affairs.

CHAPTER THREE

A Leader of the Jewish People

T he Besht did not view himself as the leader of a movement, not only because in his day the Hasidic movement did not yet exist, or because it had never even occurred to him to found such a movement, but mainly because he perceived himself as bearing responsibility for the welfare of the Jewish people as a whole. What was the nature of this calling? How did it manifest itself? What were the areas over which the Besht had responsibility and what means did he have available for dealing with them? What parts of the broad public were aware of his mission? These are the questions at the center of discussion in this chapter.

The Besht's Epistle: One Letter That Was Two

The most important source from which one may form a sense of the Besht's self-image as a leader of the Jewish people is the famous letter he sent his brother-in-law, R. Gershon of Kotov. This letter is known in the literature as the "Besht's Epistle." R. Gershon emigrated to the land of Israel in 1747 and maintained a correspondence with the Besht. From this correspondence, two letters that R. Gershon sent to the Besht have survived,[1] along with one letter that the Besht sent to R. Gershon. It is hard to exaggerate the importance of the Besht's Epistle as a source of insight into his character. Not only does it shed light on various aspects of his personal life; at its core there is a detailed report of the Besht's ascents of the soul. The account of the journey of the Besht's soul through the Upper Worlds reveals to us a fascinating picture of his inner life in general and of the essence of his mission for the Jewish people in particular.

The Epistle was first published as an appendix to *Ben Porat Yosef* by R. Yaakov Yosef of Polonne, a book issued in Koretz in 1781. In addition to the printed version of the Epistle, two versions in manuscript form have survived. One of them was set to print by Rabbi David Fraenkel in his *Michtavim MehaBesht Zal Vetalmidav*, which was issued in Lvov in 1923. This edition was reprinted by Mordechai Shraga Bauminger in 1972 on the basis of a transcription of the same manuscript.[2] The second version was discovered several years ago by Yehoshua Mondshine within a Hasidic manuscript dating to 1776.[3] The differences between the two manuscript versions and between the two manuscripts and the printed edition have been the basis of a debate among scholars as to the authenticity of the various texts. The details of this argument are beyond our purview here.[4] It suffices to remark that the treatment of the Besht's Epistle, as presented below, is based on the stance taken by Yehoshua Mondshine on this issue.

Mondshine showed that the differences between the two manuscript versions of the Epistle are the result of the Besht's actually writing two different letters, with a gap in time separating the two. In the first of the two "epistles," the Besht described the ascent of the soul that he had experienced in 1747. While the date of this letter is unknown, it was certainly written before 1750. In 1750, the Besht received a letter from his brother-in-law from which he learned that the epistle in which he had described the 1747 spiritual ascent had not arrived at its destination. The Besht therefore decided to describe the same ascent of the soul once again in a second epistle. This second epistle was written in 1752. And as the Besht had, meanwhile, experienced another ascent of the soul—in 1750—in the second epistle he included an account of this event as well. The result is that the historian seeking to reconstruct the inner life of the Besht has two epistles at his disposal, each offering a distinct testimonial. Nevertheless, one may draw inferences from one epistle to the other, as some of the same events are at the basis of both.

The Encounter with the Messiah and the Besht's Mission in the Upper Worlds

What can we learn from the Besht's Epistle, in both its versions, about how the Besht conceived his mission on behalf of the Jewish people? We begin our investigation of the Besht's Epistle by considering the manuscript version discovered by Mondshine, which was the first of the two epistles sent by the Besht. As said, at the core of this epistle is a detailed account of the 1747 experience of the ascent of the soul. The Besht begins by stressing the unusual intensity of that experience: "I beheld wonders such as I had never seen since I was able to reason, and that which I beheld and learned upon rising there, it is impossible to describe and recount even in person." Despite that, the Besht was able to give a detailed report of what he saw and heard once he had descended to a lower level:

> Yet when I returned to the lower Garden of Eden and beheld many
> souls of the living and of the dead, both familiar and unfamiliar to
> me, immeasurable and innumerable, running to and fro to rise from
> world to world via the pillar familiar to those who know mysteries,
> with such great and vast joy that the mouth does not suffice to relate

and the physical ear is too heavy to hear, and there were also many wicked ones who repented and were absolved of their sins, as the hour of favor was then great; I myself was quite surprised at how many had their repentance accepted, some of whom you knew as well, and amongst them too there was extreme happiness and they too ascended in the said ascendancies; and everyone together asked of me and beseeched me (to the point of embarrassment) saying: Your honorable Torah eminence, the Lord has granted you the extra intelligence to discover and comprehend these matters; you shall ascend together with us and be our helper and provider; and owing to the great joy I saw amongst them I decided to rise along with them.[5]

At the center of this passage is a vision of a large swarm of souls seeking redemption. The Besht is surprised to discover that included in this multitude there are also souls of the wicked who have repented. In the course of their efforts to rise from one world to the next, the souls turn to the Besht and ask him to "be our helper and provider" in the ascent, as he is thought to be competent and experienced in such matters. Evidently, this was one of the prominent features of the mission to which the Besht was assigned in his experience of ascent: to assist the souls of sinners who are seeking salvation.

Later in the letter appears a striking illustration of how the Besht viewed his own spiritual exaltedness. The Besht again tells of the great joy that overtook the Upper Worlds in the course of his ascent. He asked of the souls he encountered to explain the celebration, but received no reply. Later he mentions that the celebration and delight that filled the Upper Worlds was similar to that which Israel had experienced at the time of the reception of the Torah at Mount Sinai. With the cause of the great rejoicing left unclear to him, a suspicion crept into his heart: "And I took fright . . . for I said to myself: perhaps it was for my sake and the time had come (Heaven forbid) to disappear from the world; possibly it would be proper to do so for this reason."[6] Thus, the Besht's first surmise was that it was his pending departure from this world and the ascent of his great soul to take up permanent residence in the Upper Worlds that was the cause of a joyousness equal to that which obtained at Mount Sinai! Later in his voyage, however, he learns that this was not the cause of the rejoicing.

What follows is the portion of the letter that is most frequently cited, describing the Besht's conversation with the Messiah:

[U]ntil I arrived and rose to the actual palace of the Messiah King and I actually saw face to face what I had not seen thus far from the day I [acquired] reason . . . and they also revealed to me wonderful and awesome things in the profundities of Torah that I had not seen or

heard and that no ear had heard of for some years and it occurred to
me and I decided to ask him if it was perhaps because of preparations
for his coming that there was this goodness and happiness and rejoicing and when will Sir be coming and the answer from His Eminence
was that this could not be revealed but by this you shall know: once
your learning becomes publicly known and is revealed in the world
and your fountains have overflowed beyond what I have taught you
and what you have achieved, and others too are able to perform
yihudim and ascents just as you can, then all the *Qlipot* shall terminate and it will be a time of favor and salvation; and I worried about
this and it greatly pained me on account of the long time it would take
before this became possible; yet while I was there I learned three
charms and three holy names which are easily learned and explained,
so I calmed down and thought that perhaps by this means my colleagues too would be able to come to the level and rank that I have,
that is, would be able to have ascents of the soul and to learn and perceive as I have, yet I was not given permission my whole life long to
reveal this and I asked on your behalf to teach it to you and was not
permitted to at all and I was fast forsworn from this.[7]

This dialogue between the Besht and the Messiah has been at the core of the
debate among scholars over the role played by Messianism at the outset of
Hasidism. Dubnow drew upon the dialogue to support his position that
Hasidism replaced national redemption by a personal salvation; that is, by the
individual's religious-spiritual elevation. Here is how he interprets the Besht's
exchange with the Messiah:

> The national element is dissolved here within the religious element,
> in particular the redemption of the individual, the redemption of
> souls. Once the Hasidic doctrine has become widespread and many
> have attained the level of sanctity reached by the Besht, the "period of
> favor and salvation" shall arrive. . . . Hence, the spread of Hasidic doc-
> trine is the means for achieving the salvation of souls.[8]

Ben Zion Dinur took the opposite stance. Drawing on the exchange
between the Besht and the Messiah, he argued that Hasidism was indeed a
Messianic movement in the full, nationalist-historical sense of the term. What
the Besht learned from the Messiah was something Dinur labels a "doctrine of
redemption." The promulgation of this doctrine in the present world is the
means by which the Besht would "Hasten the End" and cause the Messiah to
arrive. As Dinur puts it:

> The Besht's task according to the Epistle is thus perceived as being a
> prophetic-Messianic one: not only is he graced with a general prophetic
> vision . . . but he has further been assigned a prophetic-Messianic

mission: to ready the age for Redemption by propagating the teachings he has been graced with through his prophetic attainment.[9]

Another scholar who discusses the Besht's Epistle in this connection is Yeshayah Tishbi.[10] Tishbi rejects Dubnow's interpretation—that national redemption is to be supplanted by personal salvation—as entirely without foundation. Tishbi goes on to assert that he has no doubt "that according to the Letter the Besht intended to hasten the End."[11] Yet Tishbi added the following qualification to this assessment:

> Contrary to Dubnow's supposition on the one hand and to that of Horodezki and Dinur on the other—that the Messianic task assigned to the dissemination of the Besht's "teaching" and "discoveries" refers to the [propagation of] Hasidic doctrine as we know it today from the writings of his students and his student's students—I believe, instead, that the letter refers only to *yihuddim* and to ascents of the soul, via charms and Names, in the manner accomplished by the other Kabbalists and *baalei shem* of that period.[12]

It would seem that the Besht conceived of his ability to perform *yihuddim* (mystical unifications) and ascents of the soul as a means, the objective of which was to hasten the End. Accordingly, believes Tishbi, the Besht did not "pave a new road toward the effectuation of Redemption," as Dinur had argued, and his stance on this issue is merely "the final manifestation of the old way."[13]

Avraham Rubinstein devotes an entire article to a detailed treatment of the Besht's Epistle.[14] He rejects Tishbi's conclusions, his main allegation being that "we have never heard that the founder of Hasidism sought to hurry the End and hasten Redemption through magical performances." As to the significance of the dialogue between the Besht and the Messiah, Rubinstein argues that one ought not to regard it as a "hastening of the End." The Besht did not enter the Messiah's chamber with Messianic intentions, nor was his initial experience there Messianic in nature. Rubinstein accordingly affirms: "To give an actual-Messianic interpretation to the question of the Besht would be to take it out of context."[15]

It seems to me that Tishbi was right to question the presumption that the Besht's Epistle informs us about some "Hasidic doctrine." Indeed, the use which both Dubnow and Dinur make of the concepts "Hasidic doctrine" and Hasidic "Doctrine of Redemption" in this context is anachronistic. The dialogue between the Besht and the Messiah revolved around secrets that the Messiah taught the Besht. And although the content of these secrets is not disclosed in the letter, it is clear from the gist of things that they concerned Names and "Intentions" through the power of which the Besht was able to attain his ascents of the soul. Certainly, such Names and Intentions do not constitute the chief content of any "doctrine of Hasidism" nor do they serve as the foundations of such.

It also seems to me that Rubinstein was right to reject Tishbi's conclusions. Indeed, the sources available to us yield no basis for supposing that the Besht sought to hasten redemption by means of Names and ascents of souls. Rubinstein is further correct when he asserts that the letter at hand shows no signs of being concerned with hastening the End, as the context of the Besht's encounter with the Messiah is devoid of Messianic anticipation.

Further evidence of the non-Messianic nature of the Besht's Epistle may be adduced here. The Epistle contains an exchange between the Besht and R. Gershon of Kotov on the subject of the Besht's possible immigration to the land of Israel. As mentioned, when R. Gershon arrived in the land of Israel he attempted to establish the identity of the figure whom the Besht had seen through his powers of farsightedness: described as "a *Hacham* who has arrived in Jerusalem from a country to the west and who is a spark of the Messiah." When R. Gershon realized that what the Besht had seen was the immigration of R. Hayim ben Atar, he reported this fact to the sages of Jerusalem and they were "astounded to hear of it." In this context R. Gershon went on to write the following:

> In brief, your name is already known in the gates of Jerusalem and the local sages requested of me that I write you to encourage you to come here to take up residence and to tell you they are hungry for the sight of your countenance, but what can I do as I know your nature is such that you have to pray with your *minyan*, besides the other things that make me despair that you ever will come to the Holy Land unless the King Messiah comes (speedily in our days may it be), and that is my great sadness as I wonder when we shall ever meet face to face.[16]

It turns out that the Besht's Epistle contains a response to this point—perhaps to these very lines or to similar ones in a letter that has not survived. The Besht writes: "for the Lord knows that I have not despaired of voyaging to the Land of Israel if the Lord so desires it so as to be together with you yet the times do not permit this."[17] Evidently, neither the Besht nor R. Gershon, one of the people closest to him, associated the thought of traveling to the land of Israel with any sort of Messianic mission. Both in the passage cited above and in other passages in his letter, R. Gershon expresses deep pain at the separation from his beloved and esteemed brother-in-law. Yet he was aware of the Besht's circumstances and had in effect resigned himself to the fact that he was not about to come to Jerusalem, unless the Messiah arrived first. Hence, he does not expect that the Besht will hasten the Messiah's arrival, either by immigrating to the

land of Israel or by not immigrating to it.[18] In the Besht's response too, travel
to the land of Israel is discussed in a personal context; that is, as part of his hope
to be near his beloved brother-in-law, and not in some other fashion.

Hasidim and other Jews emigrated to the land of Israel for various and
sundry reasons. There were some who were motivated by the desire to hasten
the End, while for others this was not a consideration at all. At any rate, it
stands to reason that in cases where Messianism was the primary motivation
for an actual or a hoped-for immigration, one would expect this to be clearly
stated in writings pertaining to it. Yet neither the statements of R. Gershon nor
those of the Besht mention any spiritual-religious motive for the Besht's possible immigration to the land of Israel. Perhaps the motive was sufficiently
obvious that they had no need to explicitly mention it;[19] if that were the case,
they would have been content to mention only the personal aspect of the voyage. However, if R. Gershon had grounds for supposing that an immigration
by the Besht would have been in the context of a Messianic mission, he would
not have written that he despaired of the Besht ever coming unless the Messiah himself was about to arrive. Likewise, if the Besht had interpreted the Messiah's statements as conferring upon him a Messianic mission, one would have
expected this to have come up in the course of the discussion of any contemplated travel to the land of Israel. More generally, I believe that the attempt to
ascribe full-fledged Messianic import to the dialogue between the Messiah and
the Besht is unsupported. Furthermore, I shall try to show that the Besht, in
the Epistle at hand, takes a decidedly non-Messianic approach.

Any attempt to analyze the meaning of the Besht's dialogue with the Messiah ought to consider it within its actual context; that is, as part and parcel
with the experiences reported by the Besht both before and after the dialogue.
As I have said, in the first section of the Epistle the Besht describes the multitude of souls who hoped to find salvation in the Upper Worlds and the
appeals they made of him. In his report of this vision the Besht expresses both
his own sense of his spiritual exaltedness and an important element of what
he took to be his mission. Later, the Besht dwells on the vast joy that filled the
Upper Worlds, and wonders whether this has something to do with his
impending demise. This portion of the letter, which gives a clear sense of the
Besht's positive self-image, is likewise devoid of any Messianic overtones. The
Besht's entry into the Messiah's chamber is described as yet a further stage to
which his soul had now climbed. Indeed, he was graced there with sights
never seen in all his life! And as he had still not discovered the cause of the
joyousness, it occurred to him that it possibly augured the imminent Coming of the Messiah. This then prompted the question: "when will Sir be coming?" Thus it appears that the basis of this question is not an aspiration for

the Messiah's immediate arrival but rather curiosity as to the cause of the heavenly celebration.

What is the meaning of the response the Messiah gave to the Besht? How did the Besht himself interpret the Messiah's words? The Messiah told the Besht that the Redemption shall come when the esoteric knowledge that he has revealed to him, knowledge through which the Besht would be able to perform *yihuddim* and ascents of the soul, had become widespread in the world. Many others would then be able to perform *yihuddim* and ascents of the soul and they would join the battle against the *qlipot* until these are shattered. To this, the Besht responds: "I worried about this and it greatly pained me on account of the length of time this was liable to take." This dialogue was preceded, as mentioned, by the various manifestations of the Besht's exceptional spiritual rank: his ability to help souls find salvation in the Upper Worlds, the wonderful secrets revealed to him during that same ascent of the soul, and the speculation that the joy in the heavens had to do with his imminent demise. It would seem, consequently, that the Messiah's reply is also to be taken in this spirit. That is: one need not expect the Redemption to take place in the near future, as it is inconceivable that such secrets as the Messiah revealed to the Besht would soon be known to all and sundry!

Furthermore, even individuals of rare virtue, (that is, the narrow band of members of the Besht's inner circle) were not permitted to know these three names and three charms that would have empowered them to undergo ascents of the soul and to perform deeds in the heavens. And as if that were not enough, the Besht apparently even had to keep all of this knowledge from his beloved friend and brother-in-law R. Gershon. If we reexamine the Messiah's words in light of the above we may read them as follows: Had there been more people of your spiritual rank, more people capable of functioning in the Upper Worlds as you are, it would have been possible to overcome the *qlipot* and the Redemption would soon be brought to the world. Yet no persons of so exalted a rank exist!

The conversation between the Besht and the Messiah takes on a further hue if we consider it in the context of the Bauminger version of the letter. After beginning on a personal note, the Besht turns to a description of his ascent of the soul. It turns out that the very first image there already tells us much about the essence of the Besht's mission:

> [For] Samael rose to give evil counsel with great delight as never before and he worked his work, issuing decrees of forced conversion upon several souls who would be killed by strange deaths and I was horrified and literally risked my life and asked my teacher and rabbi to go with me for it is a great danger to go and ascend to the Upper

Worlds for from the day I stood on my own I had not ascended by such great ascents and I rose step after step until I entered the palace of the Messiah where the Messiah studies Torah together with all the Tannaites and the Righteous Ones and also with the Seven Shepherds and there I beheld a very great happiness and I did not know what this happiness was all for and I was convinced the happiness was (God forbid) on account of my demise from the present world and I was later informed that I was not yet deceased as they like it up there when I perform yihudim below by means of their holy Torah and what the rejoicing meant I do not know to this day. And I inquired of the Messiah, when will Sir be coming, and he replied, once your Torah has spread through all the world etc.[20]

The edicts of destruction that were put into effect as a result of Samael's evil counsel are spelled out later in the letter. They involved the blood libels that led to the conversion of certain Jews and to the execution of others. In his quest to block Samael's evil counsel, the Besht risked his life and strove to rise to ever higher echelons of the Upper Worlds, until he reached the palace of the Messiah. It was there that he encountered the great celebration, the cause of which he suspected to be his impending demise. While this guess proved false, the basic grounds for his speculation were confirmed: the Besht's spiritual rank was indeed remarkably high and the *yihuddim* he performs in the present world were causing considerable satisfaction in the heavens. It is at this point that the question is raised: "When will Sir be coming?"

Apparently, then, the two themes that are the background for the Besht's dialogue with the Messiah are his efforts to defend Israel from Samael's evil counsels, and the heavenly confirmation of his high spiritual rank. Accordingly, it seems to me that one should understand the question, "When will Sir be coming?" as follows: When will the Redemption arrive and the persecutions and evil decrees finally end? The Messiah's reply does not promise the Redemption in the near future, yet it does yield further confirmation of the Besht's exceptional spiritual rank. The coming of the Messiah must await the spread of the Besht's "doctrine," and, as we have already seen, such an event was not an imminent affair. Hence the Besht must carry on by himself, with the fateful mission assigned to him, as he alone is able to act in the Upper Worlds on behalf of the Jewish people.

Confrontations with Samael

One of the principal expressions of this mission of the Besht is, as said, the confrontation with Samael. This confrontation is represented somewhat differently in each of the two editions of the Epistle. We begin with the account as it appears in the manuscript version. Immediately after describing the vision of souls seeking salvation the Besht relates: "and also I beheld all the Ministers of the nations of the world who came and surrendered like servants before their masters before the archangel Michael."[21] At first the picture may seem comforting, as the Angel Michael is the lord of the ministers of nations and thus can limit their power to injure Israel. Yet when the Besht again looks at this scene, Samael reveals himself to him. This passage describes the confrontation between them:

> And I also beheld, after beholding the said ministers of the nations, I beheld Samael among them as well, and he came as a slave, vanquished and compliant before the archangel and before all the righteous ones etc. and the fury of the Lord of Hosts was arrested in my heart like a fierce blaze for the fact that there had not been Godly vengeance returned to his tormentors for the martyrs etc., and I could not resist from asking him, you have killed in body why did you need to kill in soul, tricking them to convert, and he answered with great meekness before the said great Minister, this I did by the counsel and permission of the great and awesome minister Gabriel for the sake of All of Israel . . . and I was greatly pained by the evil of this report, and I prayed before God.[22]

It would thus appear that Samael's stance as a "slave" "capitulating" before the Angel Michael was perhaps misleading. Not only has he brought about the deaths of quite a few Jews, but he has also caused the forced conversion of others. This fact arouses the wrath and fury of the Besht. The Besht is portrayed here not only as someone who identifies personally with the suffering of the people put to death or forced to convert, but also, and perhaps chiefly, as someone who struggles as an advocate for the Jewish people as a whole. From this perspective one can understand his being mortified that vengeance was not taken against the Gentiles.

The Besht's protests apparently made a great impression on Samael; he therefore says, half as explanation and half as apology, that he acted as he had with the permission of the Angel Gabriel,[23] and for the sake of all of Israel. The meaning of Samael's explanation will become clear later on. At any rate, the Besht finds Samael's explanation unsatisfactory and he turns to God in prayer. Thus far the sequence of events is as described in his first letter (i.e., in the manuscript version). Now in his second letter (i.e., in the Bauminger version), the Besht paints a clearer and more detailed picture of events:

> I prayed there why has God done thus and wherefore the great wrath owing to which several souls of Israel have been handed to Samael for execution and several of them for conversion and then for execution

and they permitted me to directly inquire it of Samael himself and I asked Samael what was the point of this and what he thought of the fact that they were being converted and afterward being killed, and he replied that his intentions are for a heavenly cause for if they were allowed to stay alive after converting then when there was some future edict then they would not sanctify God's name but would instead convert so as to save themselves therefore his method of operation was to have those who convert be killed afterward so that no son of Israel would convert and would instead sanctify the Name of God and so it was by our sins later on that in the community of Zaslav there was a libel against several souls and two of them converted and were afterward put to death. And the rest sanctified the Name of Heaven in a great sanctity and died strange deaths and afterward when there were libels in the community of Szepetowka and the holy community of Dunajow they did not convert having seen what took place in the holy community of Zaslav but rather all of them gave over their lives to sanctify the Lord and sanctified the Heavenly Name and withstood the test and thanks to it our Messiah will come and take his vengeance and redeem his land and his people.[24]

It would thus seem that the confrontation between the Besht and Samael revolved around the blood-libel that occurred in Zatslav in 1747. This was an event of exceptional severity. The interrogated suspects were cruelly tortured and brutal executions were carried out. The Besht inveighs against the fact that several of the suspects were executed despite having converted in hopes of saving themselves. Samael replies that he did this "for a heavenly purpose," that is, so that in future blood-libels Jews would not be tempted to convert. Subsequent events confirm that Samael was right, as the Besht admits. Yet acceptance of Samael's explanation is not the same as being resigned to the occurrence of the events. The Besht prays, protests, and complains about the edict before he hears Samael's explanation, and prays for the Redemption and revenge after hearing it. Furthermore, it is noteworthy that in the picture drawn by the Besht, he is the only one to contest the evil decrees imposed upon the people of Israel and to challenge Samael on that score. None of the heavenly entourage helps him out with this.

In the early eighteenth century, a wave of blood-libels inundated Poland. Jews were arrested and tortured, forced to confess to their crimes, and sent to their death. This wave was one among other circumstances that cast a pall on the life of Jews in Poland during this period.[25] It was this bitter reality that was behind the Besht's efforts to intercede in the Upper Worlds on behalf of the Jewish people. The Epistle represents the Besht as someone who is deeply distressed by the general suffering. Further, he acts out of a deep inner conviction that he has a unique ability to influence the public fate. Evidently, this belief in his own powers was reinforced by the awareness of his remarkable mystical experiences, as well as by the repeated confirmations of his spiritual rank received in the course of his travels in the Upper Worlds. The fact that he was unsuccessful in preventing the blood-libels in these communities did not deter him from his mission.

In the ascent of the soul of the year 1749, the Besht again risked his life for the Jewish people, this time with greater success:

> And on the Rosh Hashana of the year 5510[1749] I made an ascent of the soul as is known and beheld a great evil counsel, in which Samael was nearly given permission to lay waste countries and communities entirely and I risked my life and prayed, let us fall by the hand of God and please not at the hand of man and they permitted me to have this be exchanged for a great pestilence and a plague the likes of which had not been known in all of Poland and the rest of the countries near us and so it was that the plague expanded greatly . . . and I arranged with my fraternity to have *ketoret* recited at dawn prayers so as to nullify the said edicts and it was revealed to me in a night vision: It was you yourself who chose this, let us fall by the hand of God etc., and how is it you want to nullify it now, for "an accuser cannot etc. [become a defender]" and from then on I did not recite the *ketoret* and did not pray on this matter except on Hoshana Raba when I went to the synagogue together with the whole congregation and I took several oaths owing to the terror and once I said the *ktoret* so that the plague would not spread to our environs and in this we succeeded by the grace of God.[26]

If we compare the ascent of the soul the Besht experienced in 1749 to the one he experienced in 1747, we find that both cases follow a set pattern: in the course of journeying through the Upper Worlds, the Besht encounters evil counsels and decrees threatening the Jewish people. The Upper Worlds serve also as the arena in which he acts so as to counter such decrees and counsels. The Besht risks his life, complains and objects, prays and bargains. In the 1749 ascent he succeeds in overturning the anticipated calamity decree. Possibly the decree the Besht sought to avert was associated with the wave of Heidemak rebellions that inundated certain regions of Poland in early 1749.[27] If these rebellions formed the real-world background of the 1749 ascent, the calamity the Besht feared is indeed similar to the ones that took place in 1648 and 1649. At any rate, thanks to his intercession in the Upper Worlds, he was able to get the anticipated calamitous event replaced with a "great pestilence," that is, with the plague. Apparently, the reference is to a plague that spread through certain regions of Poland during that period. When this actually took place the Besht, together with his fraternity, tried to combat the plague by reciting the *Pitum Haktoret* (the priestly incense service) at dawn prayers.[28] Yet he was forced to desist from this after being reprimanded in a "night vision" for abrogating his agreement to have the calamity exchanged for a "pestilence." In the end, the Besht contented himself with merely reciting the *Pitum Haktoret* during the Hoshana Raba holiday, thereby keeping the plague from spreading into the region where he lived.

Ecstatic Prayer as a Context for Ascents of the Soul

Thus far, we have dwelled on the Besht's experiences of spiritual ascent as depicted in his letters. Naturally, such an account concentrates on the internal dimension of these experiences. Yet in one tale from *Shivhei Habesht* we also find information on the Besht's spiritual ascent as observed by the people surrounding him at that time. This story also teaches us something about the aims of the Besht's missions in the Upper Worlds and the methods he employed to achieve them. Given its importance to our topic, we cite the tale here in full:

> One time on the Eve of Yom Kippur, the Besht saw that a great evil decree was being counseled: Israel was to lose the Oral Law. And he grew very sad throughout the eve of Yom Kippur. Toward nightfall, when the entire town came to receive a blessing from him, he blessed one or two and said: I can not go on, on account of my sadness; and he did not bless them. He went to the synagogue and preached chastisements to them and fell before the Holy Ark and cried: Woe! They wish to take the Torah from our hands. How shall we survive among the nations for even half a day?! He was furious with the rabbis and said that they were to blame, for they fabricate falsehoods from their hearts with their false premises. . . . And later he went to the *Beit Midrash* where he uttered further chastisements. They recited the *Kol Nidrei* service, and after the *Kol Nidrei* he said that the evil counsel was growing stronger.
>
> He hurried all the other leaders of prayer along so that he, who was always the one to conduct the *Neilah* service, would be able to begin *Neilah* while it was still broad daylight. Prior to *Neilah*, he began to utter chastisements, and wept and leaned his head backward on the prayer dias and sighed and cried out. Afterward he began to pray the silent *shmoneh esreh* and then began the *shmoneh esreh* recited out loud. And his custom was always, during the Days of Awe, not to look at the holiday prayer book; instead the Rabbi, R. Yekil of Miedzybóz, would prompt him with the verse from the holiday prayer book and

he would repeat it. When he reached the phrase "Open us a gate" or the phrase "Open the gates of heaven to us," R. Yekil read the phrase out loud and did not hear it repeated, at which point he fell silent. The Besht began to gesture violently, bending backward until his head nearly reached his knees, and everyone was afraid he would fall over; they wanted to hold and steady him but were afraid to do so. And they reported this to R. Zeev Kotses of blessed memory who came and looked at his face and indicated that he was not to be touched. His eyes bulged out and his voice bellowed like a bull being slaughtered, for about two hours. And suddenly he awakened and straightened up, prayed in a great hurry and concluded the service.

When Yom Kippur was over, everyone came to greet him, as was the custom always; and they asked him about the evil counsel and what its outcome was, and he reported that "during the Neilah prayers I was able to pray and to pass from world to world unhindered for the entire length of the silent *shmoneh esreh*. And during the vocal *shmoneh esreh* I also continued until I came to a certain palace, and I had just one more gate to pass in order to arrive before the blessed Lord, blessed be He, and in that palace I found the prayers of fifty years which had not risen to their destination, and now that we had prayed on this Yom Kippur with proper *kavvannah* all the prayers ascended and each prayer glowed as the bright dawn. I asked the prayers: why did you not rise beforehand? They replied, we were ordered to await Your Eminence to guide us. I said to them: come with me."

The gate was open; he told the townsfolk that the gate was wide as the entire world. "When we began to move with the prayers, one angel came along and shut the door and bolted the gate." He told them the bolt was as big as Miedzybóz. "I tried to turn the bolt so as to open it but was unable to do so. I ran to my Rabbi (mentioned in *Toldot Yaakov Yosef*) and beseeched him as follows: Israel is in such dire straits and now they won't let me in! If the times were otherwise I would not try so hard to enter. And my Rabbi replied: I shall accompany you, and if the gate can be opened I shall open it. And when he came and twisted the bolt, he too was unable to open it, and he then said to me: What can I do for you? And I began to complain to my Rabbi: How can you fail me at a time like this? And he replied: I don't know what I can do for you, but you and I will go to the Messiah's palace and maybe we'll find help from that quarter. And I went quite noisily to the palace of the Messiah. And when our righteous Messiah saw me coming from afar he said to me: Don't shout. He gave me two glyphs. And when I came to the gate thank God I was able to release the bolt and open the gate and I drove in all the prayers. And as a result of the rejoicing for the ascension of all the prayers the Accuser fell

silent and I did not have to plead the case, the decree was canceled,
and all that remained of it was the trace of the decree."[29]

Before I turn to an examination of the content of the ascent of the soul
described here, I should comment on its external form. Evidently, the Besht
experienced his ascent of the soul while passing in front of the ark during the
Neilah service of Yom Kippur. Furthermore, it is entirely certain that at least
at some stage, this prayer was of an ecstatic nature. This was manifested by the
strange noises emanating from the Besht and the violent movements of his
body to and fro. When the ecstatic trance reached its climax, the Besht
remained suspended in a nearly comatose state. Hence it was an ecstatic prayer
that evidently served as the framework, and perhaps also a sort of springboard,
for his experience of an ascent of the soul.

Is the account presented in this story typical of all the Besht's ascents of the
soul? We do not have the means to respond definitively to this question. It is,
however, safe to assume that the other experiences of spiritual ascent took
place during ecstatic prayers as well. There are two reasons for this assumption: first, as will become clear later on, ecstatic prayer was the framework and
conduit through which the Besht's "*dvekut*" was manifested. Second, the phenomenon of ecstatic prayer serving as a channel and setting for an ascent of
the soul is one that is familiar to us from the history of various religions.[30]

I now turn to an analysis of the content of the story at hand. At the core of
the ascent of the soul are the efforts the Besht makes to overturn the expected
edict that the Oral Law is to be withdrawn from the people of Israel. Below I
shall suggest certain real-world events that seem to have been the background
to this edict. Yet in any event, clearly the Jewish people would not be able to
survive without the Oral Law. Accordingly, in girding himself to the task of
overturning this edict, the Besht is taking upon himself a fateful mission.

What is the meaning of the Besht's charge against the rabbis? Possibly his
words about the "false premises" that they "fabricate from their heart" are a
reference to the method of *pilpul* (Talmudic sophistry) that was prevalent
among the scholar class in Poland.[31] If this supposition is correct, then the
Besht was charging the rabbis that their "premises" (that is, the presumptions
on which their argumentative sophistry was based) are false. At any rate, the
fact that the Besht viewed the rabbis as blameworthy deserves our notice.

If, in the two ascents of the soul described in the letter, the Besht only learns
of the accusations and edicts in the course of journeying through the Upper
Worlds, in this tale, knowledge of the anticipated edict precedes his ascent.
Moreover, it appears that the Besht launched the ascent of his soul in order to
be in a position to work to overturn the edict. Yet upon arrival in the Upper
Worlds his mission takes a detour: he discovers that fifty years' worth of

prayers had not arrived at their destination! How did those prayers manage to get lost? An explanation is hinted at by what the Besht says next: "now that we had prayed on this Yom Kippur with proper *kavvannah* all the prayers have ascended." Evidently, the prayers that had failed to arrive at the Holy Throne had been uttered without the proper intention. This charge might appear to be a severe critique on the quality of the prayers of the era except that later in the story, it turns out that even properly intended prayers (that is, those uttered by the Besht and the remainder of the congregants of the *Beit Midrash* in Miedzybóz) are not enough to raise the lost prayers to their destination. These prayers were instructed to await the Besht to carry them up with him. What we have here, then, is a further indication of what the Besht took his mission to entail and of the spiritual rank he considered himself to possess.

In his quest to raise the prayers, the Besht meets an unexpected obstacle: the gate leading to the palace toward which the prayers are supposed to reach turns out to be bolted. In his distress, the Besht seeks the aid of "his teacher," Ahia Hashiloni,[32] yet the latter is unable to resolve his difficulty. Ultimately, it is the Messiah who reveals to the Besht "glyphs," that is, a name or names, through the power of which he is able to open the gate and carry up the prayers. The ascent of the prayers leads to cancellation of the edict.

Attention should also be paid to the nature of the assistance the Messiah provided to the Besht. As in the Epistle, here too the Messiah equips the Besht with esoterical-magical information that empowers him to act in the Upper Worlds. The Messiah again emerges as a non-Messianic figure: instead of bringing about revolution and salvation for the people of Israel, he contents himself with helping the Besht to fulfill his mission. The two prominent motifs in the Besht's account of his journey through the Upper Worlds are the magnitude of the obstacle that stood in his path and the determination he showed in the efforts to overcome this obstacle. This determination carries with it a suggestion of deep emotional concern for the sufferings of the general public. The Besht complains in front of his rabbi and enters the Messiah's palace making a great noise. So loud is this noise, that the Messiah quickly begs him not to shout.

The historical events that were the background of the ascents of the soul depicted in the Besht's Epistle were, as noted, the blood-libels and the Heidemak persecutions. What was the real-world background for the ascent of the soul described in this story from *Shivhei Habesht?* Can one point to a factual basis for the evil counsel that the Oral Law was to be withdrawn from the people of Israel? It is nearly certain that the events that put their stamp on this ascent of the soul and influenced its contents concerned the clash with the Frankists and the subsequent burning of the Talmud. In 1754, in the town of Lanskorn in Podolia, a fraternity of Frankists was caught in the act of performing lascivious rites. When the fraternity's antinomianism came to light, the leadership of the communities began to persecute it. In their distress, the Frankists turned to the aid of Dembowski, the bishop of Kamenets. This bishop ordered the rabbis of the communities to present themselves for a "debate" with representatives of the Frankists. Following the "debate," the bishop rendered a verdict that the Talmud contains material that was incendiary and offensive on topics sacred to Christianity and that it was therefore to be burned. The verdict was enforced in the town square of Kamenets in October 1757, with the rabbis of the communities in the Lvov region made to witness the spectacle.

Although on that occasion only a limited number of books were burnt, the event left an especially deep impression on the Jews of Poland. Moreover, this same Dembowski was soon appointed bishop of Lvov and there was a genuine threat that his sentence would be carried out in the entire region under his jurisdiction. Fears about this edict were so great that some Jews sent all the volumes of the Talmud they possessed across the Turkish border.[33]

The link between the Besht's ascent of the soul described above and the burning of the Talmud in Kamenets was pointed out by *Shivhei Habesht*'s compiler, apparently on the basis of a tradition that had come down to him from the Besht's circle. According to this tradition, the harsh events in Kamenets were only the "trace of the edict." In other words, the Besht had succeeded in reversing the brunt of the edict, and the burning of the Talmud in Kamenets was a sort of residue left over from it.[34] Although the tale describing the ascent of the soul does not explicitly refer to the burning of the Talmud in Kamenets, it does seem that the tradition linking the two is firmly grounded. Perhaps the basis of this tradition was the proximity in time between the two events; perhaps it had origins in the Besht himself. One can learn something of the interest the Besht took in the Frankists' affair and his response to their conversion to Christianity from the following tale:

> And about those who converted I heard from the rabbi of our community that the Besht said that the *shekhina* is weeping and saying: so long as the limb is attached there is hope of some cure. But once the limb has been amputated it can never be redeemed, and each individual of the People of Israel is a limb of the *shekhina*.[35]

I now turn to a summary of my findings concerning the Besht's ascents of the soul and the role they served in the context of his activities on behalf of the Jewish people. The singularity of the spiritual ascents that the Besht underwent is striking when set against the previous cases of such spiritual ascents (the examples from which he presumably drew his inspiration). The earliest

of these are the spiritual ascents of the "Chariot Descenders," as described in
the *Hekhalot* literature. The Besht's connections with this literature are apparent in, among other things, the picture of the Upper Worlds given in the
accounts of his spiritual ascents. The same holds true for individual ingredients of this experience: the dangers associated with ascending to the highest
echelons; the presumption that in the course of a spiritual ascent, sacred
Names of magical quality are revealed to one, and so on. The *Hekhalot* literature thus portrays the Chariot Descenders as persons graced with the revelation of mysteries of an especially occult nature. Furthermore, upon returning
from their voyages to the upper chambers, the Chariot Descenders report the
secrets that had been revealed to them to their students, as their students are
incapable of achieving access to these secrets on their own.[36]

Ascents of the soul filled a similar function in the life of the ARI. Thus *Toldot
Haari* recounts:

> [The ARI] also was so graced that each night, when his soul would
> ascend to the heavens, the Angels of Service would come and accom-
> pany [his soul] to the edges of heaven, and they would inquire which
> Yeshiva he wanted to go to. Sometimes he would say R. Shimon Bar
> Yokhai's Yeshiva or that of R. Akiva or that of R. Eliezer the Great or
> that of Tannaites or Amorites or Prophets; they would conduct him
> to whichever Yeshiva he preferred. The following day he would report
> to the Sages what he had absorbed at that particular Yeshiva.[37]

We find, then, that the main purpose of the ascents of the soul experienced
by the ARI was to study secrets in the heavenly yeshiva. The ARI would subsequently teach these secrets to his students and so would fulfil his mission.
The ARI's immigration to the land of Israel is likewise described as a step that
has the objective of discovering secrets still more profound than those that
were revealed to him while a resident of the Diaspora. It was in the land of
Israel that he also met R. Hayim Vital, the person to whom he was meant to
transmit these secrets.[38]

Against the background of these precedents, which were almost certainly
on the Besht's mind, it is striking to note how peculiar his own spiritual ascents
were. The Besht too is favored with the disclosure of marvelous secrets. Unlike
the Chariot Descenders and the ARI, however, he is not in the least expected
to disclose the mysteries of the Upper Worlds to his students. To the extent that
he does raise the topic of secrets with the members of his circle, as he does in
the letter to R. Gershon, it is to bring out the exaltedness of his own soul and
to clarify the essence of his mission. Indeed, the main objective of his soul's
journey through the Upper Worlds was to allow him to act on behalf of the
entire Jewish people. While traveling in the Upper Worlds, the Besht perceives

evil edicts that are being counseled against the Jewish public and works to overturn them, carries souls seeking salvation up to higher eschelons, and guides lost prayers onward to their ultimate destination.

We are thus faced with a new conception of the meaning of an ascent of the soul. An ascent of this kind does not have the exposure and revelation of Torah secrets as its primary content; instead, intercession in the heavenly courts and efforts to influence the fate of the Jewish people favorably are the objectives of journeys to the Upper Worlds. The means the Besht employs in his effort to achieve these objectives are quite various: the application of Holy Names, direct confrontation with Samael, bargaining in the heavenly courts, and, of course, prayer. In at least one instance, we have found that the external setting of an ascent of the soul was one of ecstatic prayer. Such ecstatic prayer takes place in the midst of a public prayer service. Perhaps it seems strange that the Besht is able to undergo so remarkable an experience while passing in front of the ark with the entire congregation in prayer all around him. On the other hand, perhaps no other occasion would have been so appropriate for an ascent of the soul of the kind the Besht underwent as the Neilah service on Yom Kippur. This service serves as the climax of the prayers of the High Holidays and provides the final opportunity for favorably altering the verdict of the heavens. In this fateful hour, the Besht acts as the envoy of the entire congregation of Israel, rising to carry out his sacred mission in the echelons of the Upper Worlds.

Failures on the Score of Blood-Libels; Successes on the Score of the Heidemak Attacks

Certain stories in *Shivhei Habesht* provide information about other features of the Besht's acrtivities on behalf of the Jewish people as a whole. Of special notice are the tales about the Besht's attempts to counter blood-libels by applying his faculties of sight and of hearing from afar.

The following event took place in the community of Zaslav while the Besht was staying there. A non-Jew was found dead in a field; certain townspeople attempted to persuade the duchess that he had been murdered by Jews. The duchess was skeptical of these charges, and insisted that a thorough investigation be conducted. The town's Jews learned of the affair and were seized with panic; they sent a messenger to bring in the Besht. The latter replied to the messenger that he does not "hear" of a blood-libel being mentioned in the duchess's court. A few days later, however, the Besht does "hear" of a discussion of the blood-libel in her court. The Besht hastens to bathe in a *mikvah* and later tells the townspeople they have nothing to fear. The townspeople nevertheless send a lobbyist to the duchess's court. This lobbyist discovers that the duchess had ordered the court physician to perform an autopsy to find out whether or not the deceased had died of natural causes. The townspeople, wary of relying on the Besht's reassurances, bribe the physician, who indeed finds that there were no grounds for accusing the Jews of murder. Yet this is not the end of the story. The town's Jews ask the Besht (censuriously, one presumes) why he had not foreseen the discovery of the corpse, which would have spared them considerable anxiety. The Besht replied: "While I was in the *mikvah* I prayed about just this, why this issue had previously been concealed from me; the reply I received was that I was being punished for having been slothful during the funeral eulogy for a *Talmid Hacham* named R. Hayim of Brod."[39]

The story reflects the expectation that the Besht should have been able to assist the Jews of Zaslav in two respects. First, with his powers of seeing and hearing from afar, he ought to have been able to foresee the imminent danger and give some advance warning of it. Second, he ought to have been able to alter the course of events through his prayer. The story appears to be an expression of the image that the Besht held of himself, an image that presumably would have achieved a certain circulation among the broader public as well. At any rate, according to the tale, the town's Jews were afraid to rely on the Besht's reassurances and chose instead a tried and tested procedure: advocacy and bribery. The Besht himself confessed to his failure to see the event in advance. The explanation he puts forward only serves to accentuate the sense of failure.

Another of the Besht's failures involved the blood-libel that took place in the community of Pavlysh. When the community learned of this blood-libel, R. David, the rabbi of Korostyshev, escaped, fearing that he too would be linked to the libel. He initially planned to flee as far as Walachia, but when he reached Miedzybóz the Besht detained him there. The Besht repeatedly asserted that the accused were destined for safety and that no harm would come to them. Instead, however, the accused were tortured and put to death. When R. David received a letter describing this outcome of the libel, he showed it to the Besht. Of the Besht's reaction, we read as follows:

> He grew despondent. It was a Friday, before the Holy Sabbath, and he went to the *mikvah* and cried deeply and recited the afternoon prayers with such great bitterness that his men of virtue could no longer lift their heads and said: perhaps when he begins the prayer of welcome for the Sabbath, the welcome will be joyous. And he prayed the Sabbath prayer of welcome and the evening service with a bitter heart still, and wept while saying grace over the wine and sitting at table, then went to his room to sleep, and stretched out on the ground and

lay there for a long while. The household members and the guests remained until the candles began to go out.[40]

R. David, who lingered for many hours beside the door to the chamber in which the Besht had laid down, later reported a conversation that the Besht conducted with souls that revealed themselves to him in the middle of the night. These were the souls of the "martyrs," that is, of those who had sanctified God's name and were put to death in the course of the blood-libel. Among other things, R. David heard the Besht tell the martyrs: "I decree upon you that you shall go and take vengeance upon the Prosecutor." The martyrs rejected the Besht's demands. They explained that so as to avenge themselves they would have to be reincarnated and live in the present world, and they were afraid of doing so. Later on, the Besht asked the souls of the martyrs why he had been mislead in the heavens and why it was not revealed to him that those accused in the blood-libel were destined to die. The souls replied, that had the Besht known in advance what was going to happen he would have engaged in intense prayer and had the edict overturned. Yet the consequence of this would have been the effectuation of a still greater calamity. The compiler of *Shivhei Habesht* adds yet another explanation: "And from the rabbi of our community I heard that the Besht said that he was promised in the Heavens that the edict would be overturned, yet there was some preacher in the holy community of Brod who made a living off of captives and raised [heavenly] ire which resulted in the captives being put to death, by our great sins."[41]

It appears that the story at hand contains an echo of the blood-libel that occurred in Pavlysh in the year 1753.[42] The depiction of the Besht bitterly grieving over the events, and calling for revenge against the Gentiles, is consistent with the image of him we have seen from his letter to R. Gershon of Kotov. It is instructive that the Besht again proposed, directly or indirectly, various explanations for his inability to prevent the blood-libel or to predict its outcome. The multiplicity of explanations strongly suggests the depth of his disappointment. The gap between his perception of himself as someone capable of defending the Jewish people from calamity, and the severity of the events that overtook the Jews of Poland during those years, presumably caused him distress and frustration. It was apparently this sense of failure and helplessness that was at the root of the Besht's repeated calls for vengeance against the Gentiles.

Yet the Besht could boast of successes as well. *Shivhei Habesht*'s compiler heard of one of these from R. Yaakov Yosef of Polonne:

> When there was a war in those times between the Greek and the Ishmaelite the Besht said: I saw two ministers combating and the Ishmaelite minister gained the upper hand, and I saw the Greek minister leaving in fury and [I feared that] a great calamity will come of this to

Israel heaven forbid. And I prayed for it to turn out the opposite, for the Greek minister to be victorious. There were only two Jews whom I was unable to deliver from their hands.[43]

It was, accordingly, the prayers of the Besht that decided the outcome of the battle between the Russians and the Turks, in the Russians' favor. In this way the Besht was able to avert the threat that the Russians, returning in defeat from the battlefield, would take out their anger on the Jews. Another story about a victory of the Besht was heard by *Shivhei Habesht*'s compiler from R. Alexander, his father-in-law. The event took place in an early period of the Besht's life, before he had settled in Miedzybóz. Once, one Sabbath eve, the Besht saw that robbers were about to invade the town. He warned the townspeople and they hurried to escape before the Sabbath began. The following day, when the robbers came, they found a town empty of Jews.[44]

The robbers mentioned in this tale are evidently Heidemaks. Heidemak gangs hiding in the forests constantly threatened travelers, and from time to time even attacked urban settlements as well. Certain stories express the Besht's role in defending the public and individuals from this threat. In one such tale, the Besht paused someplace in the forest, in a region where several Jews had been murdered. He explained his behavior saying that he was seeking in this way "to expel the *qlipa* of murder from that place."[45]

Especially interesting is a story that *Shivhei Habesht*'s compiler heard from Rabbi Yaakov Yosef of Polonne. The event took place in 1766, some six years after the Besht had passed away. At the time, R. Zvi, the Besht's son, was suffering from a personal crisis. When his father revealed himself to him in a dream and told him that he knew of this crisis, R. Zvi asked him why he had not come to his aid. The Besht made the following reply: "There is no time to speak with you for I must go nullify the libels of robbers called Heidemaks." R. Yaakov Yosef further related that several weeks afterward, as the Passover holiday commenced, a blood-libel was issued in the Sdeh Lavan community. The members of the community sent word by messenger to ask him to pray on their behalf. R. Yaakov Yosef assented to their request, and attests that while he was praying the *Shekhina* hovered over him and that he was therefore certain the edict would be cancelled.[46]

It would seem, accordingly, that R. Zvi's dream, and the appeal made to R. Yaakov Yosef to nullify the blood-libel through prayer, attest to just how deeply ingrained the image of the Besht had become as someone who could protect the Jewish community from calamity. The Besht's son did not doubt that his father, after his death, was continuing to fill this mission of his; and the members of the Sdeh Lavan community sought deliverance from the prayers of someone who was considered one of the Besht's closest students.

Intervention in the Leaseholding
Business and Supervision of *Shekhita*

Two further fields in which the Besht worked for the service of the public were
the business of leaseholding and the supervision of *shekhita* (ritual slaughter
of livestock; the slaughterer is a *shochet*). At first sight, these seem to be distinct domains, far removed from each other. The former has to do with economic life and the private dealings of individuals, while the latter is a matter
of ritual and concerns relations between man and his Maker. Nevertheless, so
far as the intervention of the Besht is concerned, one may note significant parallels between his activities in these two fields.

First, each of these realms were ones in which the characteristic problems
of Jewish life in the rural areas of Ukraine were manifest. The Besht was able
to learn of them through his frequent travels, travels during which he lodged
in hamlets and villages and had exposure to the difficult realities of Jewish life
in its various guises. Second, in each of these two realms, the Besht's activities
filled a vacuum of sorts in the functioning of the official leadership of the communities. And finally, both in the case of the leaseholding business and the
supervision of *shekhita,* the Besht acted on the basis of his personal authority
and put to use the special powers with which he was blessed.

I turn now to an appraisal of the Besht's involvement in each of these two
domains.

THE LEASEHOLDING BUSINESS

As is well known, the institution of leaseholding was extremely significant
to the economic life of the Jews of Poland.[47] The expansion of Jewish settlement across Ukraine in the sixteenth and seventeenth centuries was affected
to a considerable extent by the economic opportunities made available to
them on the estates of noblemen. However, as an economic enterprise, leaseholding had certain drawbacks. One common problem was unfair competition by Jews who set their eyes on the leases of other Jews. Such individuals
would offer the nobleman a supplement to the rent so that the lease would
be transferred to them; the consequence was that the other Jewish leaseholder was threatened with the loss of his livelihood. The mechanism the
leadership of the communities applied to regulate the leaseholding business
and to prevent unfair competition was the *hazaka* (prior possession) regulations. Yet in the course of the eighteenth century the community leadership weakened and found it increasingly difficult to enforce these
regulations, especially as they clearly conflicted with the economic interests
of the noblemen who owned the estates. This was the background to the tales
in which the Besht acts to protect leaseholders whose livelihood was at risk.

It is, presumably, no coincidence that in two of these tales the leaseholders whom the Besht hastens to assist are widows.[48]

Apart from the threat of unfair competition, Jewish leaseholders lived in constant fear that they would be unable to pay their rent to the landlords. When this occurred, the noblemen did not hesitate to impose harsh prison sentences on the Jewish debtors. Certain stories from *Shivhei Habesht* imply that in this matter too the Besht came to the aid of the leaseholders.

An instructive example of aid of this kind may be found in the letter written by R. Yehiel Michal, the Besht's son-in-law, to R. Gershon of Kotov. In the course of the letter, R. Yehiel Michal tells of what had happened to his father, R. Baruch, and R. Yaakov Yekil, who were in debt to the "famous lord." As they lacked the means of paying the debt, the lord had them shackled in "iron chains." Deliverance came for the two prisoners when the lord of Miedzybóz paid their debt and wrote letters of recommendation on their behalf. This rescue too R. Yehiel ascribes to the Besht: "And this all happened thanks to the prayers and requests of the Master my Teacher my Father-in-law, for it was thus foretold by my Teacher and Father-in-law in advance that the Holy One Blessed Be He would perform miracles for them and so it was by the grace of God."[49]

SUPERVISION OF *Shekhita*

The background to the Hasidic leaders' activity as concerns *shekhita* has been elucidated in Khone Shmeruk's article, "The Social Significance of Hasidic *Shekhita*."[50] By examining the regulations of the *Vaad Medinat Lita* and the *Vaad Medinat Mehrin* (Moravia), Shmeruk discovered that there had been a steady deterioration in *shekhita* performance in these areas in the generations preceding the emergence of Hasidism. The origins of this phenomenon had to do with the expansion of Jewish settlement into the rural areas and the consequent increase in the number of ritual slaughterers who functioned at some distance from the rabbis and the scholars. The authors of the regulations complain that slaughterers are inadequately versed in the *shekhita* laws and do not enforce them rigorously enough. Worse, there was a suspicion that certain slaughterers might be closet Sabbateans, who set themselves the goal of deceiving the public into eating nonkosher meat. Given these dangers, the authors of the regulations called for raising the training standards for slaughterers and for stricter supervision by the rabbis of the communities over the rural slaughterers. The multitude of regulations issued on the subject of *shekhita* indicate that the problem endured from the middle of the seventeenth century up through the outset of Hasidism.

Shmeruk asserts that although there are no extant records of new *shekhita* regulations issued by the *Vaad Haartzot* in Poland, "it is nearly certain that conditions there were no better than they had been in Lithuania and Moravia. And in Podolia and Volhynia, the regions in which Hasidism emerged, conditions were apparently even worse."[51] Shmeruk based this assertion on the "internal and external traumas" that struck the Jews of Poland in the eighteenth century; that is, the Heidemak attacks on the one hand and the outbreak of the Frankist movement on the other. On this point, he cites further explicit testimony by R. Yaakov Yosef of Polonne.[52] This evidence leaves no doubt that the breakdown of the *shekhita* system, about which the authors of the regulations in Lithuania and Moravia complain, did not skip over the regions that would serve as the cradle of Hasidism.

Given these facts as background, one can understand the custom the Hasidim and the pious had of examining the blade used for slaughter each time they chanced to eat in a strange place. This practice was also common among members of the Besht's circle, and evidence of it is scattered throughout *Shivhei Habesht*.[53] Naturally, the Besht too observed this custom. A typical instance may be found in the tale of the Besht's visit to Sluck at the invitation of the leaseholders R. Shmuel and R. Gedaliah. When the housewife wished to prepare a feast to honor their guest, the Besht asked for the slaughterer to come and show him his knife. This demand infuriated the townspeople: "And the townspeople were enraged that he even considered examining the knife of the local slaughterer especially given that this was a large community."[54] The fury of the people of Sluck is unsurprising, as the Besht's demand to examine the knife was tantamount to casting doubt on the *kashrut* of the entire town's *shekhita*. Nevertheless, his request to view the knife should perhaps be considered a precaution taken on his own behalf.[55] The Besht's intervention in oversight of the slaughterers, however, carried an entirely different connotation.

Certain tales in *Shivhei Habesht* link the Besht's action on the subject of *shekhita* to his abilities to see from afar and to uncover secrets. In one case, the Besht exposes a *shochet* who was careless about the inspection of the lungs.[56] Another instance where the Besht exposes a *shochet* who had caused many to sin is found in the following tale:

> I heard from the rabbi of our community that the Besht sent word to the rabbi of the holy community of Bitshuv that their *shochet* was of the sect of Sabbetai Zvi (may his name be cursed) and is feeding them nonkosher meat, for after showing him the knife he strikes the knife against a mallet so as to damage it. And the rabbi looked into the matter and it was so.[57]

R. Yaakov Yosef tells of another case: The Besht warned him several times to keep his eye on a certain *shochet,* who was careless and did not follow the *shekhita* laws strictly enough. Heeding the Besht's warning, Rabbi Yaakov Yosef kept an eye on that *shochet* and caught him being negligent. The story ends with the religious court taking evidence about the *shochet*'s behavior, following which he is removed from his post.[58]

The compiler of *Shivhei Habesht* heard from his father-in-law R. Alexander—the main figure in the incident—about the Besht's involvement in the appointment of a *shochet*. Recall that R. Alexander was the Besht's scribe. After filling this function for eight years he was forced to find other employment, as he had a hard time providing for his family from what he was earning working for the Besht. Through the Besht's intercession, R. Alexander was given the post of *shochet* of the community of Sdeh Lavan. After a while he won the post of *shochet* for the Nemirov community, again after being recommended for it by the Besht.[59]

Of the nature of the Besht's intercession in R. Alexander's appointment to the post in Sdeh Lavan, we read as follows:

> And the *Maggid* of said holy community . . . R. Avraham Podlisker by name, was a great and famous *Tsadik*. Once, they were unable to approve of any knife for *shekhita*. They sent for several slaughterers from several communities and no one could show them a knife of which they approved. Once, the Besht came . . . and told them he would present a knife to them, and he presented them a knife and they approved of it. . . . And the Besht promised to send them a *shochet* and he sent them my father-in-law of blessed memory.[60]

It seems that the circumstances of R. Alexander's appointment as *shochet* of Sdeh Lavan were such that members of this community, apparently under the influence of R. Avraham Pudelisker, were exceptionally strict in matters of *shekhita*. Once the Besht was able to satisfy them about the choice of a knife they were inclined to rely on his recommendation for the position of *shochet* as well. Perhaps the relations between the Besht and Sdeh Lavan's rabbi also played a part in this affair.[61] At any rate, the Besht was able to influence the appointment of Sdeh Lavan's *shochet* in part because of his reputation for being well versed in the *shekhita* laws and strict in enforcing them.

We learn of an unusual initiative of the Besht's to have a *shochet* dismissed from his post, from the following story:

> Once the Besht traveled to Kaminka and near the town heard the Decree: the *shochet* of said holy community is to be dismissed. . . . When he came to the house of R. Baruch, R. Baruch prepared himself and slaughtered several animals; one animal was deemed unkosher and was hung in the hallway. The Besht went to smoke a pipe in the hallway. And R. Baruch entered the hallway and the Besht told him to cut him a piece of meat from this animal and to roast it

for him. R. Baruch was convinced he was joking. He said: His honor will not eat from this animal. The Besht said: I most certainly will eat from it. When he saw that he had spoken seriously he said: This animal is not kosher! The Besht said to him: yet this animal is asking of me that I eat from it. Pray tell me, what was the cause of its not being kosher? And he sent for the slaughterer and asked him: What had rendered this animal unkosher? And he said, there's a difference of opinion among the *poskim,* some say it is kosher and some say it isn't. He ordered them to slice him a piece of meat so that he will make a roast of it. And the Besht saw that his people were uncomfortable with this and said, send for R. Shmuel Moreh Zedek of the holy community of Polonne and bring a letter from him before he roasts it. And they immediately sent off a messenger riding a good horse and he went and recieved a letter from the *Moreh Zedek* that the animal is kosher. And he fired the *shochet* and refused to find him alternative employment.[62]

According to the story, the Besht had the *shochet* fired from his post because in deeming the animal unkosher he was being unnecessarily strict. The *shochet* knew, or should have known, that in cases of doubt such as this he ought to deem the animal kosher, on the basis of the principle: "the Torah takes pity on the possessions of Israel."[63] By ignoring this principle the *shochet* had caused financial damage to the owner of the animal. By the way, it is instructive that the Besht did not presume to act on the basis of his own mastery of Halachic literature. His verdict that the animal was kosher was based on the special capacity for "sight" he was endowed with. Yet the Besht's associates had trouble accepting the idea that an unkosher animal could be rendered kosher on the basis of invisible evidence. This was why the Besht referred them to a qualified Halachic figure.

The examples cited here suggest that the Besht's authority in the supervision of *shekhita* was grounded in his personal charisma. Apparently, the fact that he was versed in the *shekhita* laws—as a result of experience gained from the period in which he himself served as a *shochet*[64]—and the reputation he had earned as someone scrupulous about the blade used to slaughter the meat that he eats, also played a role in this regard. Yet for the most part it was his personal prestige that allowed him to intervene and to carry influence in a field that was by rights under the jurisdiction of the rabbinate of the communities. It should also be noted that in the majority of cases mentioned here the Besht did not act so as to challenge or ignore the rabbis. On the contrary, the rabbis of the communities recognized his authority and welcomed his assistance in the performance of their duties. One may affirm, therefore, that the Besht's activities in the field of *shekhita* showed signs of a pattern that was destined to characterize the relation between Hasidic leaders and the community institutions in the areas into which Hasidism spread.[65]

More broadly, the Besht's intervention in the leaseholding business and in *shekhita* was a further expression of the same consciousness of mission and responsibility toward the Jewish people to which we drew attention above. However, unlike his actions in the Upper Worlds, which took place in isolation from the public, his activity in these realms brought him into direct contact with the public and caused a certain alteration of their habits. Here the Besht's conception of himself as a public leader earned a certain measure of external, social realization. Furthermore, one may affirm in retrospect that the Besht's involvement in these two realms influenced a mode of behavior that was destined to characterize Hasidic leaders for generations to come.

The Motif of The Popular *Tsadik*

The Besht's intervention in the leaseholding business and in the supervision of *shekhita* was associated, as we have said, with his frequent travels throughout Ukraine. In the course of these travels he came into immediate contact with all layers of society and had exposure to many facets of Jewish life that those who kept to their *Beit Midrash* were at best dubiously cognizant of. Indeed, one of the characteristic features of the Besht's contact with the broad public, as expressed in *Shivhei Habesht,* is his sensitivity toward the sufferings of common people. Certain stories describe the Besht as one who helps sinners who have fallen on hard times to repent. A further manifestation of the Besht's special approach to ordinary folk may be found in tales at the core of which is a figure who may be termed a "popular *Tsadik*." We have in mind here the tales within which the Besht uncovers the exceptional spiritual rank of a common person. One of these stories centers around a woman from the town of Satanow: "Once the Besht traveled to said holy community and near town saw a light over one of the townspeople. He stood still and observed that this light hovered over a certain woman." When he pursued the matter further and asked the townspeople about it, it turned out this was the woman called "Die Frume Rivele," who was known in town for collecting alms for the town's poor.[66]

Another story tells of a craftsman who made socks "and would pray regularly at the synagogue, summer and winter; even if there were not ten people in the synagogue, he would still pray, alone." Once the Besht chanced upon that town and saw this artisan making his way in the early morning toward the synagogue. The Besht recognized his eminent status and "was very much astounded." In reply to the Besht's questions, the craftsman related that he does not emerge from the door to his house except to go to synagogue, and while he is occupied in his craft he recites chapters of the Psalms, to the extent he remembers them by heart. After interrogating him some more, the Besht said of him: "He is the foundation of the synagogue until the Redeemer comes may it be soon in our day Amen *Selah.*"[67]

What is apparently the most familiar illustration of the motif of the popular *Tsadik* may be found in the famous story about the youth and the flute. The gist of the tale is as follows: A certain villager used to pray during the High Holidays in the synagogue at which the Besht prayed. The villager had a son who was having trouble learning to read and did not know how to pray. When the boy reached thirteen years of age, his father brought him with him to town for the Yom Kippur prayers. For many hours, the boy remained in the synagogue without being able to participate in the prayers. During the Neilah service, when the Besht, as was his custom, passed in front of the ark, the boy took out the flute upon which he used to play when setting out to the fields with the sheep, and made a loud noise. The congregation responded in shock. The Besht, for his part, concluded the Neilah service sooner than usual. After the prayer he said:

> And this boy with the sound of his flute uplifted all the prayers and relieved me [of the task]. . . . For he does not know how to say a thing. . . . And by the strength of his desire played the flute from the truth of the core of his heart without distraction, wholly dedicated to His Blessed Name, and the Almighty looks to the heart, and by this means all the prayers were carried up.[68]

At first reading, this story provokes disbelief. As with other tales published in the collection *Gdolim Maase Tsadikim* [Great are the deeds of the righteous], this story too has been graced by an editing with a discernibly fictional component. The narrator develops and "stretches" the plot so as to intensify the element of drama. In addition, the suspicion arouses that the motif has been reproduced from some earlier story. We have in mind the famous tale from *Sefer Hasidim* about a shepherd who does not know how to pray and instead would say: "Master of the Universe. It is open and known before you that if you owned animals you would give them to me to watch over. For everyone else, I watch over animals for pay. But for you I would watch them for free because I love you." A *Talmid Hacham* heard the shepherd's prayer, scolded him, and taught him the official prayers. This *Talmid Hacham* had a dream in which he was instructed to tell the shepherd to return to his former manner of prayer.[69] Nevertheless, for all the similarity between the stories, it may be asserted that the presence of similar motifs in different historical contexts does not necessarily imply that one of them is based on the other. Furthermore, the teller of the tale about the Besht could not have learnt the story from *Sefer Hasidim*, as this story was only incorporated into the Parma edition, which was first published in 1891.[70]

As to the fictional aspect of the story, it seems to me that this fact does not negate the possibility that it has a nucleus of historical truth. The historical setting for the tale seems plausible enough: rural Jews did indeed come to town to pray with a *minyan* during the High Holidays. We also know from another source about the Besht's custom of passing in front of the ark during the Neilah service of Yom Kippur.[71] The same applies to the Besht's point of view that it was his job to "carry up" the prayers.

More than anything, what strikes me about the story as plausible and consistent with what we know of the Besht is its conclusion: that the pure intentions of this boy who did not know how to pray made a great impression in the Upper Worlds. This assessment is bolstered by another tale, this time from *Shivhei Habesht*, which leads toward a similar conclusion. We have in mind the story about the *darshan* (preacher) who informed on the Jews:

> I heard from the rabbi of our community who heard from the Hasid our teacher Zeev of Alik: Once on a Sabbath the Besht was in said holy community as a guest and the host was a community leader-alternate. And on Sabbath, the homeowner went for the afternoon service to the synagogue to hear the sermon from a visiting *darshan*. And the Besht waited for him to come home from synagogue for the third Sabbath meal. And during that time [the Besht] heard that the *darshan* was informing upon the Jews. And the Besht was furious, and told the beadle to go call for the homeowner. And the beadle revealed to several people that the Besht was furious with the *darshan*. And the *darshan* saw that people were slipping away one by one and ceased to deliver his sermon. And the following day the *darshan* came to the Besht, who greeted him and asked who he was. He replied: I am the *darshan*; why were you angry with me? The Besht leaped from his place and with tears spilling from his eyes said: Will you speak ill of the Jewish people?! Know that a ordinary Jew goes to the market day after day, and in the evening when darkness falls he takes fright and says: woe is me for I have missed the time for afternoon prayers. So he goes into some house and prays the afternoon service without knowing what he says. Nevertheless the Seraphim and Ofanim are astounded by this.[72]

It was the element of *admonishment* in the *darshan*'s sermon that angered the Besht. The phrase "informed on the Jewish people [Israel]" expresses the Besht's perspective, that sermon-givers who go too far in their chastisings have the status of prosecutors against Israel before the Divinity. For present purposes, what is especially relevant is the assertion that the Besht makes so as to repudiate the *darshan*'s statements: The simple Jew wanders about the market all day trying to earn an income for his family. Yet when night falls and he is threatened with having missed the time for the afternoon service, he takes fright and rushes to one of the prayer houses and prays. During the prayer he "does not know what he says," as this is a simple Jew for whom even the language of the prayer is unclear. Nevertheless, his prayer makes a great impression in the Upper Worlds.

It seems to me that, as in the case of the tale of the boy and the flute, one must be wary about the moral one draws from this tale. It would be a mistake to interpret these stories as idealizing the common folk and their ignorant state. On the other hand, there is a recognition here of the superiority of innocent prayer-intentions, even when these are unconnected with any formal knowledge. It is clear that this positive appraisal of the prayer of the simple Jew would not have been possible without the shift that took place at the outset of Hasidism regarding prayer-intentions; namely, the abandonment of Kabbalistic prayer-intentions (which were based on esoteric knowledge) and the stress on the value of intentional purity.[73] The Besht was thus able to shift from the traditional perspective reflected in the Mishnaic dictum "nor is the commoner a Hasid" (Tractate Avoth, 2:5), and to suggest instead that in certain cases the commoner too is a kind of Hasid—if his prayer is pure.[74]

Let us return to the Besht's criticism of the darshan and his chastisements. It is to be stressed that this was not the only criticism uttered in this spirit. Recall that the Besht accounted for his failure to rescue the Jews who were executed during the blood-libel in Pavlysh by claiming that a certain darshan took money for a sermon about the blood-libel and in this way "aroused [heavenly] ire."

An important source that sheds light on the Besht's perspective in relation to reprovers and their chastisements is provided by the writings of R. Yaakov Yosef of Polonne.[75] Consider the following statements that R. Yaakov Yosef attributes to the Besht:

> That one must beware of moral chastising; that one must love [the people] and chastise them out of love, as a father who loves his son teaches him stern morals. Yet those who seek to aggrandize themselves, heaven forbid, by this means . . . for instance by enjoyment of profits and suchlike, which are not for a heavenly cause . . . I heard from my teacher that this brings about, God forbid, ire between Israel and their Heavenly Father. And as I mentioned in the interpretation of "And the people spoke against God and Moses" etc., "and the Lord sent against the people the Snakes and Seraphites" (Numbers 21), these refer to two types of chastisers. This reading is patterned on a tale I heard from my teacher: A king banished his only son and sent his two servants after him. And one [servant] returned and spoke ill of the son to his father, etc. And the second had much the same to say, except that he spoke from the side that expressed

sympathy with the king's pain and said that the banished son had
been gone so long he had forgotten royal graces. . . . Then the king
was filled with mercy, etc.[76]

The fable attributed to the Besht illustrates his point of view about the
empathy a leader must manifest toward his public. This approach combines a
deep sense of responsibility for the public well-being with an attitude of for-
giveness and tolerance for its failings. This stance is consistent with the toler-
ant approach the Besht exhibited toward those driven to sin by their personal
misfortunes, and with his recognition of the spiritual stature of the righteous
commoners, those individuals noted for their love of their fellow man and for
their love of God.

Summary and Conclusions

The backdrop for the Besht's labors on behalf of the Jewish people was the bleak
social and political reality of Jewish life in Poland in the eighteenth century.
Calamities such as the blood-libels, the Heidemak attacks and outbreaks of
plague repeatedly struck at the Jewish community. The unmasking of the antinomianism of the Frankists, the conflict with them, and the subsequent burning
of the Talmud, although one-time events, profoundly shook the people of the
period and left deep scars upon them. In addition there were the economic difficulties and the social tensions associated with the leaseholding business, along
with the problems of ensuring that *shekhita* in the rural areas would be kosher.

With these circumstances as the background, the Besht took upon himself
the mission of working for the public good and of acting as its defender. Further, the Besht regarded himself as someone capable of acting as a bridge and
medium between earthly existence and the Upper Worlds. This mission
involved saving the souls of sinners and carrying up prayers that had lost their
way. What caused the Besht to take this mission upon himself? Whence did he
derive the enormous self-confidence needed for doing so? As said, at the foundation of the Besht's self-image, as someone whose destiny it was to act for the
benefit of the entire Jewish people, was an internal certainty that the exceptional powers and esoteric knowledge with which he was blessed were granted
him so that he might use them for public benefit. The Besht's consciousness
of this sense of mission received confirmation and support during his ascents
of the soul.

In the course of fulfilling his mission, the Besht displayed a deep emotional
identification with the sufferings of simple people. His conception of himself as
serving the role of public defender intensified his sense of personal failure when-
ever he was unable to avert a disaster. This bitter feeling, which presumably also

carried an element of personal humiliation, is manifested in his efforts to explain the failure and in the oft-repeated calls for revenge against the Gentiles. Alongside the deep identification with the sufferings of the public, the Besht shows a special sensitivity toward individuals who have fallen on hard times. Especially striking is his appreciation for the simple Jew who worships his creator with a pure devotion.

In my discussion thus far, I have been stressing the way in which the Besht himself perceived his mission. However, it is proper to ask the opposite question as well: What was the extent to which this perception was acknowledged by society? Who knew that the Besht was a leader of all the Jewish people? Did the Besht bother to announce this publicly? To what extent did the Besht require the cooperation of the public?

It stands to reason that so far as dealings with the Upper Worlds were concerned, the Besht did not require any public confirmation. Society did not appoint him to fill this function and he was not accountable to it for his achievements. The Besht was the one who judged himself on the degree of his success or failure. Nevertheless, he clearly did need a group of supporters who would take his side in his efforts, celebrate his achievements, and share in his misery when he failed. He naturally found such group support in his circle of followers. This is clearly reflected in the letter to R. Gershon, in which the Besht tells in detail of his travels through the Upper Worlds. Likewise, the Besht informed R. Gershon of how he redeems and uplifts the souls of the dead who reveal themselves to him in the course of Friday afternoon prayers. We also have seen that the Besht told R. Yaakov Yosef of his impact on the outcome of the war between the Russians and the Turks. R. Dov Ber, the *maggid* of Mezerich, told his student R. Shlomo of Lutsk that the Besht showed him the names of angels listed in the book *Raziel the Angel* and said to him that through this book he knew "which angels are appointed annually to govern the world, in order to learn how he should act with them and how to make use of them."[77]

These examples and the others like them clearly indicate that the Besht felt a need to include the members of his circle in the various experiences involving his mission on behalf of the entire Jewish people. These associates, naturally, conveyed the information to the other people with whom they came into contact. Needless to say, the members of the Besht's circle believed in his mission as a leader of all of Israel, and presumably also induced such belief in others in their sphere of influence. A further circle of people who were disposed to acknowledge the Besht's calling were the residents of his town of Miedzybóz, and in particular those who prayed at the *Beit Midrash* that he regularly attended. This congregation was witness to the Besht's experience of ecstatic prayer, would have seen the external manifestations of his ascents of the soul, and would have heard from his lips an explanation of the content of this experience. We learn of how the Besht was perceived by one of the congregants of the *Beit Midrash* in Miedzybóz from *Shivhei Habesht*'s compiler:

> I heard from the son of R. Yaakov of Miedzybóz who is called R. Yekil that one time his father led him to the *Beit Midrash,* and the Besht was there standing in prayer in front of the Ark. And he spoke to him thus: Son, look and observe, for in this world no such sight will be seen until the arrival of our righteous Messiah, for he is our R. Shimon Bar Yohai and his comrades.[78]

Tales and rumors about the Besht were presumably widespread among the residents of Miedzybóz, the town in which the Besht resided for some twenty years. A further circle of people who were exposed to the figure of the Besht, and who presumably also heard of his activities on behalf of all of Israel, were the Jews of the hamlets and villages he frequented and in which he lodged in the course of his travels. In general, it seems that the Besht's name, as a person who operates in both heaven and earth on behalf of the Jewish people, was known to a certain degree to the public in those regions in which he lived and worked.

In my discussion of the ascent of the soul from the year 1747, I contested the idea that the Besht's dialogue with the Messiah involved any sort of Messianic conceit or purpose. My stance about this receives further confirmation when considering the Besht's behavior from a broader perspective. The Besht had no plan! He did not work toward any sort of final date or event of a revolutionary cast. Nor were his activities a part of any kind of ongoing process (as, for instance, is the process of *Tikkun* described in the Kabbalah of the ARI). All of his actions take the form of responding to chance events as they occur. The world in which the Besht functions is an irredeemable one: Jews suffer from the predations of the nations of the world, most people are shackled to their material conditions, and the people of Israel are blocked by odd partitions from their Heavenly Father. The Besht accepts this irredeemable universe as an established fact and does not have the conceit of being able to alter its rules and regulations fundamentally. On the contrary: he derives the essence of his calling from the world's very irredeemability, as it is he who is capable of defending society from calamities and it is he who can serve as the bridge between earthly existence and the Upper Worlds.

Finally, it is worth again observing that in all his activities on behalf of the general public the Besht did not avail himself of any institutional authority. The Besht acted from the power of his personal charisma. Viewed in retrospect, one may say that the Besht presented a model of leadership that was to come to typify Hasidism for generations.

CHAPTER FOUR

The Besht as Mystic and Pioneer in Divine Worship

I t was his mystical experience, more than anything else, that was at the core of the Besht's spiritual world. This experience was also what gave shape to the new form of spirituality that the Besht passed on to his students and to the members of his circle; in many respects it set the tone for the Hasidic movement in its first generations. In this chapter I shall attempt to reconstruct and characterize what might be termed "the Besht's path as a mystic."

In the background to my discussion here lies the presumption that one ought not to approach the study of the Besht as though he were a philosophical figure. A philosopher is a person guided primarily by questions about ideas, whereas a mystic has longings and strivings for the mystical as his dominant concerns. To be sure, the Besht did deliver sermons in which philosophical views were expressed, yet these too were closely linked to the experiential dimension of his life. What is the connection between these two components, the ideas and the experience? It may be affirmed that the ideas the Besht expresses reflect his attempts to interpret the mystical experiences he underwent and to justify the methods he employed so as to attain them. Additionally, the Besht's sermons, with the ideas implicit in them, served the further objective of communicating his path of divine worship to his fellow men.

Even if one accepts the appraisal that the Besht's philosophy is derived from his experience, and took the form of interpretations or rationalizations of it, it nevertheless is the case that once having articulated his personal experiences through intellectual constructs, such constructs would have at times served to guide and mold the contents of the experiences themselves. Indeed, we find that the mutual relations between the element of the intellectual and the element of the experiential in the life of the Besht are somewhat complex. For all that, the ideas the Besht advances do not stand on their own and they are to be evaluated in close proximity with the experiential component of his life. Thus my phrase, "the Besht's path as a mystic," refers at once to the experiential dimension of the Besht's life, to his philosophical views, and to the mutual relations sustained between them.[1]

In seeking to reconstruct the Besht's path as a mystic, we must first address the question of the nature and singularity of this path. How are we to characterize the mystical experience that the Besht underwent? Can we point to general features that were especially typical of it? How did the Besht interpret his experience and what theosophical platform did he employ as a basis for his interpretations? In seeking to overcome the obstacles in the path of the mystic, did the Besht break new ground? What explanations did he put forward to justify the novelty of his approach?

Alongside questions about the singular nature of the trail blazed by the Besht in spirituality and worship, a question also arises about the degree to which this path was original. Yet here again I must stress: the Besht was not a philosopher and author; he was, rather, a mystic and a spiritual leading light. Thus, certain restrictions or qualifications are to be applied to the assessment of the originality of his contributions. First, innovations in ideas are not to be considered in isolation from the dimension of personal experience. Second, the question is not whether a certain idea advanced by the Besht is new in some absolute sense, but whether it constituted a genuine innovation in the social and cultural milieu in which he lived and acted. Furthermore, the question is not whether each and every detail of the Besht's path may be classified as novel, but whether innovation is discernible in the total assemblage. These qualifications are called for because the question guiding us here throughout is, Why did the Besht consider himself as someone who had been given the mission of passing on a novel form of worship and spirituality, and why was he indeed regarded as a pioneer in religion by his associates and his followers?

Before I turn to a direct discussion of these questions, I shall survey the perspectives of some of the scholars that have dealt with the subject of *devekut* in early Hasidism. This survey shall serve as the background for my attempt to sketch a new picture of the Besht's path as a mystic.

Dvekut at the Outset of Hasidism:
The Current State of Scholarship

As in other branches of the scholarship of Jewish mysticism, it was Gershom Scholem who left his mark on an entire generation of scholars and readers in all that concerns the topic of early Hasidism. In his article on *dvekut* (literally, an "adherence" or "merging"—of the soul with the Divinity), Scholem made certain assertions that have come to be conventions within the scholarly literature.[2] Scholem's main conclusions may be summarized in the following four points.

First, the most important innovation made by Hasidism at its outset, the one which set the tone for its unique form of spirituality, concerns its idea of *dvekut*. Second, Hasidism added nothing to the primacy of the religious ideal of *dvekut*. What Hasidism did fundamentally alter, however, was the conception that had previously existed in the Kabbalah as to the "place" *dvekut* occupied. The Kabbalists held that *dvekut* was a matter solely for persons of rare virtue, and that even such individuals were able to achieve it only after having undergone an extensive process of spiritual purification and development. Along came Hasidism, which taught that *dvekut* was a point of departure attainable by any Jew. Third, this change in the "place" of *dvekut* accounts for the attraction Hasidism held for the "ordinary Jew." In other words, the liberation of *dvekut* from the narrow confines of the Kabbalists, and the placement of it at the disposal of the broad Jewish public, was an important factor in the growth of Hasidism as a popular movement. Fourth, an unavoidable consequence of the "democratization" of the concept of *dvekut* was its degeneration. Or as Scholem phrases it:

> If *dvekut* is demanded of everyone, and effectively is imposed upon the masses, it must unavoidably take on simplistic and crude forms. . . . And as not each and every person was capable of attaining such heights and such spiritual postures by means of introspection and contemplation, external stimulants were needed, even when this amounted to imbibing liquors.[3]

Although Scholem is not aiming his words here at the Besht specifically, and his discussion deals with early Hasidism more generally, there is no doubt that he intends his assertions to apply to the Besht as well; one may even say, to the Besht first and foremost. That this is so may be seen from the evidence that Scholem marshals to support his remarks, which the main consists of statements attributed to the Besht. Thus the question that preoccupied Scholem seems to have been, What innovation did Hasidism make in relation to the Kabbalah? This question is consistent with his perspective according to which Hasidism was a further stage, in effect the "last stage," in the development of Jewish mysticism. Moreover, it seems that Scholem was seeking to explain why Kabbalism always remained something of an esoteric and elitist movement, whereas Hasidism developed into a movement that won a broad following. Scholem was able to answer both questions, as said, through his affirmation that *dvekut* had been turned into a spiritual-religious ideal made available to all and sundry. And as he was content with this answer, he saw no point in asking the further question whether the Besht had contributed anything to the nature and content of mystical experience. On the contrary: so far as the content of *dvekut* was concerned, Scholem repeatedly stressed the continuity between Hasidism and the literature of the Kabbalah.[4]

Now, while no one challenges Scholem's claim about the centrality of *dvekut* in early Hasidism, certain scholars have contested his assertion that Hasidism indeed assigned to *devkut* a novel "place." These scholars challenge the idea that early Hasidism viewed *dvekut* as a spiritual-religious ideal that was freely available to all. In their opinion, the Besht did not relinquish the view that *dvekut* was the province of individuals of rare virtue alone.[5] Yet this makes the question about the originality of Hasidism all the more pertinent. Can one point out characteristic features that were singular to the Besht's mystical experience?

Yosef Weiss followed in Scholem's footsteps both as concerns the centrality of *dvekut* in early Hasidism and as regards the new "place" that Hasidism found for *dvekut*.[6] Weiss, however, saw fit to raise a question that did not bother Scholem:

> Where did early Hasidism acquire its religious world built on *dvekut?*
> Where is the unmediated historical link by which the Besht is bound?
> Where did R. Israel Besht obtain those very ideals and ideas which he champions? . . . Could it be that he drew sustenance not only from books but also from the people of his own culture and environment?[7]

In line with these questions, Weiss offers a reconstruction of the spiritual-religious environment in which the Besht lived and operated. This environment, according to Weiss, consisted of a fraternity of *maggidim* (preachers) with whom the Besht maintained a partnership of ideas. Moreover, Weiss holds that this partnership did not necessarily consist of the Besht having an influence on the members of the circle of *maggidim*, but involved no less an influence of the *maggidim* upon the Besht.[8]

In the course of providing his reconstruction of the spiritual-religious world of the members of this fraternity, Weiss sheds light on the nature of their mystical experience, which in Weiss's view was at the core of their partnership with the Besht. As an illustration, Weiss puts forward the figure of R. Nahman of Kosov, whom he describes as "the principal speaker on matters of *dvekut*" among members of the circle. R. Nahman's view of *dvekut* was that it consisted of an effort to have one's thought be continually concentrated on God. This conception is expressed in, among other things, a statement attributed to him by R. Yaakov Yosef of Polonne: "I heard that the *Hasid* Our Teacher and Rabbi Nahman Kosover provided a certain person each week a fixed stipend so that when he was among people he would be reminded by a hint that he should not forget the Name YHWH which must forever be before his eyes."[9]

Apparently for R. Nahman, the goal of maintaining a perpetual focus of thought upon God was to be achieved through the technique of concentration on the name of YHWH. Yet if *dvekut* is understood as such a perpetual concentration upon God, this raises the problem of how *dvekut* is compatible with earthly endeavors. Weiss explains that R. Nahman sought to resolve this difficulty by a "division of consciousness into internal and external layers." In other words, the preoccupation with earthly affairs is to be confined to an external layer of consciousness, while the internal layer of consciousness retains its focus upon God.

This is, in essence, Weiss's view of the kind of *dvekut* the fraternity of *maggidim* and the Besht held in common.[10] I shall later try to counter the assertion that the Besht conceived of *dvekut* as a continual focus of thought upon God. However, even if we were to agree that the circle of *maggidim* and the Besht held certain ideas on this topic in common, there is still room to ask, Was there nothing in the Besht's approach to *dvekut* that was different from the approach taken by the *maggidim*? If there was nothing singular in his approach, why was it specifically the Besht's head that was crowned with the title of "Founder of Hasidism"? Why did the leaders of Hasidism in subsequent generations consider themselves to be students of the Besht and not students of R. Nahman of Kosov, R. Menahem Mendel of Bar, or of other members of the circle? Was the Besht's contribution really confined to his having bequeathed to others the approach to *dvekut* that had been common in the circle of *maggidim*? Did he contribute nothing new of his own on a subject that everyone agrees was central to the launching of Hasidism? Weiss indeed does note that the Besht's perspective about "elevating straying thoughts" was an innovation that marked him off from the others in the circle of *maggidim*.[11] Yet for all the importance of this innovation, it is rather unlikely that it sufficiently accounts for the special place occupied by the Besht at the outset of Hasidism. It would seem that in his zeal to demonstrate the Besht's dependence on the circle of *maggidim*, Weiss has tended to belittle the originality of his contribution. Yet it stands to reason that it is the very originality of the Besht that holds the key to understanding the role he played in Hasidism's beginnings.[12]

The topic of *dvekut* in early Hasidism has been examined from a new point of view by Mendel Piekarz.[13] His treatment of this topic is in line with his distinctive approach to Hasidism as it is displayed in his *Biyemei Tzmihat Hahasidut*. What distinguishes Piekarz's approach is his identification of a system of ideas similar or identical to that found in Hasidic literature, within the *drush* and *mussar* (homiletics) literature composed in the generations that preceded Hasidism. In keeping with this approach, Piekarz writes the following:

> Examination of the *drush* and *mussar* literature from the period of the emergence of Hasidism, and in particular the writings which preceded Sabbateanism, proves that the first teachers of Hasidism were merely continuers of the hope that religious life would be based upon values of interior spirituality, upon personal religious experience. . . . The importance of the ideological component in Hasidism ought

never to be denigrated in the slightest, yet in our opinion what is decisive about the portrait of its spirituality is not the mystical ideology it
contains, the legacy of its predecessors . . . but rather the novelty it
contains, that is, the efforts made by the fathers of Hasidism and their
students to implement the trend toward internalization in religious
life through a social-religious movement that was new to Judaism.[14]

Piekarz points to certain literary sources that may have influenced the conception of *dvekut* held by the founders of Hasidism. He ascribes particular
significance to the book *Shnei Luchot Habrit* by R. Yeshayah Horowitz. After
reviewing several of the ideas in this work, which bear a discernible affinity
to the ideas current in early Hasidism, Piekarz summarizes his findings with
the assertion: "there is thus no difference of principle between the topic of
dvekut in *Shnei Luchot Habrit* and the remarks of the founders of Hasidism
and their students, except for the trend toward external social realization";
that is, the idea of the dvekut of the Hasidism to their *Zaddik*.[15] Moreover,
alongside the stress on Hasidism's intellectual dependence on the writings of
preceding generations and the confinement of its innovation to the doctrine
of the *Zaddik,* Piekarz tends to downplay the significance of the mystical element in early Hasidism.[16]

I fear that the conclusion Piekarz reaches is too sweeping and extreme. No
one doubts the importance of the discovery of literary sources containing ideas
that played a significant role in early Hasidism. However, it is quite a large step
from there to the conclusion that Hasidism's entire novelty is confined to its
having turned those ideas that were the "legacy of its predecessors" into a platform for a "new social-religious movement." A collection of ideas from various books does not by itself constitute an intellectual platform for a movement.
What is further required is that there be a person or persons who have the stam-
ina and vision to mold those ideas into a coherent philosophy: a doctrine with
an order of priorities, a set of internal associations, and a reference to some
external reality. Moreover, it stands to reason that the religious innovation that
the "founders of Hasidism" passed on to their followers, the one that played so
crucial a role in establishing Hasidism as a movement, was not arranged
around a collection of ideas drawn from books; rather, it was based, first and
foremost, upon the mystical experiences they themselves underwent.

Evidently it was the founders' own experience that affected the manner in
which their ideas were formulated. Accordingly, in seeking to trace out the
process of the development of early Hasidism, attention should be paid to the
nature of the mystical experience of the founders of Hasidism and to the religious ethos they created. The discovery of texts that served as a source of inspiration to them, important though this is, is insufficient. Similarly, as will

become clear below, I do not share Piekarz's views as to the weight of the element of mysticism in the origins of Hasidism. On the contrary, it seems to me that the mystical element was at the core of the religious-spiritual legacy the Besht bequeathed to his students.

A review of the scholarship by Scholem, Weiss, and Piekarz helps make it clear why there has not been a thorough inquiry into the question of the Besht's innovations as a mystic. Scholem limited his inquiry into the novelty of Hasidism—and of the Besht within it—to what concerns the "place" of *dvekut*. Weiss tended to emphasize what the Besht had in common with the circle of *maggidim,* whereas Piekarz was focused on revealing the connections between the founders of Hasidism and the *drush* and *mussar* literature of preceding generations. Similarly, other scholars who have investigated the origins of Hasidism have not attended to the Besht's innovations as a mystic. In the entry on "the Doctrine and Literature of Hasidism,"[17] Yeshayah Tishbi and Joseph Dan discuss the basic tenets of Hasidism; yet their treatment covers Hasidism as a whole and there is no special discussion of the Besht in particular. For her part, Rivka Schatz-Uffenheimer in "Hasidism as Mysticism"[18] discusses R. Dov Ber, the *maggid* of Mezerich and his school. Where the Besht is cited in this work, it is to round out and give detail to the picture of the *maggid*'s mystical world; the question of the Besht's specialness as a mystic is barely approached in her work.

Hasidic mysticism in general and that of the Besht in particular are discussed by Moshe Idel in his *Hasidism—Between Ecstasy and Magic.*[19] The methodological novelty of this book has to do with its effort to elucidate the essence of Hasidism by revealing its wellsprings in early Kabbalist thought. Idel proceeds as though the founders of Hasidism had before them a choice of "models" or paradigms that were implicit in the Kabbalah, and proceeded by adopting and coordinating the ideas and methods from this range of choices. Accordingly, he gives a phenomenological account of these "models" and of their later incarnations in Hasidism. This approach, which Idel labels "panoramic," is presented in his book as an alternative to the historical approach. Accordingly, although Idel's treatment does shed light on some of the mystical techniques the Besht employed, it is not a historical reconstruction that focuses specifically on the Besht's path as a mystic.

A discussion of the mystical aspect of the Besht *is* at the core of an article by Rachel Elior: "R. Yosef Karo and R. Israel Baal Shem Tov: Mystic Metamorphosis, Kabbalist Inspiration and Spiritual Internalization" [in Hebrew].[20] The question that serves as the point of departure for Elior's article is, From where did the Besht's mysticism draw its inspiration? The answer, according to Elior, is to be sought in a book by R. Yosef Karo, the *Maggid Meisharim.* In her opinion this book, which tells of Karo's experiences as a mystic, had "a decisive impact on the formation of the spiritual world of the founder of Hasidism." To support her claim, Elior lists what seem to her various examples of similarity and affinity between the Besht and R. Yosef Karo. I find Elior's conclusions difficult to accept; as will become clear below, I hold that the Besht's innovation as a mystic is especially perspicuous when set against the ethos characteristic of the Kabbalists of Safed—R. Yosef Karo included. At any rate, because of her stress on the Besht's ties to R. Yosef Karo, Elior does not focus on the question of how the Besht differed from his predecessors.[21]

The Besht's Path as a Mystic

As I try to make out what was singular about the Besht's path as a mystic, I find it appropriate to set it against the path and perspective taken by other Jewish mystics—both the Besht's contemporaries and the mystics of previous generations. As a point of departure, I shall consider the concept of *dvekut* that was held by some of the more prominent Kabbalists of sixteenth-century Safed. This topic has been elucidated by Mordechai Fechter.[22] The importance of these figures to my topic is not confined to the fact that they formed an important stage in the development of Jewish mysticism. These figures left a deep stamp upon the Hasidic and Kabbalist circles of later generations, including that of the Besht.

As one would expect, the concept of *dvekut* held by the sages of Safed in the sixteenth century was not homogenous; it took various forms. One may, nevertheless, point to several distinguishing attributes common to many versions of this concept. First, *dvekut* is to be achieved through study of the Torah and especially of the secrets in it. This follows from the presumption that a metaphysical correspondence exists between the soul of man and the Torah, and a relation of identity between the Torah and the Divinity. Accordingly, a person graced by the revelation of Torah secrets while studying bonds himself with the Torah and, through it, with God. The *dvekut* thus achieved is indirect; moreover, the entity that the soul bonds to in this approach is the *sphirot* in general or the *Shekhina* in particular, not the Godhead itself.[23]

Second, according to some of Safed's sages, *dvekut* may be attained through a constant focus of attention upon the Divinity. In the case of Yosef Karo, the *maggid* repeatedly demands of him that his thought adhere to God "continually without any sort of interruption at all." This demand is to be explained by the theurgenic effect that *dvekut* of this kind produces: through the power of his *dvekut,* Karo greatly nourishes several Upper Worlds, and when his *dvekut* flags, havoc is wreaked in the heavens. The ideal of constant *dvekut* received

poetic expression in the following lines from Elazar Azcari's mystical journal:
"And lit by the light of Thy face continually, speaking with Him, walking with
Him, keeping silent with Him and awaking with Him and sitting with Him
and standing with Him and going to sleep with Him and letting all one's movements be for Him."[24]

Third, the *dvekut* of which the sages of Safed speak carries mystical import,
as its objective is the soul's bonding with the Divinity. For all that, in most cases
this is not a mystical experience in which consciousness of the "I" is lost in the
merger of the soul with God. A person who bonds with God via the revelation
of Torah secrets, and a person who bonds to Him through perpetual attention
to His Holy Name, is still capable of distinguishing between subject and object.[25]

Fourth, the majority of the Sages of Safed shared the point of view that the
path to *dvekut* involves a constant struggle against the corporeal appetites and
instincts. Such a struggle is consistent with the picture of the Demonic Powers as entities that seek to ensnare man and lure him to sin. The *maggid* warns
Karo as follows: "Therefore strengthen yourself against the Evil Instinct and
Samael and the Snake who hunt after you for it is you they desire and you must
govern them."[26] An important weapon in the battle against instinct is self-
mortification and fasting, for by weakening the body the soul is strengthened.
Another important means in this struggle is withdrawal from the society of
man into seclusion. In general, the attainment of *dvekut* depends upon repentance and purification, on spiritual preparations that liberate one from the
chains of the corporeal. Accordingly, the struggle against the corporeal
through abstinence and self-mortification is a central issue in the world of
these Kabbalists, one that left its stamp on their entire religious experience.[27]

These ideas about *dvekut* were voiced in the Kabbalist *mussar* literature.
Through this literature they affected also the Kabbalists and the Hasidim of
the seventeenth and eighteenth centuries.[28] It is unsurprising, therefore, that
some of these ideas also achieved currency among persons who lived near the
Besht in time and place. Recall that the conception of *dvekut* as continual focus
of thought upon God was widespread among the *maggidim* described by Yosef
Weiss as the Besht's intellectual partners. A typical expression of this approach
may be found in R. Menahem Mendel of Bar's interpretation of the verse,
"Happy is the man the Lord does not think of as sinful" (Psalms 32:2): "It
means that no sin is to be found in him except this—that his thought does not
cleave to Him, Blessed be He. And where it says 'does not think the Lord of,' it
means that he [fails] to uphold 'I have set the Lord [before me always],' and
this is considered a sin in him."[29] What this suggests is that Menahem Mendel
of Bar interpreted the verse "I have set the Lord before me always" (Psalms 16:8)
as an obligation to keep one's thought continually focused upon God. This

conception of the essence of *dvekut* was held also by R. Menahem Mendel of Peremyshlyan, one of the members of the Besht's circle. He says the following:

> And there is one more principle: not to study a great deal, for in the First Generations when they had powerful minds . . . they did not need to trouble themselves about Reverence, as Reverence was constantly present to them and they were able to study a great deal. But we, who have weaker minds, if we let our thoughts drift from their *dvekut* with God Blessed Be He and study a great deal, Heaven forbid we may stop thinking about the Reverence of God. . . . Therefore, one should limit one's study and constantly think of the greatness of the Creator. . . . And not think many thoughts in one's mind, but only the one thought.[30]

The radical declaration that Torah is not to be studied a great deal follows from the conception of *dvekut* as a continual focus of thought upon God. Because the spiritual effort required for *dvekut* of this type is inconsistent with the study of Torah, in the traditional sense of the term, it was inevitable that these two values be given priority. And as *dvekut* is the supreme value, the necessary inference is that Torah should not be studied too much.

The point of view that self-mortification is a necessary means in the battle against instinct was likewise prevalent among the Kabbalists and Hasidim of the Besht's time and place. There are even indications that this conception played a significant part in the lives of several persons who were close to the Besht. Thus, for instance, R. Nahman of Horodenka used to mortify himself by bathing in a cold *mikvah* on winter days.[31] Two of the most important of the Besht's students, R. Yaakov Yosef of Polonne and R. Dov Ber of Mezerich, maintained ascetic habits. Evidently the Besht too practiced self-mortification at an early stage of his career, before he turned to his special method of divine worship.[32] Indeed, it is against the background of these perspectives that the singularity of the Besht's path is most clearly seen.

I have identified four key aspects of this path. First, the Besht abandoned the point of view that *dvekut* consists of a continual focus of thought upon God. In its place, he adopted a form of *dvekut* achieved in the course of an ecstatic mystical experience, something that by its very nature is intense, brief, and inconstant. Second, unlike indirect *dvekut* (that is, adherence to the *sphirot* or to the *Shekhina* through study of Torah and discovery of its secrets) the Besht advocated a direct *dvekut* with the Godhead itself. The highway to such direct *dvekut* is enthusiastic prayer. The climax of prayer of this kind is, as said, the experience of mystical ecstasy. Third, inspired by his experience of mystical ecstasy, and as part of an attempt to interpret it, the Besht adopted a far-reaching conception of divine immanence. According to this conception, the

Kabbalist adage "no site is clear of him" is to be understood in its strictest sense, that is: the Godhead saturates all worlds, without gradations or divisions. Fourth, on the basis of pragmatic considerations deriving from his personal experience, and drawing upon his radical conception of immanence, the Besht abandoned asceticism and self-mortification as the predominant means of combating instinct. The new strategy the Besht developed on the question of the attitude to take toward the material dimension of human life is based on the denial of the existence of evil as a self-subsistent demonic entity. Among the prominent features of this strategy, one may list gratification of the body as a means of elevating the soul, the uplifting of straying thoughts, and worship through corporeality.

Thus far I have been presenting an outline of the Besht's path as a mystic. At this point it is worth stressing again that by speaking of the Besht's "path" I do not mean only the ideas the Besht believed in but also his religious-spiritual ethos. This ethos was nourished by an mystical experience of great intensity, and it found a philosophical and literary expression in the sermons the Besht delivered to the members of his circle. These sermons are of considerable importance, both because they indirectly describe the mystical experience itself and because it was by their means that the Besht interpreted his experiences to himself and to his peers. Clearly these literary and philosophical expressions filled an important role in the Besht's effort to bequeath his path as mystic to others. Consequently, it is proper to include them in what I call "the Besht's path." Nevertheless, we must beware of being drawn into a discussion of them as if they formed an independent system of ideas, cut off from the flow of life or from religious experience.

Before turning to a detailed discussion of the Besht's mystical experience, I ought to characterize, however briefly, what I have been labeling "mystical ecstasy."[33] Drawing upon the accounts of various mystics, scholars of religion have described mystical ecstasy as the highest of all stages of the experience of an approach to God. The special nature of this experience may be clarified through a comparison with the mystical union achieved via contemplation. The mystic who seeks to achieve proximity to God through the power of contemplation and concentration on the divine subject, strives to achieve release from the external world and to repress it to the edges of his consciousness. Yet this external world continues to exist somewhere on the margins of his mind. Similarly, in such a state of mystical union, the mystic continues to maintain the distinction between subject and object, between the soul and the Divinity. In the case of mystical ecstasy, by contrast, the mystic achieves a complete break with all that surrounds him; the external world ceases to exist for him. Moreover in this state, consciousness of the "I" as a defined and distinct entity is lost.

Hence this is an exceptional or hypernormal state of consciousness, in which the ego merges with the divine nothingness. The experience eludes description, yet is associated with a supreme bliss, a boundless joy and serenity.

Mystical ecstasy is sometimes discussed in terms of three of its dimensions: the physiological, the psychological, and the spiritual. Physiologically, ecstasy is a deep trance in the course of which rates of breathing and heartbeat slow down, and the body grows cold and torpid, remaining frozen in the same posture. At times during an especially deep trance a total loss of sensation may occur. Psychologically, ecstasy is described as the total concentration of consciousness upon a single point, or in other words: a complete unity of consciousness. The ego's contraction into a single idea or aspiration is so deep and consuming that all else disappears and is eliminated from awareness. As all external matters are lost, the road is paved for a mystical union with God. Spiritually, the ecstatic experience is associated with an exceptional clarity, remarkable intuition, a knowledge unfettered by the limitations of the senses, and a hypersensory perception of the divine existence in all its purity. By its nature, the experience is such that it cannot be achieved by ratiocination and words do not suffice to describe it. Nevertheless, the experience is of such intensity that the mystic feels compelled to give an interpretation of its content. When he attempts to interpret what has happened to him, the mystic draws upon the symbols and concepts of the specific religious tradition to which he belongs. The impersonal nature of the experience of mystical ecstasy encourages the mystic to articulate an image of God that is likewise impersonal. One should also note that although willpower plays an important role in the effort to initiate an experience of this kind, it plays no role in its termination, as the experience itself is involuntary.

Ecstatic Prayer

Certain informative accounts of the Besht's mystical experiences have been conserved within *Shivhei Habesht*. In light of these reports one may assert that the primary conduit through which the Besht strove to achieve *dvekut* was that of ecstatic prayer. By this I mean not only prayer conducted in private, but also prayer in public. Moreover, the form of the *dvekut* the Besht attained was, at least at its climax, that of mystical ecstasy. These features are brought out in the following account:

> I heard this from Our Teacher and Rabbi Falk the famous Hasid of the holy community of Titshilnek, who heard it from R. Avraham the rabbi of the holy community of Dabuasary, who previously was the prayer leader in the *Beit Midrash* of the holy community of Miedzybóz. Once

they had to recite the Hallel prayer, as it was the first day of the month or one of the interim days of Passover. And this R. Avraham was leading the morning service in front of the Ark while the Besht was in his regular place. And it was his [the Besht's] custom to recite the Hallel prayer by himself in front of the Ark. During the vocalized *shmoneh esreh,* the Besht was seized with a violent shaking and trembled and went on trembling as he always did during his prayer; whoever beheld him during his prayer saw his trembling. And when R. Avraham finished the *shmoneh esreh* and the Besht remained in his place and did not move onward toward the Ark, R. Wolf Kotses the Hasid came and looked at his face and saw that it was burning like a torch and that his eyes were bulging out and were open and motionless as if he was dying heaven forbid. And this R. Zeev motioned to Rabbi Avraham and they took him each by an arm and walked him over to the Ark. And he went with them and stood before the Ark and trembled somewhat and began to recite the Hallel, quaking all the while. And afterward when he had concluded the *Kaddish* he stood and trembled for a long time and they had to put off reading the Torah until he calmed down from his trembling.[34]

The Besht's trembling during prayer was not a onetime event. On the contrary, from the story at hand as well as other reports it would seem that this was a regular occurrence. In the present story, however, besides the trembling further symptoms were apparent: a burning face, eyes that bulged and were immobile, sensory loss to the point of complete dissociation from the environment, and an inability to function. These manifestations are symptomatic of an experience of ecstasy. It goes without saying that a mystical experience with such manifest external symptoms would have drawn the attention of those present. Further, the prayer service was brought to a halt until the Besht returned to his senses and was able to fill his role as the leader of prayers.

This report is notable for its lack of any attempt at interpretation of the events. R. Avraham, from whom *Shivhei Habesht*'s compiler heard the story, confined himself to a description of the sequence of events from the point of view of the witnesses to the spectacle. Yet the compiler also saw fit to append other reports besides that of R. Avraham. The following report suggests how R. Yaakov Yosef of Polonne understood the Besht's trembling during the prayers:

And not only this but I heard from the rabbi of the holy community of Polonne, the author of the book *Toldot Yaakov Yosef,* that once there was a large pitcher of water standing near where the Besht was praying, and they saw the water move back and forth in it, verily the *Shekhina* hovered over it and caused the earth to tremble, as it is

written: "For the reason that the Lord descended upon it in fire. . . .
And the mountain shook mightily" (Numbers 19:18).[35]

The phenomenon of trembling, which in this tale has devolved from the
praying Besht on to his surroundings and could be seen in the water next to
him, was thus interpreted as an event having a clear mystical import: "the
Shekhina hovered." This interpretation is based on the trembling said to have
taken place at Mount Sinai during the giving of the Torah. The events at Mount
Sinai, the climax of biblical revelation, have always functioned as symbol and
source of fascination for Jewish mystics. In a way, each mystical experience is a
return of sorts to the state of affairs at Mount Sinai on an individual basis. For
all that, in this case it appears that Mount Sinai is being invoked only as a ref-
erential embellishment, and that R. Yaakov's sense of the mystical import of the
Besht's quaking relates more to the direct impression he formed. One readily
surmises that the significance that R. Yaakov Yosef assigned to this trembling is
one that would have been shared by additional persons in the Besht's circle.

To what extent could the Besht's ecstatic prayer affect persons who were
standing nearby? An indication of this may be seen in what happened to R.
Dov Ber, the *maggid* of Mezerich. Here is how this event was described by the
maggid himself:

> Once on a holiday . . . the Besht was praying in front of the Ark with
> great fervor, for as I had heard several times from his chosen [follow-
> ers], he was louder than everyone and would pray with great cries,
> And the Rabbi and great *Maggid* could not bear it for he was quite ill.
> And he left the *Beit Midrash* and entered a small house in the *Beit
> Midrash* and prayed there in private. And before the *Mussaf* service
> the Besht went to the small room to dress himself in the *Kittel*. And
> the *Maggid* said that he was aware that the Divine inspiration was
> with him and that when he looked at him, could tell that he was not
> in the present world. And when [the Besht] put on the *Kittel*, the *Kit-
> tel* wrinkled up on his shoulders and the great *Maggid* grasped the *Kit-
> tel* to smooth out the wrinkle. And when he touched it he began to
> tremble and he gripped the table that was there and the table too
> began to shake with him. And after the Besht left he had to pray and
> to ask of the Blessed Lord to remove this thing from him for he had
> not the strength to endure it.[36]

It would thus appear that in addition to the trembling, the Besht's prayer
was characterized by loud cries as well. Like R. Yaakov Yosef, the *maggid* too
interpreted these external symptoms as an expression of "divine hovering."
Being a man of decidedly mystical inclinations, the *maggid* could readily discern that the Besht was "not in this world." The climax of the tale is of course

the trembling that took hold of the *maggid* himself. This episode is illustrative both of the magnetic power that the Besht's ecstatic prayer had and of the *maggid's* susceptibility to be swept into this emotional vortex.

Further informative testimony about the Besht's ecstatic prayer is contained in the story about the ascent of the soul that the Besht experienced on Yom Kippur, which I have previously discussed. The event occurred during the Neilah prayers when the Besht himself was serving as the leader of prayers. Suddenly the Besht fell silent:

> [He] began to gesture violently, bending backward until his head nearly reached his knees, and everyone was afraid he would fall over; they wanted to hold and steady him but were afraid to do so. And they reported this to R. Zeev Kotses of blessed memory who came and looked at his face and indicated that he was not to be touched. His eyes bulged out and his voice bellowed like a bull being slaughtered, for about two hours. And suddenly he awakened and straightened up.[37]

In the course of the prayer the Besht sank into an ecstatic trance, as he had in the instances cited above. This was preceded by a stage of emotional stimulation, as manifested in the loud and peculiar noises and the unusually violent gestures. Clearly these external signs of the Besht's prayer left a deep impression on the congregants of the *Beit Midrash* in Miedzybóz and made them uncomfortable. In this particular case the members of the congregation sought the advice of R. Zeev Kotses, who was one of the Besht's associates and could be presumed to have had experience and familiarity with situations of this kind.

The sources available to us do not permit a precise determination of when the Besht adopted this manner of prayer. However, it would seem that ecstatic prayer became a hallmark of the Besht at a relatively early stage of his career. We learn of this from a passage included in the collection of stories about the time the Besht revealed himself:

> Afterward he took up residence in the holy community of Tluste and there too served as *Melamed.* And he was unable to have a *minyan* in his house and he gathered some people to his place and prayed with them. . . . And prior to the prayer he would go to the *mikvah* even during the period of Tevet and during the prayer sweat would drip off of him like beads.[38]

The large beads of sweat that dripped off the Besht are of course signs of the emotional intensity that marked his prayer. Moreover, just as we have found in the stories cited above, the prayer here was a public one. As said, this account is associated with the process of the "revelation" of the Besht; that is, the early stages of his fame as a *baal shem*. The person from whom *Shivhei Habesht's* compiler heard this story was R. Alexander, the Besht's scribe during that period. Evidently R. Alexander based his account on something he had heard from the Besht himself or from people who knew him during those years.[39]

Thus far I have been relying on testimony concerning the Besht's ecstatic prayer as observed and interpreted by persons in his proximity. I now turn to an examination of texts that illuminate the point of view taken by the Besht himself. I begin with a passage that refers to the external manifestations of ecstatic prayer:

> Rabbi Israel Baal Shem Tov may he rest in peace said: When a man is drowning in the river and makes certain gestures to try and extricate himself from the waters which are carrying him off, surely the people who see him will not make fun of him and his movements; so when one is praying and makes gestures the person should not be ridiculed, as he is saving himself from the waters of malice, i.e., the *qlipot* which come to distract him from his thoughts while he prays.[40]

At its basis, this passage is an attempt to defend those who pray in an ecstatic manner from those who would make fun of them. The fact that the unusual movements and sounds aroused reactions of ridicule is itself unsurprising.[41] Yet it seems that the Besht was bothered by these reactions, and hence saw fit to explain and justify the external symptoms of ecstatic prayer. The peculiar gestures are a means, the purpose of which is to focus thought upon the divine subject and to purify the soul of "straying thoughts." In other words: ecstatic prayer is supposed to help the person praying achieve liberation from the characteristic consciousness of earthly life and to attain an unmediated proximity with the realm of the divine.

A further aspect of the external manifestation of ecstasy is brought out in a fable attributed to the Besht:

> I heard a fable from my master my grandfather of blessed and righteous memory. There was someone who played a fine musical instrument melodiously and with great tenderness. And those who heard him could not contain themselves for all the melodiousness and delight to the point where they would dance almost to the ceiling owing to the greatness of the delight and satisfaction and melodiousness. And anyone who was nearby and who would draw still closer in so as to hear this musical instrument would receive greater delight and would dance all the more mightily. And during this there came a deaf man who could not hear at all the sound of the melodious musical instrument, but only saw the impassioned dance of the people; they seemed to him insane. And he told himself: what good does this

gladness do? And verily if he had been wise and knew and understood that the cause was the greatness of the pleasure and the melodious sound of this musical instrument then he too would have been danc-ing there.[42]

Here again the Besht is attempting to defend those who seem to the alien observer to be "insane" on account of the external manifestations of their ecstasy. However, by contrast with the passage previously cited, in the present fable ecstatic dance symbolizes the mystical experience itself. The movements of the body at this stage are no longer the product of voluntary choice and ini-tiative, but are an inevitable consequence of the power of the "delight" associ-ated with proximity to God. Indeed, the involuntary nature of the experience of ecstasy is one of its hallmarks.

It thus appears that the Besht distinguished between two different sorts of symptoms of ecstasy that arise in the course of prayer. In a way these are var-ious stages of the same process. During the first stage the gesticulations and loud cries are a means the person praying consciously and deliberately employs to stimulate his soul. The Besht held that without bodily arousal a spiritual arousal would not occur.[43] As the spiritual stimulation intensifies, the symptoms of ecstasy become involuntary and uncontrollable. The climax of the experience of ecstasy becomes the setting for awareness of direct contact with the Divinity. This is the experience of mystical ecstasy.

What is the nature of the spiritual experience that the gesticulations and loud maxims in prayer are meant to stimulate? Evidently, apart from clearing the consciousness of straying thoughts, powerful emotions are also awakened, the content of which is a yearning for proximity to God. One can learn some-thing of the intensity of these feelings from the Besht's statements to the effect that one who succeeds in praying the morning and *Mussaf* services with "dvekut," (that is, with the proper enthusiasm and spiritual turmoil) ought not be disheartened if he is unable to maintain the same level of prayer dur-ing the afternoon service as well, "given the weakness his body and mind has suffered."[44] Furthermore, the demanding and exhausting nature of ecstatic prayer requires that one make a sparing and calculated use of one's bodily and spiritual powers. Consequently, although recital of psalms and study of Torah are considered important preparations for praying, one must not indulge in them excessively "lest one not have the brains needed for praying."[45]

ABANDONMENT OF LURIANIC *Kavvanot*

The spiritual stimulation we have been speaking of is the *kavvanah* or "intention" in the Hasidic sense of the term. The Hasidic embrace of *kavvanah* of this kind, and its recasting as the spiritual content of prayer, involved the abandonment of the Lurianic *kavvanot*.[46] The Kabbalist conception of *kav-vanah* had rested upon the presumption that each commandment or prayer has a particular "destination" and particular "mission" to perform in the Upper Worlds. The Kabbalist, who is fluent in the secrets of the prayers and commandments, is supposed to accompany the utterance of his prayer and the performance of the commandment with his *kavvanah*, the content of which is that very "destination" and very "mission." Through the power of these *kav-vanot* the force and effect of his actions would be multiplied in the Upper Worlds. In the generations preceding the emergence of Hasidism, the Lurianic *kavvanot*—those devised by the ARI and his students—were commonly employed by the Kabbalists. It goes without saying that the concentration required of a person attempting to pray with the accompaniment of Kabbal-ist *kavvanot* is not readily compatible with the turbulence and emotion of the ecstatic praying in the manner of the Besht.

The shift having to do with Lurianic *kavvanah* at the outset of Hasidism has already been discussed by Yosef Weiss and Rivka Schatz-Uffenheimer.[47] These scholars both affirm that Hasidism abandoned Lurianic *kavvanah* because it did not suit its conception of *dvekut*. Yet because Rivka Schatz-Uffenheimer focuses in her book on the *maggid* of Mezerich and his school, her remarks make it appear as though it was the *maggid* who first adopted the new stance concerning *kavvanah*. Weiss, conversely, does assert that the Besht had already ceased to employ Lurianic *kavvanot*. Nevertheless, Weiss maintains that the Besht's stance on this topic was vague and that it was the *maggid* who took the crucial step. Weiss reached this conclusion on the basis of the fact that the *mag-gid* has explicit things to say on this issue,[48] whereas nothing comparable exists for the Besht. Yet given the evidence that does exist regarding the ecstatic nature of the Besht's prayer, the ineluctable conclusion is that it was the Besht specifically who ceased to employ Lurianic *kavvanot*. What the *maggid* has to say on this topic—on which he takes after the Besht—is thus not to be seen as expressing an innovation of his own but rather as an effort to give an a pos-tiori justification to a custom that had already taken root.

The choice to have ecstatic prayer supplant prayer that is accompanied by Kabbalist *kavvanot* reflects a far-reaching change: a transformation not only of the character but of the very purpose of prayer. The Kabbalists viewed the principle objective of prayer in terms of its influence on the Upper Worlds. The Besht, by contrast, maintained that the primary purpose of prayer was the "delight" it produced; that is, the private experience and spiritual ascent that the person praying undergoes, the climax of which is mystical ecstasy. A suc-cinct expression of this point of view is given in the following words: "From the Besht: the reward of a *mitzvah* is a *mitzvah*, as a man has no greater reward than the delight he feels from the *mitzvah* itself when he performs it with joy. . . . The chief virtue is to take a greater delight in the worship of the Lord than in all other pleasures."[49]

The mystical import of the term "delight" (*taanug*) and the bold link drawn between such "delight" and ecstatic prayer, is clarified by a sermonizing interpretation that the Besht gives to the verse "and from my flesh I behold the Lord" (Job 19:26). "By the Besht of Blessed Memory: 'from my flesh . . . behold': just as a physical union is not consummated unless the member is aroused and there is desire and joy, so in the spiritual union, i.e., during Torah and prayer, when it is done with the member aroused and with joy and delight, then it is consummated."[50] The Besht's words affirm that just as the corporeal and spiritual manifestations of erotic desire are necessary prerequisites for achieving a "physical union," so the bodily and spiritual manifestations of ecstatic prayer are vital means of achieving "spiritual union." The representation of ecstatic prayer as sexual intercourse leaves no doubt that the climax of such prayer is the experience of mystical ecstasy.[51]

THE DIALECTICS OF RISES AND FALLS IN WORSHIP

One of the most prominent features of *dvekut* of this kind is the brevity and interrupted nature of the experience,[52] which sharply distinguishes it from the conception of *dvekut* as a continual focus of thought upon the Divinity. Indeed, as one who had experienced the supreme bliss involved in mystical ecstasy, the Besht had trouble reconciling himself to its brevity. A revealing illustration of his fretful thoughts on this subject may be found in the following passage:

> From the Besht of Blessed Memory: About "And the animals run and return" (Ezekiel 1:14). The soul, having been quarried from a holy place rightly yearns to return to the site of its quarry, and lest it be nullified in reality it has been bound up in matter, so that it will also attend to material concerns such as eating and drinking and conducting business and so forth . . . for a delight that is perpetual becomes a habit and ceases to be a delight; therefore there are rises and falls in a man's worship of the Blessed Lord so that he will have the delight which is the main purpose of worshipping the Blessed Lord.[53]

The basic question being posed in this sermon is, How is one to reconcile the soul's natural tendency to seek a continuous communion with God with the fact that even a person who achieves *dvekut* must content himself with an experience of brief duration? As I have said, the background to such a "philosophical" question is, almost certainly, the personal experience of the Besht himself. He felt the post-*dvekut* plunge himself, and wondered how it could be

accounted for. He proposed two explanations, each of which is independent
of the other.

The core of the first answer is the phrase "lest [the soul] be nullified in reality"; that is, concern that a sustained *dvekut* might cost the mystic his life. How
is this risk to be understood? Two interpretations may be preferred, a theoretical and a practical one. The theoretical interpretation is that in cleaving to
God the soul abandons the body; thus the ineluctable consequence of pro-
longed *dvekut* is death. The practical interpretation notes the physical and
spiritual effort involved in the ecstatic praying that is the prelude and means
to *dvekut*. The intensity of this effort is aptly expressed in the following maxim:
"It is a great mercy of the Blessed Lord that a man survives after praying, for
by rights he ought to perish from loss of strength . . . from the intensity of the
vast *kavvanot* that he inflects."[54] Accordingly, the purpose of the descent from
the heights of *dvekut* and the return to material existence is to guarantee that
the mystic, quite literally, does not perish.

The second answer proposed by the Besht has to do with the spiritual content of the experience of *dvekut,* that is, with "delight." For only by descending
from the heights of *dvekut* may one obtain the perspective from which
"delight" of this kind can be adequately appreciated. The descent is necessary
for the ascent. The appearance of the verse "and the animals run and return"
in the Besht's speech is thus meant to imply that the sequence of rises and falls
is a manifestation of laws that were set in place for good reason.[55]

The dialectic of rising and falling that occurs in divine worship, which is
implied in the phrase "and the animals run and return," is also suggested by
the concepts of "Greatness" and "Smallness." The repeated mention of these
terms in the Besht's parlance is an indication of their importance. It is worth
articulating how this pair of concepts enriches the phenomenology of rises and
falls in worship. The example from the following passage may shed light on
this point: "And behold, in a time in which Greatness is in the world, then He
the Blessed One adheres to a man directly, which is not the case when Smallness prevails in the world; then a man must struggle mightily to be able to draw
near to the Blessed One."[56]

The concepts of "Greatness" and "Smallness" thus reflect two basic spiritual
states. "Greatness" is the mystic's supreme sense that the gates of heaven are
opening before him and he is succeeding in rising and realizing his yearnings
for unmediated contact with the Divinity. "Smallness," by contrast, denotes the
sense of disappointment and helplessness of one who has failed in his efforts to
free himself of the shackles of material existence. If the phrase, "the animals run
and return" stands for the idea that a fall from *dvekut* is inevitable, "Smallness"
alludes to the sense of failure and to the difficulty of again soaring up to it. This

failure may well cast the mystic to the depths of despair. Here the Besht has a remedy to offer: the "Greatness" and "Smallness" in one's experience are not merely attributes characterizing the particular mystic but are laws that reign throughout the "universe." The very recognition of the dialectical nature of mystical life can help a mystic liberate himself from "Smallness": "for the animals run and return and the *anima* of man is determined by the principle of Smallness and Greatness and when he pays attention to the fact that he is in a state of Smallness this very knowledge sweetens the Judgments at their roots."[57]

If the mystic attends to the fact that his failure does not necessarily reflect his personal limitations, and that the condition of "Smallness" is a temporary and necessary one in the process of rises and falls in worship, this knowledge can restore his self-confidence and aid him in again climbing toward proximity with God.[58] A further recommendation the Besht has for one caught in a state of Smallness is to make use of "humorous words."[59] Sadness and depression are liable to turn failures in worship into a habit, whereas gladness can serve as a springboard to the cherished *dvekut*. The repeated appeal the Besht makes to the notions of "Greatness" and "Smallness" suggest that despite the interpretations he put forward on this topic the issue did not cease to worry him. Among other things, the Besht was bothered by doubt as to whether he was fit to serve as a spiritual leader during the times he was in a state of "Smallness." His worries on this score and the resolution he found for them are hinted at in the following sermon:

> I heard from my Master my Grandfather of Blessed Righteous Memory, that once there came to him a certain man and asked him to tell him some Torah, and he responded with this verse: "For the lips of the priest shall hold wisdom and Torah shall be sought from his mouth as he is the angel of the Lord of Hosts (Malachi 2:7). . . . The Sages offered the following interpretation: If a Rabbi resembles an angel of the Lord of Hosts, Torah will be sought from his mouth and if not, not (*Moed Katan* 17a). And he posed the question, how may such a Rabbi who resembles an angel of the Lord of Hosts be found in this era. . . . And he of Blessed Memory said that the interpretation is as follows: If the Rabbi resembles an angel of the Lord of Hosts, he is like an angel who stands perpetually on one step . . . and yet there is a state of Smallness and a state of Greatness and this is what he said: if the Rabbi resembles an angel, then he is in a state of standing like an angel, and even though it is impossible to stand perpetually on a single step for one falls sometimes into Smallness, still even his Smallness is a Greatness too for another person; it is only by comparison with his own Greatness that it is Smallness. . . . Then one may ask and request of him that he say some Torah.[60]

The solution thus involves the relativity of the states of "Greatness" and "Smallness." Just as each and every individual raises himself in worship in comparison with his own level, he also falls in terms of his level. Accordingly, a great man's fall is not the same as a small one's. When a great man is in a state of "Smallness," he is still sufficiently great to be able to serve as a source of spiritual authority for others.

A sharp expression of the Besht's worries about falls in worship appears in remarks heard from him by his grandson, R. Ephrayim of Sadilkov:

> Once I heard from him on a Sabbath Eve when he said in the course of giving an interpretation to the verse "Who shall ascend with us skyward" (Deuteronomy 30:12) and he hugged and kissed me ... and said as follows: I swear this to you,[61] that there is a person in the world who hears Torah from the Holy One Blessed be He and his *Shekhina* and not from an angel and not from etc.[62] and does not himself believe that he will not be cast out from before the Holy One Blessed Be He heaven forbid for easily one can be cast into a bottomless chasm.[63]

These lines surely tell something of the Besht's conception of himself as a mystic of the first order. Unlike those who are graced with revelations of the indirect sort, such as the revelation of Elijah, of the *maggid* and suchlike, the Besht is blessed with the ability to hear Torah directly from the Almighty. Except that this same wonderful experience comes accompanied with a terrible fear of falling. The depiction the mystic gives here of himself is of someone who walks on the edge of a chasm and who faces the threat of falling in at each and every step.

Thus far I have been dwelling upon several characteristic manifestations of the Besht's mystical experience that can also serve to confirm the assertion that, at its climax, this was an experience of ecstasy. The physical symptoms of this experience are depicted in the accounts of the trance that the Besht sank into in the course of his prayers. His close students, who were witnesses to this spectacle, describe the Besht as being blessed with "divine inspiration" and as someone "not in this world." The Besht himself hinted at the ecstasy of his mystical experience when he used the metaphor of sexual intercourse to describe it. This metaphor is consistent with his repeated statements that the main purpose of the worship of God is the "delight" associated with it. Mystics who have attained the experience of ecstasy attest to being flooded with a sensation of supreme contentment. Likewise, the Besht's worries about the transient nature of *dvekut* suggest that this was an experience of ecstasy, which by its nature is short and episodic. Quite probably it was the intensity of the ecstasy that sharpened and accentuated the sense of fall that came afterward. The philosophical explanations that the Besht developed, those that found expression in the verse "and the animals run and return" and the pair of terms "Smallness" and "Greatness," could perhaps soften the distress of the descents and assist in the efforts to ascend, but they could not entirely suffice in dispelling the fears of falling. On the contrary, it appears that the recurring doubts over the dialectical phenomenon of rises and falls was one of the more striking features of the Besht's path as a mystic.

DIVINE IMMANENCE

The ecstatic quality of the *dvekut* that the Besht experienced is illuminated also by the theosophical explanation he offered for it. We are referring to the sweeping interpretation the Besht gave to the Kabbalist adage, "no site is clear of him." This interpretation is nicely illustrated in a fable cited and commented on by R. Yaakov Yosef of Polonne:

> As the Besht of Blessed Memory said—a fable he told prior to the blowing of the *shofar:* There once was a wise and great king who built imaginary walls and towers and gates, and commanded the people to come to him through the gates and the towers, and instructed that royal treasures be distributed at each and every gate. And there were some people who came to one gate and took the money and went away while others etc., until his son and friend made efforts to go specifically to his father the king. Then he saw that there was no partition separating him from his father for it was all a hallucination.[64]

In the fable at hand a royal palace is portrayed, with the king's residence at its center and fortifications and watchtowers surrounding it in a series of circles. One readily gathers that the king is the Almighty and the command "to come to him through the gates and the towers" are the commandments of worship. The walls and the towers are the partitions that separate man from his Maker, that is, the instincts and appetites or, as it was interpreted by R. Yaakov Yosef, "the straying thoughts and distractions from Torah and prayer."[65] The king's servants sought to obey his command and to come to him, yet were able to surmount only a few of the fortifications, each to the extent of his abilities. Only the king's son struggled mightily enough to be able to reach the king himself. It may seem that only a quantitative difference separates the king's son from the rest of his servants, yet in fact there is a difference of quality between them, as they represent two types of worship of God. The king's servants are observant Jews who uphold the *mitzvot*. Their reward is the treasure scattered about the walls. The "son and friend" of the king, on the other hand—who represents the Hasid or the Besht himself—does not settle for less than unmediated proximity to the Divinity, that is, for *dvekut*.

The sting in the fable comes, of course, at its conclusion: after succeeding through great efforts to get beyond the walls and towers, the king's son discovers that they were mere hallucinations. Evidently, then, the Besht denies independent existence to any nondivine entity that appears to divide between man and God. The divisions are "hallucinations," and it is the Divinity that created them as such. Recognition of this truth can potentially give a boost to a person who seeks to surmount the partitions. It is in this spirit that R. Yaakov Yosef interpreted the Besht's fable:

> And the moral is clear: that the Holy One Blessed Be He is concealed in various garbs and partitions, while it is known that the Blessed Name fills all the land with his Majesty (Isaiah 6:3), and every movement and thought all comes from Him the Blessed One . . . and no partition separates man from Him the Blessed. In this knowledge and by it all evildoers shall perish. (Psalms 92:10).[66]

Several scholars have already focused on the importance of the idea of divine immanence in early Hasidism.[67] Of special relevance are the remarks of Rachel Elior, who stresses the tension between this new conception and the one from the tradition of the Kabbalah:

> The basic presumption of Hasidic thought is the supposition of immanence or the presumption of the equal presence of the Divinity everywhere: the divine element subsists in every action and in every thought. Attention has long since been drawn to the centrality of the idea of immanence in Hasidism, yet evidently it has yet to be realized that the presumption of immanence . . . entirely uproots the point of the Kabbalist hierarchy in general and of the Lurianic dualism in particular, and nullifies the ontological weight of the doctrine of constriction [tsimtsum] just as it collapses the significance of the world of sphirot and the Kabbalist transcendentalism.[68]

It seems to me that it was the Besht who broke the ground for this revolutionary conception of immanence in Hasidism. Moreover, it stands to reason that this new conception did not spring from the musings of a thinker confined to the narrow limits of theosophical speculation, but rather was an outgrowth and reflection of the mysticism experienced by the Besht himself. Like other mystics, the Besht sought to interpret his experiences and to formulate them in the language of ideals and symbols that were current in the religious culture in which he lived. As such it is understandable that he should draw upon ideas and symbols from the realm of Kabbalah. Yet how is one to understand the leap of thought from the hierarchal and stratified conception of divine presence in worlds, pervasive in Kabbalist thought, to the radical conception of immanence as put forward by the Besht? Put otherwise: it was the

Besht's own experience of mystical ecstasy, an experience in which his soul merged unimpeded with the divine spirit and all "partitions" disappeared as though they had never been, that disclosed to him the truth about the presence of the divinity in all things. It was through this experience that the Besht could conclude that earthly life in its various manifestations is nothing more than a hallucination.[69]

The knowledge that the partitions that divide man from God are a kind of hallucination has the potential, as we have said, of helping those seeking *dvekut* to surmount the obstacles set in their path. Yet this assertion also entails a risk: an over-simplistic understanding of the idea of divine immanence can lead a person to infer that *dvekut* is attainable easily or without a large spiritual investment. Apparently it is concern over such a mistaken conclusion that is at the basis of the following text: "From the Besht: 'You are our Lord' (Jeremiah 14:22; the verse can be read, '*You He our Lord*'). Interpretation: When a man is convinced he is in the presence of God, and employs 'You,' then he is far from God, far from the concealed 'He'; whereas when he believes he is hidden and distant from the Lord, from the 'He,' then he is close and present to God, to 'our Lord.'"[70]

This homily revolves around the following problem: Why does the verse employ two appellations for the Divinity, "You" and "He"? The Besht's answer is that he who turns to God using the language of presence—he who believes himself to be in God's proximity—is in fact distant from Him. Whereas he who turns to God using the language of separation (that is, with an awareness of distance) is the very one who is closer to God. Thus consciousness of distance from the Divinity is what arouses the required spiritual imperative for seeking *dvekut*. This dialectical stance concerning the proximity and distance between the human and the divine is also suggested by the remarks with which Rabbi Yaakov Yosef introduces the fable of the walls cited above:

> One must understand: For the Blessed One fills all the land with his majesty, no site is clear of him, and where man is, there his Blessed Majesty is found, and if so why should prayers have to be received by angels who move from palace to palace? The reply is: that the Holy One Blessed Be He arranged it thus so that it would appear to man as though he were distant, and he would make efforts to draw much closer.[71]

The difficulty that Rabbi Yaakov Yosef confronts is the product of the contradiction between two competing conceptions of the Divinity: the transcendental conception, which was current in the *Hekhalot* literature and is expressed in the depiction of angels who guide prayers from one palace to another; and the immanent conception, suggested by the phrase "no site is clear of him." In resolving this difficulty R. Yaakov Yosef affirms that it is in fact the immanent conception that expresses the state of affairs as they actually are.

The transcendental conception, by contrast, is a sort of optical illusion. Yet this illusion is a pedagogical artifice that the Almighty employs: the illusion of distance is designed to stimulate man to invest the necessary effort to attain proximity to God. More generally, although the idea of divine immanence plays a decisive function in the path toward *dvekut,* nothing about it diminishes the effort that is required of those who seek to take this path.

The Nature and Purpose of Evil

The radical concept of divine immanence let the Besht contemplate a reassessment of the nature and purpose of evil. In the Kabbalah, evil was considered to be a metaphysical phenomenon that enjoys a certain degree of independent existence. Moreover, the war between the forces of the Evil Side and the forces of Sanctity is one of the marked features of Kabbalist dualism.[72] Yet this conception of evil was at odds with the harmonicist position that was at the basis of the Besht's interpretation of "no site is clear of him."

The Besht himself points out the contradiction between these two: "From the Besht of Blessed Memory: Since the *Shekhina* encompasses all of the worlds, Matter, Plant, Animal and Speaking, and all creatures good and evil, and the true unity is the *Shekhina,* how can two opposites be contained in one subject good and evil which are two opposites? . . ."[73] At the basis of the reply the Besht offers to this question is the declaration that evil does not in truth have an independent existence, as "evil is the seat of the good." To clarify and illustrate his assertion, the Besht cites the verse: "And Pharaoh approached and the Children of Israel raised their eyes and behold Egypt had set out after them and they feared greatly and the Children of Israel cried out to the Lord" (Exodus 14:10). It was the fear of the Egyptian army pursuing them that caused the Children of Israel to cry out to the Lord. A further example: "By observing the behavior of the wicked, one gains satisfaction in one's own righteousness, and thus is pleased and gratified by evil."[74] The conclusion toward which the Besht is building by means of these examples is, "When evil is a cause of good it becomes a seat of the good and all is absolute good."[75] And in the words of Tishbi and Dan: "This perspective entirely eliminates the dualistic division of Divinity and World; the war between good and evil constricts itself to the realm of human psychology alone."[76]

Having rejected the demonic character of evil, the Besht was in a position to formulate a new strategy for confronting the earthly or corporeal dimension of human existence. Indeed, his innovations on this topic are among the most striking features of his path as a mystic. I shall begin with an account of his stance toward the phenomenon of asceticism and self-mortification.

REJECTION OF ASCETICISM AND SELF-MORTIFICATION

The polar opposition between spirit and matter, between the soul and the body, was a fundamental assumption in the perspective of the Kabbalists in the generations that preceded the emergence of Hasidism. The soul aspires by its very nature to return to the source from which it had been quarried in the Upper Worlds. Yet it is imprisoned in a body of flesh and blood that keeps it locked to the realm of earthly existence. Worse, the body is the abode of appetites and instincts that lead a man to sin and distance him from God. The conflict between body and spirit is closely affiliated with the battle of the Giants: the war between the forces of Holiness and the forces of the Evil Side. Just as one who manages to elevate himself through worship of God earns an influx of sanctity from on high, so one who falls into sin becomes trapped in nets of uncleanliness and provides them with nourishment. The demonic conception of the Evil Instinct and of sin, and the supposition that the body is the abode of instincts and appetites, led to the development of asceticism and self-mortification as the predominant methods of combating instinct. As the experience of the corporeal is what binds man to the forces of the Evil Side and distances him from the forces of holiness, the more he is able to reduce and weaken the body, the better. These perspectives, which were common in the early stages of the Kabbalah's development, figured substantially in the world of the Kabbalists of Safed in the sixteenth century. A religio-ethical ethos developed in that world that emphasized the importance of the struggle against corporeal appetites and viewed asceticism and self-mortification as essential techniques in that battle. This ethos also found expression in the Kabbalist *mussar* literature and left its stamp on the perspectives and modes of life of Kabbalists and Hasidim in the seventeenth and eighteenth centuries.[77]

Against this background, the Besht's perspective on the essence of the Evil Instinct is striking. An expression of this perspective appears in the following tale:

> From the Besht. Once there was a king who ruled strictly, and sent one of his servants to test the subject states by pretending he was a servant in rebellion against his master. And several of the states took up combat against [the servant] and mastered him while others went along with him. And in one state there were wise men who sensed that this was all at the behest of the king. —The moral is clear: There are some who combat the Evil Instinct . . . and resist him until they are able to master their instinct by the degree of the combat and great self-mortifications; and there are others who sense that he is carrying out the will of the Creator.[78]

The recognition that the Evil Instinct is not an independent demonic entity but rather a tool in the hands of God, makes combat against it with the weapon of self-mortification unnecessary. This is the conceptual basis of the justification for rejecting self-mortification. To this the Besht added a practical justification: the ascetic mode of life is associated by its very nature with a mood of sadness that forms a spiritual barrier to *dvekut*. It is in fact joy that stands to serve as a hoist for uplifting the soul to the divine realms. It seems that this assertion, which appears in various guises over and over in the Besht's remarks, had its grounds in his personal experiences.[79]

The lessons of his experiences were ones the Besht sought to share with others. Thus, for instance, the Besht attempted to wean R. Yaakov Yosef of Polonne of his habit of fasting. Here is what the Besht wrote to him on this topic:

> And behold the impress of his holy hand I have received . . . and in it is written that his Highness speaks as though he is forced to fast. And my entrails grew angry from what I read. And I hereby add by a most holy oath, conjoined by the Holy One Blessed Be He and the *Shekhina*, that he must not endanger himself in this way as this is a bitter black and sad deed, and the Divinity does not hover where there is depression but rather where there is the joy of a *mitzvah* as his highness knows these are matters I have taught several times.[80]

The Besht not only rejected self-mortification; he mandated the use of material pleasures as a means of spiritual elevation. This point of view is brought out in the following fable:

> I heard from my Rabbi on the subject of Sabbath that eating and drinking is a *mitzvah*, as is implied by the following fable. A prince who had been taken captive received a note in his father's handwriting and wanted to rejoice; he therefore provided the masses much drink so that they would be happy and then he too could rejoice. The moral is clear: the soul can not rejoice in the spiritual until the material has rejoiced in the corporeal.[81]

Hence it is specifically through bodily pleasures that the soul is set free of its chains and allowed to rise to the heights of the Upper Worlds. Drink is depicted here as a sort of bribe that must be paid to the body to keep it from interfering with the soul's achievement of its desire.

An example illustrating the role this perspective played in the life of the Besht and the members of his circle is found in the following tale:

> One time on *Simhat Torah* the Besht's men of virtue were celebrating and dancing and drinking wine from the Besht's cellar. And the Besht's righteous wife said, no wine will be left for *Kiddush* and *Havdalah*. The Besht said to her jokingly, you are right, go tell them to stop and to go home. And when she opened the door and they were

dancing in a circle, and she saw that a fire blazed about them like a screen, she took the utensils and went herself to the cellar to bring them as much wine as they wished.[82]

The drinking of wine as a spiritual stimulant was, evidently, a typical behavior for the Besht and the members his circle. Nevertheless, clearly the Besht did not ascribe an independent value to the pleasures of the body. Their entire value was as a means of spiritual elevation.

The Besht's attitude toward asceticism and self-mortification reflects a new emotional posture toward the material dimension of human life. Unlike a "standpoint" or an "intellectual position," the concept of an emotional posture designates a broad outlook that can come to be expressed in a variety of topics or ideas. This new spiritual attitude is characterized by a feeling of comfort with regard to the material. Unlike the outlook that was widespread among Kabbalist circles, in both the Besht's day and in previous eras, the Besht did not consider the corporeal to be a menacing or repulsive phenomenon. Contact with the corporeal does not necessarily bring about spiritual downfall. On the contrary, material existence can be elevated and consecrated, and thus converted from an obstacle set in the mystic's path into a springboard by which he can soar toward the cherished spiritual ascendancy. This new attitude was the basis of two prominent elements of the Besht's path as a mystic: worship through corporeality and the elevation of straying thoughts.

WORSHIP THROUGH CORPOREALITY

The term "worship thorough corporeality" denotes a corporeal act that is given validity and value as heavenly worship through the power of the intention that accompanies it.[83] Here is what Rabbi Yaakov Yosef attributes to the Besht on this topic:

> I heard from my Teacher: "All that you find your hand empowered to do, do (Ecclesiastes 9:10). . . . For a man is as a ladder planted on earth, so as to perform earthly acts in the material, and his head reaches skyward, so that with his head he can direct his intentions skyward to bind the act with the thought for by this it is made into a union above."[84]

The topic here is thus a mundane act; that is, an act that does not have the status of being either a commandment or an infraction of a commandment. Such an act has the potential of being consecrated, and so, through the power of "thought," of being rendered of equal value to a *mitzvah*. The content of thought of this kind is the intention to bind the corporeal act, and by its means corporeal existence as a whole, to the divine realm. This is, without a doubt, one of the more impressive indications of the weight that the Besht ascribed to *kavvanah* in the worship of God. The radical novelty of the idea of "worship through corporeality," as conceived by the Besht, can be illuminated by comparing the perspectives taken by several figures on this issue.

Gershom Scholem and Yosef Weiss held that the Besht understood *dvekut* in the sense of continual concentration of thought upon God. On the basis of this presumption, they associated the Besht's idea of worship through corporeality with the idea of *dvekut*. That is to say, worship through corporeality is a way in which one can extend and maintain the state of *dvekut* while carrying out one's earthly affairs. Scholem, seeking a precedent for this point of view in the world of the Kabbalists, cites Nachmanides' commentary to the verse "to love the Lord your God, to walk in all his ways and to adhere to him" (Deuteronomy 11:22). Here is the passage from Nachmanides: "And perhaps "adherence" [*dvekut*] here is to mean that you must remember the Lord and his love always, and not separate your thought from him when you go when you rest and when you wake up; until the conversation one holds with humans shall be in one's mouth and tongue yet one's heart is not with them but before the Lord." Explaining these lines, Scholem wrote: "Certainly Nachmanides did not mean to say that it is possible to attain *dvekut* by social interactions. Yet it is clear that he thought that one can attain *dvekut* in a social context as well, despite the fact that this context itself is generally considered an obstacle which is to be surmounted through supreme effort." This idea, Scholem goes on to say "acquired considerable import with the Besht."[85]

Yosef Weiss discusses the idea of worship through corporeality in the Besht in the course of his discussion of the conception of *dvekut* in the circle of *maggidim*. As a point of departure, he considers the traditions that follow the way of R. Nahman of Kosov, which urge that thought is to be concentrated upon God even at a time of dealings with people. Evidently R. Nahman's way was an application of the idea we found in Nachmanides. The Besht's position as regards worship through corporeality is described by Weiss as "a far-reaching and even categorical extension" of the stances of Nachmanides and R. Nahman. If these two had contemplated the possibility of sustaining the state of *dvekut* even into the times of social interaction, the Besht held that the "corporeality," which may coexist with *dvekut*, encompasses "each deed and action that a man performs."[86]

Another scholar who links the idea of worship through corporeality with *dvekut* is Yeshayah Tishbi. Tishbi touches on this subject in the course of his effort to uncover "traces of Rabbi Moshe Hayim Luzzato in Hasidic doctrine." He cites several passages from RaMHaL's writings to demonstrate that such writings might have served as a source of inspiration for Hasidism. Among other texts, he cites the following passage from *Mesilat Yesharim:*

> That a man is to be separated and withdrawn entirely from the material and adhere always in each and every hour to his Lord . . . and even at a time when he is engaged in the material acts that his body makes necessary to him, his soul is not to depart from its adherence to the Supreme. . . . For a man who consecrates himself with the sanctity of his Creator, even his corporeal acts return to being matters of genuine sanctity.[87]

There is no doubt that the perspective that grounds this text is one that urges maximal austerity and withdrawal from the life of the present world. It is for that very reason a status of sanctity is to be assigned to corporeal matters. This status holds, however, only for one who has confined his material needs to the minimum essential to his bare existence. Such a man is in a position to consecrate his material needs by making them essential to his adherence to God.

Thus the statements of Nachmanides, the paths of R. Nahman of Kosov, and the writings of RaMHaL all share a certain viewpoint: the idea that *dvekut* may be maintained notwithstanding the engagement with the material world. Yet the Besht's point of view as regards "worship through corporeality" was entirely different from theirs. Not only did the Besht not advocate asceticism; for the Besht, "worship through corporeality" has nothing at all to do with the subject of *dvekut*. Accordingly, he is not concerned with how the material may be consecrated as an essential means of attaining *dvekut*, nor even with the problem of how *dvekut* may be maintained in the context of mundane preoccupations. Unlike all these others, the Besht urged that earthly conduct as such was to be converted into divine worship. Because the Besht rejected asceticism, and because he conceived of *dvekut* as a brief and inconstant affair, he sought to elevate the materiality with which he came into contact by means of "worship through corporeality."[88]

A further quote from the Besht can help illustrate this line of thought:

> I heard from my Teacher of Blessed Memory an explication of the verse "all that you find your hand empowered to do, do" (Ecclesiastes 9:10). Hanoch Matatron used to dedicate each stitch to the Holy One Blessed be He and His *Shekhina* etc. . . . and in doing so, would bind the material deed from the lower world, by the thought that it is "empowered," to the spirituality of the Upper World, and thus fulfill the verse "in all your ways" in materiality "know him" (Proverbs 3:6): this is to form a union of the Holy One Blessed be He and the Divinity.[89]

The Midrash portrays Hanoch as a cobbler who performed *yihuddim* with each and every stitch that he stitched.[90] The Besht does not appeal to this Midrash by chance: it demonstrates the possibility of granting a state of sanctity to the most mundane action imaginable. The two verses cited in this passage were ones the Besht was especially fond of, and he repeatedly draws upon them in his discussions of "worship through corporeality." What the texts have in common is an activist stance. This is an activism that seeks to elevate the material state within which man lingers and to have it be bound to the Upper Worlds. The issue therefore is a sort of mission assigned to the mystic. It is not he himself who is to be redeemed by means of the "worship through corporeality" but rather the world in its earthly guise. The Besht considered this mission to be a matter of daily practice, as one may learn from the testimony of R. Yaakov Yosef: "I heard My Teacher's detailed guidance about this, how to also attend to each corporeal matter and to uplift and bind it."[91] It appears that the Besht showed R. Yaakov Yosef how to implement the principle of worship through corporeality practically by conjoining the appropriate thought to each corporeal act.

The scholars were right to define worship through corporeality as an expansion of the field of divine worship that indicates a new dimension for the application of the concept of sanctity.[92] The radical aspect of this idea has to do with the antinomian potential implicit in it. One of the firm foundations of Jewish tradition is the clear boundary that has been set between the sacred and the profane. The supposition that through the power of *kavvanah* one may sanctify what the *Halachah* has not sanctified raises a challenge to this perspective. It is no surprise, consequently, that the opponents of Hasidism criticized this idea.[93] And indeed, the leaders of Hasidism of subsequent generations qualified and restricted the "worship through corporeality," limiting it to *Zaddikim* alone.

ELEVATING STRAYING THOUGHTS

The radical conception of divine immanence, and the rejection of the idea of evil as a self-subsistent demonic power, served as the intellectual platform for the Besht's formulation of his original perspective vis-à-vis "straying thoughts."[94] This widespread notion in the *mussar* and Hasidic literature referred to sinful thoughts or merely mundane reflections that break into a man's consciousness while he is praying and interfere with his ability to concentrate. Among Kabbalists the reigning perspective was that such "straying thoughts" originated from the forces of the Evil Side. Further, any prayer that has been tainted by such straying thoughts is "kidnapped" by these forces and provides them with nourishment.

It is therefore unsurprising that many generations of Kabbalists and Hasidim were troubled by the phenomenon of straying thoughts. All were agreed that a person must make the greatest possible effort to banish such straying thoughts and repress them, and to the extent possible even prevent them from penetrating one's consciousness. One effective means to this end was thought to be self-mortification. With this general perspective as the background, the resolution the Besht proposes to this problem is striking in its difference:

> The point is that a man is obligated to believe that the earth entire is full of his glory Blessed be He, *no site is clear of him,* and all a man's thoughts partake of His existence Blessed be He and each thought is an entire level. And when there enters into a man's thought, while he is engaging in prayer, some foreign and wicked thought, it has come to the man so as to be redeemed and elevated. And if he does not believe in this, he has not fully accepted the yoke of Heavenly reign, for he disbelieves (heaven forbid) in the Blessed One.[95]

Evidently the principle, "no site is clear of him," implies that straying thoughts also have a divine origin, and it is only man's limited consciousness that has distorted them and given them their negative guise. Accordingly, he who banishes straying thoughts is denying their origins in divinity. The inference is, that one ought not banish or reject the straying thoughts but instead elevate them and return them to their divine origins.

The Besht was aware of the danger that one is liable to find oneself entrapped by the straying thoughts while praying without being aware of how to elevate or convert them into pure thoughts. He therefore qualified his initial statements:

> He should consider: if at the time that the foreign thought came, it immediately occurred to him how to redeem and elevate it, then he should embrace and elevate it; but if it did not occur to him how to redeem and elevate it, then presumably it came to distract the man during his prayer and confuse his thoughts; he then has the right to reject such a thought.[96]

The passage at hand is an interesting example of how the Besht was prepared to pull back from a position of theosophical principle if ethical or pragmatic considerations demanded it. Given his statement of principle that straying thoughts also originate from a sacred realm, one would not have thought that there was room for compromise on this issue. Nevertheless, the Besht recommends rejection of the foreign thought when no means has been found to elevate it.

The way in which the Besht qualifies the elevation of the straying thoughts in certain instances leaves no room for doubt that this was a matter of regular practice for him and not merely an abstract idea. This was also the spirit

in which the Besht's recommendations were taken by his contemporaries and
his associates. Another illustrative testimony is one that *Shivhei Habesht's*
compiler ascribes to R. Nahman of Hordonka, who was a member of the
Besht's circle:

> Once I heard from R. Nahman of Horodenka: When I was a great
> Hasid I went every day to a cold *mikvah* which in the present age no
> one would tolerate such a *mikvah*. And when I came home and found
> the *mikvah*[97] very hot, so much that the walls nearly burned down, I
> didn't feel the heat for about an hour. And nevertheless I was unable
> to free myself of straying thoughts until I had been converted to the
> wisdom of the Besht.[98]

It thus seems that R. Nahman adopted the new method proposed by the
Besht with regard to straying thoughts as an alternative to the old method that
had been current among the Hasidim and Kabbalists, that is, self-mortification. In R. Nahman's experience, the Besht's method was effective where the
old way had failed.

That the Besht's innovation on the subject of elevating straying thoughts
was seen as a practical alternative to techniques employed by Hasidim and
Kabbalists—including persons considered to have been followers of the
Besht—is supported also by a remark made by R. Ephrayim of Sadilkov. He
contrasts his grandfather's new approach with the method employed by R.
Menahem Mendel of Peremyshlyan. The latter had claimed that one could
"break up" straying thoughts by concentrating upon the name YHWH. This
was indeed a different technique than the one used by R. Nahman of Horodenka; common to both approaches, however, is an idea that straying thoughts
are fundamentally evil and are to be banished from consciousness. In contrast
to the technique of R. Menahem Mendel of Peremyshlyan, R. Ephrayim presents the method handed down to him by his grandfather:

> And I say according to what was handed down to me, that all thoughts
> are entire levels and they come to a man because they desire to be
> redeemed. And when a man considers this and knows that the Lord
> Blessed be He, and Blessed be his Name, is the root of all the thoughts
> and from him come all thoughts, he can return them to their roots,
> as is known from my grandfather of Blessed Memory, and convert all
> thoughts to good and uplift them to sanctity.[99]

Apparently, it is the recognition of the divine origin of straying thoughts that
can serve as the hoist for uplifting them.

At times the Besht associated the elevation of straying thoughts with the
Lurianic idea of elevation of the sparks. Thus, for instance, he explained that

the straying thoughts that appear during prayer are "from the secret of the breakup and the 288 sparks that a man must sift daily."[100] Evidently, the straying thoughts first originated in the sacred sparks that were scattered during the breakup. Accordingly there is an correspondence between the obligation to sift and uplift the sparks and the obligation to uplift straying thoughts. It would be a mistake, however, to infer that the Besht developed his special approach to the subject of straying thoughts at the inspiration of the Lurianic doctrine of the uplifting of the sparks. A more plausible surmise is that his approach grew out of his novel concept of divine immanence (with which it has a deep affinity), and that the association with the uplifting of sparks is merely an attempt to give the practice a retroactive justification. Furthermore, the association the Besht makes between uplifting straying thoughts and uplifting sparks is an example of a phenomenon to which other scholars have drawn attention: that when Hasidism adopted ideas from the Lurianic Kabbalah, the ideas often lost their metaphysical significance and took on a psychological meaning.[101] Indeed, the "sparks" and the *qlipot,* which the Besht identified with the straying thoughts, may no longer be classed as metaphysical phenomena, but rather as phenomenon whose locus is entirely within the human soul. The idea of uplifting sparks, more than it was a source of influence for the idea of uplifting straying thoughts, seems rather to have been reinterpreted so as to conform to it.

In concluding my treatment of the subject of straying thoughts, I cite the remarks made by Yosef Weiss: "For the subject of the evil thoughts and their redemption is at the forefront of the Besht's interest and serves as a key of sorts to understanding his entire doctrine."[102] Weiss is correct in calling attention to the Besht's considerable preoccupation with the topic of straying thoughts, although I doubt that this indeed is "the key to understanding his entire doctrine." Evidently, in his zeal to demonstrate the Besht's links to the circle of *maggidim,* and indeed the association of both the *maggidim* and the Besht to Sabbatean ideas,[103] Weiss overlooked the natural and obvious context of the subject of straying thoughts: prayer. If the Besht continually recurs to the topic of straying thoughts, it is first and foremost a reflection that in the Besht's doctrine, prayer functioned as the main channel for achieving dvekut. It seems to me that it is in prayer specifically that one finds the key to comprehending the path of the Besht.

Intentions of the Letters in Prayer

My account of the role of prayer in the Besht's path as mystic will not be complete without addressing the technique of focusing intention on the letters of the prayer and the Torah.[104] The reference here is to a certain method of direct-ing *kavvanah* that the Besht recommended as a path for achieving *dvekut*. The assumption at the root of this method is that the letters of the prayers, as well as the letters of any text included in the concept "Torah," are potential recep-tacles for the presence of divinity. This special virtue of the letters of the Torah and prayer is based on the fact that their roots are to be found in the Upper Worlds. By means of the proper *kavvanah* one may bind the letters to their upper roots and draw divine presence back with them.[105] Thus a person who prays or studies Torah can have his soul merge with the divinity that is implicit in the letters and in this way adhere to God.

This idea appears in many traditions attributed to the Besht by R. Yaakov Yosef. Before addressing these traditions, it would be proper to quote what the Besht himself says of this matter. In a letter to his brother-in-law, R. Gershon of Kotov, the Besht included the following instruction:

> While you are praying or studying, in each and every utterance and issuance from your lips understand how to make a unification of it, for in each and every letter there are worlds and souls and divinity which rise and commune and bind each other to Godliness and after-ward the letters commune and unify thoroughly and form a word and are completely unified with Godliness and you will include your soul with them at each and every level of the above.[106]

These statements suggest that it is not the content of the words of the prayer that need to be at the focus of the attention of the person praying, but rather the divinity residing within the letters. This entity is described here as being composed of three aspects arranged in a hierarchy: worlds, souls, and divini-ties. Yet these aspects are contained within each other; the divinity, which is at the top, encompasses them all. In other formulations of this idea we are explic-itly told that the Light of Infinity resides within the letters, and it is possible that the Besht had this in mind in using the concept "divinity." The Besht guided R. Gershon to "include" his soul with the divine entity residing in the letters by means of *kavvanah*, which is to be conjoined to the utterance of each and every letter.

The technique of focusing *kavvanah* on the letters of the prayer and the Torah as a means of achieving *dvekut* is presented somewhat differently in the following: "The subject of *dvekut* in Him Blessed be He by means of the let-ters of the Torah and the prayer which his thought and insides should adhere to the spiritual inside, that is within the letters, in the manner of may he kiss me with the kisses of his lips': spirit is to adhere to spirit. . . . And when he lingers on a word it is *dvekut* as he does not want to be separated from that word."[107] The simile of the kiss illustrates the possibility of the soul's encounter with the "insides" of the letters; that is, the divine essence that is concealed within them. Regarding the thought mentioned here, the Besht says: "For in a place where a man thinks thoughtfully there he is entirely."[108] The reference is thus to a maximal concentration of spiritual powers, which the person praying pours into the letters as they are being enunciated.

At times this action is manifested in a drawing out of the enunciation of the words in a prayer. This phenomenon, which evidently was one of the features of the Besht's prayer, at a later stage took on the form of a directive: "*Dvekut* is when he says a single word he lingers greatly on that word, for on account of the *dvekut* he does not wish to separate himself from the word, and therefore lingers greatly on that word."[109]

As Idel has shown, we have before us a technique that stresses the vocal aspect of prayer and assigns great significance to having each and every letter be uttered out loud and individually.[110] It is likely that this phenomenon is what is at the heart of ecstatic prayer. The bodily manifestations of ecstatic prayer were meant, as we have said, to arouse the powers of the soul. The pouring of intention into the letterforms of the prayer during their utterance, with the aim of binding oneself to the divinity hovering within them, is the inner content of such prayer.

From a psychological point of view, such prayer serves as a track on which the usual state of consciousness can make a gradual transition to the cherished state of absolute isolation from one's surroundings, full forgetting of the self, and surrender into the naught. This process is hinted at in the following passage:

> In prayer one must place all one's powers in the enunciation, and go on this way from letter to letter until corporeality is forgotten and one thinks the letters conjoin and link up with each other, and this is a great delight. . . . And this is the world of Formation. Later one comes to the letters of Thought, when one no longer sounds out what one is saying; here one has arrived at the world of Creation. Afterward one arrives at the measure of Naught, in which all one's corporeal powers are lost; this is the world of Nobility, the degree of wisdom.[111]

The words "formation," "creation," and "nobility" are not being used here in the original sense of these terms, in which they refer to different degrees of the Upper Worlds; rather, they denote different stages in the process of mystical ascendancy. Initially one concentrates on the letters in the course of enunciating the words of the prayer. Gradually the letters lose their "corporeality," (that is, their concrete form) and seem to link themselves to each other. In the next stage one ceases to make a noise during the prayer and finds oneself silently "shouting."[112] A good illustration of the phenomenon of cutting oneself off and losing selfhood is provided in the following: "Rabbi Israel Baal

Shem Tov said . . . When I adhere my thoughts to the Creator Blessed Be He I allow the mouth to say what it wishes, for I then bind the utterance with the root of the Supreme, with the Blessed Creator."[113] Evidently, at a certain stage of the process the mystic loses control over the power of speech and the mouth speaks on its own. The letters, which at the beginning of the process serve to aid the ascent of the soul, now serve as a pipeline through which divine inspiration can flow toward the soul of the one praying.[114]

Summary

In this discussion I have sought to describe and characterize the various components of what might be termed the Besht's path as a mystic. By contrast with the then current view that *dvekut* could only be manifested through a perpetual concentration upon God, the Besht considered ecstatic prayer as the predominant means of achieving *dvekut*. In the initial stages of such prayer, the fierce gesticulations and loud noises serve as means of inducing spiritual arousal. The prayer-intentions are focused on a yearning to unite with the divine presence that hovers within the shapes of the letters of the prayer. Increasingly, prayer becomes an experience of involuntary ecstasy, as manifested by the shaking of the body. The climax of such prayer is mystical ecstasy, which is an especially intense experience of union of the soul with divinity, to the point of complete severance from all the surroundings. *Dvekut* of this kind is no longer an indirect attachment to the Divinity via the *sphirot* but rather a direct merger with the Godhead. Nor is its purpose the fulfillment of a certain theurgic task; its sole objective is the vast pleasure associated with this experience—or, as the Besht puts it, the "delight" of it.

The nature of mystical ecstasy is such that it is brief and episodic. The Besht worried over this dialectic of risings and fallings in worship, as can be seen in his frequent invocations of the verse "and the animals run and return" and of the concept-pair "Greatness" and "Smallness." The theosophical translation of the experience of mystical ecstasy gives rise to the radical conception of divine immanence: Divinity indeed saturates everything; any appearance of division between the soul of man and Divinity is the merest hallucination. Taking this idea a step further, the Besht denied the existence of evil as an independent demonic entity. In so doing he cleared the road for the formulation of a new approach to addressing the material dimension of human existence.

The essence of the new approach is the recognition that matter does not have to be isolated from spirit or to be repressed. Instead, the material can be uplifted and consecrated, and converted by that means into an opportunity for spiritual ascendancy. This revolutionary approach rested upon three related and mutually supporting elements: (a) the empirical observation that asceticism and self-mortification were not delivering all that was expected of them; (b) the recognition that the various manifestations of material reality are merely "costumes" or "hallucinations," while in fact the Godhead is everywhere, filling every thing; (c) recognition of the power of human "thought" to determine the status of material reality, as reflected in what R. Yaakov Yosef cited of the Besht: "I heard explicitly from my teacher: where a man thinks, there he entirely is."[115] A mundane action may thus be converted into a worshipful act through the agency of "thought," which reunites the material with its origins in divinity. For similar reasons, "straying thoughts" need not be banished or "broken" as they too may be brought back up to their sources in divinity.

The characteristic novelty and originality of his path as a mystic, as well as the extraordinary intensity of the experiences he had, helped ground the Besht's recognition that it was his mission to lead others to follow in his path. The Besht viewed himself as a harbinger and trailblazer in matters of prayer and spirituality. Indications of this view may be seen in, among other things, the instructions he includes in his Epistle to R. Gershon of Kotov about the *kavvanah* he should use with the letters of the prayer, as well as in his request of Yaakov Yosef of Polonne that he desist from further acts of self-mortification. These instances also provide a sense of how the Besht interacted with some of his disciples and members of his circle. The many sermons the Besht delivered to those who came to hear his homilies should likewise be seen as part of his effort to disseminate his mode of worship to them. Accordingly, the question that all the above prompts is, What was the target audience for the Besht's activities as a spiritual pioneer? This question will be the focus of the next chapter.

CHAPTER FIVE

The Besht and His Circle

B eing an original mystic and a pioneer in divine worship, the Besht also viewed himself as imbued with a spiritual message to be conveyed to others. Who were the people with whom the Besht hoped to share the lessons of his personal experiences? What audience did he target for his work as a leading light in divine worship and spirituality? Did the Besht really seek to have *dvekut* be a legacy for each and every Jew, as Gershom Scholem has suggested? In the previous chapter I already noted that this point of view is no longer accepted by the majority of scholars.[1] I now would like to suggest several of the considerations that have led me as well to reject this idea.

First, the stance that Scholem attributes to the Besht—that any Jew can or even must arrive at *dvekut*—is revolutionary. Consequently, one would have expected the Besht to have mentioned it explicitly, and even to have attempted to provide a justification for it. To the best of my knowledge, however, in the material attributed to the Besht no explicit remarks on this subject are to be found. Second, it is hard to believe that the sermons attributed to the Besht, those in which he gives expression to his personal experiences in all that concerns *dvekut,* were meant for the broad public. Given the content and character of these sermons it would seem that they were aimed specifically at the spiritual elite. Third, if we consider, one at a time, each of the figures mentioned by the sources as having been students or associates of the Besht, we see clearly that these individuals are not members of society's broad classes. On the contrary, given the social background and mode of life of these figures it appears that they belonged to Hasidic and Kabbalist circles. It may therefore be affirmed that it was not the Besht who transformed his associates into Hasidim, but rather the fact that they were Hasidim to begin with which induced them to form an association with the Besht.

These considerations lead me to the conclusion that the intended audience for the Besht's work as a leading light in divine worship consisted of a narrow band of associates—the group to which the scholarship gives the label, "the Besht's circle." What sort of circle was this? Who were the persons that it comprised? What topics preoccupied its members? What patterns of social behavior typified it? These questions will be at the focus of this chapter. Yet before I attempt to respond to them, it is important that I form a clearer understanding of what Hasidism and Hasidic fraternities were like in the generations preceding that of the Besht, as well as in a time and place nearer to the Besht himself. The picture that will then emerge will provide a clearer sense of the background out of which the Besht's circle grew and will allow a more accurate listing of the features that were special to this circle.

Kabbalist Hasidic Fraternities in Sixteenth-Century Safed

One ought, first of all, to recall that the concepts "Hasid" and "Hasidut" referred originally to an individual's personal virtue and had nothing to do with membership in a movement or trend of any kind. The biblical term "hasid" derives from the word "hesed" and designates someone who customarily acts kindly or charitably to others. Along with this sense, there are places in the Bible in which the concept "hasid" is used passively; that is, as someone toward whom God has acted kindly or who has been graced with His proximity.[2]

In Talmudic literature, the term *hasid* refers to a person who makes efforts to carry out the religious commandments above and beyond what is required. The efforts such a person makes may be manifested in both in the realm of his relations with God and in the realm of his relations with his fellow man. Thus, a hasid's behavior deviates in certain respects from normal patterns of behavior. At times, such behavior may border on extremism.[3] Consequent to the usage of the Talmudic Sages, the term "hasid" took root in its meaning as someone whose worship of God has an especial intensity and quality. This was not an institutional designation, but rather expressed the spontaneous evaluation by a public of one of the individuals within it. The concept "hasidut" refers to the lifestyle and degree of spirituality of the hasid. As to the contents of Hasidism, over the generations various and sundry conceptions developed in its regard.

The most famous instance of Hasidim and Hasidism from the Middle Ages is the one well known as the "Hasidim of Ashkenaz."[4] This designation refers to an elitist circle that existed among the Jews of Germany in the twelfth and thirteenth centuries. In the world of these Hasidim, decisive significance was assigned to the aspiration to worship God above and beyond what the Halachah requires. During that period, this aspiration was also given institutional sanction by means of the idea of "the will of the Creator." The Hasid is one who makes efforts to discover hints of the will of the Creator in the Torah and then to implement this will in his life. The adoption of the terms "Hasid" and "Hasidut" by the Hasidim of Ashkenaz reflects their assessment that their own manner of divine worship was especially lofty, and could be linked to the image of the Hasid of which the Sages had spoken. It follows that the use of the term "Hasidim" to refer to a group did not supplant the original sense of this term, as an appellation denoting individual virtue. Likewise, the concept of "Hasidut" continued to refer to the way of life and level of spirituality toward which a Hasid aspires.

In the sixteenth century, the concepts "Hasid" and "Hasidut" began to be colored by Kabbalist influences. From this period on, it became possible to speak of a "Kabbalist Hasidism" or of a "Hasidic Kabbalism." The clearest illustration of a Hasidism of this type is provided by the Hasidic fraternities that flourished in Safed in the sixteenth century. From the point of view of my discussion, these fraternities have a particular significance, as they served as a source of inspiration and a model of emulation for the individual Hasidim and fraternities of Hasidim in subsequent generations.

As a general rule, the Hasidic fraternities existing in Safed in the sixteenth century could be distinguished by the following attributes:[5]

1. It was for the sake of engaging in the Doctrine of Kabbalah and attempting to influence the Upper Worlds that these fraternities were founded and maintained. With this end in mind, the fraternities cultivated and adopted ritual practices and an ethical ethos shaped under the influence of the Doctrine of Kabbalah.

2. One implication of the deep involvement that these fraternities had with the Doctrine of Kabbalah is that its members must have been drawn from the spiritual elite. These organizations were thus exclusivist and elitist in demeanor.

3. The internal relations within the fraternities were ones of brotherhood and mutual assistance.

4. The relations these fraternities had with the broader public were complex: on the one hand, they set themselves apart from the public, both by not revealing the Torah secrets they had acquired and by their unique ceremonial rites and moral ethos. On the other hand, they considered themselves to be working on behalf of the public and as its representatives.

5. As a rule, these fraternities came to be organized around the figure of a charismatic leader. The principal task of such a leader was to discover Torah secrets and to formulate modes of ceremony and moral practice built around them.

6. At times, the organization of the fraternity took on an aspect of stricture and formality. An expression of this was the Confederation Document, a contractual document that bound all members of the fraternity.

Having listed these general characteristics, I shall now consider some particular instances. I begin with the fraternity that consisted of the ARI's students. The hope for the disclosure of Torah secrets was a primary aspiration of the students who grouped themselves around the ARI. Here is how matters are described in *Toldot Haari:*

> He also was so graced that each night, when his soul would ascend to the heavens, the Angels of Service would come and accompany [his soul] to the heavenly Yeshiva, and they would inquire to which Yeshiva he wanted to go. Sometimes he would say to the Yeshiva of R. Shimon Bar Yokhai or to that of R. Akiva or that of R. Eliezer the Great or that of Tannaites or Amorites or Prophets; they would conduct him to whichever Yeshiva he preferred. The following day he would report to the Sages what he had absorbed at that particular Yeshiva.[6]

It thus would seem that the main function of the ARI was to serve as a sort of conduit for the transmission of Torah secrets. Yet relations between the ARI and the members of the fraternity were characterized also by the gap between what the students sought to learn and what the ARI was able or willing to teach them. This point is illustrated in the following tale: Once, the students begged the ARI to disclose to them Torah secrets that had recently been revealed to him. The ARI replied that even if he were to live another eighty years he would not have the time to teach them all the secrets that had been revealed to him on the topic of Balaam's ass.[7] The ARI declined to reveal certain secrets to his students not only because of their limited prowess but because of the dangers that were involved. This is the lesson to be learned from the tale told by R. Hayim Vital: "I asked my teacher of blessed memory to instruct me about a certain Unification so that I might attain an attainment. And he said to me, you are not ready yet, but I pleaded with him, and he supplied me with a certain Unification; in the middle of the night I arose and performed the Unification, and I felt overcome by a shaking in my body and my head and my reason began to fail. . . . And in the morning my Teacher of Blessed Memory said, didn't I tell you so?"[8]

The Hasidic Kabbalists of Safed were noted, as said, also for their ceremonial rites and a moral ethos that set them apart from the broader public. These practices were given further institutional expression in the form of *takanot:* religious regulations and behavioral injunctions.[9] Examination of such regulations reveals a spiritual-religious ethos in which asceticism and abstinence are paramount. Asceticism in this context refers to the attempt to isolate oneself as far as possible from life in the present world and to devote oneself entirely to the heavenly order.[10] The phenomenon of abstinence, for its part, is reflected primarily in the repeated admonitions to fast.[11] As to the objective of such fasting, one of the authors of the regulations writes as follows: "And the purpose of the fasting is: a. To weaken the might of materiality; b. At the time the Temple stood, one had given sacrifices, and now one is to give of one's own fat; c. For when a man sins mercy is separated from the Judgment, whereas when he fasts and repents he combines them."

It appears that the first of these explanations is also the most important of the three. The weakening of the body, the repository of instinct and a stronghold of the Other Side, gives strength, *eo ipso,* to the powers of the soul that craves to return and rejoin its origins in the Upper Worlds. The two additional explanations—the metaphor of fasting as ritual sacrifice and the claim about how fasting influences the Upper Worlds—are indications of how firmly ritualized fasting had become among Safed's Kabbalist Hasidim.

A typical expression of the trend toward asceticism and abstinence may be seen in the following regulation: "Minimal meat and wine are to be consumed on weekdays even at night as this gives power to Samael."[12] This statement is an illustration of the causal link that exists between gratifying bodily pleasures and empowering the forces of contamination. The demonic significance the Safed Kabbalists ascribed to material life was one of the formative elements of their moral ethos. Besides the explanations mentioned above, abstinence was considered important to the process of repentance.[13] The point of view that self-mortification purges one of sin was given ritual form in the custom practiced in Safed on the eve of the new moon:

> On the Eve of the New Moon, all the people participate, men, women, and students. And there is a place in which they gather that day, where they sit all day long reciting *slihot* [repentance verse] and supplications and making confessions and self-beatings. Some of them put a large stone on their bellies as a reminder of punitive stoning; one chokes his throat with his own hands, while another puts himself in a sack and is dragged outside round the synagogue.[14]

The basis of these extreme manifestations of the effort to become cleansed of wrongdoings was, no doubt, an especially acute consciousness of sin. Yet such feelings of guilt were also sharpened and augmented by a belief that one's transgressions give force to the powers of the Other Side, and hence even cause the Day of Redemption to be delayed. In other words: the inclination to repent and purify oneself derived not only from the hope for personal exaltation, but also, and perhaps mainly, from a heightened awareness of the effects of sin in the metaphysical plane and from a sense of one's responsibility for the fate of the Jewish people.[15]

Among the regulations the Safed Kabbalist fraternities enforced, some of the more prominent are those that accentuated the isolation of their members from the broader public. Examples are the practices of dressing in white on the Sabbath and holidays, of putting on *Talit* and phylacteries during afternoon prayers, of conversing exclusively in the Holy Tongue, and so forth.[16] Certain regulations stress the responsibilities that members have toward each other. Before praying, each member must individually accept the commandment to "love they neighbor as thyself." Although "thy neighbor" in the commandment refers to every Jew, this was taken as having especial weight when the "love of friends who engage in Torah together" was concerned.[17] The mutual commitments of fraternity members are also reflected in the regulations that urge members to assist each other with the doubts and obstacles that arise in the moral-religious sphere.[18]

In sum, the Kabbalist Hasidic fraternities that flourished in Safed in the sixteenth century appear to have been elitist organizations that were introverted and set themselves apart from the remainder of the public. Their isolationism was sustained by the esoteric doctrines they held, from the ethos to which they subscribed, by their sense of fraternity and mutual responsibility, and by the personal attachment to the leader. Apart from all these, more formal means of communal bonding were also at times employed.[19]

Hasidism and Hasidim in Eighteenth-Century Poland

Ben Zion Dinur appears to have been the first to have commented about the existence of Hasidic fraternities in Poland prior to the Besht and to have noted the Besht's associations with certain of these fraternities.[20] Dinur even proposed a detailed characterization of these fraternities. Three of their characteristics stand out: their preeminent concern with the Kabbalah, their adoption of Hasidic practices showing the influence of the Kabbalist Hasidim described above, and their cultivation of a sense of a close-knit community.[21]

In the *Memoirs of Solomon Maimon*,[22] the Hasidim are described as persons who "devote their entire lives to the fulfillment of the commandments and the moral virtues with especial strictness." An additional feature that Maimon attributes to the Hasidim is their ascetic way of life. One of Hasidism's manifestations that left a deep impression on Maimon, and presumably on many of his contemporaries as well, was the practice of severe self-mortification so as to atone for sin. In general, the self-mortification took the form of severe and extended fasts.[23] Maimon tells of ascetic Hasidim whom he encountered or heard about in the 1760s. The book by R. Pinchas Katzenelbogen[24] contains a description of Hasidim in the first decades of that century. Katzenelbogen too points out that fasting was a typical method of purification for the Hasidim of his day.[25] It will be recalled that frequent fasting was a practice that also characterized several members of the Besht's circle, such as Rabbi Yaakov Yosef of Polonne and the *Maggid* Dov Ber of Mezerich. It also appears that the Besht practiced fasting in an earlier stage of his life.[26]

Something of what the Hasidim of the Besht's day were like can be learned also from the case of the clash between R. Yaakov Yosef and the members of the Shargorod community, in which he served as rabbi. The details of this affair will concern us later. At this stage, it suffices to note that the Hasidim who lived in this community tended to pray separately and applied the laws for ritual slaughter more stringently than the rest of their brethren. A further custom of the Hasidim mentioned in connection with this affair, and that other sources also touch on, is that of the Third Sabbath meal. I refer to how this meal was removed from the family setting and transformed into a central event in the world of the Hasidic fraternity. At the heart of the Third Sabbath meal, and what granted it its quality as a spiritual rite, was the telling of *divrei Torah* in the course of the meal.[27]

Another important attribute of the Hasidim of Poland around the time of the beginning of the Hasidic movement has been pointed out by Yaakov Hasdai, who comments on the frequent use of the terms "servant of God" or "serving God" in the *drush* literature of the period. On various grounds, Hasdai came to believe that this phrase designated a certain defined group within the larger body of Hasidim.[28] I am not convinced of the certainty of this conclusion; perhaps the term "servant of God" is merely a synonym for "Hasid," as Halpern suggests.[29] At any rate, what is important for us is Hasdai's assertion that the people thus designated devoted all of their time to divine worship and hence faced considerable difficulties in providing for their families.[30] As these Hasidim saw it, the preoccupation with mundane affairs, including that of earning an income, stood in opposition to the ideal of maximal devotion to the worship of God.

Thus far I have mostly been concentrating on Hasidic figures as individuals. What were their organizational frameworks like? For this question one may point to two of the examples that have been discussed in the scholarship: the Hasidic fraternity that existed in the setting of the Kloyz of Brod and the fraternity of Hasidim in Kotov. I begin with the first of these two.

The most famous document to mention the Hasidic fraternity associated with the Kloyz of Brod is the *herem* circular in which the new Hasidism was banned. This circular was disseminated in the Brod community in the spring of 1772. The circular stresses that it is prohibited to deviate from the current version of the text of the prayerbook—yet it exempts the Hasidim who reside in the Kloyz from this rule. It describes them as "filled with the revealed Torah, with Talmud and Poskim, and also masters of the secrets of the Kabbalah . . .

but their main focus and study is the revealed Torah, Talmud and Poskim; they are famous for their piety, know their Lord, and pray with Kabbalist *kavvanot*." These Hasidim are permitted to continue on their way and to pray using the ARI's version of the prayer. Likewise, the Kabbalists's habit of dressing in white on the Sabbath, a practice that was severely condemned when engaged in by the New Hasidim, was permitted for residents of the Kloyz.[31]

The social aspects of the Kloyz phenomenon have been examined by Elhanan Reiner.[32] His research suggests that the Kloyz was a study framework meant for mature, advanced scholars and that it was financed by the donations of one or several individuals. In this sense, the Brod Kloyz was one institution among many. What was special about this Kloyz was that it served as the abode of a Hasidic fraternity who joined study of Halachah to that of the Kabbalah and observed Hasidic practices. Reiner is right to observe that the *herem* circular reflects the recognition of society that the Kloyz residents had special rights to segregate themselves and to observe Hasidic customs not followed by the wider public.[33] The plaudits the *herem* circular bestows upon the sages of the Kloyz clearly indicate that this was a fraternity marked by exceptional prestige. The stress the drafters of the circular place on how proficient Kloyz members were in Halachic literature is meant, presumably, to distinguish them from the New Hasidim, who were accused of causing distraction from Torah. It is clear, however, that what characterized the Kloyz sages was the way in which they combined study of the Halachah and Kabbalah at the same time.

Another attribute of the sages of the Brod Kloyz was the wealth and prestige of the families from which they came. This fact presumably also influenced the degree of authority these sages enjoyed among the broader public. Indications of such authority include the involvement of the Kloyz sages in the Emden-Eibenschütz debate and the Cleve *get* affair, as well as the part they played in the publication and dissemination of books of Kabbalah.[34]

A comparison of the Brod Kloyz Hasidic fraternity to the Hasidic circle in Kotov can bring out the differences between them. The Kotov circle's members did not enjoy the same degree of authority and public influence as did the Brod Kloyz sages. This difference stemmed, among other things, from the fact that Brod was one of the more important of the Jewish communities of Poland, unlike Kotov, which was merely a small town in southwest Ukraine. Moreover, the Kotov Hasidim, though they were members of the spiritual-religious elite, did not come from privileged or influential families. For the purposes of my discussion, however, this fraternity was of special importance, given the relationships that were formed between the Besht and certain of its members. Of these figures, the most prominent are R. Moshe, Kotov's rabbi; R. Nahman of Kosov; and the *mokhiah,* R. Aryeh Leib of Polonne. In all likelihood R. Gershon

of Kotov, the Besht's brother-in-law, was also a member of this circle. I shall dis-
cuss the nature of the ties the Besht had with these figures later on. At this stage,
I shall attempt to characterize the circle itself on the basis of the scholarship that
Yosef Weiss has devoted to this subject.[35]

The Hasidim of Kotov were described by their contemporaries as the
havura kadisha (the circle of the sacred) or as the *bnei havura* or *anshei havura*
(sons or members of the circle). These designations highlight their status as an
organized body segregated from the general public. Yet we know little of the
attributes marking this circle. If we infer from what we do know of R. Nahman
of Kosov to the other members of the circle, it would seem that they had the
custom of praying using the ARI version and that they were preoccupied by
the striving for *dvekut*.[36] As with other Hasidic fraternities, the Hasidim of
Kotov also took communal Third Sabbath meals. This meal was held in the
house of R. Moshe, the community rabbi, and lasted till well after the end of
the Sabbath. In the course of the meal the Hasidim held conversations on matters of divine worship.

A further attribute of the Kotov Hasidim was their desire for purification
from sin, including hidden sin. A reflection of this desire can be seen in an
episode centering on R. Nahman of Kosov. The gist of the tale is as follows:
R. Nahman confronted members of the fraternity with knowledge of their
hidden sins. This enraged them, as they suspected him of arriving at this
knowledge by means of "prophecy," and thus of violating the fraternity's
"agreement" not to prophesize. R. Nahman, for his part, maintained that he
had not violated the agreement as the information had come to him via the
spirit of one of the deceased from the town.[37] The Kotov Hasidim's practice
of using the "spirits" of the deceased so as to learn of hidden sins is hinted at
in another story as well.[38] As a rule, in the course of striving for moral purity,
including redemption from hidden sin, the Hasidim of Kotov made use of
knowledge they arrived at by means of metaphysical entities. Furthermore,
the agreement of the members of the fraternity not to "prophesize" suggests
that some of them professed to capacities for discovering the thoughts and
hidden sins of their comrades.

Socially, the Kotov Hasidic fraternity was noted for the internal cohesion of
its members, on the one hand, and for its segregation from the general public,
on the other. This segregation is reflected in, among other things, the derision
toward Hasidim voiced by outsiders.[39] The derisive remarks may have been
connected with the strange motions the Hasidim made as they prayed. At any
rate, it seems that the behaviors that distinguished the Hasidim from the general public were not merely cause for admiration but also the source of tension.

A further social attribute of the Kotov Hasidic fraternity was that they were leaderless. The members of the fraternity viewed each other as equals.

Two Documentary Sources Concerning the Hasidic Fraternities in Poland

An important contribution to our understanding of the nature of the fraternities of Hasidim that existed in a time and place near to the Besht's was provided by the two period documents discovered and discussed by Gershom Scholem.[40] What is special about these sources is that they describe what appear to be a new breed of Hasidim and Hasidism, displaying practices of a kind similar to those the Besht observed.

The first source is incorporated within the introduction written by R. Shlomo of Chelm to his Halachic work *Merkevet Hamishneh*.[41] The author devotes a considerable portion of the preface to a characterization of various "sects" within the class of "scholars." For our purposes, the important passage is the following one:

> And some of them are empty of all knowledge and [what there is] is small and feeble. Neither in Torah secrets nor in Talmud do they excel. Astray do they lead. And wild their cries. Which skip over mountains. With prayers and pleas. In songs and tunes. And vocals and harmonies. Ten registers shifting. And actions peculiar. Wrapped in white. And a fringe threaded blue.... Sighs which break a man's body in half. Hands waving to and fro. Trunks swaying like trees in the forest.... And suchlike that our ancestors never dreamed of. With our own eyes we have seen them, these virtuous ones of our times. Yet unread and unlearned. One is called a Sage, the other a Rabbi. Whoever adds most gestures and gesticulations. Who is praised and adored by commoners. Women and children. Stimulating the senses. Before the idiot and feeble-minded. They tell some of his praises to him. O Hasid, O humble one.... And the whole world counts as nothing to him. He butts north and west. Saying I am sans-pareil. My cedar shall not be felled. I who see through the bright skylight. In studying prayer and spiritual purity. And who does not behave as you do. None is your like or your equal. For thee the Lord anointed with oil of joy above thy peers. Are the chosen one of your gates. Capital expenses (in both senses) are permitted you. In secret rooms. Do all you can for you are empowered. Like the green grass I have granted you all. And of all you can see, partake. For they have not been created but to serve us. With their soul, their might and their funds.[42]

What sort of Hasidim are being described in this passage? We may list out their features as follows:

1. These people have set themselves apart from the wider public through their Hasidic paractices. Among other things, they dress in white on the Sabbath and holidays.

2. By R. Shlomo of Chelm's standards, these Hasidim are not learned in Halachah and Kabbalah.

3. It is the vehemence and passion of their prayer that characterizes them above all. Such prayer involves much singing, melodies, and exaggerated gestures. It is ecstatic in nature, resembling the prayer we have seen that the Besht engaged in. (One gathers from the tone taken by R. Shlomo that he viewed the various manifestations of prayer of this sort as alien and degenerate.)

4. Their ecstatic prayer has earned these Hasidim the admiration of the uneducated classes. The common folk even mistakenly think that Hasidim of this kind are "spiritual prodigies," masters of Halachah and Torah secrets.

5. As if that were not enough, some of these Hasidim believe themselves blessed with prophetic powers. They accordingly consider themselves proper objects of honors and financial support.

R. Shlomo's tone in describing these Hasidim clearly indicates that he had severe reservations about them. Evidently, as someone who was an unquestioned *Talmid Hacham* and of a rationalist turn of mind, R. Shlomo had trouble finding even the faintest positive qualities in these people. On the contrary, their mixture of unscholarliness and wild emotional outbursts aroused in him feelings of unease and disgust. The need that R. Shlomo felt to announce in public what sort of people these are and to warn about them is understandable. Yet R. Shlomo tempered his severe condemnation of the Hasidim with the following words: "And not everyone heaven forbid do I condemn. For one man in a thousand I have found. Whose thought is meet. Whose motives are pure. These are the residues upon whom God calls. Their faces do I fear. May blessings fall upon their heads. May my posterity be as theirs."[43] Evidently the "residues" that the author favorably marks for special distinction are Hasidim of the type found in the Kloyz of Brod. Thus it seems that the degenerate form of Hasidism, the faults of which R. Shlomo spells out one by one, were perceived by him as a departure from the way of the old Hasidism—the authority and superiority of which he also recognized.

The second source that deals with Hasidim of a time and place close to the Besht's is contained within *Mishmeret Hakodesh,* a work written by R. Moshe b. R. Yaakov of Satanow.[44] This is a *mussar* text that sets forth the values and ideals of Kabbalist Hasidism. In the course of his discussion of the actual and hoped-for state of affairs in divine worship, the author describes various phenomena that appeared in his day. Among other things, he discusses Hasidim of a type similar to those who had aroused the wrath of R. Shlomo of Chelm. R. Moshe, however, viewed these Hasidim in a more positive light.

Yet even R. Moshe finds fault with an aspect of their ecstatic prayer: "And I saw many of the generation's pure ones who took it to their hearts to pray with *dvekut* to God by means of joy and tearful prayer, without taking care to recite the words properly."[45] R. Moshe is warning about corruption in the recitation of prayer words and insists that the words are to be recited grammatically. Still, the passionate prayer itself he holds in high regard. This is attested to by the designation "the pure ones of the era." Similarly, he describes ecstatic prayer in a positive, or at least not in a critical, manner. Furthermore, R. Moshe sees fit to defend these Hasidim against those who would ridicule them for the peculiar body movements that accompany their prayer. He defends enthusiastic prayer from the suspicions that such behavior is "done for the sake of pride." To counter such suspicions, R. Moshe affirms: "One whose soul adheres to God, Blessed be He, does not allow himself to lazily repose but rather [behaves] as it is written: "And David twists with all might before the Ark of God'" (2 Samuel, 6:14)[46]

Yet later on the author of *Mishmeret Hakodesh* lists several of the manifestations of Hasidism that in his opinion are worthy of censure: "And I have seen those who worship God in their prayers with all their hearts and it is nothing to them to waste two or three hours in idle conversation at times when speaking of morals, and they drink fountains of wine and say that it was not for the evil ones that pleasures were created (may ash fill such mouths)."[47] It appears that the Hasidim referred to here are identical or similar to those whom the author had previously spoken of, as both groups were noted for the passion of their prayer. Yet these are noted also for their "idle conversation" and their imbibing of wine. It comes as no surprise that as someone who identified with Hasidism of the ascetic sort, R. Moshe's ire would have been raised at Hasidim who drink to excess, and all the more at people who justify indulgence in all earthly pleasures by the statement, "it is not for the evil ones that pleasures were created." Yet what does he mean by the "idle conversation" he ascribes to them? Why does it outrage him so? We learn this from what he goes on to say:

> And in particular, for the time they waste from Torah the punishment
> is quite severe, for they cause others to sin with them and to hold to

idle ways. . . . And even discussions of morals ought not to be conducted excessively if time for Torah is wasted by it, for from morals
he will shift to idle matters and morals themselves are not the main
part of Torah. For the essence of what is sought from Torah are laws
and details and specifics. And through excessive preoccupation with
morals he lessens the time spent on Bible and Mishna and Halachah
which are the body of the Torah; he will end up with thorns covering
all, permitting what is proscribed. . . . And especially the volatile wines
which burn his very soul.[48]

If we suppose that the two accounts we have before us deal with the same
group of people, it will follow that the second account can be used to fill out
and interpret the first. Recall that R. Shlomo of Chelm asserted that the
Hasidim who engage in enthusiastic prayer are proficient in neither Halachah
nor Kabbalah. One might have thought that the people he is speaking of were
complete ignoramuses. Yet from R. Moshe's statements it would seem rather
that the people in question came from the scholarly class; otherwise what
point would there be to blame them for wasting time meant for Torah? This
appraisal of their background is one that R. Shlomo of Chelm shares: he
includes these Hasidim in his discussion of the various groups that the scholarly class comprised. Thus, these were people whose time—so one would have
expected from their social standing—should have been entirely dedicated to
Torah study. Instead, they waste their time in idle conversation and discussions
of morals. Evidently these two preoccupations were linked; this is what R.
Moshe hints at when he says, "For from morals he will go on to idle matters."
It seems that he does not have in mind conversations about profane matters
but rather the discussions that these Hasidim held on topics of divine worship.
Evidently, conversations of this type were held in the course of study of the
mussar literature.[49]

As already noted, it was Gershom Scholem who uncovered these two source
texts and he was the first to discuss them. I offer here several of the principal
conclusions that Scholem reached with regard to them. First, Scholem
affirmed that a certain section of *Mishmeret Hakodesh* contains clear hints of
the Besht, although his name is not explicitly mentioned there. Scholem was
so sure of this identification that he asserted that "in the book *Mishmeret
Hakodesh* we have, preserved in our hands, the first historical evidence of the
Besht's public activity."[50] This identification has been conclusively disproved
by Hayim Liberman.[51] Second, as to the Hasidim that the two source documents describe, Scholem asserts that they were not members of the "movement" founded by the Besht, but rather belonged to antecedent Hasidic circles.
In his opinion, there is no evidence suggesting that it was the Besht who first

employed the "way and manners" of these Hasidim, and it is more plausible to suppose he "received them ready-made."[52] This assertion by Scholem seems to me to hit the mark. Indeed, there is nothing to indicate that it was specifically the Besht's circle that was spoken of. Moreover, the joint testimony of Shlomo of Chelm and Moshe of Satanow would indicate that the phenomenon was of considerable scope; yet the Besht's circle at the time comprised only a few people. Third, it is hard to agree to one of Scholem's further conclusions: that the Hasidim mentioned in the two sources mentioned are "commoners," or in his words, "Commoners and untutored Hasidim and seekers of God through primitive enthusiasm."[53] On what basis does Scholem render this verdict? His language suggests that he took R. Shlomo of Chelm's words at face value when the latter spoke of these people being ignoramuses. Likewise, it appears that, to Scholem's tastes, ecstatic prayer is something "primitive."

Now, as to the degree of learnedness of these Hasidim, we have seen that both R. Moshe of Satanow and R. Shlomo of Chelm place them in the scholarly class, even if, by the standards of both authors, they do not sufficiently engage in study of Torah—they spend too much time on *mussar*. As to ecstatic prayer, it is hard to accept the judgment that prayer of this kind is any more "primitive" than prayer which is accompanied by Lurianic *kavvanot*.[54]

I now summarize my findings and consider their implications. I have found that the phenomena of Hasidim and of Hasidut, in the older sense of these terms, was not unfamiliar to the Jews of Poland in the first half of the eighteenth century. The characteristic practices of these Hasidim had been shaped by the influence of the Kabbalist Hasidic fraternities that had flourished in Safed in the sixteenth century.

A few of these practices: special rites that included praying following the version of the ARI; dressing in white on the Sabbath; frequent ritual bathing; and intensive engagement in study of Kabbalah, in addition to study of the Halachah. We have also seen that these Hasidim, or at least some of them, organized themselves into fraternities that maintained an isolation from the general public. Their isolationism took various forms: sites of their own for study and prayer, as with the Brod Kloyz; special meetings to discuss the topic of divine worship, as in the case of the Third Sabbath meal for the Kotov Hasidic fraternity; or prayers in a separate *minyan*, as with the Hasidim of Shargorod. A further form the isolationism of the Hasidic fraternities in Poland took was the special strictures the Hasidim applied to themselves in all that concerns the subject of *shekhita*.

Alongside the old type of Hasidut, a Hasidism arose in new form. Its features were the following: cultivation of an ecstatic style of prayer; rejection of asceticism; and focus on morals texts and the discussion of divine worship at the expense of preoccupation with the Talmud and *Poskim*. As said, these hall-marks are reminiscent of several of the characteristic features of the Besht's spiritual path.

What these findings suggest is that the Besht did not operate in a vacuum. The various manifestations or forms of Hasidim and Hasidut I have been dwelling upon tell about the context within which the Besht arose, the one that sustained him and in which he acted. All or most of the members of the Besht's circle operated within this context. The new road the Besht paved in divine worship was one he sought to bequeath to persons who may be defined as Hasidim of the old type.

Moreover, if we assent to Scholem's assertion that the accounts of R. Shlomo of Chelm and R. Moshe of Satanow do not refer to the Besht and his circle, it follows that some of the characteristic attributes of the Besht's way were not unique to him. In other words, it would seem that so far as ecstatic prayer and the rejection of asceticism were concerned, the Besht was not alone. Indeed, it is conceivable that on these topics he was influenced by other Hasidim. In any event, however, it was the Besht who developed the intellec-tual basis of the new mode of divine worship, and it was he who, by the power of his authority, was able to bequeath this new way to those who were destined to make it a path that many would follow.

The Members of the Besht's Circle

R. GERSHON OF KOTOV

At this stage of my discussion I turn again to the Besht's circle. I begin by sketching a portrait of certain members of the circle. In the course of doing so, I shall attempt to portray the relationships that developed between each of these individuals and the Besht. On the basis of these findings, I shall try to form comprehensive conclusions about the nature of the Besht's circle.

Among the figures closest to the Besht was his brother-in-law: R. Avra-ham Gershon of Kotov. Certain stories from *Shivhei Habesht* present the ini-tial contact between these figures as a sequence of harsh confrontations. Thus, for example, R. Gershon was reputedly against his sister's marriage to the Besht. It was R. Gershon's father who had promised his daughter's hand in marriage to the Besht; R. Gershon, who was not informed of this, was obliged to carry out his father's wishes against his will. As the story tells it, R. Gershon was a dignified *Talmid Hacham* whereas the Besht, who was engaged in living as a hermit at the time, seemed to him an ignoramus. Mat-ters went so far that R. Gershon tried to convince his sister to obtain a divorce from the Besht.[55]

The tension between R. Gershon, the scholar with a prestigious family lineage, and the Besht, who then was posing as an uncouth villager, is the setting for several tales of the "revelation" of the Besht. One example is the following story:

> Once, the Besht sought out the rabbi of the holy community of Kotov
> and borrowed the Book of Zohar from him. On his way home, he
> encountered his brother-in-law R. Gershon, who asked him: What are
> you carrying under your arm? He didn't want to tell him. R. Gershon
> descended from the wagon and pulled the Book of Zohar out from
> under his arm. He took the book away from him, with the question:
> What do you need the Book of Zohar for? Later . . . the Besht came to
> town to pray in the *Beit Midrash*. During the *Shema* he let forth a huge
> sigh. After the prayer service, he was asked by R. Moshe the rabbi of
> said holy community: What was that great sigh I heard you make in
> the middle of the prayer? And speaking kindly to him he heard the
> the truth [from the Besht], that the mezuzah is not kosher. And he
> found that it was so, and gave him that Book of Zohar, with the bless-
> ing that he would not again encounter said R. Gershon.[56]

In impounding the Book of Zohar from the Besht, R. Gershon was behaving in accord with the accepted point of view that a commoner is not fit for dealing with a book such as this. The Besht, for his part, reacted by revealing that the mezuzah was unkosher, thus disclosing his powers of sight from afar. It is no accident that the person to whom the Besht reveals himself is R. Moshe, who besides being the town rabbi was also a Kabbalist and Hasid. These features made R. Moshe the person most qualified to recognize the Besht's unusual powers, as a result of which the Book of Zohar was returned to him. The story's irony builds on the gap between the inferior and contemptible image that R. Gershon held of the Besht, and his true superiority as revealed to R. Moshe.[57]

The question to be asked is, What degree of truth is there to this story and the others of its kind? Is the tension between the Besht and his brother-in-law no more than a literary fiction, meant to accentuate the marks of the "revelation" of the Besht—or does it have some basis in reality? This question becomes all the more acute given that the Besht's correspondence with R. Gershon leaves no room for doubt that the two brothers-in-law maintained relations of amicability and respect toward each other.

At first glance, it would seem that the tension between R. Gershon and the Besht is no more than the product of Hasidic lore: most of the tales that describe the tension between the two figures carry a discernibly fictional tone.[58] On second thought, however, it seems that even if several of these tales have sailed off into the realms of the imaginary, there is still a nucleus of truth to them. As it happens, the Besht *was* lacking in a prestigious family line, and by the standards of his time and place was not considered a *Talmid Hacham*.[59] It therefore would not have been remarkable for R. Gershon to have been less than comfortable with the match his sister had made with the Besht. Supporting evidence for this hypothesis comes from the tradition according to which R. Gershon's sister was a divorced woman at the time she married the Besht.[60] If there is truth to this tradition (and it is hard to imagine that *Shivhei Habesht* would put such a "stain" upon the Besht's wife if there were no grounds for it) then from the point of view of the bride's family, the match with the Besht would have been regarded as a sort of compromise. According to the matrimonial values of the time, a divorced woman could not expect to find a spouse of a status similar to her own.

It is therefore not inconceivable that at an earlier stage of their acquaintance, R. Gershon's attitude toward the Besht was one of suspicion and disapproval, and that only in the course of time, once he was made aware of his qualities, did he shift his tune and become the Besht's friend and pupil. If this hypothesis is correct, then the tension between R. Gershon and the Besht is what fed the Hasidic legend. Naturally the legend would have fashioned the events after its own manner and made use of it for its own purposes.

Who was R. Gershon of Kotov? What place did he occupy on the social and cultural map of the period?[61] First of all, it must be noted that by the concepts of the times, R. Gershon was considered a genuine *Talmid Hacham*. True, the claim that he was the leader of the rabbinical court in Brod is in all likelihood an exaggeration,[62] and it is unclear what degree of veracity there is in the tradition that has him serving as a judge in Kotov. Yet one may assert that R. Gershon was regarded as a rabbinical authority in Brod, as he played a role in a famous Halachic dispute in which some of the most important rabbis participated.[63] A further indication of R. Gershon's status as a *Talmid Hacham* may be seen in the fact that the Ashkenazic sages in Jerusalem implored him to become their "Rabbi and President and Chief and Patron."[64]

In addition to being a scholar, R. Gershon was a Hasid and Kabbalist. His Hasidic practices included fasting, abstention from relations with his wife, prayer in accordance with the ARI's version, and employment of Lurianic *kavvanot*.[65] Further testimony about R. Gershon's standing as a Hasid are provided by the designations that R. Yehonatan Eibenschütz applies to him: "The famous Rabbi and Hasid, a Torah prodigy and Divine Kabbalist."[66] The Besht too describes him as "the Rabbinic wonder, the Hasid, famous in Torah and piety."[67]

It seems that for a certain time R. Gershon was a member of the Kloyz of Brod. The Kloyz ledger indicates that he served as a leader of prayers there.[68] R. Gershon's links to the Brod Kabbalists are also suggested by the fact that he was related by marriage to the family of R. Moshe Osterer, a prominent figure among members of the Kloyz. While a resident of Kotov, R. Gershon was associated with that town's Hasidic fraternity,[69] and when he became a resident in Jerusalem R. Gershon joined the Kabbalists who studied Torah secrets in the *Beit Midrash* "Beit El."[70]

This sketch of the portrait of R. Gershon would not be complete without mention of his skills as a mystic and magician. In a previous chapter we cited a tale in which the Besht redeems the souls of sinners who appear to him in the course of his prayer. The story goes on to relate that R. Gershon was envious of the Besht and sought to perform the same feat himself. However, when masses of souls appeared to him while praying, he was seized with a panic and fainted.[71] Although this tale is supposed to show the Besht's superiority over his brother-in-law, it at the same time conserves a tradition that shows R. Gershon as one who considered himself capable of performance in such matters. If in this case R. Gershon's ambitions turned out to be misplaced, in at least one other case he was able to "surprise" the Besht. The story is about a time when R. Gershon spent the Sabbath in Annopol. Upon his return from there, he tells the Besht: "I there achieved a great light from R. Shimshon,"[72] by which is meant that he had been visited by the soul of R. Shimshon of Ostropoli, a well-known Kabbalist who had been killed by Cossacks in the year 1648. To this the Besht deprecatingly replied: "You are kidding yourself." Yet a while later the Besht himself visited the same place, likewise saw the "light" and realized that his brother-in-law had been correct.[73]

Certain stories from *Shivhei Habesht* attribute magical powers to R. Gershon. One such story involves the Kotov Hasidic fraternity; its gist is as follows:

> In Kotov there was one man by the name of Tectiner who was always speaking out against the circle of Hasidim. One time, R. Aharon, the Besht's brother-in-law, heard him and quarreled with him. And this man leaped up and grabbed the beard of said R. Aharon. His brother, R. Gershon, stood and put a ban on him and a few days later that man died.[74]

R. Leib, the son of R. Gershon, is the source of another story, one that gives expression to the image R. Gershon held of himself. The story takes place at a time when the land of Israel had been stricken by a drought. R. Shalom Sharabi, the leader of the Kabbalist circle in Jerusalem, announced a fast and gathered the public for communal prayers. At his instruction, R. Gershon passed in front of the ark. While reciting *slichot*, R. Gershon walked away from the ark. When he was asked why he had done so, he replied that while praying he could sense that his prayers were being received and that rains were destined to fall for several days. He accordingly moved away from the ark, as he feared appearing "impudent." Indeed, the story goes on to relate, rains did come following those prayers. Thus not only did R. Gershon's prayers impress the heavens and cause rain to fall; he was aware of this in advance, in a manner reminiscent of the Besht.[75]

In sum, by his formal training, his lifestyle, and his social standing, R. Gershon was a scholar, Hasid, and Kabbalist of the type that earned the recognition and esteem of the Jews of Poland in the eighteenth century. Furthermore, even his emigration to the land of Israel fits a pattern of behavior typical of the Kabbalist Hasidim of those generations.[76] Likewise, we have found that R. Gershon considered himself and was depicted by others as one graced with mystical and magical powers. Even if he was not a mystic and miracle worker of the rank of the Besht, he nevertheless had ambitions and achievements in this department. It comes as no surprise, therefore, that R. Gershon associated himself closely with the Besht and sought to achieve spiritual growth by his aid. Similarly, it was natural for the Besht to have found a student and friend in R. Gershon, someone to whom he could tell of his unusual experiences and share his accomplishments in matters of divine worship.

The closeness of the relationship between the Besht and R. Gershon of Kotov may be seen in the letters the two exchanged during the period in which R. Gershon resided in the land of Israel.[77]

Reading these letters, what is most striking is the expressions they contain of the friendship and respect in which these two figures held each other. The two brothers-in-law do not stint with their declarations of mutual affection and love. The Besht begins his letter with the words: "To my beloved, my brother-in-law, and my friend dearly cherished as my own soul and heart," while R. Gershon writes: "My beloved brother-in-law, friend of my soul, cherished one of my heart, light of mine eyes." The two express longings for each other. The Besht writes: "I would gladly say much more and wander on at length but on account of the tears I have in recalling your departure from me I cannot speak." R. Gershon replies in the same coin: "And I miss you as if you were my own son." R. Gershon also voices the wish that the Besht would follow him to the land of Israel, though he knows the chances of this are slim. To this the Besht replies: "for the Lord knows that I have not despaired of voyaging to the Land of Israel if the Lord so desires it so as to be together with you yet the times do not permit this." Meanwhile, the Besht attempts to console himself with the exchange of letters with his brother-in-law: "And now my beloved brother-in-law, friend of my soul who is closer than a brother to me, wish your brother well, and do not withhold your hand from your brother who hungers to hear thirstily your pleasant words."

R. Gershon says prayers for the Besht and for the members of his household, and begs the Besht to pray for him as well: "And on Rosh Hashanah and Yom Kippur I prayed for you and for all who accompany you. . . . Only this I ask, that they pray for me as well and for the members of my family that I be graced to raise my children in the Holy Land to the Torah to the *huppah* and to good deeds." Whereas the Besht writes to his brother-in-law: "And so pray for me . . . and for my offspring in the Diaspora." Evidently the Besht sought from R. Gershon's prayer the extra weight accorded to prayers made in the land of Israel, while R. Gershon hoped to enjoy the special exaltedness of the prayers of the Besht.

The fraternal relations between the bothers-in-law were expressed also in the assistance they provided to each other, each in the realm of his expertise: this one as a scholar and that one as a *baal shem*. R. Gershon taught Torah to the Besht's son, Zvi Hirsch.[78] The Besht returned the favor by supplying R. Gershon with amulets. We learn about this from the request R. Gershon included in his letter to the Besht for the latter to send him a "general amulet." By this he meant an amulet the power of which would last several years, as opposed to the amulets he had been receiving from the Besht on an annual basis. Furthermore, during his period of his residence in the land of Israel the Besht would occasionally send a gift of funds to his bother-in-law.[79]

Thus far we have dwelled on the fraternal and amicable relations between R. Gershon and the Besht, relations that at the family level were ones of equality and mutual respect. Yet as regards their spiritual rank and the assistance they were able to provide each other on matters of divine worship, the Besht was clearly the superior figure. This gap between them was also manifested in how they addressed each other: the Besht addresses his brother-in-law using the designations appropriate to someone deemed a scholar and Hasid; whereas R. Gershon addresses the Besht using the designation: "rabbi of all those in the Diaspora." Recall also that when R. Gershon arrived in the land of Israel he took pains to corroborate the prophetic statements the Besht had relayed to him before he had left for his trip, and made efforts to spread his fame among the sages of Jerusalem as a worker of miracles.[80]

A passage from the Besht's Epistle illustrates the sort of guidance the Besht provided R. Gershon on matters of divine worship. This passage has been mentioned in a previous chapter, but given its relevance I cite it here once more: "Yet this I shall inform you; and let the Blessed Lord assist you, and may your paths be in God's presence and lose not sight of them especially when in the Holy Land. While you are praying or studying, in each and every utterance and issuance from your lips intend to make a unification of it, for in each and every letter there are worlds and souls and divinity which rise and commune and bind to each other and afterward the letters commune and unify thoroughly and form a word and are truly unified with Godliness and you will include your soul with them at each and every level."[81] The Besht thus sought to pass on to his brother-in-law the method of prayer based on the hypothesis that the prayer's letterforms serve as a sort of repository for the Divine Presence. It will be recalled that this mode of prayer was the means the Besht employed to achieve *dvekut.* Nor was this the only instance in which the Besht gave guidance to R. Gershon on matters of divine worship. On the contrary, it appears that he spoke to him quite often on these topics. Evidence to this effect may be seen in the following passage from the Besht's Epistle to R. Gershon: "Yet I ask of you to review the words of morals I told you several times and to always have them present in mind and to think of them and be scrupulous with them, surely you will find in each and every maxim all sorts of delicacies for it is no empty matter what I told you."[82] The tone and phrasing of this line clearly reflects the position of authority and paternalism that the Besht adopted toward R. Gershon in all that concerns matters of divine worship. Given the expressions of admiration that R. Gershon displayed toward the Besht, one may readily surmise that he indeed accepted the Besht's authority in this domain.

The bonds between the Besht and R. Gershon lasted for many years. They began in the 1730s, when the Besht married R. Gershon's sister and lived near Kotov. When the Besht set up residence in Miedzybóz, in the early 1740s, he invited R. Gershon to live in his home. R. Gershon resided in the Besht's home for several years and during that time also taught Torah to his son. After R. Gershon immigrated to the land of Israel, in 1747, the two brothers-in-law kept up a correspondence with each other. They met one more time when R. Gershon came to Poland for a visit in 1757.[83]

In sum, the sources available to us portray R. Gershon of Kotov as an established scholar and Hasid of the old type. The close and lasting bonds he formed with the Besht were nourished by a combination of family affiliation, personal friendship, and spiritual partnership. And although these were bonds of personal intimacy and mutuality, still, the Besht's superior position is quite apparent, both in regard to his spiritual rank and in regard to his ability to guide and direct R. Gershon in divine worship.

R. MOSHE OF KOTOV, THE POLONNE *Mokhiah,* AND R. NAHMAN OF KOSOV

By contrast with the relatively large amount of information we have about the Besht's ties with R. Gershon, we know only little about his links to the other Hasidic figures who resided in the town of Kotov. Nevertheless, a few lines can be sketched about the Besht's associations with several of them: R. Moshe of Kotov, R. Yehuda Leib (a.k.a. the Polonne *mokhiah*), and R. Nahman of Kosov.

I begin the discussion with a passage that claims to describe the event of the "revelation" of the Besht. The passage appears following a convoluted story, in the course of which the Besht reveals his true identity to a student of R. Gershon of Kotov. At that point, the Besht instructed the stunned student:

> Go to the large sect of Hasidim in the town and also to the Rabbi of the community and say the following: There is a great light in the proximity of your community. It would be appropriate for you to follow it and bring it into town. And when these words were heard by all the Hasidim and also by the Rabbi, they all decided that the Besht was the man . . . and all went to his village to ask him to come to town. The Besht had advance sight of this and went to town. . . . And when they met each other, they all went down to a certain place in the woods and made a chair out of the branches of a tree and sat him down on it and accepted him as their Rabbi.[84]

The story from which this passage is drawn is one of the most fictional of the tales in *Shivhei Habesht*. Thus, for example, the dramatic account of the coronation ceremony in which the Besht is rendered leader of the "sect of Hasidim" has an utterly fictitious sound. Nevertheless, it seems to me that in its way the story does convey a historical truth of relevance to our subject. The Hasidim mentioned in the story are undoubtedly the Hasidim residing in Kotov, and the referred-to rabbi of the community is none other than R. Moshe, rabbi of Kotov.[85] It stands to reason that the function this story assigns to the Kotov Hasidim (i.e., recognition of the Besht's stature) is a function these Hasidim indeed filled during the years in which the Besht lived near Kotov. This was the period in which the Besht took his first steps as a *baal shem* and a mystic, and it would have been natural for him to have sought to earn recognition from the Hasidim of the nearby town.

Seen in this light, R. Moshe of Kotov had an especially important role to play; besides being a member of the Hasidic circle he served also as the rabbi of the community.[86] Indeed, three of *Shivhei Habesht*'s tales associate R. Moshe with the "revelation" of the Besht. One of them is evidently a reflection of a true event: the story in which R. Moshe is mentioned as among those present when the Besht exorcised a dybbuk from a woman in Kotov.[87] The two other tales are fictional in nature. One of them is the story involving the Book of Zohar, cited previously. The second tale follows a similar plan: R. Gershon of Kotov gets angry at the Besht for not having put on phylacteries on *hol hamoed*. In fact, the Besht had adopted the Kabbalist practice on this topic. Yet, because the Besht was "concealing" his identity during that period, he pretended to have acted out of ignorance. R. Gershon brought the Besht to R. Moshe, the community rabbi, so that the latter would reprimand him. However, when he appeared before R. Moshe, "the Besht removed the disguise and the Rabbi saw a great light and stood up before him."[88]

A tradition that circulated among the Jews of Kotov tells that R. Moshe was the first person to have recognized the Besht's true nature and to have spread the news of his revelation.[89] This tradition is consistent with the historical nucleus which is the basis of the tales in *Shivhei Habesht;* namely, that the Besht disclosed himself to R. Moshe of Kotov before he achieved his public reputation. R. Moshe recognized the Besht's special qualities, spoke of them to others, and in so doing contributed to the spread of the Besht's fame as a *baal shem* and mystic.

Something of the relationship between these figures can be learned also from the letter the Besht sent to R. Moshe. This letter is undated but was written during the period in the Besht resided in Tluste.[90] The picture that the letter suggests is of two figures who respect each other and who regularly correspond. Among other things, the Besht recommends that R. Moshe use a certain medicine. He incidentally explains that use of this medicine is conducive to divine worship. He states these things in a tone of authority. It would thus seem that as far as the subjects of medicine and divine worship are concerned, the Besht considered himself qualified to advise R. Moshe and even to provide guidance to him.

R. Moshe of Kotov passed away in 1738.[91] It follows that his relationship with the Besht would have been confined to the 1730s, during the period before the Besht went to live in Miedzybóz.

Another member of the Kotov Hasidim who joined the Besht's circle was R. Yehuda Aryeh Leib, also known as "the Polonne *mokhiah*" or simply "the *mokhiah.*" When the *mokhiah* was a resident of Kotov he earned an income as a *melamed* and apparently also as an itinerant preacher.[92] Later he was appointed as preacher of the Polonne community. His association with the Besht commenced in the 1730s and lasted until the Besht's death in 1760.

The tales about the *mokhiah* that appear in *Shivhei Habesht* derive in the main from his student, Rabbi Gedaliah of Lince. Consequently, there is reason to suppose that these tales are based to a considerable extent on what R. Gedaliah heard from the *mokhiah* himself. How then is the *mokhiah* depicted in *Shivhei Habesht?*

Certain tales hint at the *mokhiah*'s Hasidic mode of life. He was afflicted by worries about the "straying thoughts" that spoiled his prayer intentions. When he wished to describe a man as virtuous, he would say of him that "he never saw an emission in all his days." It was the *mokhiah,* too, whose influence caused R. Yaakov Yosef to become a Hasid. The *mokhiah* delivered a sermon, and his reprimands seemed directed at R. Yaakov Yosef personally. In this way the *mokhiah* discovered that he had the power of reading the thoughts of others. The reprimands deeply moved R. Yaakov Yosef, and as a result he began to observe Hasidic customs.[93] I shall later return to this episode in greater detail. At any rate, the story about the *mokhiah*'s ability to read minds is just one of several tales that reflect the attraction the domain of the magical held for him. Among other things, we read about the *mokhiah*'s conceit that he is unafraid of direct conflict with demons; about the soul of a dead man that came to him in a dream and revealed secrets that were later confirmed; about his having asked the Besht to teach him "the language of beasts and birds and the language of trees"; and about his claim to be able to extract the writings that the Besht had enclosed in a rock in a mountain if he so desired. These were the writings containing the magical knowledge used by the Besht.[94]

In light of the above, it is unsurprising that the tale of how the *mokhiah* came to be affiliated with the Besht is bound up with an event of a magical nature. I have already mentioned this story in the chapter that deals with the Besht as a *baal shem*. It will be recalled that the *mokhiah* took up residence in a house that was haunted by a demon. The very fact that he moved into such a residence could be considered an act of boldness on his part; nonetheless the *mokhiah* was forced to abandon the house when the demon threatened to injure his children. It was only the Besht who was able to defeat the demon; from that time forward the *mokhiah* "remained his disciple."[95]

In sum, the *mokhiah* was drawn by the realm of the magical and even claimed to have capabilities in this field. His connection to the Besht was fed, at least in part, by the recognition of the latter's status and superiority as a worker of miracles. The *mokhiah* came to recognize the Besht's magical abilities in the 1730s; presumably he also contributed to the establishment of the Besht's reputation as a *baal shem*.

The association between the Besht and the *mokhiah* was to last for many years. Several stories in *Shivhei Habesht* suggest that the association was continuous and intimate. The *mokhiah* often visited the Besht's home, took meals with him, and joined him in his travels. Moreover, the *mokhiah* was considered to be one of the Besht's close students and protégés.[96]

The third Hasid from the Kotov circle who was associated with the Besht was R. Nahman of Kosov.[97] The sources we have available depict R. Nahman as a genuine Hasid and mystic. It is to be recalled that among the Kotov Hasidim, R. Nahman was considered to be graced with the power of "prophecy"; that is, with an ability to reveal the secret sins of others. Another of R. Nahman's notable attributes was the special quality of his prayer, which excited everyone who heard it. We learn about this from the following story, among others: R. Nahman had a relative named R. Yudele. One Sabbath morning, the two went to bathe in the *mikvah:*

> R. Nahman was very quick and R. Yudl was something of a lazybones. While he was taking off his clothes, R. Nahman stood in front of the platform praying. And when R. Yudl came out of the *mikvah* he heard R. Nahman singing a tune for the *haaderet vehaemuna,* and he got excited and ran to the *Beit Midrash* in only his smock, with no clothes on, and danced for about two hours.[98]

Even the Besht recognized the preeminence of R. Nahman's prayers. "The Besht said: Wherever R. Nahman has been, they know what prayer is, and wherever R. Nahman has not been, they know not what prayer is.[99]

Central to the world of R. Nahman was the striving for *dvekut.* In accordance with the main conception of *dvekut* held by Hasidim of the old type, R. Nahman attempted to keep his consciousness continually focused upon God. Moreover, he developed special techniques for attaining this goal, and his statements on the topic are cited in the books by R. Yaakov Yosef. R. Nahman's originality on the subject of *dvekut,* and the many citations attributed to R. Nahman by R. Yaakov Yosef, have led Yosef Weiss to describe him as the "foremost among the speakers on the topic of *dvekut*" in the Besht's circle.[100]

Shivhei Habesht cites a story that turns on a confrontation between the Besht and R. Nahman.[101] This confrontation was, in effect, a sort of test in which the Besht was asked to demonstrate his ability to read R. Nahman's mind. As the story tells it, the Besht indeed managed to read R. Nahman's thoughts. If so, it would seem that the role assigned to R. Nahman does not differ from that assigned to R. Moshe of Kotov and to the *Mokhiah.* He, like they, is one of the people who recognized the Besht's singularity and hence who contributed to the establishment of his status as a miracle worker and as carrier of the Holy Spirit.

R. YAAKOV YOSEF OF POLONNE AND THE *Maggid* DOV BER OF MEZERICH

Within the Besht's circle, a special place is reserved for R. Yaakov Yosef of Polonne. He, more than anyone, contributed to the preservation and promulgation of the Besht's doctrines. In his works, R. Yaakov Yosef cites many dozens of sermons and sayings he heard from the Besht. For that reason, these writings are of primary significance for the efforts to understand the spiritual world of the Besht.

The very fact that in his works R. Yakov Yosef mentions so many things he heard personally from the Besht attests to the closeness of their association.

The Besht rarely delivered sermons in public, so evidently R. Yaakov Yosef heard these sermons in smaller fraternities or in private conversations. Moreover, at least some of the statements that R. Yaakov Yosef attributes to the Besht take the form of personal guidance. This is hinted at in the following formula: "And this matter I recalled and received from my teacher mouth to mouth and it may not be explicated in a book, know and understand."[102] As will become clear later on, there are other expressions that indicate the intimacy of the bond between the Besht and R. Yaakov Yosef. Nevertheless, the relationship that these two personages maintained was not the sort characteristic of colleagues of equal status but rather one more fitting to the interaction of a rabbi with his pupil.

How and why did Yaakov Yosef come to be the close student of the Besht? The answer to this question is found in an episode cited in *Shivhei Habesht* that is attributed to Yaakov Yosef in person:

> I heard this from the famous Rabbi the Hasid and Wise One of the holy community of Polonne who was the rabbi of the holy community of Shargorod. He heard that the Besht had come to the holy community of Mohilev. He said to himself: I shall travel there myself, for he was not then yet a Hasid. He traveled and arrived on a Friday before morning prayers. He saw the Besht smoking a pipe, and was perplexed by this. Later, during the prayers, [I] wept a great weeping such as I never had wept in all my days, and grasped that it was not on my own account that I was weeping. Afterward the Besht voyaged to the land of Israel and I remained desolate until he returned. Then I began to travel to him and stayed with him for some time. The Besht used to say that I needed elevation. I stayed for about five weeks and asked, when will his highness elevate me?[103]

These few words describe a dramatic event that changed the life of R. Yaakov Yosef. The knowledge that the Besht was residing in a nearby town encouraged him to travel to see what he was like. Evidently his curiosity was piqued by the rumors he had heard of the Besht's virtues and powers. The initial encounter was disappointing. R. Yaakov Yosef presumably expected that a man of so towering a reputation would be found, before morning prayers, engaged in study of Torah. Yet here was the Besht, smoking a pipe. The astonishing shift commenced during the prayer service. The fact that R. Yaakov Yosef wept as he had never wept before indicates that he was overcome by an especially powerful set of emotions. He was also certain that he himself was not the source of the overwhelming emotions, but that they rather originated from the Besht. Evidently it was the Besht's passionate prayer that had such an effect on R. Yaakov Yosef and swept him into so intense a storm of emotions.

The immediate result of this experience was a sense of his dependence on the Besht. R. Yaakov Yosef became aware of this dependence when the Besht traveled to the land of Israel and he felt himself bereft and alone. When the Besht returned from his voyage, R. Yaakov Yosef began to visit him frequently and even stayed with him for a period of several weeks. It seems that he attempted to adopt the Besht's manner of prayer, and that this is the meaning of his question "when will his highness elevate me?"

The authenticity of this tale derives first of all from its being told to the compiler by R. Yaakov Yosef himself. The story also sounds plausible in light of the knowledge we have of the Besht's ecstatic prayer and the effect it had on people nearby. It will be recalled that R. Yaakov Yosef was the one who described the Besht's prayer as a "hovering of the divine presence."[104] What nevertheless raises a doubt about its authenticity is another story from *Shivhei Habesht*, one that seems to present an alternative account of how R. Yaakov Yosef came to be a Hasid. According to this other version, R. Aryeh Leib, the Polonne *mokhiah*, is the one who brought about the turnabout in Rabbi Yaakov Yosef's life. The gist of the story is as follows: the *mokhiah* spent the Sabbath in Shargorod as a guest in the home of R. Yaakov Yosef, who was then serving as the community's rabbi. The *mokhiah* asked his host to be present at a public sermon he would be delivering that Sabbath. During the sermon, Yaakov Yosef felt as though the *mokhiah*'s words were being aimed at him personally. This surprising and unsettling experience led him to recognize the *mokhiah*'s spiritual powers, to the point that he decided to affiliate himself with the *mokhiah*. Under the *mokhiah*'s influence, Yaakov Yosef began to adopt Hasidic practices.[105]

It thus would seem that we have two different and conflicting accounts of how R. Yaakov Yosef came to be a Hasid: the first refers this development to the influence of the Besht, while the second associates it with the *mokhiah*'s influence. Closer consideration, however, leads to the conclusion that two separate events are involved here, two stages, in effect, of a single process. Upon hearing the *mokhiah*'s sermon, Rabbi Yaakov Yosef became a Hasid, but of the old type; while after his encounter with the Besht, R. Yaakov Yosef fell under the influence of his special mode of divine worship, and became his disciple.

We learn from how the story continues that following the *mokhiah*'s sermon, R. Yaakov Yosef began to observe Hasidic customs. This fact precipitated a severe conflict with the members of the community. Matters reached the point where R. Yaakov Yosef was chased out of the town of Shargorod just prior to the Sabbath and had to spend the Sabbath in one of the nearby villages.[106]

What was this conflict about? What fault did the townspeople of Shargorod find in their rabbi that made them chase him from their town? Certain authors have mistakenly held that the people in Yaakov Yosef's town were opponents of Hasidism and persecuted it on that account.[107] This explanation suffers from anachronism: the opposition to Hasidism began only in the 1770s whereas the confrontation with Rabbi Yaakov Yosef took place in the 1740s. Those same authors make the further mistake of not distinguishing between the two events mentioned here, and link R. Yaakov Yosef's conflict with the Shargorod community to his decision to affiliate himself with the Besht. Yet the conflict arose following Yaakov Yosef's becoming a Hasid of the old kind, and the event took place before he became personally cognizant of the powers of the Besht.[108]

One can learn of the nature of the conflict between R. Yaakov Yosef and the members of his community from remarks that he himself included in one of his sermons:

> What my eyes, not those of a stranger, saw, is that war will be always be waged against one who aspires to sanctity and asceticism by praying in his own *minyan,* as it is impossible to pray in a congregation which is carrying out the Commandments from habit [rather than inspiration.]. . . And as to *shekhita,* the people are not strict enough, for here anyone does the slaughtering, even those ignorant of the laws of *shekhita* and the Godless . . . [109]

It appears that following his metamorphosis into a Hasid, R. Yaakov Yosef ceased to pray in the community synagogue and set up a separate *minyan* for himself. Likewise he refused to eat the same slaughtered meat that the rest of the community did. Later in the sermon it is implied that this isolationist behavior is what incurred the community's wrath, to the point where R. Yaakov Yosef was discharged and another rabbi was hired in his place. The extremity of this reaction ought not to surprise us. Although it was not unusual for Hasidim to segregate themselves from the public and to be strict in matters of *shekhita*—something often regarded with approval—nevertheless, for a rabbi to separate himself from the members of his community because their prayers are deficient and their *shekhita* dubiously kosher would have been to insult his community deeply.[110]

The sources reviewed thus far suggest that the process of R. Yaakov Yosef's transformation into a disciple of the Besht occurred in two stages. In the first stage, R. Yaakov Yosef began to adopt the Hasidic practices that characterized the Kabbalist Hasidim of the old type. Among other things, these practices included strictness regarding *shekhita* and the quality of one's prayer. This development took place, as noted, under the *mokhiah*'s influence. Only during the second stage did R. Yaakov Yosef become personally aware of the Besht. Perhaps it was the *mokhiah* who told him of the Besht and aroused his desire to meet him. In any event, the experience of praying in proximity to the Besht caused a transformation in the life of R. Yaakov Yosef.

When did R. Yaakov Yosef begin his affiliation with the Besht? I can give no certain answer to this question. There is reason to suppose, however, that it occurred between 1747 and 1752. This estimate is based on a letter the Besht supplied to R. Yaakov Yosef to take with him to the land of Israel in 1752. In the letter, addressed to his brother-in-law R. Gershon, the Besht recommends R. Yaakov Yosef to R. Gershon and asks the latter to assist him upon his arrival in the land of Israel. Given the praises the Besht showers on R. Yaakov Yosef, it would appear that R. Gershon had not met him before leaving Miedzybóz for the land of Israel in 1747. R. Yaakov Yosef thus came to recognize the Besht at some point at the end of the 1740s or the early 1750s. The close ties between them lasted up until the Besht's death in 1760.

It is worthwhile to cite here what the Besht wrote in praise R. Yaakov Yosef: "The famous Rabbi, the Hasid, our teacher Yosef Cohen Tzedek, a servant of God[111] . . . whose actions are desirable before God Blessed be He, and all his deeds are for a heavenly cause."[112] The Besht does not refer to R. Yaakov Yosef's status as rabbi and scholar, preferring instead to stress his virtues as a Hasid.

A source that sheds light on the relationship between the two figures is the letter the Besht sent to Yaakov Yosef, a section of which was cited above. I now cite the letter in full:

> To the hand of my beloved, the love of my soul, the great luminary rabbi, the righthand pillar, the mighty hammer famous in Hasidism, the perfectly wise and wonderful miracle worker, who cleaves to the walls of my soul closer than a brother to me, the Master Yosef Hacohen. And behold the impress of his holy hand I have received, and I have seen in one glance the top two lines in which it is written that his eminence speaks as though he is forced to fast. And my insides grew angry from what I read. And I hereby add by a most holy oath, conjoined by the Holy One Blessed Be He and the *Shekhina,* that he must not endanger himself in this way as this is a melancholy and sad deed, and the Divinity does not hover where there is depression but rather where there is the joy of a *mitzvah,* as his eminence well knows for these are matters I have taught him several times, and he should take these matters to heart. And about the fragments of his thought which lead him to this, I shall counsel you and let the Lord be with you, heroic warrior. Each and every morning while studying he should adhere himself to the letters with a complete adherence to the worship of his Creator Blessed Be He and Blessed be His Name, and then the Judgments will be sweetened at their roots, and the Judgment will be lighter upon him. And of your flesh do not ignore—heaven forbid

do not fast [more] than is obligated and necessary. And if you heed
my voice the Lord shall be with you. And with this I will cut things
short and say Peace from one who seeks your welfare always, so sayeth
Israel Besht.[113]

The letter before us suggests that the two figures corresponded extensively.
Actually, the Besht's remarks are in response to R. Yaakov Yosef's claim that he
has to fast because of the "Judgments." The concept of judgments in this context may be understood as Evil Counsels produced by sins or sinful thoughts.
In seeking to overcome such judgments, R. Yaakov Yosef was employing a
method that had long been accepted in Kabbalist and Hasidic circles. The novelty here, of course, is in the stance taken by the Besht, which affirms that one
need not avail oneself of self-mortifications in order to combat the judgments
successfully. This was not the first time that the Besht instructed R. Yaakov
Yosef to refrain from fasting. On the contrary, the Besht notes that he had
already made his position on this subject clear to R. Yosef "several times." Perhaps what is new in the present letter is the proposal of an alternative to self-
mortification: "sweetening the Judgments at their roots." That is to say: the
Besht's guidance to R. Yaakov Yosef is that he overcome the judgments by
revealing their divine origins. This objective is to be achieved by adherence to
the divine light that hovers within the letters of the Torah and the prayer.[114]

What can one learn about the nature of the relationship between the Besht
and R. Yaakov Yosef in light of the letter at hand? It would seem that beyond
the honorifics, which reflect the conventions of the times, the opening words
express a warm and personal relation with the addressee. Such is also the dominant tone in the body of the letter. Nevertheless, when he seeks to dissuade
Yaakov Yosef from fasting, the Besht takes an aggressive and determined tone,
as would be expected in relations between a rabbi and his pupil. Moreover, the
Besht's anger at the fact that Yaakov Yosef is still fasting reveals an emotional
involvement on his part. It seems that the Besht had a deep interest in his student's welfare. One may summarize, therefore, that the Besht's relation toward
R. Yaakov Yosef was characterized by a combination of intimacy, on the one
hand, and an authoritarian and sharp stance on the other. R. Yaakov Yosef too
accepted the relationship he had with the Besht as the relations of rabbi to
pupil. This is clearly expressed in the many dozens of sermons which he attributes to "my teacher."

A further example of the personal guidance that the Besht provided R.
Yaakov Yosef is to be found in the tradition that *Shivhei Habesht* attributes to
Rabbi Gedaliah of Lince:

And I heard from the rabbi of our community the Master Gedaliah
of Blessed Memory, that several times the Rabbi [Yaakov Yosef]

wished to journey to the Holy Land, and the Rabbi Besht said he should not go. And he told him you will be able to use the following sign: Each time the desire to travel to the Holy Land overcomes you, you will know for sure that there are Judgments on the city heaven forbid and that Satan is bothering you to keep you from praying for the city. Therefore, when the desire to travel to the Holy Land overcomes you, pray for the city.[115]

We know about R. Yaakov Yosef's intentions to travel to the land of Israel from the letter the Besht gave him in 1752, to deliver to his brother-in-law R. Gershon. It is unclear why the journey did not take place. At any rate, R. Gedaliah's statements suggest that R. Yaakov Yosef did not abandon his hopes to travel to the land of Israel and on occasion considered carrying them out. What now appears is that it was specifically the Besht who attempted to divert him from this scheme. The fact of the Besht's intercession on this matter is itself a further indication of his closeness to R. Yaakov Yosef. At the same time, it gives expression to the position of authority and the paternalism he showed in his relations with his students. As one with the power of "seeing" and revealing the metaphysical meanings of events, the Besht reveals to R. Yaakov Yosef that there are hazards associated with his plans to travel to the land of Israel, and recommends that he continue to stand on the watch.

In instructing R. Yaakov Yosef to remain in his place and pray for the peace of the city, the Besht is assigning to him one of his own characteristic roles; the Besht considered himself a person charged with the public welfare whose prayers could prevent calamities from occurring. It would thus seem that the Besht attributed great powers to R. Yaakov Yosef's prayers as well. Incidentally, in discussing the advice the Besht gave to Yaakov Yosef regarding travel to the land of Israel, it is hard not to speculate that this advice also sheds light on the failure of the Besht's own plans to travel to the land of Israel. Put otherwise: perhaps the Besht interpreted the failure of his trip as a heavenly message about the public mission he had to fill in Poland.

By contrast with the relative wealth of sources that refer to the ties between R. Yaakov Yosef and the Besht, there are only two tales in *Shivhei Habesht* that deal with the ties between the Besht and Dov Ber, the *maggid* of Mezerich. The more important of these is the one that describes how the *maggid* came to be affiliated with the Besht. According to the story, the *maggid* grew seriously ill as a result of his extended fasts. R. Mendel of Bar, who chanced upon the *maggid*'s place of residence, advised him to go to see the Besht and be cured by him. According to another version, it was the *maggid*'s family members who urged him to travel to seek a cure from the Besht. One way or the other, the event

THE BESHT AND HIS CIRCLE

following which the *maggid* affiliated himself with the Besht took place during the period of his convalescence. The core of the story is as follows:

> One time [the *maggid*] fainted and they spent half the day trying to revive him. . . . And afterward R. Yaakov and the above-mentioned friends came to visit him and asked him what had caused his fainting. . . . He told them: Besht sent his beadle to fetch me at midnight, and I came and found him seated with a small candle by his head and he was wearing a wolf-skin inside out. And he asked [me]: have you studied the wisdom of the Kabbalah? I said yes. And he had a book laid before him on the table, and he instructed me to read out to him what was in the book. And the writing in the book was in small sections, with each section beginning "R. Yishmael said, I was told by Matatron the interior minister. . . ." And I read out a page or two to him. And the Besht said: not like that, I shall read it out to you! And he read it out to me. And while doing this he was seized with a shock and awoke and said: here we are dealing with affairs of the Chariot [*maasei merkavah*] and I am sitting down. So he read it standing up. And while he spoke, he lay me down in a bed like a circle and I no longer could see, yet I heard sounds and saw great bolts of lightening and flares. And so it was for about two hours. And I grew very frightened and began to faint from fear.[116]

What is the meaning of the test the Besht applied to the *maggid?* In what way did the *maggid* "fail" the test? What is the lesson the *maggid* was supposed to have learned from this event? It seems that the *maggid* made the mistake of taking an intellectual approach to a text that dealt with Torah secrets. For the Besht, by contrast, any involvement with a text of the *maasei merkavah* was to be approached in the mode of Revelation.[117]

The tale, as presented to us, has been through several incarnations. Nevertheless, there is no reason to doubt that it gives expression to a genuine event. Perhaps the Besht and the *maggid* had argued over the proper way of dealing with Torah secrets. At any rate, the *maggid* evidently was witness to one of the Besht's mystical experiences, and his observation of this event deeply impressed him. This experience was presumably ecstatic in nature, which apparently is what accounts for the loud noises and the bolts of lightening.

A further dramatic meeting between the two figures took place during the prayer service:

> I also heard from the preacher the Master Eliahu of blessed memory that when he first came to the great *maggid* of the holy community of Mezerich he told him this story, and said: Once on a holiday—perhaps it was the first day of Passover or it may have been *Shmini Atzeret*,

I had to say the blessing for either rain or dewfall—the Besht was praying in front of the ark with great fervor, for as I had heard several times from his chosen [followers], he was louder than everyone and would pray with great cries. And the Rabbi and great *maggid* could not bear it for he was quite ill. And he left the *Beit Midrash* and entered a small house in the *Beit Midrash* and prayed there in private. And before the Mussaf service the Besht went to the small house to dress himself in the *kittel.* And the *maggid* said that he was aware that the divine inspiration was with him and that when he looked at him he could tell he was not in the present world. And when [the Besht] put on the *kittel,* the *kittel* wrinkled up on his shoulders and the great *maggid* grasped the *kittel* to smooth out the wrinkle. And when he touched it he began to tremble and he gripped the table that was there and the table too began to shake with him. And after the Besht left he had to pray and to ask of the Blessed Lord to remove this thing from him for he had not the strength to endure it.[118]

The background to this story is familiar to us from other tales: the Besht passes in front of the ark in the *Beit Midrash* of Miedzybóz while leading the holiday prayers. In the course of doing so he sinks into the trance of an ecstatic prayer, the symptoms of which are loud noises and a trembling body. To the *maggid* the Besht seems at such a time to be like someone "not in this world" and graced with "divine inspiration." In other words: the *maggid* interprets the Besht's ecstatic trance as an event of clear mystic significance. It turns out that the very sight of the Besht's ecstatic prayer sweeps the *maggid* into so intense a storm of emotions that at the touch of his shoulder he too is infected with a trembling.

What the two stories have in common is the direct encounter between the *maggid* and the Besht at a time when the latter was in the midst of an experience of mystical ecstasy. One ought not to be surprised that this aspect of the Besht should have so deeply impressed the *maggid,* as he was a mystic in his own right.

One learns about the sort of relationship the *maggid* had with the Besht, as viewed by the *maggid,* from an account by a student of the *maggid*'s, R. Shlomo of Lutsk, included in the latter's introduction to the book *Maggid Dvarav Leyaakov.*[119] R. Shlomo reports that the *maggid* would habitually sing the Besht's praises. Among other things, he once said: "Does it surprise you that he had revelations from Elijah, and revelations at other very high levels as well? And he began to hint at what sort of level a revelation from Elijah is and how supremely high it is." The *maggid* went on to speak of what the Besht had taught him: "And once I heard from his holy mouth, that the Besht of Blessed and Righteous memory had taught him the language of birds and the conversation of trees etc., and also studied the secrets of Holy Names and Unifications with him." The *maggid* goes on to list in great detail the secrets that the Besht revealed to him. R. Shlomo asks him, why does he not reveal his spiritual rank, as did the Besht? The *maggid* replied: "That he [the Besht] also disclosed only the faintest bit of himself and that the revelation from Elijah he did not disclose, only it is possible that prior to his death I alone achieved [awareness of this revelation] by the grace of God when I came to him."

It seems to me that one can draw the following inferences from Shlomo of Lutsk's account. First, the *maggid* recognized the Besht's spiritual rank as a person graced with the revelations of the highest levels of the Upper Powers and as an unrivaled master of the secrets concerning Holy Names, the performance of Unifications, and suchlike. Second, the *maggid* considered himself to be a student of the Besht, at least as regards knowledge of these secrets. Third, the *maggid* claims that when he visited the Besht he discovered the fact that the Besht had been graced with an Elijah-revelation, although the Besht himself had yet to disclose this to others. It may be inferred that the *maggid*'s visits with the Besht reflected the closeness of their relationship. Fourth, the *maggid*'s habit of telling his students about the Besht's greatness indicates, first of all, how deep an impression the Besht's personality made on him. It would also appear that the *maggid* attempted to base his authority as a leader upon his close ties with the Besht.

R. NAHMAN OF HORODENKA AND R. MENAHEM MENDEL OF PEREMYSHLYAN

One of the most prominent figures in the Besht's circle of associates was R. Nahman of Horodenka. One can learn about the extent of R. Nahman's Hasidism, as depicted by the members of the Besht's circle, from what R. Yehiel Michal of Zloczow tells of him:

> That R. Eliezer of Amsterdam[120] went to the Holy Land for the sake of R. Nahman of Horodenka, as he said: when we both shall be in the Holy Land we shall bring the Redeemer. And when he came to the Holy Land all the townspeople came toward him. And when he saw R. Shimshon b. R. Nahman and asked him where is your father, he told him he had traveled abroad.[121]

The idea that if two persons of a spiritual elevation are present together in the land of Israel the Messiah is liable to come is not an exceptional one in the thought of the period. However, for our purposes what is important is the fact that R. Nahman was perceived as one of the two persons who had the power of causing the arrival of Redemption. The image of R. Nahman as a "great Hasid" is also suggested by what he himself relates of what he had learned from the Besht:

> Once I heard from R. Nahman of Horodenka: When I was a great
> Hasid I went every day to [bathe in] a cold *mikvah,* such a *mikvah*
> which in the present age no one would tolerate. And when I came
> home and found the place very hot, so much so that the walls had
> nearly burned down, I didn't feel the heat for about an hour. And nev-
> ertheless I was unable to free myself of straying thoughts until I had
> been converted to the wisdom of the Besht.[122]

The compiler of *Shivhei Habesht* heard the above from R. Nahman in person and thus it has the status of a "first-person confessional." The general
account suggests that bathing in a cold *mikvah* was one of the means employed
by R. Nahman to mortify himself. In this way he sought to master the "straying thoughts," that is, mundane reflections or sinful thoughts, that break into
the flow of consciousness and damage the prayer-intentions. It will be recalled
that this was a common practice in the world of the Hasidim of the old type.
What was singular about R. Nahman was the extremity of the mortifications
that he applied to himself. Evidently this is what he meant by speaking of himself as having been a "great Hasid." It is possible that in speaking of these matters R. Nahman used the term "great Hasid" ironically, as he had since freed
himself of the perspective that advocates self-mortification. At any rate, by the
concepts of the old-style Hasidism—which R. Nahman was identified with
during that period—the severity of self-mortification was indeed an indication of the degree of one's Hasidism.

The principal lesson of the story at hand is that these severe self-mortifications did not help R. Nahman at all. It was only by means of the "wisdom of
the Besht" that he was able to free himself of straying thoughts. I refer to the
Besht's point of view that straying thoughts have a sanctified origin; therefore,
rather than being banished from consciousness they are to be elevated and
restored to their origins in the upper heavens.[123] One may presume that the
Besht's influence on R. Nahman of Horodenka was not confined to the battle
against straying thoughts, but encompassed the entire practice of asceticism.

Now, although R. Nahman is depicted as someone who recognized the
superiority of the "wisdom" of the "Besht" and who was influenced by it, the
Besht treated him as a person of a rank equal to his own—so certain stories
suggest. The common denominator in such tales is the belief the Besht had in
the power of R. Nahman's prayer. An example may be seen in the following
story: the Besht and R. Nahman set out on the road together. When the time
was reached for the afternoon prayer service they found themselves in one of
the villages. The Besht asked the servant to check if it would be possible to
pray in the house that was next to where they had stopped. The servant found
that the house was full of non-Jews and thus that one could not pray there.

Meanwhile R. Nahman got off the cart, entered the house wrapped in *tallit* and *tefillin*,[124] and stood in prayer. When the Besht learned of this he said: "He will surely cause some affliction to befall the Gentiles." And indeed, a short while later a fire broke out in the nearby fortress and all the Gentiles present in the house rushed off to put it out. When the house was clear of Gentiles "the Besht too went to pray there."[125]

Another story, which again suggests how highly the Besht regarded the quality of R. Nahman's prayer, describes a conflict between the two:

> Rabbi Nahman of Horodenka had the virtue that he would say about every thing he saw or that occurred to him: it was good, it was for the best. His faith was as firm as an iron bar. Once, soldiers were billeted among the Jewish residences in the holy community of Miedzybóz. The Besht told him: pray that the soldiers won't be billeted among the Jews. He [R. Nahman] told him that it was for the best. The Besht told him: How nice that you weren't alive in Haman's generation; you would have said of that decree too that it was for the best. And nothing better occurred than that Haman was hung, which too was a good thing.[126]

The Besht had reservations about R. Nahman's passivity, which had origins in his fatalistic belief that all was for the best. What R. Nahman took as a Hasidic virtue, the Besht regarded as a dangerous divorce from reality. It is possible that the dispute between the two is a reflection of the fundamental difference between the lone Hasid and the leader, who considers himself to be responsible for the public welfare. At any rate, in this story too the Besht is depicted as one who deals with R. Nahman as though he were his equal, owing to the power of his prayer. It would seem, then, that the relations between the Besht and R. Nahman, as preserved in the memories of the tellers of the stories, are not the relations of rabbi and student but rather the relations of two colleagues. For all that, certain stories contain the recurring theme of R. Nahman's recognition of the Besht's special rank. One such tale is the following: "During the Besht's funeral, R. Nahman was very worried about the fact that he was unable to see anything. And when he came back from the graveyard he beheld great wonders."[127] It seems that R. Nahman had expected to see the great turmoil being caused in the Upper Worlds as a result of the final ascent of the Besht's soul to take up permanent residence there.[128] Besides recognizing the Besht's greatness, the story gives expression to R. Nahman's self-image as someone with the power to "see" the goings-on in the Upper Worlds.

R. Nahman's attitude toward the Besht and his self-image are also reflected in the following tale:

I heard from the rabbi of our community, that when R. Nahman
wanted to travel a second time to the Holy Land he went with R. Yosef
of Kaminka to visit the tomb of the Besht. . . . And when he returned
from the graveyard he rejoiced with a great rejoicing and said: The
Besht has instructed me to travel to the Holy Land. R. Yosef was
greatly perplexed and said: Where did he speak with you? R. Nahman
was perplexed in return: Didn't you see him speaking with me and
standing by my side?![129]

The voyage to the land of Israel mentioned here took place in the summer of
1764. Actually, R. Nahman was one of several Hasidim to emigrate at that time
to the land of Israel.[130] R. Nahman's companions for the voyage also included
another of the Besht's associates: R. Menahem Mendel of Peremyshlyan.

The sources available to us portray R. Menahem Mendel as being not only
a Hasid but also a charismatic figure, able to fascinate students and believers.
We learn about several of R. Menahem's Hasidic attributes from *Shivhei
Habesht*. Thus, for example, it is told that before making his way to the land
of Israel he went to take his leave from R. Yaakov Yosef of Polonne, and stayed
as a guest in his home for several days. R. Yaakov Yosef observed the custom
of passing in front of the ark during prayers with the *minyan* he held in his
home. R. Menahem Mendel asked permission to pass in front of the ark, and
R. Yaakov Yosef relinquished his rights in honor of the guest. In explaining this
gesture, which apparently was an exceptional event, R. Yaakov Yosef extensively praised the prayer of R. Menahem Mendel.[131]

Another of R. Menahem Mendel's pious measures was that of keeping
speech to a minimum. The compiler of *Shivhei Habesht* is able to tell that R.
Menahem held strictly to this habit for a dozen years. He preferred to reply in
writing to those who addressed him, "and when he did speak, would hold back
his expression and collect himself before letting the words leave his mouth."
The compiler of *Shivhei Habesht* is also able to tell of R. Menahem Mendel's
humility. During the same visit at the home of R. Yaakov Yosef, R. Menahem
Mendel complained to his host about the excessive honors he was being
shown. He was referring to how the people in the communities through which
he passed came out to greet him. R. Yaakov Yosef's reply to him was that "the
Besht always used to pray that people would speak ill of him. R. Mendel said
he had thought of the same counsel."[132]

Some further fragments of information about R. Menahem Mendel are
contained in the testimony of a relative of his, who resided in his home for an
extended period.[133] This report suggests that R. Menahem Mendel "would
remain awake all night long, engaged in study. Before dawn he would go to
the *mikvah,* and at first light he would pray the morning service with the

early-risers' *minyan.*" Of special interest to us is what the relative of R. Menahem Mendel tells of his manner of prayer: "He grew very angry at people who
clapped their hands while praying, and except for the sharp bowings moved
not at all during the *shmoneh esreh* prayer but would stand there as if lifeless."
Apparently, R. Menahem Mendel did not approve of hallmarks of ecstatic
prayer. How are we to understand R. Menahem Mendel's anger at those who
tended to clap their hands and move to and fro while praying? Does this mean
he had reservations about the Besht's mode of prayer? Or perhaps R. Menahem Mendel was angered by those who behaved in this way because he suspected them of arrogance in their superficial imitations of the Besht? We have
no way of knowing. At any rate, it is clear that R. Menahem Mendel followed
his own path in this regard, a way quite different from that of the Besht.

Menahem Mendel's family member also speaks of his motives in emigrating to the land of Israel: "He traveled to the Holy Land because people had
begun to journey to see him to deal with affairs." It appears that as a result of
the reputation he had begun to acquire as a Hasid and holy man, supplicants
of various sorts began to turn to him, believing him to be a miracle worker.[134]
Yet R. Menahem Mendel was unwilling to apply himself to this profession,
either because he did not see himself as qualified for it or because the occupation was not to his liking. His voyage to the land of Israel was thus meant as a
means of freeing himself of the expectations of these supplicants and of the
pressures they placed on him. This explanation, of course, in no way gainsays
any positive motives R. Menahem Mendel may have had for emigrating to the
Holy Land. As we have noted, emigration to the land of Israel was then considered to be an act of Hasidism.[135]

When was the bond between R. Menahem Mendel and the Besht formed?
It is almost certain that this occurred in the Besht's final years. This inference follows from the fact that the gap in their ages was about thirty years.[136]
It would thus seem that R. Menahem Mendel affiliated himself with the
Besht when he was in his late twenties or early thirties. The sole extant testimony about R. Menahem Mendel's visit to the home of the Besht also dates
to this period.[137]

The compiler of *Shivhei Habesht* is unable to tell us how R. Menahem
Mendel's came to affiliate himself with the Besht, nor do we have any declarations from R. Mendel himself about his debts to the Besht. Nevertheless, R.
Mendel's association with the Besht can be discerned in what R. Mendel attributes to him in his book *Hanhagot Yesharot.* To this is joined also the testimony
provided by R. Meshulam Feibush, the author of *Yosher Divrei Emmet.* R.
Meshulam lists the three figures whose influence he received on matters of
divine worship. The three are the *maggid* of Mezerich, R. Menahem Mendel of

Peremyshlyan, and R. Yehiel Michal of Zloczow. Among other things, he describes these figures as "the learned of the age, miracle men, possessed of the Holy Spirit . . . all [of whom] drank from the same fountain, it being the divine Rabbi Israel Baal Shem Tov of blessed and righteous memory."[138] Apparently, in the years preceding his emigration to the land of Israel—that is, in the early 1760s—R. Menahem Mendel's reputation as a person of spiritual quality had begun to spread, and those seeking guidance on Hasidic manners made efforts to seek his counsel. One such person was R. Meshulam Feibush. R. Meshulam Feibush, in turn, from what he heard of him, was able to describe his teacher R. Menahem Mendel as someone who had drunk at the fountain of the Besht.

R. YEHIEL OF ZLOCZOW AND R. PINCHAS OF KORETZ

Two other figures who were members of the Besht's circle were R. Yehiel Michal of Zloczow and R. Pinchas of Koretz. Alhough each of these figures is worthy of individual threatment, I prefer to discuss here the features they shared. Both R. Yehiel Michal and R. Pinchas came to Hasidism from a distinguished scholarly background; both affiliated themselves with the Besht when he was at a relatively advanced age; both were influenced by his path in divine worship and presented themselves as his disciples; both were destined to become charismatic leaders; and both, like the Besht, became miracle workers.

Of R. Yehiel Michal's association with the Besht one may learn from statements attributed to him in person:

> I heard this from the rabbi and Hasid R. Yehiel Michal of the holy community of Zloczow—who spoke here in the town of Lince when visiting for the wedding of the son of our Teacher Zeev—that he was commanded from the heavens to accept the Besht as his rabbi and to go to learn from him, and he was shown springs of wisdom which streamed toward him. And when the Besht passed away, he was commanded to accept the great *maggid* R. Dov as rabbi, and he was shown those very springs which had gone to the Besht now streaming to said Rabbi and *maggid*.[139]

These remarks, attributed to R. Yehiel Michal, are of course important for a discussion of how the *maggid* of Mezerich rose to a position of leadership. Yet for the purposes of my discussion it suffices that they give an indication of R. Yehiel Michal's association with the Besht. The vision of springs of wisdom flowing to the Besht, and later to the *maggid,* reflects R. Yehiel Michal's notion that these two figures were graced with divine inspiration. At the same time, R. Yehiel attests of himself that he was graced with guidance from the heavens and was able to "see" the goings-on in the Upper Worlds.

R. Yehiel Michal's statement of an association with the Besht is somewhat casual and doesn't specify exactly what it was that he learned from him. R. Pinchas of Koretz, by contrast, quite clearly specifies how he had been influenced by the Besht. According to traditions that originated in the circle of students of R. Pinchas, he was devoted to the way of asceticism and self-mortification. He was inspired to take this path by R. Yosef Karo's *Maggid Meisharim.* The Besht taught R. Pinchas that asceticism causes damage to one's divine worship. Below are two sayings attributed to R. Pinchas that reflect the transformation that took place in him in this regard: "From the day on which people began to go in the way of the Besht, many of the things that R. Yehuda Hehasid had warned about were nullified" and "One must eat and worship the Blessed Lord by eating."[140]

From the traditions preserved by the circle of students of R. Pinchas the picture that emerges is of a charismatic leader with an extremely high image of himself. Thus, for example, he told his students that when he was a guest in the home of the Besht on the Shavuot holiday prior to the demise of the Besht, he refrained from bathing in the *mikvah*. If he had bathed, he would have prevented the Besht's death. R. Pinchas even tended to accentuate his independence of the Besht. Among other things he instructed his students to put on *teffillin* on *hol hamoed,* and related that he had argued with the Besht on this point. However, side by side with the accentuation of his elevation and independence vis-à-vis the Besht, R. Pinchas often would tell his students of the marvels that the Besht performed.[141]

R. DAVID FURKES AND R. ZEEV KOTSES

R. David Furkes is described in *Shivhei Habesht* as the preacher of Miedzybóz. He was one of those who prayed in the same *Beit Midrash* as the Besht. One learns about the status of R. David in this *Beit Midrash* from the fact that he was among those who led the service on Yom Kippur. He took care not to eat meat unless he had seen and examined the *shekhita* knife in person, as was the Hasidic custom.

Certain stories indicate that R. David frequently stayed in close proximity to the Besht. From time to time he joined him in his travels out of town, accompanied him on his way to the bathhouse, was a regular guest in his home and took meals with him. On occasion he happened to be near the Besht when the latter was undergoing his unusual experiences. Naturally, R. David reported what he had seen to others. Thus, for example, he told that "one time the Besht prayed while on his travels by the eastern wall of a house and near the western wall there were barrels full of the harvest and people could see that the wheat was shaking."[142] Another event occurred near the time of the Besht's death. R. David went in to ask him a question. While the Besht was answering R. David noticed that his face was burning like a torch. The scene was so frightening that R. David tried to escape. Later the Besht explained what was going on: Elijah was standing to one side of him and his teacher, Ahia Hashiloni, on the other side.[143] It thus seems that the extended time spent near the Besht and the personal closeness between them is what made R. David the witness, narrator, and interpreter of the Besht's mystical experiences.[144]

Another Hasid who was a permanent resident of Miedzybóz and one of the Besht's associates was R. Zeev Kotses. The tales in *Shivhei Habesht* depict R. Zeev too as someone who is constantly by the Besht's side. The bond between them was familial as well: an orphan girl raised in the Besht's home married an orphan boy raised in the home of R. Zeev. One of the tales depicts R. Zeev as a scholar. The story runs as follows: The Besht accompanied Rabbi Yehiel Michal Margaliot to the town of Horodna, as the latter had been invited there to serve on the rabbinate. As was to the custom in those days, the new rabbi delivered a sermon in the synagogue. One of the townspeople tried to heckle the preacher by raising arguments and asking tough questions. R. Zeev Kotses, who came along with the Besht on that trip, interrupted and answered the questions. It is to be noted that in this tale, as in others, the Besht does not profess to be a scholar. When scholarship is needed he avails himself of others. This particular time it was R. Zeev who defended the honor of the Besht's preferred rabbi.[145]

Yet the main function assigned to R. Zeev, as a Hasid closely affiliated with the Besht and an intimate acquaintance of his, was to serve as a sort of broker between the Besht and the congregants of the *Beit Midrash*. A typical illustration appears in the following tale (discussed above in another context): Once, the Besht was supposed to lead the prayers for the Hallel service. As the congregation waited for him, a trembling overtook the Besht and he was unable to approach the prayer platform. R. Zeev stepped into action: "there then came the Hasid Rabbi Zeev Kotses who glanced at his face, which was burning like a torch, and his eyes were bulged open and motionless like someone in death throes heaven forbid. And this R. Zeev hinted to Rabbi Avraham, and they each took him by the arm and walked him to the platform."[146]

A further example is provided by the story of the Besht's ascent of the soul, which occurred as he was passing in front of the ark during the Neilah service of Yom Kippur. In the course of the prayer the Besht began to make vigorous movements to and fro. The congregants in the *Beit Midrash* worried that he was going to fall over and wanted to support him. Yet they were afraid to touch him, as he was in the middle of an ecstatic event. Again R. Zeev is called into action: "And they told R. Zeev Kotses of blessed memory and he came and looked at his face and indicated that he was not to be touched."[147] The common denominator in these two instances is the consternation the congregants in the *Beit Midrash* suffer as the Besht, who is standing right there among them, sinks into an ecstatic trance. R. Zeev Kotses is thus recognized as one who is qualified to guide the public how to act in cases like these.[148] One may perhaps add that the special bond between R. Zeev and the Besht, as the residents of Miedzybóz saw it, was also reflected in the fact that his burial plot was located alongside the Besht's.

The Form and Nature of the Besht's Circle

Thus far I have been delineating the figures of a few persons who were affiliated with the Besht and have been seeking to inquire about the kind of relationships they formed with him. The question that is now in order is, What can be learned from these clarifications about the form and character of the Besht's circle as a whole?

It seems to me that the first assertion to be made is that even though these people were practically all Hasidim of the old type, they did not join together to form a Hasidic fraternity, either of the sort that had existed in Safed in the sixteenth century or of the sort found in Brod or in Kotov in the eighteenth century. Simply stated: these people lived in different geographic areas, often at a considerable distance from each other. Moreover, their contact with the Besht did not entirely overlap even chronologically. Some had their affiliation with him confined to the 1730s, the period when the Besht lived in or around Kotov. Such was the case for example, with R. Moshe of Kotov and R. Nahman of Kosov.[149]

As was mentioned, both R. Gershon of Kotov and the Polonne *mokhiah* affiliated themselves with the Besht during this period. Yet the relationships these two had with the Besht lasted for many years, in effect up until the Besht's death. By contrast, several of the Besht's associates became affiliated with him only in the forties, after he had settled in Miedzybóz; prominent of these was R. Yaakov Yosef of Polonne. Others became affiliated with him only in his final years. These included, evidently, the *maggid* of Mezerich and R. Menahem Mendel of Peremyshlyan.

Not only did the Besht's associates reside in different places, affiliate themselves with him in different periods of his life, and maintain ties with him for different periods of time; they differed from each other in the nature of their connections to him. Some of them stayed close by his side, while others were linked to him more loosely. Some of them kept their spiritual autonomy and maintained a friendship on a more equal basis, while others recognized his eminence and treated him as their rabbi and teacher. In sum, there was a decided difference between the circle of the Besht's associates and Hasidic fraternities, whose members lived together in one place, met regularly in a certain location for study and prayers, and were formed around the personality of the charismatic leader.

Having asserted that the Besht's circle did not take the form of a Hasidic fraternity or commune of the types mentioned earlier, is there still reason for using the term, "the Besht's circle"? Perhaps the "circle" never existed and is nothing more than an invention of scholars and writers? I believe that the concept of the Besht's circle is both justified and practical. It is justified because it indeed represents a historical reality; it is practical because it helps us to understand the influence the Besht had on his contemporaries and on people of subsequent generations. However, in order to make productive use of the term, it is crucial that I accurately define it.

The Besht's circle may be described as a relatively wide ring that had several subsidiary rings within it. The widest ring, that which forms the outer boundary of the circle, is drawn based on the combination of two criteria: persons who could be classed as Hasidim of the old type and persons who were intimate with the Besht to one degree or another. The combination of these two criteria is called for given the function that the circle served in the life of the Besht. The circle was meant to function as the framework and setting for the emergence and establishment of the Besht's reputation as a miracle worker and original mystic, one who is paving a new path in divine worship. To this end, what was first of all required was Hasidim of the old type; that is, people who had a spiritual background in common with the Besht. Only people of this kind could recognize the Besht's singularity as a mystic and the innovative nature of his path in divine worship. Furthermore, it was essential that these people come to know the Besht in person and spend some time with or near him, for the Besht's spiritual message was conveyed primarily by the inspiration of his personality and experiences. These qualities could be clearly appreciated only by those who were in direct contact with him. In addition, the fact that certain members of the circle acknowledged the Besht's unusual powers was important in the establishment of his status as a miracle worker.

I turn now to a more detailed specification of the functions the circle played on behalf of the Besht. The circle was meant

1. to serve as the audience before which the Besht could expose his magical powers and achievements as a mystic, to tell of his experiences, to interpret them and draw conclusions that were relevant also to others;

2. to recognize the Besht's unusual qualities and powers and make the public aware of them;

3. to accept the Besht as a rabbi and master and to adopt various elements of his path in divine worship;

4. to publicize and promote the Besht's path in divine worship.

I have listed the various functions in ascending order in terms of the commitments they contain toward the Besht's personality and path. One may therefore say that the various people whom the Besht's circle comprised were distinguished from each other by the scope of functions they filled, and perforce also by the depth of their commitment toward the Besht and his path.

What was the nature of the group that the Besht himself designated as "*hahavura sheli*" (my fraternity)? Given the conception I have advanced here, one should regard the *havura* as one ring among the several that made up the circle. In a certain sense this was the innermost ring. What made this ring more special than the others?

As said, it was the Besht himself who employed the term "my *havura*." He noted this in one of the letters to his brother-in-law, in which he told of the ascent of the soul that he had experienced on Rosh Hashanah of 1749. In the course of his travels in the Upper Worlds the Besht discovered that a severe plague was about to break out in various regions of Poland. Later in the letter he tells how he prepared to act so as to prevent the spread of the plague: "I arranged with my fraternity to have *ktoret* recited at dawn prayers so as to nullify the said edicts."[150] It appears then that the recital of the *ktoret* during the morning prayer service, which the Besht and the members of his fraternity used to hold at dawn, was supposed to halt the spread of the plague. The function assigned to the members of the *havura* was thus to assist the Besht in carrying out ritual activities having a theurgic significance. The conclusion necessarily follows that the people concerned are those who permanently reside near the Besht and pray with him in the same *minyan*. Otherwise, how could he have made use of them in times of emergency?

Another designation the Besht used with regard to the members of his *havura* was *anshei segula* (virtuous men, or men of quality). This term is used in the first letter he sent to his brother-in-law and it appears in the context of the conversation he held with the Messiah. To the Besht's question, "When will sir be coming?" the Messiah's reply, it will be recalled, was that he was destined to come when numerous people knew of the unifications that the Besht had been taught and could perform ascents of the soul just as he could. This response disappointed the Besht, for it was unreasonable to expect the multitude to attain so elevated a rank. In seeking to overcome this obstacle the Besht conceived of the following plan:

> But of what I heard, three things and three Holy Names should be easy to learn and explain, and I calmed down and thought it might be possible by this means for Men of Virtue to come to the level and rank that I have, that is, would be able to have their souls ascend to the skies and learn and achieve just as I do, and I was not given permission all my life long to reveal this and I asked this on your behalf to teach you and they did not permit it at all.[151]

The "men of virtue" mentioned here are evidently the members of the *havura*. It seemed that in this case too the Besht assigned to them a task of a theurgic nature. What is also suggested here is that among these "men of virtue" R. Gershon was especially close to the Besht. The designation of the members of the fraternity as "men of virtue" also appears several times in *Shivhei Habesht*. However, before looking at these instances, let us examine an external source that refers to the Besht's fraternity: a Halachic responsum that R. Meir, the rabbi of Konstantin, sent to the Besht. The responsum addresses itself to the question regarding *shekhita* that was raised in Miedzybóz and sent on to R. Meir. In the opening of the responsum R. Meir wrote the following:

> To the Champion of Judah and Israel, who labors mightily for great and small, the pioneer of remedy and relief, he is none other than the prodigal rabbi, famed for his good name, Israel, may God preserve and save him; and to his colleagues, rabbis, beloved all—including the prodigal Rabbi Gershon, may God preserve and save him, and the others whose name I know not: my blessings to you all.[152]

R. Meir of Konstantin may not use the term *havura*, but it is clear he is referring to a select group of high-ranking individuals associated with the Besht. From the phraseology it appears that these are people who are routinely found in proximity of the Besht. Still, it seems that R. Meir did not know the members of the fraternity, with the exception of R. Gershon of Kotov who is mentioned by name. The date of this responsum can be established as being the first years of the Besht's residence in Miedzybóz.[153] It thus would seem that during this period the Besht was thought of by R. Meir of Konstantin as a famous *baal shem*, around whom a fraternity of Hasidim had gathered. It is nearly certain that the mere fact the fraternity was mentioned was meant to glorify and elevate the Besht.

The term "men of virtue" or "his men of virtue" appears, as said, several times in *Shivhei Habesht*. In places *Shivhei Habesht*'s compiler uses the term "his people," and it appears that this is how he translated the Yiddish term "seine menschen." As to the phrase "men of virtue," it seems that the compiler chose it in consequence of the Besht's usage in his letter to his brother-in-law. A further designation that *Shivhei Habesht*'s compiler uses in relation to the fraternity is *bnei gilo* (roughly, "colleagues"). Here too he seems to be following the lead of the Besht's Epistle. At any rate, from the various tales in which these terms appear it seems that they refer to a restricted group of people who were in close proximity to the Besht. Let us cite several examples: "On *Simhat Torah* the Besht's men of virtue were celebrating and dancing and drinking wine from the Besht's cellar." When R. Yaakov Yosef was chased out of the town where he served as rabbi and was forced to spend the Sabbath in a nearby village, the Besht "said to his men of virtue: let us travel to this village, for I know he is greatly suffering and we shall spend the Sabbath with the rabbi of the holy community of Shargorod." When the Besht failed in his efforts to nullify the blood-libel in Pavlysh—that is, when it turned out that the convicts were executed despite the Besht's prophecy that they were destined to be rescued—the Besht responded with great weeping and bitterness "to the point that his men of virtue could not raise their heads." When the Besht was suffering miserably "his colleagues [*bnei gilo*] thought he was suffering because his wife had died." Likewise we find the Besht sitting "at a meal with his men." On the morning of the day on which the Besht died, "he sent for his men of virtue to all be assembled," and instructed them how to handle his burial.[154]

Who were the people who made up the *havura?* In light of our assumption that the *havura* comprised, in the main, Hasidim who permanently resided in Miedzybóz, it is likely that R. Gershon of Kotov was the foremost member of this fraternity. This pertains, of course, to the years during which R. Gershon lived in the Besht's home, before he emigrated to the land of Israel. Two additional persons who belonged to the *havura* from among the residents of Miedzybóz were R. David Furkes and R. Zeev Kotses. It will be recalled that these two persons are mentioned in *Shivhei Habesht* as Hasidim who lived in Miedzybóz and had reservations about the Besht upon his arrival in town.[155] Above we suggested that this story reflected the need of the Besht to earn the recognition of these Hasidim who lived in Miedzybóz. Now the significance of this recognition becomes clearer: R. David Furkes and R. Zeev Kotses were meant to accept the Besht as the leading figure among the Hasidic fraternity living in town. It is worth recalling that according to the archival material discovered by Rosman, these two Hasidim received a regular stipend from the public coffers, along with a small group of residents of Miedzybóz. Rosman has suggested that this stipend be seen as an expression of the fact that they belonged to the fraternity of Hasidim of Miedzybóz led by the Besht, a fraternity that won the recognition and support of the community.[156]

I seek here to define the *havura* as distinct from the "circle." What made the *havura* special was that its members lived near to the Besht; therefore contact with him was frequent and immediate. In consequence they were also witnesses to the Besht's unusual experiences and could tell of them to others. In this regard the members of the *havura* may not have been essentially different from any other members of the circle; given their proximity to the Besht, however, they had more opportunities to form impressions of his personality and experiences and to share their impressions with others.

Several roles stand out as being special to members of the *havura*. First, they were the regular participants in the Besht's *minyan*. In effect, they formed the human environment and the spiritual atmosphere that the Besht required in order to pray in his special manner. Second, in times of emergency the Besht could call on their aid for activities of a theurgic nature. It is thus unsurprising that when R. Gershon of Kotov listed the factors that kept the Besht from emigrating to the land of Israel he wrote: "I know it is your nature that you have to pray in your *minyan*."[157]

Moreover, as the Besht's constant companions, who were identified with him and seen as subject to him, they filled important functions: in confirming his self-image and in forming his public image. From this point of view it is important to stress that if one or another of those who made up the circle's outer rings may have enjoyed a spiritual independence vis-à-vis the Besht, within the "*havura*" everyone recognized his authority. In all likelihood the Besht himself considered this fact to be of some importance. A picturesque expression of this may be found in the following anecdote: "The story is told that the Besht, rest in peace, said to R. Wolf Kotses: Nothing separates you from me but the thread of a hair, but through that thread of a hair you shall never pass."[158]

At the beginning of this chapter I advanced the claim that the Besht's circle was unlike the Hasidic fraternities that had flourished in Safed in the sixteenth century or like those found in Brod or Kotov in the eighteenth century. This assertion was based on the reasoning that the people concerned did not live in geographical proximity to each other nor did they regularly meet with each other in a special place for purposes of prayer and study. The question that now arises is, Can one regard the Besht's *havura* as a Hasidic fraternity of the type we have discussed? At first it appears that this question is to be answered in the affirmative, as these people did reside permanently in a single location and tended to hold daily prayers in their own special *minyan*. Nevertheless, it seems to me that one must qualify the similarity between the Besht's fraternity in Miedzybóz and the Hasidic fraternities of the type discussed, for the Besht also maintained extensive and continuous contact with those of his associates who resided outside of Miedzybóz. Some of them would "travel" from time to time to see the Besht or to spend a Sabbath or holiday with him. The Besht himself would also pay visits to his associates in their hometowns. It thus would appear that the members of the *havura* who resided in Miedzybóz did not enjoy exclusivity in their contact with the Besht. Furthermore, given the frequent visits of certain of the members of the circle in Miedzybóz, it stands to reason that the border between them and the members of the *havura* would have been blurred.

At first sight, the Besht's fraternity might seem as though it were a typical Hasidic *havura,* given its existence in a particular location, namely, the *Beit Midrash* of Miedzybóz. Indeed, it is nearly certain that the Besht and the members of his fraternity held their special *minyan* inside this *Beit Midrash*.[159] However, even if the Miedzybóz *Beit Midrash* was identified with the Besht and his fraternity, and even if they did use it for various purposes, this building did not function only as their special place. On the contrary, the various accounts in *Shivhei Habesht* that touch on the *Beit Midrash* in Miedzybóz suggest that it served as the zone of encounter both between the Besht and the members of his fraternity, and between them and the other people who prayed there—most of whom were not part of the fraternity.

Given the facts and considerations adduced here, it seems to me that one of the striking attributes of the Besht's circle was its very nongeographical character. It was the Besht's personality that lured people from various locations and unified them into a single social entity. It may therefore be said that through this style of leadership the Besht contributed to the formation of the Hasidic court, which was later destined to lure people to it from distant locations. Or perhaps it would be more accurate to say that the Besht presented a model of leadership that the Hasidic movement was destined to adopt.

Naturally enough, the picture presented here as regards the individuals whom the Besht's circle comprised is a partial and to some extent arbitrary one. The reason for this selectivity has to do with the nature of the sources available to us. The book *Shivhei Habesht,* from which I have drawn most of my information regarding the members of the circle, devotes considerable space to certain members, such as R. Yaakov Yosef and the Polonne *mokhiah,* and little to others, such as the *maggid* of Mezerich and R. Menahem Mendel of Peremyshlyan. One may argue that the space *Shivhei Habesht*'s compiler devotes to certain people is a reflection of their degree of closeness to the Besht. That may be true in certain cases. However, there is no doubt that there were additional factors that affected the space devoted to each of the various figures in this book. The first of these, so it would seem, is the degree of closeness that certain members of the circle had to the keepers of the traditions and to the tellers of tales who fed them to *Shivhei Habesht*'s compiler. In addition, for a certain person to be mentioned in *Shivhei Habesht,* he had to be either at the center of or a witness to a "tale"; that is, an event or saying that was of interest to the keepers of the traditions.

Accordingly, one cannot rule out the possibility that some persons who would have been included in the Besht's circle by the criteria suggested above, appear in *Shivhei Habesht* as marginal figures, or do not appear there at all.[160] As it happens, a document that gives a certain further dimension to the circle is the will of R. David Halpern of Zaslav.[161] R. David began service as rabbi of the Ostra community in 1736. In 1746 he left this post and moved to Zaslav, where he resided until his death in 1765. In the years during which R. David was a resident of Zaslav, a close relationship was formed between him and the Besht. Both by the nature of these ties and by his spiritual rank, R. David ought to be considered a member of the circle. R. David's bonds with the Besht and with persons associated with him would later be expressed in his testament, in which he bequeathed substantial sums of money to several members of the circle.

Here is the list of the Besht's associates as contained in the testament, arranged in order of appearance and with the amounts granted to each: R. Yehuda Leib the Polonne *mokhiah,* R. Dov Ber the *maggid* of Mezerich, R. Yehiel Michal of Zloczow and R. Pinchas of Koretz: one hundred and fifty zlotyes each. R. Zeev Kotses of Miedzybóz, 100 zlotyes. R. Menahem Mendel of Peremyshlyan, 200 zlotyes. R. Nahman of Horodenka, 150 zlotyes (the latter two are designated in the will as the "poor men of the Holy Land"). R. Zvi, the Besht's son, 100 zlotyes.

What is the significance of this list? What criteria did R. David apply when choosing which associates of the Besht to bequeath his money to? What is the meaning of the differences in the amounts assigned to different individuals? I have no way of offering definitive answers to these questions. Nevertheless, it stands to reason that of all the Besht's associates, R. David believed that these were the most important. Another look at the list of people included in the will leads to the conclusion that they may be divided into two subgroups: those who were of particular importance because they had been especially close to the Besht and those who were considered eminent figures in their own right. The first group consists of R. Zeev Kotses and R. Zvi, the Besht's son. The second group consists of R. Yehuda Leib the Polonne *mokhiah,* R. Dov Ber the *maggid* of Mezerich, R. Yehiel Michal of Zolotschov, R. Pinchas of Koretz, R. Menahem Mendel of Peremyshlyan, and R. Nahman of Horodenka. In all likelihood it was no coincidence that the second group is comprised of charismatic figures, several of whom also displayed talents for leadership. As

R. David passed away in 1765 (that is, five years after the death of the Besht), it is not impossible that the will reflects the standing these people had in the first half of the 1760s, when a few of them had begun to lead Hasidic circles as a means of carrying on the Besht's way. In any case, R. David of Zaslav's will gives us an additional means of considering the Besht's circle. It appears that to R. David, and presumably to others as well, the members of the circle who were its dominant figures were not necessarily the ones who lived by the side of the Besht. This gives further support to my assertion about the nongeographical character of the circle.

The Besht's circle differed, as said, from the Hasidic fraternities whose attributes were sketched out in the first section of this chapter. Now another claim is in order: this circle was also unlike the Hasidic court that was to take form in the 1760s and 1770s. True, certain members of the circle, those who were not residents of Miedzybóz, tended to travel from time to time to visit the Besht and spent a Sabbath or holiday in his home. The home of the Besht also served at times as a meeting place for members of the circle who were permanent residents of Miedzybóz. Unlike the later Hasidic court, however, the Besht's home never became a fixed destination for pilgrimage. Not only were the visits in the Besht's home random in nature and lacking in the hallmarks of institutionalization; the Besht himself often took the initiative and, as mentioned, would pay visits to the members of his circle who lived in other towns.[162]

How may one characterize the internal relations that existed within the Besht's circle? It would appear that the fraternity in question had a feeble organizational structure and spontaneous and informal internal relations. The feeble structure of the circle was reflected in, among other things, the fact that the emigration of individuals within it to the land of Israel at various times did not cause any sort of breach of the framework. The informal nature of the circle is also noticeable in the relations between the Besht and various individuals, even those who accepted his authority and regarded him as their rabbi and teacher. Thus, for example, the letters exchanged by the Besht and R. Gershon of Kotov reflect an atmosphere of relaxed intimacy and do not contain the slightest trace of reserve. Relations within the circle were also characterized by a sense of brotherhood and mutual assistance. The clearest illustration of this was how the Besht traveled with several members of the fraternity to the village in which R. Yaakov Yosef was forced to spend the Sabbath when chased from Shargorod. So furious was the Besht at the people of Shargorod for having hurt R. Yaakov Yosef that he refused ever to spend the Sabbath in that community.[163] The feeling of partnership and fraternity among members of the circle were displayed also in the visits to each other, both during the Besht's lifetime and after his death. An example of this are the departure visits that

R. Nahman of Horodenka and R. Menahem Mendel of Peremyshlyan paid to their friends when they were about to set out to the land of Israel.

What attributes did members of the circle have in common? What bound them to each other, in the absence of a particular location, regular meetings, a common order of study, and the other such attributes typical of the Hasidic fraternities? What did the members of the circle speak about when they met one another? The answers to these questions are to be found in this and previous chapters. We have seen the Besht telling his associates of the ascent of the soul he experienced and of the other revelations he was graced with, guiding R. Gershon of Kotov about *kavvanot* in prayer, warning R. Yaakov Yosef not to fast, praising the prayers of R. Nahman of Kosov, and revealing secrets to the *maggid* of Mezerich. In fact, many of the sermons that R. Yaakov Yosef cites in the name of the Besht are expressions of the latter's personal experiences and display his aspiration to have the morals of these experiences be conveyed to his associates. We have seen that many such sermons deal with the striving for *dvekut* and the means of attaining it. There are solid grounds for supposing that the setting for these sermons were the private conversations held by the Besht with the members of his circle.

We have seen the Besht's associates speaking of the unusual incidents that occurred to the Besht and supplying interpretations to them. They would also tell each other what they had learned from the Besht. Among other things, they would discuss the quality of prayer, the elevation of straying thoughts, and so forth.[164] In sum, the figure of the Besht, his powers, experiences, and manner of divine worship are what formed the core of the discourse of the members of the circle.

Of course, the Besht's circle is not to be thought of as identical with the movement of Hasidism, as Hasidism did not really become a movement until the 1760s and 1770s; that is, the two decades after the Besht's death. Given the findings of this chapter, however, I may assert that the Besht's circle played a decisive role in all that concerns the establishment of the Besht's reputation as a worker of miracles and a mystic of the highest rank, and as someone who paved a new path in divine worship. Moreover, certain members of the circle later were to turn the Besht's mode of divine worship and the wonder of his figure into the core of their activities as leaders of Hasidic fraternities. In light of all of this, one may assert that the Besht's circle served as the seed from which the Hasidic movement was destined to grow.

CHAPTER SIX

The Historicity of *Shivhei Habesht*

D o the sources available to us provide an adequate basis for forming a historical reconstruction of the Besht? This question has preoccupied scholars of Hasidism since the time of Shimon Dubnow and continues through the present. The Besht himself did not leave us writings that could have shed light on his upbringing, education, or the phases of his life. Nor were his teachings written out by himself; these have come down to us through writings of his students. Now, in addition to the difficulty produced by the scarcity of reliable and detailed texts, of the sort we would have hoped to find for a historical figure of the rank of the Besht, there is the further problem of the peculiarity of one of the sources we do have at our disposal. I refer to the collection of stories known by the name *Shivhei Habesht* (Praises of the Besht).[1]

Shivhei Habesht, a book first published in Kapost in 1814, contains some two hundred and fifty tales about the Besht and his associates. Its author, R. Dov Ber, the *shochet* of Lince, heard the stories from various persons, wrote them down in Hebrew, and placed them in the order he saw fit. It is nearly certain that he completed this project of his in the second half of the 1790s. More than fifteen years passed before R. Israel Yaffe, the "printer" (that is, the editor and publisher) brought the book to press.

Given the paucity of sources about the Besht, it is needless to remark that scholars of Hasidism have repeatedly asked themselves, Can one learn, and what can one learn, about the Besht and his associates from the stories in *Shivhei Habesht?* This question arises against the background of concerns and considerations that have cast serious doubts on the usefulness of the book as a historical source. Several such concerns are the following:

1. The *legendary* aspect of the book is quite conspicuous and frequently manifested in the stories that center around miracles and marvels.

2. The legendary aspect of the book is likewise discernible in its motifs, many of which are familiar to us from earlier literary sources.

3. In its content and aims, the literary genre to which the book belongs is the *hagiography;* that is, literature that describes the

life of the holy person through idealizations, out of hopes that the holy figure will serve as a model and object of emulation for readers.

4. A gap of some fifty-five years separates the death of the Besht from the date of *Shivhei Habesh*'s first publication. During this entire period, the stories shifted from person to person in oral form, before they were finally written down, edited and printed. There are grounds for suspecting that the stories as we have them today reflect a conception of the Besht fashioned by later generations more than they supply evidence about the Besht as a historical figure.

It is, accordingly, unsurprising, given these and similar considerations, that some scholars have reached the conclusion that *Shivhei Habesht* is utterly unreliable as a source and that anyone seeking to learn about the Besht as a historical figure can gain nothing from it. In practice, however, few people have behaved as though this were the case. Most scholars of Hasidism have attempted—each in his way—to separate the legendary aspects of the stories from the implicit historical elements, sifting out reliable data from the tales about the Besht and his associates. Indeed, if we survey the evolution of scholarship on this topic, we can discern a process that is largely one of an increasing recognition of the historical value of *Shivhei Habesht*.

Owing to the significance of this topic, I review here several of the more prominent stages in this process. Alongside the delineation of the stance of each scholar on the historicity of *Shivhei Habesht*, attention will be paid to the way in which the figure of the Besht is portrayed by that particular scholar. This review will permit us to form an opinion of the relation between these two issues. In addition, the survey of the scholarship on *Shivhei Habesht* will serve as a point of departure for a presentation of my own views on the subject.

Stages in the Acknowledgment of the Historicity of *Shivhei Habesht*

Of the various factors that have kept scholars from relying upon *Shivhei Habesht*, most significant has been their rejection of the element of the miraculous in the book. By this I mean the wondrous performances that the tales ascribe to the Besht, both those directly linked to his work as a *baal shem* and those that exceeded the regular bounds of this occupation. The rejection of the element of the miraculous was especially notable among the first scholars to engage in the scholarship of Hasidism. There was one simple reason for this:

scholars of Hasidism in the late nineteenth and early twentieth centuries, like everyone else engaged in the study of Jewish history in those days, were closely associated with the rationalist cultural heritage of the Haskalah movement. And the Haskalah movement was famous for its abhorrence of supernatural phenomena in general and of magic in particular.[2]

It thus comes as no surprise that scholars who have had trouble acknowledging the credibility of *Shivhei Habesht*, given its magical and miraculous ingredients, were also made uncomfortable by the Besht's having been a *baal shem*. Anyone seeking a clear illustration of the discomfort with *Shivhei Habesht*'s miraculous elements should look to Shimon Dubnow. Here is how Dubnow opened his discussion of the Besht:

> Out of the mists there appears to us the historic form of the founder
> of Hasidism; out of mists of the wondrous tales with which popular
> legend had wreathed its favorite hero. A dense mask, spun by the fan-
> cies of his contemporaries and his successors, conceals from our eyes
> the true picture of the Besht, until at times it seems to us as if this per-
> son had never existed but was entirely a figure of legend.[3]

Dubnow hastens to explain to the reader that he himself is not prone to so radical a conclusion: not only did the Besht's friends and students attest to his existence, but so, too, did his opponents. Furthermore, even in the "legendary biography" of the Besht (i.e., in *Shivhei Habesht*), one can, in his opinion, discern "the portrait of a living man who is affected by his environment and affects it," if only one examines it with a "critical eye." Yet this qualification does not alter Dubnow's basic appraisal of *Shivhei Habesht*, as being "legendary biography." And here is how Dubnow explains the possible origination of biography of this kind:

> Fifty-five years after the day the Besht died, there appeared in print a
> book which relates the story of his life in legendary form . . . just as
> the first evangelicals were published two generations after the death
> of the Christian Jesus. The sequence in which legendary biography is
> created is the same for the two periods, although seventeen centuries
> divide them. Over dozens of years, marvelous tales about the child of
> Podolia spread steadily among the people, just as had happened for
> the child of the Galilee in his day; each and every story as it left the
> mouth of the first teller was not that far removed from reality, but in
> the course of being transmitted from person to person by the faithful
> and impassioned public, it grew entangled by embellishments and
> exaggerations. Later, redactors came and set down the tales in writ-
> ing in various forms, and story-pamphlets spread among the com-
> munities of believers as "sacred writings."[4]

We find that what has transformed stories not far removed from reality into the "dense mask" of legend is a combination of two factors: first, the fifty-five years during which the stories shifted about from person to person before being written down, edited, and printed; and second, the "embellishments and exaggerations" that accrued to them in the course of their oral and written migrations. These "embellishments and exaggerations" are the wonders and miracles that the tales ascribe to the Besht and to some of his associates. And as, within Dubnow's view of the world, there can be no truth to any of these, it follows that the "marvels" imputed to the Besht can only be products of the fancy of the "passionate faithful," and that these merely proliferated with the passage of time.

With this perspective as his point of departure, Dubnow stated the principle that is to guide the scholar who seeks to make use of *Shivhei Habesht:* he must "extract the seed from the garbage of legend."[5] And by what criterion is one to distinguish "seed" from "garbage"? This comes out most clearly in the pages in which Dubnow sketches the Besht's biography. It is the simple distinction between the element of the supernatural—which is deemed "garbage"—and everything that does not offend rationalist sensibility. Given such a criterion, the use to which Dubnow puts *Shivhei Habesht* is quite limited. It is largely confined to an effort to extract certain details regarding the Besht's biography. To that end, he peels off the coat of the "legendary" that enshrouds the tales and discovers in them certain particulars about the Besht's date of birth, the various means by which he earned his living before he became a *baal shem,* and so forth.[6]

And how did he approach those tales in *Shivhei Habesht* that express the element of the magical in the figure of the Besht? How did Dubnow conceive of the relation between the fact of the Besht's being *baal shem* and his role as the founder of Hasidism? To this question Dubnow had a clear response: as a rule, *baalei shem* were people who deceived the ignorant masses for their own pecuniary gain. The exception to this rule were those *baalei shem* who tried to win over their public to some idea and plied their trade as a means of promoting their doctrines. The Besht was one of these: "R. Israel Baal Shem first earned an income from this trade out of poverty, but once he felt a need to share the doctrine of Hasidism with the broad public, he realized that his fame as a "miracle man" was precisely what would let him incline the masses to accept his teaching."[7] We find that Dubnow was prepared, to a certain extent, to clear the Besht of the stain of magic thanks to the honest use to which he put it. While the Besht's practice as a *baal shem* and the Hasidic doctrine he sought to promote are two different, even entirely unrelated matters, one must still forgive the former because it functioned as a means to the latter.

Not everyone was prepared to adopt Dubnow's perspective about the historical nucleus to be found in the tales of *Shivhei Habesht*. One scholar who gave an incisive and explicit expression of the opposite view was Yitzhak Schiffer.[8] Schiffer's discussion took as its starting point the well-known distinction that Ahad Haam had made between the "historical person" of Moses and his "archeological" person. By this is meant the distinction between the image of Moses formed in the course of the ages and the person as he actually was.[9] Schiffer agreed with Dubnow that the legendary figure of the Besht indeed played a role in the history of Hasidism. Yet this legendary figure was entirely ungrounded "archeologically"; that is, it had no basis in historical reality. The person who in fact ought to be considered the founder of Hasidism is none other than R. Yoel Baal Shem;[10] the legend about the Besht as founder of Hasidism was only an invention of Rabbi Yaakov Yosef of Polonne, a student of the Besht. Schiffer's denial of a role for the "archeological" (the actual) Besht in the history of Hasidism is closely linked to his perspective on the question of the historicity of *Shivhei Habesht*. Here is what he says:

> If, however, we seek to state the "archeological" truth regarding the Besht, we must completely subtract from the investigation the book *Shivhei Habesht,* which is a sort of "history of holy persons" and is as ripe with exaggerations as a pomegranate. All those "historical seeds" which people try to sift from it, are so fogged in and clouded by rhetoric to the point where the majority are of no interest to the investigator who seeks to expose the true portrait of the historical Besht.[11]

As said, this stance, though not the only one of its kind, did not become the main route taken in Hasidism scholarship.[12] To the contrary, the dominant trend in the development of the scholarship has been the opposite. An important illustration of this point may be seen in the chapter of Israel Zinberg's book devoted to the Besht.[13]

Zinberg opens his discussion of the Besht with statements resembling those with which Dubnow began. Like Dubnow, Zinberg asserts that the figure of the Besht "peers at us . . . out of the mist of tales of marvels." Indeed, Zinberg did share Dubnow's attitude toward the legendary and fanciful elements in *Shivhei Habesht*. He too was of the opinion that magic was a debased social and cultural phenomenon, a species of superstition.[14] Zinberg's remarks, however, represent the beginnings of the new trend, both as regards the evaluation of the figure of the Besht and as regards the assessment of what can be learned about it from *Shivhei Habesht*. Here is what he says:

> On the threshold of a new era, in the second half of the eighteenth century, in the "generation of science and enlightenment," when

sound common sense was declared the only reliable authority on man's entangled paths, the great miracle took place: a human life, the life of a simple Jew, was transformed into an imaginative legend, an *aggadah* of ancient times. So enormous was the impression made on his milieu by this itinerant village teacher and exorcist. And through this fantastic, often naively superstitious specter clearly shines a real form, remarkably beautiful in its harmonious integrity and glorious simplicity.[15]

We find that the mythological figure of the Besht is not only the product of the imaginations of fervid Hasidim, as Dubnow had maintained, but was first of all an effect of the deep impression the Besht had made on his contemporaries. And as this was the case, it is unsurprising that from beneath the shroud of legend that cloaks *Shivhei Habesht* there "clearly shines a real form."

How did Zinberg come to discern this "realistic figure" in *Shivhei Habesht*? Like Dubnow, Zinberg also sifted the "realistic" seeds of the Besht's biography while discarding the rinds; that is, the supernatural elements of the various kinds. A further technique Zinberg employed, again like Dubnow, was elucidation of the Besht's biography through placement of it within the historical context known to us from other sources. Despite these lines of similarity, however, the figure of the Besht as drawn by Zinberg is infinitely vaster and richer than the faint image that appears from Dubnow's book. This difference arises, primarily, because of the historical question that Zinberg posed: "By what were all these men so carried away? How did this common *baal shem* and writer of amulets become the legendary hero of *Shivhei Ha-Besht*, the founder and teacher of a mighty popular movement?"[16]

The manner in which Zinberg formulates his question reflects the complexity of his stance: a negative opinion of the phenomenon of magic, on the one hand, and recognition of the immense historical role played by the Besht, on the other. Hence, the Besht's significance for Hasidism is not to be understood through his being a *baal shem*, but rather in spite of it. Indeed, Zinberg was able to find the reply to his query in the teachings of the Besht: the Besht's views about the "complete merging of divinity with the world," the denial of the existence of evil, the rejection of asceticism and self-mortification, the obligations to joyfulness, the tendency to be less strict rather than more—all of these represented a religious-spiritual innovation that held great appeal for the masses.

The materials that Zinberg draws upon for his précis of the Besht's doctrine are the tales attributed to the Besht in the writings of his students; and of course the Epistle he wrote to his brother-in-law. Yet in addition Zinberg returned to *Shivhei Habesht* and cited its stories. It appears that the principle that guided him in the choice of these stories was how well they corresponded to the learned sources concerning the Besht's teachings. In any event, Zinberg went considerably further than Dubnow in the use to which he put *Shivhei Habesht*. He did not content himself with merely extracting biographical details from it; rather, he sought and found stories that expressed, in his opinion, various aspects of the spiritual innovations the Besht spread among his contemporaries.[17]

To conclude my discussion of Zinberg, I cite his severe condemnation of the simplistic conceptions of the Besht, conceptions that in his opinion were characteristic of views of both Maskilim and "Mitnagdim":

> The battlers for Haskalah, or enlightenment, greatly oversimplified the question of the nature of the founder of the Hasidic movement. They concluded that here was an ignorant swindler who wished to mislead the common people. The arid scholars, the Mitnagdim, represented the Baal Shem Tov as a plain ignoramus, and in the heat of religious disputation even decleared him a "drunken and mad prophet." A modern historian of culture, no matter what his philosophy may be, realizes quite well how naïve and crude such a characterization of the Baal Shem Tov's personality is. We emphasize the word "personality," because the Baal Shem Tov was, above all, an important, profound personality who considered the phenomena of the universe from the standpoint of a world-consciousness, a personality who felt himself co-responsible for the fate of the whole world and had the unshakeable faith that, on the basis of this responsibility, he could give "correction" (*tikkun*) to the most tragic problems of the world.[18]

What these lines suggest is that at least one important aspect of the miraculous in the figure of the Besht—that is, the self-image as someone who could influence the goings-on in the universe—is here earning a certain appreciation. More broadly, one may say of the picture of the Besht presented by Zinberg that it reflects the tension between the rationalist stance, which rejects magic and its practitioners, and the romantic stance, which takes an approving view of the role the Besht played as a leader of a popular movement. Zinberg's overall statements, however, give the impression that recognition of the greatness of the Besht prevails and overcomes the essential rejection of the element of the magical in his figure. At any rate, Zinberg's discussion provides us with a good illustration of the relation between the positive appraisal of the Besht's personality and historical role, on the one hand, and the increasing recognition of *Shivhei Habesht*'s value as a historical source, on the other.

A landmark in the development of scholarship of the Besht came with Gershom Scholem's article, "The Historical Figure of R. Israel Baal Shem Tov."[19]

The question at the root of his article and at which its title hints is, Can one point to trustworthy sources on which to ground a historical reconstruction of the Besht? Scholem answered this question in the affirmative. To that end, he assembled all the existing, independent sources concerning the Besht that he knew of. Next he went to the Hasidic sources, *Shivhei Habesht* among them. The reliability of the tales from *Shivhei Habesht* were thus lent support by means of the parallels Scholem found in the external sources.[20] Scholem's view was that "the Hasidic tradition must be treated . . . with great caution, but that does not mean that everything is to be rejected." Along with finding analogies between the Hasidic traditions and the external sources, Scholem advocated examining the development of motifs within the Hasidic tradition itself. As an example, he pointed to two tales from *Shivhei Habesht* that in his opinion represented two incarnations of a single narrative motif, the first one realistic and the second one legendary.[21]

Now, by relying on a variety of sources, external as well as internal, Scholem was able to sketch certain facets of the figure of the Besht. Here we note the most relevant:

1. Throughout his life, the Besht worked as a *baal shem* and he was even proud of his vocation. In making this claim, Scholem hoped to dismiss once and for all the attempts of scholars and authors with Hasidic affiliations to obscure the element of the magical in the figure of the Besht.[22]

2. In addition to his activities as a *baal shem,* the Besht was discovered also to be "a visionary who prays out of *dvekut* and passion and disseminates his religious ideas on the proper way of achieving adherence to the Creator."[23]

3. Not only did these two aspects of the figure of the Besht *not* contradict each other, but "from the outset his occupation as a miracle worker and healer was closely linked to his doctrines, and throughout his working life we may not separate the two."[24]

4. The last assertion is based on an identification of the Besht with "what scholars of religion in our day call the *charismatic leader.* . . . A type who, as Rudolph Otto defined it in his masterful analysis of Jesus, possesses 'the gift of healing and exorcism of spirits, of preaching, prophecy and being able to induce in others a revelation of sorts—as Jesus appeared to his disciples to be walking upon water.'"

I should remark about the shift that Scholem's stance represents as concerns the magical component in the figure of the Besht. Scholem not only rejected the attempts to obscure this component; he stressed that it was an inseparable part of the totality of the Besht's personality and attributes. Unlike Dubnow and Zinberg, who tended to distinguish between what they regarded as the inferior magical element and the positive aspects of the figure of the Besht, Scholem emphasized that the magic, the vision, and the praying with *dvekut* were all inseparably bound up with one another.

After making these points, Scholem went on to formulate his statement of principle, significant both for the understanding of the figure of the Besht and for the assessment of the status of *Shivhei Habesht*. He says the following:

> The question disputed by the scholars is: how many of these attributes of the charismatic figure are to be admitted as genuine gifts of a personality, and not as mere imaginings? It is a pity that for most of the writers the verdict on this question is left to rest on general philosophical principles, usually of a rationalist cast, instead of resulting from analysis of the facts. Enough people of this type have existed in both Judaism's Hasidic movement and in the analogous Christian movements, during the past two hundred years, for there to be scope for an unstinting scholarship of the visions of the charismatics. . . . Where is the boundary which separates the imaginary virtues from the real (even if para-normal) ones in a certain person?—this is far from clear. Yet I must say outright that in my humble opinion not only would the history of religion greatly benefit by an investigation of supra-normal, or para-psychological, visions, but that even the conventional use of the terms "imagination," "suggestion" and "auto-suggestion" does not convey the whole truth of the matter, and to the extent that it explains anything does not explain it fully. . . . It would seem that the interaction between the charismatic person and the public, while at times it gives rise to what are called miracles, is of a nature more complex than is commonly supposed.[25]

Here we have it: Scholem, well aware as a scholar of religion that the miraculous in its various manifestations is essential role to forming the relations between the charismatic leader and his believing public, is challenging the rationalist perspective, according to which every instance of the phenomenon of the supernatural is treated as a product of the imaginations of the ignorant.[26]

Scholem's programmatic assertion, about the essence of the relations formed between the charismatic figure and his believers, served as a point of departure for Joseph Dan when he approached the question of the credibility of *Shivhei Habesht*. After citing Scholem's remarks and agreeing with his critique of the rationalist approach, Dan proposed an alternative to the distinction between "authentic stories" and stories "which are inauthentic." Instead of relying on "external standards which are based on prejudices," Dan proposed that one rely on considerations that address "the inner content" of the stories. Thus, for instance, the scholar is to ask, Who is the figure to whom the tale is attributed as a source? What historical and geographical facts are to be found in the story? What plausibility is there that the person who told the tale was present when the events described took place, and was in a position to form an impression of the story's truth? And similar such questions.[27]

And what of the marvels and miracles? What standards are we to use to evaluate those? To deal with this question Dan suggested a distinction between three sorts of "marvels" that appear in *Shivhei Habesht*. They are as follows:

(a) *A marvelous experience.*—The friends, students and associates who surround the Besht . . . feel that something is taking place before their eyes which is of deep spiritual significance, and they are carried away in the flood of feelings aroused by the charismatic figure.

(b) *Marvelous knowledge.*—The charismatic leader demonstrates his awareness of concealed knowledge. This may be knowledge of what is buried in the past, of what is hidden in the hearts of man, of what is going on in the Upper Worlds, or of what is fated to be. Disclosure of such marvelous knowledge amazes the bystanders and arouses in them a sense of awe.

(c) *A marvelous deed.*—Here the charismatic leader works upon physical reality and transforms the laws of nature, effecting genuine "miracles."[28]

These remarks by Dan clearly indicate that he distinguishes between marvels of the first two types, which he considers to be human phenomena distinctly within the realm of the possible, and marvels of the third kind, which do not deserve credence. On the basis of these distinctions, Dan made a detailed examination of several stories in *Shivhei Habesht*. His findings are instructive. Dan showed that a linkage exists between stories that are "authentic," by the above-mentioned criteria, and "marvelous" phenomena of the two first types, namely, experience and knowledge. However, marvels of the third type—miraculous acts involving changes in the order of nature—characterize specifically the stories that, by the sum of their attributes, are to be classed as "inauthentic."

In truth, Dan resists being explicit about the historicity of the stories in *Shivhei Habesht*. Because his book purports to deal with these tales from a literary perspective, he qualifies himself and states:

> What really took place when the Besht stayed in such and such a place and performed such and such an act—that, it seems, we shall never know, and from a literary point of view it does not matter one way or the other. Yet from a literary point of view there is significance to whether the tale was told by someone who could have believed it indeed took place in his presence; or whether he heard it from a credible source, someone who could have witnessed the event; or whether the story is built on hearsay. . . . For our subject, an authentic story is one which emerged from the circle of friends and students of the Besht, and was told in their name, with the intent of describing exactly what took place; an inauthentic story is one which was born at a distance, in place and time, from the Besht's circle, and does not contain direct evidence about what occurred or about the temper of the Besht's circle and his environment. The class of authentic stories is no more "literary" than the class of inauthentic stories; yet the distinction between the two types of stories is necessary for examination of the various literary classes, which were conjoined in the book *Shivhei Habesht*.[29]

To be more precise about what Dan is asserting: he defines a story to be "authentic" when it was perceived to be true by the students of the Besht who related it. Such a story thus reflects the "truth" of the circle of tellers and hearers, but not necessarily the "truth" of the story's subject matter. As someone who deals with the tales of *Shivhei Habesht* from a literary point of view, Dan regards this as sufficient. It seems to me, however, that even if this was not his original intention, the considerations Dan puts forward, like the examples he cites from *Shivhei Habesht* and his analysis of them, contribute substantially to recognition of this book as a credible source—one that sheds light on what "really took place when the Besht stayed in such and such a place and performed such and such an act." Despite his qualified formulations and his stress on the literary aspect, Dan's statements contain an indication of a road, and perhaps one can even say the blessings of the road, for anyone who would use *Shivhei Habesht* as a source for a historical reconstruction of the Besht.

The use of *Shivhei Habesht* has not always been accompanied by methodological qualifications. There have also been those who relied on this book without feeling they needed to apologize at all or to spell out the considerations that guided them. One example may be found in the article by Yosef Weiss, where *Shivhei Habesht* is used for the sake of reconstructing a profile of the

Hasidic circle that existed in Kotov.[30] Weiss was skilled at being able to locate and discover persons and events within the book and to combine them into a rich portrait of that circle. Perhaps Weiss felt no hesitations about using this information because the factual details he drew upon seem to be the sincere utterances of those who told the tales. Nevertheless, one of the attributes that Weiss ascribes to members of the circle is their conceit that they possessed the power of "prophecy"; that is, of being able to reveal the secret sins of their comrades. Weiss is not in the least incredulous about this marvelous capacity and presents it as the literal truth. It seems that like Scholem, and following in his footsteps, Weiss too is aware that the manifestations of the miraculous—which includes prophecy in its various forms—are to be considered primary phenomena within religious life. Consequently, he had no qualms about acknowledging the historical reality of this aspect of the Hasidim of Kotov.

If we take a broader view of the positions of the scholars thus far surveyed, we find that the trend that emerges is one of increasing readiness to acknowledge the value of *Shivhei Habesht* as a historical source. Likewise, we find a linkage between a scholar's readiness to rely on *Shivhei Habesht* and the richness and vitality of the portrait he draws of the Besht. Beginning with Gershom Scholem, there is also a manifest readiness to regard the miraculous elements of the life of the Besht and his associates as historical realities. Naturally, acknowledgment of the import of the miraculous and acknowledgment of the value of *Shivhei Habesht* are stances of mutual support.

Since the 1980s, scholarship concerning *Shivhei Habesht* has been enriched by another interesting and fruitful line of inquiry. Certain scholars have set themselves the goal of assessing the veracity of tales within *Shivhei Habesht* in light of external sources. A review is thus in order of the findings of these scholars and their significance for our topic.

The Veracity of Tales in *Shivhei Habesht* in Light of External Sources

R. ELAZAR OF AMSTERDAM'S EMIGRATION TO THE LAND OF ISRAEL

It appears that the first person to have made a meticulous study of the veracity of a story from *Shivhei Habesht* on the basis of external sources was Israel Bartal. The tale that Bartal dealt with concerns the event of the emigration of R. Elazar of Amsterdam to the land of Israel. The core of the story is as follows:

> I heard from R. Yoel the preacher of the holy community of Nemirov
> . . . that once the Besht spent the Sabbath in Shargorod, and following the Sabbath, after the *havdalah* ceremony, told (as was his custom)

what he had seen during the Sabbath. And he said that he had seen that R. Elazar of the Community of Amsterdam had passed away. And he said to him that he had died on the previous Sabbath, which was the Sabbath of *Bereshit*. And I asked him what was the cause of his death, and he said that two people from Poland had insulted him on *Simhat Torah* . . . and spoke to him as follows: "Here you are president, but in the country of Poland you were not fit to be even a tailor's rabbi." And he accepted a death for himself, if revenge would be taken against them by the plague and the sword, heaven help us. And I asked him: What will you do with your wife, the *Rabbanit?* And he said that I should take her from them . . .

That year, the son of the rabbi of the community of Polonne arrived.[31] His father asked him: What is the rabbi R. Elazar doing? He said: he has already passed on. He inquired whether he had died on the Sabbath of *Bereshit;* he said yes. And he said how do you know this, as no man has preceded me?[32] He said to him: We knew this by the Sabbath of *Noah* already, for the Besht told it to us. And he was very perplexed. And he asked him about the wife of the aforementioned rabbi, and he said that R. Avraham Schverdlik came from Jerusalem and took her to Jerusalem. And he asked about those who had the argument with the aforementioned rabbi, and he said they were enfeebled by the outbreak of plague heaven help us and were chased out into the field where Ishmaelites came and killed them.

He also said on that same Sabbath[33] that he saw that they would print that very year a new book and he does not know the name of the book as they had yet to give it a name. And this book was composed by a member of the sect of Sabbetai Zvi, his name be cursed . . . in an appealing language so that the people will desire it and will, heaven forbid, contaminate the world by our many sins.[34]

So runs the story as it appears in *Shivhei Habesht.* Bartal investigated this episode on the basis of sources printed in the second half of the eighteenth century.[35] As it turns out, he was able to locate enough data with which to form a fairly rich picture of R. Elazar: the itinerary he followed on his journey to the land of Israel, the dispute that broke out between him and the members of the Safed community, his death, and the fate of his wife. After comparing what he found in the various sources against the story in *Shivhei Habesht,* Bartal concluded that this story can be considered "a completely 'historical tale,' the various components of which are repeatedly corroborated, though with certain variations, by the printed sources."[36] Among the verified details, Bartal listed

the death of R. Elazar of Amsterdam in Safed on the Sabbath of *Bereshit* . . . the quarrel between R. Elazar and the Ashkenazim of Safed . . . the relocation of R. Elazar's widow to Jerusalem by one of the members of the Ashkenazi community in Jerusalem . . . [and] the outbreak of plague in Safed at around the time of these events, which took the lives of those involved in the dispute with R. Elazar.[37]

How did Bartal explain the correlation between the details of the story as it appears in *Shivhei Habesht* and what was found in the other sources? In Bartal's opinion, the correlation tells us about the "ways in which the masters of Hasidic lore made use of the historical material of their day, or of a time close to theirs.[38] In other words: the "masters of Hasidic lore" took a true event that happened in their time and was known to them, and inserted an "element of legend" into it; namely, the Besht's ability to see from afar.[39] Bartal also offered an account of why the "masters of Hasidic lore" seized upon the figure of R. Elazar of Amsterdam in particular:

> R. Elazar, a figure who was above dispute both for those who were and who were not Hasidim, served Hasidic lore by being a sort of source of legitimization for the Besht and his marvelous deeds: a personage to whose authority all assented—and moreover one that was quite closely linked to the family of R. Yaakov Emden, and thus was approved of by those who accused the Hasidim of using Sabbatean materials.[40]

If Bartal considered the first part of the tale, in which the Besht reveals his power to "see" the death of R. Elazar, as showing signs of an apologetic trend, he considers this trend all the more evident in the second part of the story: there the Besht is described as someone who predicted that an anonymous Sabbatean text was about to be printed. Bartal says the following:

> It seems that the subsequent part of the story in *Shivhei Habesht,* which deals with the disclosure of the Sabbatean quality of the book *Hemdat Yamim,* contains certain elements of response to criticism of the discovery that Hasidim maintained possession of Sabbatean writings. This criticism, which could have been "Mitnagdic" or "mask-ilic," was deflected not in the "clever" ways that Gershom Scholem ascribed to the editors of the R. Adam Baal Shem tales, but rather by means of the invention of a story which rebuts the potential anti-Hasidic charge. . . . The story took shape, it rather seems, in the context of the accusations made in the late eighteenth and early nineteenth centuries about the Sabbatean texts which Hasidic circles held as sacred; it bears the marks of an "inverted" tale.[41]

In other words, by having the Besht prophesize about the printing of the Sabbatean book, while voicing condemnation of this text, the "masters of Hasidic lore" meant to clear Hasidism of the charge of keeping Sabbatean texts in their possession. In short, Bartal held that the conjunction of the "element of legend" (that is, the Besht's power of seeing from afar) and the presence of R. Elazar of Amsterdam, reflect the objectives of the "masters of Hasidic lore": to defend the Besht's reputation as a worker of miracles, and to defend Hasidim from the charge of holding Sabbatean texts.

I find this interpretation of the story at hand difficult to accept. To begin with, I believe that there are no grounds for the notion that either *Shivhei Habesht*'s compiler, or the various figures from whom he heard the tales gathered in his book, acted out of any defensiveness or felt a need to seek "a source of legitimization for the Besht and the tales of his marvels." A close and sensitive reading of this book will show that these people believed in the Besht's unusual powers, admired him on account of these powers, and felt no need to conceal such feelings or to apologize for them.

Nor, in my opinion, ought one to accept the apologetic significance that Bartal assigns to the Besht's prophecy about the printing of the Sabbatean book. Even if we suppose that the Hasidim were aware of the fact they were being accused of links to Sabbateanism, and even if we agree with Bartal's assessment that they felt a need to defend themselves from this charge, this still does not suffice to support the conjecture that the "masters of Hasidic lore" invented the story out of whole cloth and attributed it to the Besht. For who, in the end, are the "masters of Hasidic lore" referred to here? R. Yoel the preacher of the Nemirov community, who told the story, and R. Dov Ber of Lince, who heard it, set it down in Hebrew, and fixed its place in the collection. R. Dov Ber, who carefully noted the source from whom he heard each and every story, in this case added an explanation about how R. Yoel came to witness what he reported: "[R. Yoel] was always to be found by the side of the rabbi of the holy community of Polonne, in the Community of Raszkow, in the Shargorod Community and the holy community of Nemirov."[42] In other words: R. Yoel was affiliated with R. Yaakov Yosef of Polonne and was a regular guest in his home, in the various communities in which the latter served as rabbi. Hence, R. Yoel chanced to be in R. Yaakov Yosef's home in Shargorod on the Sabbath that the Besht stayed there and he heard what he related directly from the Besht.

Are we really to suspect R. Yoel of taking a story about the emigration of R. Elazar of Amsterdam to the land of Israel, familiar to him from some other source, and "implanting" the Besht within it? Or perhaps it was *Shivhei Habesht*'s compiler who took a story he was familiar with from another source and attributed it to R. Yoel. It would be best to give up all these elaborate explanations and simply to trust that the compiler of *Shivhei Habesht* indeed heard the tale from R. Yoel, and that R. Yoel indeed heard what he heard from the

Besht. Yet this too is impossible, for accepting matters literally would mean granting credibility to the Besht's ability to see from afar. Still, what are we to do if the Besht himself believed he was endowed with such an ability, and this was believed unreservedly also by his associates and students? We already know from reliable sources that the Besht often would tell his associates about the things he had "seen."[43]

Bartal has graced us with an important work of scholarship that verifies the factual basis of the story that appears in *Shivhei Habesht*. If we combine Bartal's findings with the testimonies to the effect that the Besht believed in his powers of seeing from afar, and that this was believed in also by his associates and the tellers of tales about him, why should we not take the story literally and acknowledge that it expresses the genuine historical experience of the Besht and his associates?

R. GERSHON OF KOTOV IN THE LAND OF ISRAEL

Certain stories in *Shivhei Habesht* describe events in the life of R. Gershon of Kotov from the period of his residence in the land of Israel. Yaakov Barnai sought confirmation of these tales through a comparison with other sources, foremost of which is the letters that R. Gershon sent to the Besht from the land of Israel.[44] Barnai also drew upon general knowledge of the modes of life of the Hasidim who emigrated to the land of Israel in the eighteenth century. Barnai was able to verify certain factual details contained in *Shivhei Habesht* from the other sources. This conclusion led him to the conjecture that the tales in *Shivhei Habesht* were based on letters sent from the land of Israel, or on oral traditions that Hasidim who had resided in the land of Israel and then returned to the Diaspora brought back with them. Barnai even stressed the fact that only two of the letters that R. Gershon sent from the land of Israel have survived. He speculates, accordingly, that if we had further letters available, further details of the stories in *Shivhei Habesht* would be verified.

In short, Barnai's findings reinforce the impression that the majority of the tales gathered in *Shivhei Habesht* are not to be classed as legends or "popular tales" but rather as stories originating in genuine traditions. By this term I mean traditions that reflect the genuine life experiences of the Besht and his associates.

THE BESHT'S VISIT TO THE DZIERZAWCAS

A study was recently published about the familiar story in which the Besht visits the two large leaseholders from Sluck, who were known at the time as the Dzierzawcas.[45] I am speaking of the article by Adam Teller, in which he examines this story on the basis of external sources, including archival material.[46] Following is a synopsis of the story as it appears in *Shivhei Habesht*.

In Sluck, there were two brothers named Gedaliah and Shmuel, who were employed as large leaseholders on the estate of the duke of Radzivill. Shmuel and his wife Tovele built a large new house, yet were reluctant to move in, fearing that demons had taken up residence there. On Tovele's counsel, Shmuel invited the Besht to inspect the house and purify it. During the feast that the leaseholders arranged in his honor, the Besht told Shmuel of his hopes to emigrate to the land of Israel. Shmuel expressed a willingness to assist the Besht in financing travel expenses. To his question about the amounts of money involved, the Besht replied that he needed "sixty thousand." Shmuel replied that this seemed a trifling amount. During the Besht's stay at their house, Shmuel's wife Tovele turned to the Besht and asked him to reveal "how long would their days of fortune last?" At first the Besht was reluctant to respond. Tovele insisted, however; and the Besht eventually replied that the wealth and power of the leaseholders would last another twenty-two years. When Shmuel heard this he grew furious at the Besht.

How did things turn out for the leaseholders? Shmuel and Gedaliah lent a considerable sum of money to the duke of Radzivill. The duke, however, not only had a hard time paying off the debt; the leaseholders worried that he would even turn to them for an additional loan. The two therefore decided to seek sanctuary in the court of the king of Prussia. This king promised to offer his protection once they relocated from Sluck to Breslau. In exchange, the leaseholders made a gift to the king of the promissory note the duke of Radzivill had signed. Yet the plan did not turn out well. One of the leaseholders' clerks informed on them to the duke. The duke had Shmuel arrested and instructed a military unit to head out to his residence and to confiscate all his property. The officer who was supposed to carry out this order gave advance warning to Tovele, Shmuel's wife, and left her enough time to save her jewels. Tovele put her son-in-law in charge of the jewels; he fled to Breslau, was appointed there as a rabbi, and lived in great wealth. The duke of Radzivill was not content to arrest merely Shmuel and his wife. He forced Shmuel to invite all his relatives to a wedding. Some of them fell prey to this ruse and were taken off to prison. The compiler of *Shivhei Habesht* concludes the story with the following words: "And this event took place 22 years afterward just as the Besht had said to him." This is the gist of the tale as related in *Shivhei Habesht*.

It was Israel Halpern who first examined this story with an eye to placing it in its historical context. Halpern was interested in finding the causes of the events that have become known as the Waszczylo riots.[47] This term refers to the peasants' revolt that took place in Lithuania in the 1840s and in the course of which some Jews were hurt. Pursuing a rumor that explained the revolt as Gentile jealousy at the wealth accumulated by the leaseholders Shmuel and

Gedaliah, Halpern looked into the biographies of these two individuals. As part of this effort, he considered the story associated with them as told in *Shivhei Habesht*. Halpern thus did not set out to corroborate the story in *Shivhei Habesht*, but rather hoped to draw on it as a source of information about the leaseholders. Before he turned to *Shivhei Habesht*, however, Halpern found the leaseholding brothers mentioned in two additional Jewish sources: in the memoirs of Solomon Maimon, and in remarks on the episode written by R. David of Makov.

Solomon Maimon, in the context of his account of the leaseholding business—the source of income for many of Poland's Jews—mentions the two leaseholders of the estate of the duke of Radzivill. He relates that they acquired their wealth through the efficient and ruthless management of their leaseholding affairs.[48] R. David of Makov, famous for his battles against Hasidism, included remarks critical of the Besht in his testament. Among other things he commented that the Besht was known in his day "not as a scholar but only as a *baal shem* and writer of amulets." R. David further remarks that he had heard from a certain wise old *Talmid Hacham* about the Besht's visit to the leaseholders. He says the following:

> The famous *neggidim* [affluent, powerful Jews] known as Dzierzawcas, who grew wealthy under the hands of the great and famous duke, their wealth is almost inestimable—they sought to know what the future held for them, and they sent for [the Besht] who came and sacrificed a calf on the sill of the house,[49] and he told them their wealth would last only twelve years from that time and no longer, and so it was in fact.[50]

After examining the Jewish sources, Halpern next turned to the external ones. He was able to identify further information about the fall of the leaseholding brothers and about the scope of their business ventures. In these sources he also found complaints by village leaders about acts of corruption by the leaseholders.[51]

Joseph Dan has also written about the tale of the leaseholders.[52] Following Halpern, Dan asserts that his findings "corroborate the historical background and the account of the fall" of the leaseholders. Along with Halpern, Dan notes the testimony of R. David of Makov and emphasizes its importance:

> This testimony of R. David of Makov, which concludes with the words "and so it was in fact," is one of the only testimonies in the rich Mitnagdic literature in which the Besht's marvelous abilities are admitted to. This testimony from the mouth of a *Mitnaged* certainly would not have been sounded, unless he had in his hands sources and traditions that he could not challenge.[53]

On the basis of these considerations, Dan concluded that the tale of the lease-holders as it appears in *Shivhei Habesht,* is "an authentic story corroborated by external and *Mitnagdic* sources."[54]

As mentioned, Adam Teller has recently devoted a new study to this affair. Teller was able to present a rich and fascinating historical reconstruction of the biographies of the two leaseholders from Sluck. This reconstruction relies in part on studies by Polish historians and primarily on material from the archives of the Radzivill family. Teller found that the two leaseholders indeed attained remarkable positions of power and accumulated vast wealth. Their leaseholding venture with the Radzivill family began in the 1820s and contin-ued through the thirties and early forties. The leases were of an exceptional scope in the concepts of the period. In addition, the brothers had commercial ventures in the town of Koenigsburg and real estate acquisitions in Sluck. The leaseholding brothers' enormous financial success was based on the exploita-tion of the farmers and oppression of sublessors. They did not shrink from using force against those who would not bend to their wills. They likewise intervened in the economic activities of certain Jewish communities and even took care to appoint some of their relatives as rabbis of communities.[55]

The crisis in the relations between the leaseholders and the duke of Radzivill broke out in the year 1745. The background to this crisis appears to have been the huge debt that the duke owed to the king of Prussia. Shmuel was arrested and forced to sign a confession stating that he had cheated the duke out of more than six million zlotyes, and had relinquished all his property to the duke. The duke did not manage to arrest Gedaliah, who had fled to Koenigsburg and there was under the protection of the king of Prussia. How-ever, several dozen of the leaseholders' family members were also arrested. Shmuel perished in prison after a year and a half.[56]

After reconstructing the affair of the leaseholders, Teller compared the details derived from the Polish sources with what is related about the incident in *Shivhei Habesht*. The conclusion of this comparison was that some of the details that appear in *Shivhei Habesht* are indeed corroborated by the external sources. These include the names of the brothers, their vast wealth, and the purchase and construction of their houses in Sluck (for the "purification" of which the Besht was summoned). In the second part of the story in *Shivhei Habesht,* the corroborated particulars are the name of the duke, the grant of protection by the king of Prussia, the arrest of Shmuel, the confiscation of his property, and the appointment of his son-in-law as rabbi of Breslau. Teller also found many inaccurate details in the story that are nonetheless close to the truth. On the other hand, certain particulars from the story in *Shivhei Habesht* were found to be "gross errors, originating from lack of knowledge of the details of the real affair." In light of all of this Teller conjectured "that around the time of the occurrence of the events, the Besht's Hasidim were well aware of the facts, but over the half-century or more which passed until they were written down in the final text, these facts became corrupted."[57]

What does all this imply about the reliability of *Shivhei Habesht?* When coming to venture an opinion on this subject, Teller stresses the need to distinguish between the two parts of the story, the part that revolves around the Besht's visit to Sluck and his activities there, and the part that is meant to tell what became of the leaseholding brothers and how the Besht's prophesy was fulfilled. Now, many of the factual details cited in the first part were corroborated by the external sources. Conversely, of the details cited in the second part of the story, "some of them can be corroborated, some are half-true and some are in error." Teller explains the difference in the extent of the accuracy of the two parts of story by saying that from the point of view of Hasidic tradition the first half was of great importance, as the Besht was at the center of it. Conversely, the details of the second part, the purpose of which was to tell about the fulfillment of the Besht's prophecy, are less consequential. Teller summarizes his assessment as follows: "What is special about this story is not the fact that it alludes to figures about whom we know many details, but rather the very fact that what it recounts about the activities of the Besht can be verified—at least in part."[58]

In addition to verification of the details that form the factual framework of the story on the basis of archival material, Teller bases the reliability of the story on the testimony of R. David of Makov (cited above). Teller estimates that at the root of this testimony is a Lithuanian-Jewish tradition that originated in Sluck, and that it is independent of the tradition of *Shivhei Habesht,* which originated in Ukraine. This estimate is based on the difference between the two traditions as regards the number of years during which the "good fortunes" of the leaseholders would last: twenty-two years according to *Shivhei Habesht,* and twelve years according to R. David of Makov.[59] Teller points out the superiority of the source originating in R. David of Makov; that is, that the fall of the leaseholders would take place within twelve years. Recall that the crisis with the leaseholders began in 1745. Twelve years earlier (that is, in 1733), Shmuel and his wife moved to Sluck and there bought their first home. Accordingly, Teller declares: "In all likelihood it was precisely in this year of relocation that not only would worries have arisen about the sanctity of the new home, but also curiosity as to whether their good fortune would continue to shine in the future as well."[60]

The studies by Bartal, Barnai, and Teller differ from each other in several regards. The common denominator in all is that in their reliance upon external sources of various types they verify numerous details that appear in certain stories in *Shivhei Habesht.* Nonetheless, the three scholars differ from one another in the way each evaluated the results of his research. Bartal maintained that the correspondence between the details of the story in *Shivhei Habesht* and what he was able to find from external sources is evidence of a literary manipulation carried out by the "masters of Hasidic lore." They took a ready-made, true story and implanted a "legendary element" within it referring to the Besht. Barnai estimated that the correspondence between what is told in *Shivhei Habesht* and what is suggested by the letters sent from the land of Israel indicates that these letters and others like them served as the source of the stories about the biography of R. Gershon of Kotov in the land of Israel. Teller inferred that the story cited in *Shivhei Habesht* about the Besht's visit to the leaseholders of Sluck is largely true. We thus find that even in this pathway of scholarship of *Shivhei Habesht* one can discern the trend spoken of earlier; that is, the increasing readiness to acknowledge the veracity of the stories cited in *Shivhei Habesht.*

An examination of three stories from *Shivhei Habesht* does not, of course, amount to evidence regarding the nature of the book as a whole. Nevertheless, it seems to me that it is possible to make inferences from the examined stories to a great many others. Such an inference would suggest that many stories collected in the book *Shivhei Habesht* reflect the genuine historical experiences of the Besht and his associates. Furthermore, it is not the historian's business to establish whether the Besht indeed was endowed with the powers of prophecy and far-sightedness. What the historian is to do is determine whether these abilities of the Besht played a substantial part in how he perceived himself, in how his associates viewed him, and perforce also in the relations formed between him and those who surrounded him. We can learn about all of these from the stories in *Shivhei Habesht,* such as those whose details were verified by Bartal, Barnai, and Teller.

The Current Form of *Shivhei Habesht*

The issue of the reliability of *Shivhei Habesht* as a historical source is linked, naturally enough, to the sequence of incarnations through which the book passed before reaching us. Recall that it was Dubnow who already voiced a suspicion that in the years between the death of the Besht and the printing of the book, the tales underwent substantial modification. A comprehensive survey of the wide literature on this topic would take us considerably beyond the bounds of the present discussion.[61] Nevertheless, I ought still to draw attention to the results of the studies on four questions that have direct bearing on the subject. These are (a) What was the extent and significance of the printer's editorial intervention in the printed version of the text? (b) What is the connection between the printed Hebrew version of the book and its Yiddish translation? (c) What relation exists between the print edition of *Shivhei Habesht* and the sole surviving manuscript version? (d) Did the compiler receive the text in the form of edited sets of stories?

THE PRINTER'S EDITORIAL INTERVENTION

We begin with the question of the printer's intervention. Recall that it was the Hasid R. Israel Yaffe who first brought the book to print, in Kapost in the year 1814. In the opening of the book R. Israel Yaffe added the following lines:

> Said the printer:
> Because in the manuscripts I transcribed I found—in the sequence
> of the developments and the revelation of the Besht (may his memory defend us Amen)—things which were not in order, and as I had heard in the name of the rabbi and Admor (his soul rests in the heavenly repository) everything in its proper order and well explained, I therefore shall print [it] as was heard from his holy mouth; and what deviates from this I shall follow with [the phrase] as written in said manuscripts.[62]

Several pages later R. Israel Yaffe again remarks: "Thus far [is as] I heard in the name of the Admor (his soul in a heavenly repository) the order of developments. And [of] the deeds and marvels that occurred meanwhile I shall write as written in the manuscripts that have come to me."[63]

This declaration by the printer about his editorial intervention in the text that reached him in manuscript form poses several puzzles. Who is the "Admor" whose words "heard from his holy mouth" led R. Yaffe to change the text of the manuscript? What sort of changes were these, and to what extent do they obscure the original version of *Shivhei Habesht*? Is there a discernible agenda to the printer's editorial intervention? Is his intervention confined to the first pages, ending where he explicitly says "thus far . . ."? Or did he alter the text of the manuscript in other places as well?

Persuasive and satisfying answers to these questions may be found in the statements of two scholars who have dealt with this issue: Yehoshua Mondshine[64] and Moshe Rosman.[65] Mondshine adopted the prevailing view among the scholarship of his predecessors that the Admor in question is none other than R. Shneur Zalman of Ladi, whom R. Israel Yaffe considered as his rabbi. Yet Mondshine rejects the idea that R. Shneur Zalman was involved personally in the editing of *Shivhei Habesht*. As to what kind of editorial intervention this was, Mondshine states that he "rearranged the stories from the beginning of the book to conform to the sequence in which he heard them from the

Admor." Furthermore, at least some of the tales appearing in this section of
the book were taken from the text of the manuscript. This claim was based on
Mondshine's comparison of the print edition to the manuscript, which was
not interfered with by the printer. It thus appears that the printer's intervention consisted, at least in part, in his having taken stories from where the compiler put them and moved them to the beginning of the book. The question
whether R. Israel Yaffe added stories that were not in the original manuscript
text is one that Mondshine left unanswered, as the manuscript that served as
a basis of his comparison covers only a part of the book.

Rosman agreed with Mondshine's conclusions and added an important
claim of his own: the key to the question of whether R. Israel Yaffe added material to the beginning of the book that wasn't in the manuscript he had before
him is the presence of parenthesis marks. In keeping with prevailing conventions of the period, parenthesis marks signify an editor's alterations to the existing form of the manuscript.[66] Consequently, those paragraphs that are
delimited by parenthesis marks in the beginning of the book (i.e., in the section
the printer rearranged) are paragraphs taken from the original manuscript.
Conversely, the remaining paragraphs contained in this section, eleven out of
seventeen, derive from a tradition that R. Israel Yaffe heard in the name of the
Admor. The same principle holds for the major portion of the book, the part
attributed to the compiler. Whatever is bracketed with parenthesis marks in this
section, some ten paragraphs, was added by the printer, while the remainder is
a transcription of the manuscript text as written and arranged by the compiler.[67]

The relevance of all of this to our subject is that R. Israel Yaffe's editorial
intervention in *Shivhei Habesht,* whatever its agenda may have been, was negligible in its effects. The bulk of the book represents the original text as shaped
by R. Dov Ber of Lince. Moreover, one has no trouble distinguishing between
the material that the book originally contained and what was added to it by
the printer.

THE RELATION BETWEEN THE HEBREW VERSION AND THE YIDDISH TRANSLATION

A further question that has preoccupied the scholars is, as said, that of the
relation between the Hebrew edition of *Shivhei Habesht* and the translation to
Yiddish that was published in Ostra in the same year.[68] One of the first scholars to attend to this issue was Khone Shmeruk. In an article dealing with the
tales of R. Adam Baal Shem,[69] Shmeruk discovered that the Hebrew and the
Yiddish editions of these stories had substantial differences between them.
When he tried to account for these differences, Shmeruk came to the conclusion that the Yiddish edition is not a translation of the printed Hebrew edition

but rather of a still earlier Hebrew text. Shmeruk speculated that the text the Yiddish translator had in front of him was a copy of the original manuscript of the book; that is, in the form it had prior to the printer's editorial intervention.[70] And because in the Hebrew print edition the R. Adam stories are to be found in the section in which the printer intervened, Shmeruk inferred that this intervention is what accounts for the differences between the Hebrew and Yiddish editions of the book.

Shmeruk's findings provoked Avraham Yaari to conduct a thorough comparison between the printed Hebrew edition and the Yiddish translation.[71] As a result of this comparison, Yaari asserted that the Yiddish edition "is fundamentally unlike the edition in Hebrew." This difference is to be found in the order of the stories, in their form, in deletions, additions, and also in the textual content of several of the stories they have in common.[72] On the basis of these findings Yaari reached a far-reaching conclusion: the Hebrew and Yiddish versions of *Shivhei Habesht* represent two primary editions each of which is independent of the other. Not only that, but the Yiddish edition is superior to that of the Hebrew.[73] Consequently, Yaari went on to assert:

> Anyone who henceforth comes to investigate the history of Hasidism and Jewish history in Poland using *Shivhei Habesht* as a source, will not have met his obligations if he has not closely examined and compared the Yiddish edition. . . . And certainly it would be impossible to put out a critical edition of *Shivhei Habesht* without the Yiddish text as a basic element of it.[74]

One scholar who adopted this conclusion wholeheartedly was Avraham Rubinstein. When preparing his critical edition of *Shivhei Habesht,* Rubinstein took care to include a comparison with the Yiddish translation in the notes to the text. In addition, he interpreted many difficult passages from the Hebrew version on the basis of the Yiddish text.[75]

This issue of the relation between the Hebrew and Yiddish editions of *Shivhei Habesht* was reexamined by Yehoshua Mondshine.[76] Following an exhaustive examination of the relation between the Hebrew and Yiddish editions, and drawing on studies of other texts that had been translated from the "Holy Tongue" into Yiddish, Mondshine reached a conclusion that is the opposite of that of Yaari and Rubinstein: the Yiddish edition of *Shivhei Habesht* was based upon the Hebrew print edition and not upon some earlier manuscript. Mondshine accounts for the differences between the two editions as follows:

> The translations to Yiddish were meant primarily for women and common people . . . a layer of the population whose lack of knowledge of the Hebrew language was coupled with a lack of familiarity

with the sources, lack of familiarity with famous figures, and so on.
Thus the translator had to face the task of adapting his text to readers who needed the material presented in a form that would be enjoy-
able and appealing for them to read. The contents had to be
thoroughly digested so that the reader would not have to stretch his
head too much to understand it. Hence, the tales were treated to con-
tractions, expansions, and levelings-out of the difficulties and contra-
dictions of the original; meanwhile various details which would not
interest these readers were eliminated, such as the source from which
this or that story was heard.[77]

Mondshine's explanation of the source of the differences between the Hebrew
and Yiddish editions is based on numerous pieces of textual evidence. Mondshine goes further and puts forward a wide range of arguments and evidence to
overturn the alternative account that Yaari presented. After an examination of
all of these, I find that Mondshine's position is convincing and well supported;
that is, the historian who seeks to learn from *Shivhei Habesht* about the Besht
and his associates, ought to focus his attention on the Hebrew version of the
book. The Yiddish translation is to be regarded as an interpretation of the
printed Hebrew text and as such may be of assistance. This translation, however,
does not represent an earlier and superior version of the Hebrew original.

THE RELATION BETWEEN THE PRINTED EDITION AND THE MANUSCRIPT

An important development for the historian who would rely on *Shivhei
Habesht* has been the discovery and publication of a manuscript of the book.
This manuscript came to the Lubavitch library in New York in 1980 and was
printed in facsimile form by Yehoshua Mondshine in 1982. Hayim Liberman
was the scholar who immediately declared the manuscript to be superior to
the print edition.[78] Following Liberman, Mondshine examined the manuscript and discussed its attributes extensively in the introduction he wrote for
the facsimile edition.[79] Mondshine found that many of the differences
between the manuscript and the print edition may be traced to the fact that
the version the "printer" had available contained corruptions. Generally
speaking, these corruptions were the result of transcription errors. Likewise,
in the print edition there are omissions of entire sentences; evidently, the typesetter skipped these lines because of similar words elsewhere in the text he had
in front of him. Moreover, the printer himself, and perhaps the typesetter as
well, made changes and emendations to the text in hopes of improving it.

At any rate, the numerous examples that Mondshine cites leave no room
for doubt that the manuscript is superior to the print edition. Most of the

differences between the two are slight and negligible; in a few cases, however, the manuscript serves to clarify obscurities and difficulties in the print edition. Unfortunately, the manuscript printed by Mondshine does not cover all of *Shivhei Habesht* but only the majority of it. Nevertheless, the publication of the manuscript along with notations of its differences from the print edition, as well as the extensive discussion of the character and attributes of the text of the manuscript, are extremely welcome developments for anyone wishing to rely on *Shivhei Habesht* as a historical source.

DID THE COMPILER RECEIVE EDITED "CLUSTERS" OF STORIES?

A new conception of the process by which *Shivhei Habesht* was created was proposed by Elhanan Reiner.[80] His proposal is as follows:

> In contrast to the discussion which primarily concentrates on the literary activity of the last editor of *Shivhei Habesht* and the printer's functions as publisher, I would like to advance a different idea, and to consider *Shivhei Habesht* as a collection of clusters of traditions that were transmitted by various transmitters, in various periods, in various textual forms, and that the editor's effort consisted primarily in linking these "clusters" to each other and arranging them into a single entity. The work of the *Shochet* of Lince consisted mainly, on these assumptions, of the formation of an anthology of tales which reflects, more or less, what was told and collected in regard to the Besht and his environment in the years which passed between the beginning of the collection and the time of editing.[81]

Taking this idea further, Reiner describes two stages that preceded the editorial activity of Dov Ber of Lince. In the first stage, the individual story or "praise" was created; in this stage the content is orally transmitted and is undocumentable. In the second stage the oral tales are assembled, edited around a certain theme, and set down in writing. The collections of the writings geared toward a certain subject are thus the "clusters" that reached the hands of the "final editor" who joined them into a single book.[82] Reiner even points to what seems to him the two principal clusters that deal with the Besht. The first of these was received by Dov Ber of Lince from his father-in-law, R. Alexander, who served as the Besht's "scribe"; the second was received from R. Gedaliah, the rabbi of Lince.[83]

Reiner also argues that the work of collecting the early traditions about the Besht and forming them into "clusters" was carried out primarily by associates of R. Yaakov Yosef of Polonne. That is why the figure of R. Yaakov is so prominent in *Shivhei Habesht*, whereas R. Dov Ber of Mezerich "is represented in the book only marginally."[84]

I find Reiner's remarks about the stage in which individual stories were given form through oral transmission extremely interesting. What is very much to the point is his account of the role that the *shevah* or "praise" played in the world of the people who created and transmitted it:

> The *shevah* . . . was not meant to be a depiction of the "true" biography of the hero. Such a depiction would have been quite familiar to the audience who read and heard the praises. . . . Nor was the praise meant to announce the greatness of the hero to those who are unacquainted with him; it is not a means of propaganda but rather a part of the cultural world of the public in which the figure of the mythological hero is an element of its mythology, and the transmission of the praise is part of the ritual of this public.[85]

I further agree with Reiner that within *Shivhei Habesht* one can make out sets of stories arranged around a certain topic or a certain figure. Yet what I do not find plausible is his assertion that these sets reached the compiler, R. Dov Ber of Lince, in a written and organized form, and that all that remained for him to do was to link them together and form a book. This description of the sequence of events is inconsistent with the fact that the compiler begins each tale by naming the person he heard it from. Reiner claims that "the notation of names of transmitters—and at times of a chain of transmitters—is typical of material transmitted orally." Yet the question one must ask is, Who heard the oral story? Was it the compiler of the "cluster" or the book's compiler, Dov Ber of Lince? In Reiner's approach, the words "I heard" and the notation of the transmitter's name would have to have been included in the already prepared cluster that reached R. Dov Ber. However, this solution is inconsistent with the cases in which the compiler adds various details about the circumstances in which he himself heard the story.

Furthermore, Reiner's view about the "clusters" that reached the compiler is contradicted by the compiler's own express testimony about the process of writing the book. Here is what the compiler says: "I bethought myself to write out the marvels that I heard of from men of truth, and in each account of the events I wrote whom I heard it from; and I thank the Lord for having endowed me with the power of memory, I have not omitted or added to what I heard . . . and I wrote all of this for posterity."[86] It is the compiler, then, who heard the tales from the various tellers and who wrote the names of the people he heard them from before each story. And indeed, besides the sets organized around individual tellers, such as the stories the compiler heard from his father-in-law about the "revelation" of the Besht, the book has many sets consisting of tales that the compiler heard from assorted tellers. Thus, for instance, the compiler arranged eight stories from different tellers around a common theme: the Besht's ecstatic prayer.[87] It is thus clear that the compiler, who heard each of these tales separately, was the one who gathered the stories into a cluster. Likewise there is a small cluster, comprising three tales, about the quality of R. Nahman of Kosov's prayers. In this case too the compiler heard the tales from various tellers. Moreover, the tales about the quality of R. Nahman's prayer are followed by a tale about the quality of the prayer of R. Yaakov Yosef of Polonne.[88] These are representative examples of many of the clusters of stories in *Shivhei Habesht*.[89]

In sum, the testimony the compiler gave about his working methods, the structure of many of the "clusters," and the remarks the compiler sprinkled among the tales about the circumstances in which he heard them—all these clearly suggest that it was R. Dov Ber of Lince who heard the tales from the various storytellers and that it is he who wrote them down. This conclusion is consistent with Reiner's observation about the uneven nature of the selection of tales constituting *Shivhei Habesht*. The large number of tales associated with R. Yaakov Yosef, however, and the contrastingly small number associated with R. Dov Ber of Mezerich, is not an effect of the "clusters" that purportedly reached the compiler, but rather of the simple fact that the compiler was a regular figure in R. Yaakov Yosef's household and had no direct contact with the *maggid* of Mezerich. Generally speaking, the content of the tales included in *Shivhei Habesht* was largely determined by which storytellers the compiler chanced to encounter. In effect, this means tellers who lived in the same town as the compiler, such as R. Gedaliah of Lince, or tellers who visited Lince, or those whom the compiler met in the course of his travels. The inference to be drawn is that *Shivhei Habesht* is not representative of the totality of traditions told about the Besht and his associates in the various regions of Poland.

Moshe Rosman's Pessimistic View of *Shivhei Habesht*

Given the development of the scholarship as surveyed from the beginning of this chapter up to this point, one might suppose that the historian who wishes to rely on *Shivhei Habesht* today has a well-paved road in front of him. Recall that the manifest trend in the scholarly literature, starting with Dubnow, continuing through Zinberg, Weiss, and Scholem and ending with Dan, is one of increasing recognition of the value of this book as a historical source. This trend should have been bolstered by the studies of Bartal, Barnai, and Teller, who verified numerous details of the stories in *Shivhei Habesht* on the basis of external sources. Apart from all of these, there are the conclusions that Mondshine and Rosman reached about questions concerning *Shivhei Habesht*'s various textural incarnations. The stance recently taken by Moshe Rosman in his book on the Besht comes, therefore, as something of a surprise. Rosman devotes a considerable portion of his book to a detailed and systematic investigation of the sources on which a historical study of the Besht may be based; in this context he naturally discusses *Shivhei Habesht* as well.[90] And the conclusions that Rosman came to—as regards the book's value as an historical source—are ones of considerably skepticism. Below are the main points of his approach to this subject.

Rosman describes the efforts of the various scholars to rely on *Shivhei Habesht* as one continuous failure. This failure has two aspects: methodological and empirical. Methodologically, none of the scholars has been able to enumerate convincingly the criteria by which one is to distinguish the legendary elements in *Shivhei Habesht* from the historical ones. And empirically, the conclusions that scholars reached after analysis of particular stories have been contradicted by subsequent developments in the scholarship. As an example, Rosman points to the R. Adam Baal Shem tales. Three scholars—Dubnow, Scholem, and Eliach—interpreted these stories, each in a different way; then Shmeruk came and demonstrated that the R. Adam tales were drawn from an earlier literary source. This discovery put an end to all those interpretations.

Likewise, Gershom Scholem's approach to this subject was deemed by Rosman to be a dead end. Scholem, it will be recalled, sought to corroborate certain stories in *Shivhei Habesht* on the basis of external sources. However, Rosman believes that some of the sources that Scholem took as credible are far from reliable. Rosman further argues that Scholem often relied on stories without explaining at all what his considerations were in doing so. In sum, Rosman believes that the attempts of various scholars to rely on *Shivhei Habesht* only demonstrate the problematic character of this book.[91]

Indeed, later in his treatment Rosman provides a long list of reasons and arguments that call into question the reliability of *Shivhei Habesht* for historical study of the Besht. He makes the following points:

1. The first edition of *Shivhei Habesht,* the one printed in Kapost in 1814, was not based on the original manuscript.

2. The sole manuscript that has survived differs substantially from the text of the manuscript that the printer of the Kapost edition had in front of him.

3. The printer disclosed to his readers that he intervened in the editing of the book: he changed the order of certain stories, added material from other sources, put parenthesis marks around certain passages, and made amendments to the text.

4. An examination of the content of the stories reveals that several
   of them are merely variant accounts of the same event. Likewise,
   there are stories that seem analogous to tales about celebrated
   figures from a previous era, such as the ARI.

5. Many of the tales are clearly legendary in character. Indeed, the
   translators of *Shivhei Habesht* into English, Dan Ben Amos and
   Jerome Mintz, prepared an index of the book's motifs and
   arranged them according to the order customary for popular
   tales. The proliferation of such motifs in *Shivhei Habesht*
   presents a serious obstacle for anyone who would use it for
   historical analysis.

6. Even if we suppose that the stories are "more or less" historical,
   what we have is a collection of anecdotes unlinked by any continuity or logic, lacking dates, and mostly lacking a reference to
   their context or circumstances.

Given all these considerations, Rosman concludes, a scholar who seeks to identify the historical nucleus of *Shivhei Habesht* is liable to find himself in a state
approaching despair.[92]

And what of the studies that verify factual details mentioned in *Shivhei
Habesht* on the basis of external sources? Rosman believes that these studies
are indeed superior to attempts to evaluate the reliability of the stories by internal analyses alone. However, the discovery of factual details within a story still
does not make such a story "historical." A researcher who analyzes a certain
story within *Shivhei Habesht* must never forget the fundamental aims of the
book as a whole. This is the lesson to be learned, according to Rosman, from
Bartal's study. The fact that one of the tales in *Shivhei Habesht* conserved historical details about the emigration of R. Elazar of Amsterdam to the land of
Israel does not suffice to verify what is related in it about the Besht. Recall that
Bartal interpreted the story as a response to a potential criticism of Hasidism
by Mitnagdim or maskilim. On this interpretation, claims Rosman, the biography of R. Elazar was drafted to serve the ideological needs of the Hasidic
movement in the early nineteenth century.[93]

The key factor, however, leading to Rosman's skepticism about *Shivhei
Habesht,* is the hagiographic nature of this book. In his own words:

> The first step in reading *Shivhei Ha-Behst* must be to accept that it is
> a work of hagiography, or sacred biography as the current academic
> lexicon terms it. This means that it was not written to record the biog-
> raphy of a great person in the past but to persuade people in the pres-
> ent to behave in a certain way or to accept a particular doctrine.

> Hagiography is primarily concerned with turning the exemplary life
> into a proof text for a position advocated in the present. . . . *Shivhei
> Ha-Besht* is no exception.[94]

Rosman further claims that *Shivhei Habesht* is an anthology that was edited
twice: once by the compiler (that is, R. Dov Ber of Lince) and a second time
by the printer, R. Israel Yaffe. Now, a fundamental principle of textual analysis, says Rosman, is that anthologies, and especially anthologies based on oral
traditions, tell us about their editors and their intended audiences no less than
they do about the phenomenon they purport to represent. And as the material included in *Shivhei Habesht* took form at the end of the eighteenth and in
the early nineteenth centuries, it therefore reflects the trends and circumstances of those who shaped it and those for whose purpose it was shaped.
Accordingly, continues Rosman, whatever the Besht may have done while he
was alive, and whatever the content of the tales told about him while he was
alive or shortly after his death, we have to recognize that what was conserved
from these stories, what was corrected in them, what was omitted or added to
them—all was oriented toward the vision of people who lived a generation or
two after his death.[95]

What, then, were the agendas that guided R. Dov Ber of Lince and R. Israel
Yaffe? Here Rosman again points to what they both wrote in their introduc-
tions to the book. R. Dov Ber wrote that in the past, miracles occurred frequently and that this served to strengthen faith. In present times there are
fewer miracles and faith is weakening. From this Rosman concludes that R.
Dov Ber chose to tell stories about miracles so as to strengthen faith. R. Israel
Yaffe, by contrast, decried the scarcity of righteous men, but consoles himself
that no age is without its famous *zaddikim*. And if R. Dov Ber considers *zaddikim* to be people who work miracles, R. Israel Yaffe emphasizes their roles as
public leaders. Indeed, continues Rosman, the printer was guided by the desire
to have the Besht be seen as a public leader. The stories the printer added to
the beginning of the book, those that describe the Besht's parents, his child-
hood, and the manner in which he acquired esoteric knowledge, are all linked
to the Besht's future role as a leader. The printer thus hoped to have the Besht
be presented as the paradigm of the Hasidic leader for the nineteenth century.

Rosman summarizes his discussion of *Shivhei Habesht* as follows:

> For both compiler and printer, the historical details, however accu-
> rate, were but raw material to be used rhetorically to prove a theo-
> logical or ideological point. Their first loyalty was to the spiritual
> needs of their audience, not to the task of reconstructing the his-
> torical milieu of the Besht's lifetime and writing the biography of
> the Besht.[96]

In closing, I must add that in the reconstruction of the historical figure of the Besht that he proposed in his book, Rosman remained true to his position, and scarcely made any use of *Shivhei Habesht.*

Shivhei Habesht as a Reliable Historical Source

THE PRINTER'S AGENDA

I would like to begin the response to Rosman's views with the question of the printer's agenda. Rosman was correct in asserting that the printer's intervention reflects a certain agenda that originally derived from R. Shneur Zalman of Ladi. Quite naturally, R. Shneur Zalman looked upon the figure of the Besht from the perspective of someone with the responsibilities of leading a Hasidic community. Hence there is some plausibility to Rosman's assertion that R. Shneur Zalman sought to have the Besht be regarded as the model for the Hasidic leader. This can help account for the legendlike stories that the printer added to the beginning of the book. Among these, most conspicuous are the stories designed to supply the Besht with a prestigious lineage and link him to the apocryphal *baal shem* R. Adam, who supposedly provided the Besht with secrets of practical Kabbalah.[97]

The tendentious nature of the printer's intervention is also discernible in the tale about the Besht's "revelation." If, in the section of the book that the compiler wrote, the Besht was "revealed" to be a *baal shem,* in the printer's section the magical element disappears entirely; instead the Besht is "revealed" to be a Kabbalist and mystic of the first rank. Evidently these were the aspects of the figure of the Besht that better suited the conception held of him by R. Shneur Zalman of Ladi. Yet it is also possible that concealment of the magical component in the figure of the Besht reflected R. Shneur Zalman's discomfort with the expectations of all those who flocked to him that he would remedy their material afflictions.[98] At any rate, the tale about how the Besht was "discovered," as shaped by the printer and influenced by the tradition deriving from R. Shneur Zalman, is a story clearly legendary in character.[99]

So far, I am entirely in agreement with Rosman. However, the printer's tendentious intervention need not drive off the historian who seeks to rely on *Shivhei Habesht,* as by far the majority of the book is free of this sort of bias. Recall that it was Rosman himself who made an important contribution to our awareness of the limits of the printer's involvement. The group of stories the "printer" arranged includes only the first fifteen stories that appear in the book.[100] To this one should add the ten stories incorporated within the body of the book and that are identifiable as supplemented material. All the remainder of the stories, some two hundred and twenty-five of them, were unaffected by the agenda that guided the "printer." Quite the opposite: in many of these stories what is specifically stressed is the Besht's power as a *baal shem*, a quality the "printer" apparently had an interest in playing down. Moreover, in this section of the book the Besht is depicted as an itinerant *baal shem* and no bias or anachronism (e.g., describing the Besht as a leader of a Hasidic court) is discernible in it.[101]

In sum, whatever the printer's agenda may have been, this agenda did not affect the majority of the tales in *Shivhei Habesht*. Accordingly, there is no justification for judging the book as a whole on the basis of features confined to the stories the printer edited.

THE COMPILER'S AGENDA

I turn next to Rosman's claim about the agenda that guided the compiler of *Shivhei Habesht:* R. Dov Ber of Lince. For indeed, the compiler too had an agenda; he even stated what it was in his introduction to the book. What I must do, then, is come to a conclusion about what kind of agenda this is and how it may affect the reliability of the book. Here is what the compiler declares:

> And I too noticed, from the time I became a man up to my full maturity and even old age, that day by day the miracles diminished and the marvels disappeared. For in earlier times it happened that there were people who fell into a sleep called *Hiner Bet*,[102] and when they came back to life they would tell of the wonders they beheld in the Upper Worlds. . . . And in our generation too there were righteous people who revealed hidden futures and by this belief in God and belief in the Torah would be strengthened. And now that there are fewer zaddikim . . . belief has greatly fallen off and how much heresy has spread in the world. . . . I therefore bethought myself to write out the wonders that I had heard from men of truth. . . . And I wrote all this for posterity for my sons (may they live) and my grandsons (may they live), so that it may serve to strengthen belief in the Lord and his Torah and faith in zaddikim. Therefore all who read it may truly know, that I did not write this in the manner of legends and story-tales, let the reader only observe and truly examine, using the mind's eye, each and every story of the marvels of the Blessed Lord, and he will learn from it the proper moral, to adorn his heart with the fear of God and belief in the might of our sacred Torah which the story induces.[103]

Reading through this statement of intentions, it is entirely clear that the compiler did not view the Besht as the model or paradigm of a Hasidic leader, as the interest he shows in the stories had nothing at all to do with Hasidism as a movement. The compiler attempted to collect tales about "miracles" and "marvels" because the various expressions of the supernatural within human existence provided, in his opinion, the clearest proofs of divine intervention. Zaddikim, who are granted supernatural powers by the grace of God and through their loyalty to Him and His Torah, serve as living demonstrations of the existence of God and the sanctity of his Torah.

It may possibly trouble us that in our own time, when the distinction prevails between people who are "religious" and people who are "secular," it is hard to conceive of the phenomenon of faith growing feeble in a society we label as "traditional": such a society—so it strikes us—is one in which all of its elements share religious commitments. Yet the compiler's remarks clearly suggest that his generation struck him as one in which belief had grown frail. Is the enfeeblement of faith, which the compiler laments, a genuine historical phenomenon, or is it merely the compiler's subjective impression? Perhaps the compiler's statements are a reference to the spirit of rationalism, which originated in the European enlightenment movement and whose echoes even reached as far as eastern Europe. At any rate, as the compiler saw it, the religious faith of his contemporaries had become enfeebled, and he believed that a collection of stories about zaddikim who were blessed with marvelous powers could help remedy this situation. So much for the compiler's explicit explanation for why he collected the stories. Yet it stands to reason that there was a further motivation as well that led him to collect the tales about the Besht and his associates: the miraculous element expressed in the stories, besides serving to strengthen an enfeebled faith, also aroused the curiosity of the compiler and fascinated him, just as it had fascinated those who conserved the memory of the events and spoke of them to others.

In any event, the question that must now be our chief concern is as follows: Is the agenda that guided the activity of the compiler, and that he explicitly admits in the introduction to his book, such as to jeopardize the reliability of the stories he gathered in his book? In other words: Did the interest that the compiler had in "miracles" and "marvels" lead him to invent these stories out of whole cloth, or to find miraculous tales that had spread among the people and ascribe them to the Besht and his associates? Perhaps the compiler merely selected the Besht and his associates because they already had a reputation for performing marvels? In other words: Are the miracles and marvels in the tales of *Shivhei Habesht* merely fictions, then, designed for the ends of a certain agenda? Or are they instead the reports of events grounded in a certain social and cultural reality—one that also gave rise to and sustained this agenda?

To respond to this question, I must examine the method the compiler followed in writing his book. How did the compiler conceive of his role? What was his attitude toward the things that he heard? Who were the people he heard the stories from? What sorts of stories did he decide to include in the collection? I shall try to answer these and similar questions by reading between the lines of *Shivhei Habesht* itself.

ACCURACY ABOUT THE NAMES OF STORYTELLERS

It is to be stressed at the outset that the compiler treated the stories he heard and included in his collection as the reports of genuine events. He expected a similar treatment of them from the reader of his book. Consequently, in the preface he bothered to remark that he heard the stories from "men of truth," and at the beginning of each story he took care to note the person from whom he heard it. The compiler also states: "I thank the Lord for granting me the power of memory and have neither detracted nor added to what I heard and all is true and solid and the words have not been altered by my mouth."[104] R. Dov Ber considered himself obligated to transmit faithfully what he heard, adding or omitting nothing.

Now, if one looks at how the compiler worked, one finds that not only did he take the trouble to specify the person he heard the story from, at the beginning of each story; at times he even adds details about the circumstances of the telling. Thus, for instance, he begins one of the stories with the following clarification: "I heard from my son, the Master Leib may he live, that once, R. Hirsch,[105] the son-in-law of the rabbi of the holy community of Ostra, the great luminary R. David, spent the Sabbath with us . . . and after the Sabbath he spoke, and my son heard this from him and told me the story."[106] Another example is the remark prefacing the tale that the compiler heard from R. Menahem Nahum of Chernobyl. This is, in fact, another version of the story about the Besht's ascent of the soul, which the compiler earlier had cited in the name of R. Falk. The preface is as follows: "But once, the Rabbi and Hasid our Master Menahem Nahum of Chernobyl was in our town and told this story to the crowd and I came in the middle of the story and heard from him some slightly different and also slightly new things."[107] In cases where he heard a story indirectly, the compiler is careful to note this fact: "The Hasid R. Yosef of Zornitz, known as R. Yosef Melamed, was in our town in the holy community of Lince. And as I was not in a healthy state at that time and could not sit with him, I only greeted him and did not hear this from him directly. And my friends heard it from him and told me."[108]

In a few cases the compiler is not ashamed to admit that he does not remember who he heard a certain story from,[109] yet these cases are the exceptions that prove the rule. In addition to taking care to note the names of tellers, and often also the circumstances of the telling, the compiler saw fit to explain to himself and to his readers perplexing aspects of the tales. An example is the following story:

I heard from my father-in-law that the Rabbi the Hasid our Master Gershon bathed in the sea while the ship was moving.[110] And I asked [my
father-in-law]: how was it permitted to place himself in such great danger, and he was unable to reply to me. And when R. Gedaliah came to
us I remembered and asked him about this and he replied to me: Once,
I sat with the Rabbi and Hasid the Master Zvi of Kamenets on the patio
in front of the house and I raised the topic with him and asked him as
follows: I heard that you bathed in the sea while the ship was moving,
how it is permitted to place oneself in such danger? He chuckled and
said: So what, all the deckhands washed themselves in the sea, for there
is a sack made of leather with a leather ladder in it hanging from the
ship and you climb up and down and wash yourself in it.[111]

An example of a different kind involves a story about a woman who underwent an exorcism. In the course of the exorcism the Besht asked the dybbuk—
the soul that had penetrated the woman's body—to identify himself.[112] The
dybbuk replied that he was unwilling to reveal his identity before all those
present because his sons, who live in the same town, would be disgraced. When
alone with the Besht, the dybbuk revealed his name. Here the compiler adds:
"And my father-in-law of blessed memory too was acquainted with him [and
said] that he was turned into a spirit only because he ridiculed the Hasidim of
the holy community of Kotov."[113] Evidently, by noting the fact that R. Alexander, the compiler's father-in-law, had personally known the man whose soul
was reincarnated in the woman's body, and even the sin he was being punished
for, the compiler was seeking to bolster the credibility of the story.

In a few cases the compiler heard more than one version of the same story,
and he takes care to transmit both versions and to note this. An example is the
following:

I heard from a person named R. Zeev, the brother of R. Leib the Hasid
of Lince who took up residence in the Holy Land more than thirty
years ago. . . . And R. Zeev too was a scholar and God-fearing man
who is to be believed, and also from the rabbi of our community I
heard [this] in a different version and I shall also write the Rabbi's
account of this.[114]

The comment about the credibility of R. Zeev is quite rare. This seems to
me easily explained: most of the tellers from whom the compiler heard the stories were people he knew, and the compiler felt no need to vouch for their credibility. The R. Zeev mentioned here was not a familiar figure and so the
compiler made sure to describe him as credible.

In sum, the compiler's working assumption was that the tales he gathered
in his collection came to him from reliable sources. Was this assumption well

founded? Who indeed were the tellers he heard the stories from? Did these people emerge from the fringes of society, were they random guests who gave vent to popular knowledge, or perhaps persons of a recognized public stature? And most important, how close were the tellers to the Besht and to members of his circle?

WHO WERE THE TELLERS, AND WHAT DID THEY TELL?

A systematic investigation of the names of the persons from whom the compiler heard the stories yields the following picture: of some two hundred and fifty stories included in *Shivhei Habesht,* about one hundred stories were told by persons who were rabbis of communities, thirteen were told by community preachers, and the compiler heard four stories from people who served as Hasidic leaders.[115] Of the rest, a large number were told by people who came from the upper spiritual-religious class and by *shochtim* or *melamdim.*

How were the storytellers connected with the Besht or the other members of the circle they told of? Some of the tellers, in fact, knew the Besht personally and were even considered to be his associates. Of these, the most prominent is R. Yaakov Yosef of Polonne, the Besht's unquestioned disciple, from whom the compiler heard twenty-two of the stories in the collection. At least nine of these stories consist of R. Yaakov Yosef's direct testimony of events in which he was involved personally. In the remainder of these stories, R. Yaakov Yosef either witnessed the events or heard about them from other associates of the Besht.

Another person whom the compiler frequently cites and who was an associate of the Besht is R. Alexander Shochet—the compiler's father-in-law. For eight years R. Alexander worked as the Besht's "scribe."[116] The designation "scribe" seems to refer to his role as an inscriber of amulets; yet it is clear that as the Besht's "scribe" R. Alexander served as his personal assistant, was often at his side, and accompanied him on his travels. A few of the events R. Alexander relates, mainly those that involve the "revelation" of the Besht, deal with the time before his acquaintance with the Besht began. It is thus likely that he heard about them from the Besht himself or from people who knew him during that period. At least some of the stories R. Alexander tells are to be classed as firsthand reports of what he had heard or seen in person.

Firsthand reports about the Besht—where the tellers themselves witnessed the events described—are also provided by Rabbi Meir Margaliot,[117] R. Moshe b. R. Yekel of Miedzybóz, and R. Moshe Harbater.[118] In this context one must also mention R. Moshe, the son-in-law of the sister of R. Yaakov Yosef of Polonne. Of the three stories that the compiler heard from him in person, one is to be classed as a report of something he heard directly from the Besht, whereas another conveys what he heard from the *mokhiah* about what happened to the *mokhiah* himself. Also to be mentioned is R. Yoel of Nemirov, who told two tales based on things he heard directly from the Besht.[119]

Alongside the tales about the Besht that may be classed as firsthand reports, *Shivhei Habesht* contains a substantial number of tales that are reports at second hand. These include the tale the compiler heard from someone who heard it from R. Zvi—another person who functioned as the Besht's "scribe" for several years.[120] Another example is the story that the compiler heard from his son, R. Yehuda Leib of Lince, who heard it from R. Hertz, the son-in-law of R. David, the rabbi of the Ostra community.[121] The events recounted by R. Hirsch took place in his family home and he may well have witnessed them. Among other things, R. Hirsch tells about what he heard from the Besht in person.[122]

Of special significance are the tales the compiler heard from R. Falk, the rabbi of Titchelnik. R. Falk heard one tale—the one describing the Besht's ecstatic prayer—from R. Avraham, the leader of prayers in the *Beit Midrash* of Miedzybóz, who was present during the actual event.[123] R. Falk heard another story about the Besht from his father-in-law R. Shmeril, who received the Besht's services as a *baal shem* and was himself the subject of the tale.[124] R. Falk also heard a few stories from R. Yosef Ashkenazi. This R. Yosef was an associate of the Besht, and besides being his relative he would often read to the Besht out of *Sefer Ein Yaakov*. Some of what R. Yosef Ashkenazi recounted to R. Falk occurred to him in person in the Besht's presence. The remainder is presumably based on what he saw and heard while in the Besht's proximity.[125]

Several tales the compiler includes in his book are to be classed as firsthand reports about members of the Besht's circle. These include the tales the compiler heard from the aforementioned R. Yoel. R. Yoel served as the preacher of the Nemirov community, and as said, at various stages of his life was a regular member of the household of R. Yaakov Yosef of Polonne.[126] Three tales related by R. Yoel refer to R. Yaakov Yosef and are based on the close acquaintance between them. The compiler, R. Dov Ber of Lince, was likewise affiliated with R. Yaakov Yosef, and four of the stories contained in his book are based on what he himself saw and heard while by the latter's side.[127] The compiler heard another tale—the one that depicts the Besht's fraternity dancing in his home on the Simhat Torah holiday—while in the home of Yaakov Yosef. Also a firsthand report is the tale that the compiler attributes to R. Yehiel Michal of Zloczow on his attitude toward the Besht and the *maggid*.[128] R. Leib, the son of R. Gershon of Kotov, was a further important source for the compiler; he tells of what happened to his father during his residence in the land of Israel. R. Leib's tale refers to an event in which he himself was involved. Additional tales about R. Gershon of Kotov during the period of his stay in the land of Israel were heard by the compiler from R. Pinchas Melamed, who was associated with R. Leib. Presumably R. Pinchas heard the stories directly from R. Leib.[129]

Of the firsthand reports about members of the Besht's circle, the testimony of R. Eliyahu, the preacher of the Lince community, is especially significant. R. Eliahu told the compiler what he himself heard from the *maggid,* R. Dov Ber of Mezerich. The subject of this story is the trembling that took hold of the *maggid* when he touched the Besht while the latter was in the midst of an ecstatic prayer.[130] The compiler also heard of the Besht's ecstatic prayer from the Hasid R. David Furkes, who was a member of the Besht's fraternity in Miedzybóz.[131] Another member of the Besht's inner circle who told the compiler of his connection with the Besht is R. Nahman of Horodenka.[132]

Prominent among the storytellers that *Shivhei Habesht*'s compiler relied upon is R. Gedaliah of Lince. The compiler heard sixty-six stories from him, twelve of which the compiler also heard from R. Alexander or R. Yaakov Yosef. R. Gedaliah served as the rabbi of Lince and the compiler was a regular guest in his home. In addition, R. Yehuda Leib, the compiler's son, was a student of R. Gedaliah.[133]

What is the source for the stories that R. Gedaliah told the compiler? R. Gedaliah passed away in 1804; that is, forty-four years after the death of the Besht.[134] In none of the stories that he tells of the Besht does R. Gedaliah present himself as having been witness to the events. Likewise, in his tales R. Gedaliah cites sermons he heard in the Besht's name, but never from him directly. It is thus clear that the R. Gedaliah stories were not based on direct contact with the Besht. We do know, however, that R. Gedaliah was a student of R. Yehuda Leib, the *mokhiah* of Polonne and a member of the Besht's inner circle.[135] Quite probably, then, R. Gedaliah heard at least a few of the stories from the *mokhiah.* He presumably heard the remainder from contemporaries of the Besht, who were still alive when he began to collect information about his life and works.

It was from these people that the compiler heard the tales about the Besht and the various members of his circle. It follows that the origins of the majority of the tales are well-known figures who were members of the rabbinical elite or who held religious offices. Moreover, a few of the storytellers knew the Besht and his associates in person and their accounts have the status of firsthand reports. Many other tales are to be classed as reports at second or at third hand.

We have learned, then, of the way in which the compiler noted his sources; of his commitment to the faithful recording and transmission of what he heard; and of the identities of the tellers and the close affiliation many of them had to the figures of whom they told. It seems to me, therefore, that we are justified in treating quite a respectable number of the stories cited in *Shivhei*

Habesht as testimonies and traditions, of the kind that are customarily relied upon in historical scholarship.

Nevertheless, the use of the term "tales" or "stories" in this context remains appropriate, as these reports passed from person to person in oral form before they were set down and edited. Furthermore, accounts classed as stories have a particular character by their very nature. The formation of a story commences with the choice made by the first teller to speak about an event he witnessed, or the things he heard from an important figure, and so forth. Beside selecting the event around which the story revolves, the first teller also stresses and accentuates what strikes him as important or interesting about that event. He likewise determines the rhetorical garb that the story is to wear. And if a story has passed from person to person, in principle every hearer and teller of it may add a dimension of his own. Needless to say, the compiler, who heard the stories in oral form and in Yiddish and set them down in writing and in Hebrew, contributed a share of his own to their final form. Yet notwithstanding all the above, these stories were not pulled from the air and they are not to be thought of as fictions. These tales are to be considered, rather, as testimonies and traditions, as they are the reflections of real people, of the real events that occurred to these people, and of the utterances they actually made. And of course, the stories reflect the impressions that the events and people mentioned in the stories made on those who encountered them, including the first teller.

Rosman argued, it will be recalled, that the stories are to be suspected of reflecting the ideological or theological agendas of later generations. To assess how well founded this suspicion is, one must pay attention to the topics of the stories collected in *Shivhei Habesht*. Let us begin with the stories that revolve around the element of the miraculous (the ones that purportedly serve the compiler's agenda). If we sort the marvelous tales by category, the most conspicuous are the ones in which the Besht's functions as a *baal shem*: healing the sick, battling demons and spirits, telling futures, and so forth. Another category in which the Besht's marvelous powers are manifest involves his conduct in the Upper Worlds. One instance is the tale about the Besht's ascent of the soul that takes place during the Neilah service of Yom Kippur. In the course of journeying through the Upper Worlds the Besht works to overturn a severe edict issued against the Jewish people. A further example is the tale about the throng of souls that reveal themselves to the Besht while he is praying: the souls of sinners plead with him and beg him to lift them to salvation. Many tales describe the Besht's ability to see and to hear from afar. Usually these powers are demonstrated in the course of the Besht's efforts to assist the suffering, whether individuals or communities. The element of the miraculous appears also in the tales about the Besht's ecstatic prayer. It seems that the compiler took a special interest in these tales, both because the external manifestations of ecstatic trance struck him as deviations from the course of nature, and because the Besht's associates interpreted his ecstatic prayers as events of revelation.[136]

Are the stories before us fictional, designed to serve an ideology? Or do they perhaps reflect the historical reality of the Besht and his associates? Should we lend credence to claims that the Besht healed the sick and exorcised dybbuks and cleared demons out of houses? Yet the Besht was after all a *baal shem;* if he had not acted like other *baalei shem* he would not have been able to meet the demands of his professional calling. And what about his performances in the Upper Worlds and the powers of seeing and hearing from afar? Is the critical scholar to believe in all of those too? Well, why not? There is no doubt that the Besht himself believed he had such powers. This fact is clearly indicated by his letters. Nor is there any doubt that the Besht's associates and admirers believed in these powers as well. Consequently, whatever metaphysical and theological significance these actions may have, the "wonders and miracles" of the sorts we have been listing are ensconced in the form of life within which the Besht lived and in the cultural and social reality of those who surrounded him. Given that this is the case, the miraculous element in the tales of *Shivhei Habesht* are not only to be considered a reality the veracity of which the historian is permitted to acknowledge, but one that he is in fact required to recognize. If he does not, he has failed in his obligations to understand and describe the figure of the Besht as the Besht himself and those surrounding him perceived it.

In short, the compiler's agenda is not only something that need not damage the reliability of *Shivhei Habesht* as a historical source; it is even consistent with the goals of the historian. The compiler sought to gather stories of a miraculous nature because these are the stories that have the potential of strengthening an enfeebled faith. For his part, the historian must ask of himself and the sources available to him, What was it about the Besht that so fascinated the people surrounding him? And the conclusion one is forced to is: this was an effect, among other things, of the marvelous powers he was graced with. These powers are what impressed the people around him; and those impressions are what formed the nucleus of the stories, some of which came to be heard by *Shivhei Habesht*'s compiler.

Now, besides what *Shivhei Habesht* has to teach us about the marvelous powers gracing the Besht, it contains a good deal of other information about various aspects of the Besht and his associates. We have in mind the details buried in tales that revolve around some marvelous event, and that are inadvertently disclosed. Thus, for instance, we can learn from the stories about the geographic range of the Besht's circuit as a *baal shem;* about the nature and identity of the people who employed his services; about the Besht's relations with his clientele and the tensions with doctors who worked in the same regions. From the tales of the Besht's marvelous powers we can learn also about the configuration of the Upper Worlds he saw in his visions and about his conception of his public mission both in the Upper Worlds and in the earthly environment in which he lived and worked.

Furthermore, despite his stated agenda of collecting tales about miracles, the author included in his book many stories about the Besht and his associates that do not revolve around miraculous events. These include tales that shed light on the Besht's relations with certain members of his circle, on how this circle lived, and on the qualities of the prayer of several of its constituent members. That being the case, the impression the Besht and his associates made on the people around them went beyond the narrow confines of miraculous performances. It so happens that other aspects of the figure of the Besht and his circle have become the subjects of stories. Of special importance are those stories that conserve and give voice to the Besht's self-image. By this I mean stories that transmit remarks made by the Besht on various topics; in particular, stories based on what the Besht related about experiences he himself underwent. It is hard to underestimate the importance these tales have for an understanding of how the Besht viewed himself and his mission and for an understanding of his influence on those who surrounded him.

Three Further Obstacles

Among the other obstacles in the path of the historian who seeks to rely on *Shivhei Habesht,* Rosman listed, it will be recalled, three issues. First, the sole surviving manuscript of *Shivhei Habesht* differs from the print edition. Second, some of the book's stories resemble tales about great figures from previous generations. Third, the translators of the book to English present a long list of motifs from the book that typically appear in popular tales. Let us consider each of these points in turn.

I have already dealt with the issue of the manuscript. Recall that it was Yehoshua Mondshine who printed a facsimile edition of the manuscript and closely examined its attributes. Mondshine's comparison of the manuscript to the print edition left no doubt as to the superiority of the manuscript. Indeed, in certain cases, text that is problematic in the print edition is clarified and easily explained by examining the manuscript. Are we to infer, then, that the print edition is not to be used? I do not believe so, for the following reasons. First, although the manuscript version we have available does not encompass the entire book but only a substantial majority of it, we still can enjoy its advantages only for the portion that has survived. Second, despite the clear superiority of the manuscript over the print edition, most of the differences between them are slight and insignificant. In short, clearly, if the print edition was freer of errors, there is more that we would have been able to learn from it. Now that all we have is a printed version of *Shivhei Habesht* that has errors and a more accurate manuscript version, covering a respectable amount of the book, what we should do is make the most of them both.

We now turn to the resemblance between the tales in *Shivhei Habesht* and the earlier literary motifs. In the set of stories edited by the printer, biblical motifs are easily discerned. An obvious example is the resemblance between the tale about the captivity of the Besht's father and the story about Joseph in Egypt. Likewise, the tale about the Besht being born to hundred-year-old parents is reminiscent of the birth of Isaac to Abraham and Sarah in their old age.[137] Biblical motifs of this kind, however, are to be found only in the set of stories edited by the printer; they do not characterize the remainder of the book.

And what of the tales that resemble those told about the ARI? The scholar who has dealt with this subject at length is Joseph Dan.[138] To offer an example of the similarity in the tales about these two figures, Dan pointed to a tale about souls that revealed themselves to the ARI asking that he save them, and a similar story involving the Besht. How does Dan account for this resemblance? At first, he speculates that the tale about the ARI came to be attributed also to the Besht. Yet Dan did not settle on this particular conclusion and suggested another possibility: the resemblance between the tales reflects the fact that the Besht was influenced by the figure of the ARI and took after him.[139]

Another example Dan listed is the story about the ARI's practice of prostrating himself on the graves of Tannaites and bonding with them so that they would reveal Torah secrets to him. Of the ARI's manner of bonding with the souls of the dead, *Shivhei Haari* says this: "And his *nefesh, ruah, neshama* [soul, ghost, spirit] communes with the *nefesh, ruah, neshama* of the zaddik." Dan compares this to the tale about the Besht's efforts to deliver the soul of Sabbetai Zvi. The common denominator between the two tales is the method of communication: the Besht also sought to communicate with the spirit of Sabbetai Zvi "*nefesh* by *nefesh, ruah* by *ruah, neshama* by *neshama.*"[140] It is on the basis of this similarity that Dan infers:

> If the tale about the ARI cited above had not been well known, the same tale would not have been told about the Besht, at least not in that form. Here is where the resemblance ends. From that point on there are differences, and they result from the complete Hasidic modification of the story. This modification is manifested, first of all, in the historical setting: a response to the affair of Sabbateanism, which was one of the burning topics of the day.[141]

Having inferred a link between these two stories, Dan drew a similar yet more sweeping inference:

> In the tales of the ARI and his practices one can thus see the background for the formation of the Besht's self-image, practices and habits; as well as the background for the formation of the Hasidic tale, which sought to present the Besht in the same light in which the ARI had been presented. . . . Yet Hasidism added to the tales of the ARI historical and personal details which referred to the Besht, his time and place, and modified them to fit its doctrine.[142]

It seem to me that Dan was correct about the first part of what he says; namely, that the figure of the ARI, as preserved in the memory of subsequent generations, had an influence on the Besht. This helps to explain, in part at least, the similarities in the tales told about them both. However, I do not agree in the least with the view Dan expresses in the second part; namely, that Hasidim took tales about the ARI and retrofitted them to the historical and personal circumstances of the Besht. I shall list several reasons why not.

1. The example cited by Dan proves nothing except that the technique employed by the Besht for communicating with the soul of Sabbetai Zvi resembles the one that the ARI used when trying to communicate with the souls of Tannaites. This similarity is quite understandable given the common Kabbalist infrastructure shared by both the Besht and the ARI. Yet the two stories in question differ so radically from each other that it is hard to believe that one of them is a modification of the other.

2. Dan's speculation that Hasidim adapted the tales about the ARI to fit the Besht is inconsistent with what we know about the process by which the tales about the Besht were formed. Where have we found any hint of the existence of a committee of sages engaged in modifying ancient stories and bringing them up-to-date with contemporary circumstances? The remarks that *Shivhei Habesht*'s compiler spreads throughout his work, which shed light on his methods, suggest that he acted sincerely and made efforts to transmit the stories he assembled as faithfully as possible. The element of manipulation, which is discernible in the work of the printer, is not at all to be found in the editorial work carried out by the compiler.

3. I suspect that the tendency scholars have to discover earlier sources for the phenomena they investigate is liable to lead them

to deny the creative and spontaneous power of the historical figure. Why should the Hasidim modify stories told about the ARI to make them fit the Besht? The Besht was a mystic with quite remarkable experiences in his own right; moreover he spoke of these experiences to his associates quite often. Is there anything odd about the fact that the Besht—who relates in his letter that souls of sinners "by the thousand and tens of thousand" pleaded with him to redeem them—should seek to save even the soul of Sabbetai Zvi? In short, anyone who has the Besht himself available has no need of model personages from the past as a means by which to depict his hero.

Gedaliah Nigal, in his book on Hasidic literature, also affirmed that *Shivhei Habesht* was influenced by earlier literary sources and especially by what was related about the ARI. To support this claim, he drew a table in which he listed motifs from *Shivhei Haari* and similar motifs from *Shivhei Habesht*, side by side.[143] However, examination of this table reveals that the motifs which can be explained as the influences of *Shivhei Haari* on *Shivhei Habesht* are to be found only in the set of stories in which the "printer" intervened. Some of the examples Nigal points to show only a faint resemblance while others reflect the basic fact that both the ARI and the Besht were mystics of the first order who were endowed with exceptional spiritual powers.

As we have said, Dan Ben Amos and Jerome Mintz, the translators of *Shivhei Habesht* into English, have created an index of the various motifs contained in *Shivhei Habesht*'s tales, arranged following the conventions used for the motifs of popular tales.[144] This index has several hundred motifs. Repeated examination of this list has left me perplexed about what it was that Rosman considered such a great problem for the historian seeking to rely on *Shivhei Habesht*.

Let us consider a few instances from Ben Amos and Mintz's list. Appearing in the group labeled Mythological we find, among other motifs: rewards for charitable deeds; heaven; heavenly gates. The group labeled Taboo contains, among other motifs: prohibition against having marital relations by candlelight; prohibition against traveling on the Sabbath; prohibition against mourning on holidays and festivals. The group labeled Magic includes: magical performance by means of incantation of holy names; knowledge of the language of trees; knowledge of the language of beasts; magical knowledge derived from examination of a holy text.

What do these examples teach us? Does the fact that a prohibition against intercourse by candlelight existed in various cultures and appears in their popular tales diminish in the least the historical reality of the Halachic prohibition?

Does the fact that the phenomenon of magic has many similar or identical features in various cultures invalidate the historical reality of the tales describing the Besht's magical performances? Does the existence of analogous popular tales in which sacred texts are examined to reveal hidden knowledge cast doubt on the historical reality of the Besht's claim to be able to "see" from one end of the world to the other by examining the Book of Zohar? To be sure, some of the motifs on the list are decidedly legendary in nature. Yet this alone does not suffice to falsify the historical reality of the vast majority of the motifs that the list contains.

The categorization of motifs serves, presumably, an important function in the scholarship of popular tales. Yet one doubts whether the historian seeking to learn about the figure of the Besht on the basis of *Shivhei Habesht* can derive much benefit from Ben Amos and Mintz's index of motifs; at any rate, he certainly should not regard it as an obstacle.

To summarize the discussion of the status of *Shivhei Habesht* as a historical source, I would like to again assert that a respectable portion of the stories cited in this collection are to be considered reliable testimonies and transmissions that are grounded in the personal experiences of the Besht and the people near to him. These are, consequently, tales that express and reflect the cultural and social world of the Besht and his associates. Nevertheless, I certainly am not suggesting that we consider all of the stories cited in *Shivhei Habesht* as credible, for there is no doubt that the book also contains legendary elements. (These are especially conspicuous in the section edited by the printer, but they may be found within the body of the book as well.) I believe, however, that the seasoned historian will have no trouble identifying these elements and distinguishing between them and the trustworthy parts of the book. Such a distinction may well base itself on comparisons of *Shivhei Habesht* to the other sources available to us. However, it is a distinction likely to be based, more than anything else, upon the intuition of the historian.

At any rate, it seems to me that the test of the historian is how plausible and persuasive his manner of drawing upon sources is. I hope that the sensitive and critical reader will find that the use I have made of the book *Shivhei Habesht* is reasonable and convincing. For my part, I have no doubt that a restrained and intelligent use of *Shivhei Habesht* is likely to yield much information about the Besht's personality, his spiritual world, his working methods, and the persons in his circle. The rich and diverse information that can be extracted from *Shivhei Habesht* on these subjects may not be obtained from any other source available to us.[145]

The Besht and the Founding of Hasidism

At the close of this book, I return to the question with which I opened it: Can the Besht be considered the "founder of Hasidism"?

The Besht passed away on the first day of the Shavuot holiday of the year 1760. During the two decades following his death, efforts were made to spread the Hasidic form of worship among wider segments of the public. Over the same years, the institution that came to be known as the Hasidic court also began to take form. Viewed in retrospect, one can view these initiatives as the first crystallizations of the Hasidic movement.

As the previous chapters have shown, the Besht was not a leader of a movement, nor did he even conceive of founding one. It was only posthumously that the Hasidic movement came into being. Nevertheless, it makes sense to ask whether there are good grounds for regarding the Besht as having been decisive for the emergence of Hasidism as a movement, even if this outcome was not intended by him. May one argue that it was the Besht's personality, his manner of worship and his effect on the people around him that set in motion a process which led to Hasidism's formation as a movement? In short, is the Besht worthy of the title, "founder of Hasidism"?

The perspective that is at the basis of this book, a perspective that the reader will no doubt have remarked in the course of reading it, is that the Besht ought indeed to be regarded as the "founder of Hasidism," notwithstanding the above-mentioned reservations. In the material that follows, we examine what the preceeding chapters imply on this issue and how all the various findings hang together.

The structure of our discussion has been based, it will be recalled, on the distinction between three main facets of the person and occupation of the Besht: (1) *baal shem,* (2) leader of the Jewish people, and (3) mystic and guide in matters of divine worship. This structural idea is also at the basis of the summary presented here.

The Besht's conducted his practice as a *baal shem* in a society in which magical phenomena were central and *baalei shem* were highly esteemed. This centrality was reflected in the prevalence of demonological beliefs among all classes of society and in the predominance of the view that demonic forces were best confronted by magical means. Furthermore, in this society, the persons believed qualified to effectively apply magical techniques were the *baalei shem*. The rise in the status of magic and *baalei shem* in traditional Ashkenazi society in the seventeenth and eighteenth centuries appears to be linked to the spreading influence of the Kabbalah within this society. This perhaps accounts for the society's tendency to identify magic with practical Kabbalah and *baalei shem* with Kabbalists. At any rate, during this period we see a substantial increase in the publication of books of charms, which presumably attests to an expanding demand for the use of magic to address the various afflictions of human existence. Furthermore, beginning in the late seventeenth and early eighteenth centuries, we are witness to a phenomenon that may be described as the professionalization of the *baalei shem*. By this we mean the emergence of *baalei shem* whose practice of magic was their primary occupation and chief source of income. These *baalei shem* often traveled from community to community to offer their services to the public at large. A few also had a part in the publication of books of charms.

This new category of "professional" *baal shem* also included the Besht. For him, too, the profession of magic was his main source of income; and he, too, offered his services as a *baal shem* while traveling throughout various regions of Ukraine. Moreover, in the type of maladies he was called on to treat, and in the type of medicinal and magical treatments he employed, the Besht resembled the other *baalei shem* who worked in his day. Nevertheless, one may distinguish several characteristics that set the Besht apart from the other *baalei shem*. For the Besht had an unusual endowment of powers: an ability to see and hear from afar, an ability to confront demons and other metaphysical entities face-to-face, and a self-confidence he projected to great effect on the people surrounding him. In sum, besides the esoteric magical knowledge he had at his disposal, the Besht was distinguished by his strikingly charismatic personality.

What does all this imply for the role played by the Besht in the emergence of Hasidism? Presumably, had the Besht been a *baal shem* and nothing more than that, he would not have had any effect on the emergence of Hasidism as a movement. Quite a few *baalei shem* practiced at a time near that of the Besht, and some even gained great fame, yet the name of none has been linked with the appearance of a new movement. Clearly, then, the magical element in the figure of the Besht could have been decisive only in conjunction with other traits. Having thus qualified the question, I restate it: How did the magical element in the figure of the Besht contribute to the beginnings of Hasidism?

A partial answer to this question has been suggested above, toward the end of the chapter on the Besht's practice as a *baal shem*. There it was said that because the society in which the Besht lived and worked held *baalei shem* in high esteem, the fact that the Besht was a celebrated and prestigious *baal shem* presumably served as a convenient and effective platform for his public efforts. To this I now add two further answers. First, as a *baal shem* who routinely covered wide territories as part of his practice, the Besht had direct and unmediated exposure to the "earthly" conditions of Jewish existence, an exposure the Kabbalists and mystics rarely acquired. This intimate acquaintance with the political, social, and economic conditions of the Jewish communities in Ukraine is, it seems, what was behind the need the Besht felt to act on the public behalf. Second, in retrospect one may affirm that the magical side of the Besht was to become embedded within the image of the Hasidic *zaddik* of subsequent generations. Although not all Hasidic leaders were comfortable with the notion that they had to take after the Besht in this regard, nevertheless, generally speaking the Hasidic *zaddik* was considered—by his adherents as well as by himself—to be a miracle worker who could deliver his flock on affairs worldly as well as divine.

The magical element in the figure of the Besht had a further significance. The Besht believed that his mission in life was not confined to relieving the ailments of individuals, and that he was responsible also for the welfare of the Jewish people as a whole. The Besht further believed that the unusual powers with which he was graced, those he made use of in his work as a *baal shem,* were conferred upon him so as to be used on behalf of the public. We thus find that the magical element in the Besht is also what nourished his sense of mission as a public leader.

The Besht's self-image as a leader and shepherd of the Jewish people as a whole was most dramatically illustrated in his ascents of the soul. These experiences were the primary setting for the Besht's actions to defend the Jewish people in the heavenly courts. The climax of this activity occurred with his confrontations with Samael. At the same time, these experiences reinforced the image that the Besht held of his spiritual exaltedness and his mission. These ascents of the soul also afforded him the opportunity to act as a bridge between the Upper and Lower Worlds, either by carrying up prayers that had not reached their destination or by redeeming the souls of sinners.

The realms of the Besht's work on behalf of the Jewish people were derived from the circumstances of the period and from the real-life challenges that the Jewish public had to confront. The Besht had to deal with the blood-libels, the Heidemak attacks, and outbreaks of plague—events that periodically recurred and could be considered perpetual threats to the safety and welfare of the Jews of Poland in those days. The Besht's initiative in defending the public from all of these reflects both his involvement in public life and his recognition that he had powers of his own with which to react to these matters. Yet as we have found, the Besht's efforts often were not crowned with success. His failures, which the sources do not conceal, are accompanied by bitterness and frustration—the product of the gap between his sureness of the mission he was charged with and the tragic occurrences he did not have the power to forestall. Nevertheless, we have found that the Besht boasted of successes as well in this realm.

Two further domains in which the Besht was involved were, as mentioned, the supervision over the quality of *shekhita* and assistance to leaseholders who were having difficulties meeting their debts. The Besht's involvement in these issues is also indicative of how deeply committed he was in public life, in both its religious and its economic dimensions.

In sum, we have before us a strikingly novel phenomenon: a public leader who believes he is able to deal by magical means with the hardships of society, employing both heavenly and earthly methods to achieve this end. I must here also add that in all his activities on behalf of the public the Besht did not rely on any institutional authority. That is to say: in acting for the sake of *klal yisrael* the Besht presented a striking example of charismatic leadership. The charismatic nature of this leadership is to be seen in the Besht's conception of himself, in his public image, and in the nature of the means he had at his disposal.

Among the scholars there have been, as said, several who sought to attribute to the Besht a mission of a Messianic nature. A careful examination of the sources, and especially of the Besht's Epistle to his brother-in-law, has led us to the conclusion that this perspective is unsupported. On the contrary: the picture that emerges from the sources is that the Besht perceived himself as one whose destiny it was to defend the Jewish people from the Diaspora's characteristic ravages. In other words: the Besht's mission was entirely oriented toward a world in which redemption does not occur. Ironically enough, it was the Messiah who supplied him with the magical means of fulfilling this mission. Yet the Besht had no plans or intention of altering the order of the world by hastening the Redemption. This is something he left to the Messiah.

Retrospectively, one may say that this path of the Besht set a precedent that generations were to follow. The leaders of Hasidism—most if not all of them—viewed themselves, and were perceived by their adherents, as people assigned the task of guiding their public "through this bitter Diaspora." Aside from a few exceptional cases, the leaders of Hasidism did not seek to change the order of nature, and all their efforts were aimed at enabling a reasonable spiritual and material existence in the circumstances imposed on them by the environment.

In this context, I should mention the Hasidic tradition according to which the Besht attempted to emigrate to the land of Israel, yet did not succeed in this effort.[1] The significance of this attempt, of which we have no reason whatsoever to doubt, is understandable given the cultural and spiritual milieu in which the Besht lived. The essential purpose of such an emigration is individual spiritual improvement. Among Hasidim of the old type, an emigration of this sort is considered to be an act of piety. It is in this spirit too that one is to understand the emigration to the land of Israel of R. Gershon of Kotov, the Besht's brother-in-law, in the 1840s, and the emigration of several Hasidim from the Besht's circle in the 1860s.

Now, it is extremely unlikely that the Besht assigned the extreme significance of the sort proposed by Dinur to the failure of his voyage to the land of Israel.[2] What is quite interesting, however, is the novel interpretation the Besht gave to the adage of the Sages concerning the spiritual quality of settlement in the land of Israel: "For anyone who resides in the Land of Israel is as though he has a deity, and anyone who resides outside the Land of Israel is as though he lacks a deity" (Tractate *Ketuvot*, 110b). The Besht's interpretation, as cited by R. Yaakov Yosef, is as follows:

> I heard from my teacher: "In the place of which a man thinks, there he is completely." . . . If he lives in the Diaspora and yearns and thinks perpetually of the land of Israel, then he *seems* as though he has no Deity but in fact has one, for his thought is always of the Land of Israel. Such is not the case when he is in the Land of Israel and maintains his position from the Diaspora; for then his thought is forever in the Diaspora, concerned with how to provide for his family, and then he seems as though he has a [Deity] but in fact has none for all his thought is in the Diaspora.[3]

The homiletic interpretation that the Besht is suggesting for the maxim of the Sages, an interpretation that inverts its literal sense, may be regarded as a spiritualization of the land of Israel. One can enjoy the special sanctity of the land of Israel even without residing in it, provided one's attention is focused upon it; conversely, physical residence in the land of Israel does not always guarantee the hoped-for exaltation. It is not impossible that this interpretation reflects some of the Besht's ruminations over the failure of his trip to the land of Israel.

In this context, too, one should bear in mind the admonition the Besht gave to R. Yaakov Yosef:

> Several times the Rabbi [Yaakov Yosef] wished to journey to the Holy Land, and the Rabbi Besht said he should not go. And he told him to

use the following sign: Each time you are overcome by a desire to
travel to the Holy Land, you may know for certain that there are Judgments on the city heaven forbid and that Satan is distracting you to
keep you from praying for the city.[4]

We thus find that not only is there no necessity of traveling to the land of Israel,
as one may be graced with its sanctity through the power of thought, but that
an actual voyage might be seen as betraying the mission of the leader, who
must dwell amidst his people and protect them through the power of his
prayer. In sum, neither the tradition about the Besht's attempt to travel to the
land of Israel nor the traditions that seek to explain why such travel is unnecessary, link this subject to any sort of Messianic destiny.

Alongside the Besht's magical talents, the exceptional spiritual powers with
which he was endowed, and his strong sense of mission as regards the Jewish
people, there was the special quality of his mysticism. In this realm the Besht
was revealed to be a pioneer and pathbreaker. Unlike the Hasidim of the old
type, who advocated a perpetual focus of thought upon God as the primary
means of achieving *dvekut*, the Besht adopted ecstatic prayer as a means of
inducing *dvekut*. This difference as regards the path leading to the experience
of the mystical left its stamp on the nature of the experience itself. For the
Hasidim of the old type, the striving toward *dvekut* was associated with a perpetual struggle against the distractions of everyday life; yet the ecstasy of
dvekut as experienced by the Besht was brief and episodic in nature. It was
against this background that the Besht developed his ideas on the dialectical
nature of divine worship, with its risings and fallings.

A further attribute of mystical ecstasy is its absoluteness. The mystic is
absorbed into the divine nothingness, to the point where consciousness of the
self is obliterated. I have suggested that this experience should be seen as the
grounds of the radical interpretation that the Besht gave to the Kabbalist
adage, "no site is clear of him." At any rate, this far-reaching idea of divine
immanence supported the Besht in his novel approach toward material existence. Hence, the extreme tension in all that concerns gratification of bodily
needs, that characterized the Kabbalist moral ethos and derived from recognition of the powers of the Other Side—that tension was replaced by the Besht
with the effort to sanctify the mundane, through discovery of the divine potential inherent within it. I refer to the Besht's innovations pertaining to "uplifting straying thoughts" and "worship through corporeality."

Now, even if these particular innovations did not achieve wide currency
or long endure, there is no doubt as to the significance of the revolution the
Besht wrought on the subjects of asceticism and self-mortification. Among
Hasidim of the old type, asceticism and self-mortification were believed to be

the preeminent methods for combating desire and the Other Side that arouses it. The Besht taught, conversely, that such methods cause more damage than good and that they are to be done away with entirely. This too was the spirit of his guidance to his associates.

It is also proper to draw attention to the link between the Besht's new form of mysticism and the mission he took upon himself as a public leader. Adopting ecstatic prayer as a means of inducing *dvekut,* and abandoning the view that striving for *dvekut* requires a perpetual focus upon God, liberated the mystic from the interminable battle against the mundane. Consequently, in the Besht's world there was no opposition between striving for a focused and intense mystical experience and an involvement in public life in all its dimensions.

A further comment is in order on how the Besht's conception of *dvekut* relates to his activity on the public behalf. Recall that the striving for an ecstatic mystical experience, with ecstatic prayer serving as a prelude to it, was linked to an abandonment of the use of Lurianic *kavvanot* as part of the prayer. In effect, the Besht distinguished between divine worship meant for theurgical purposes and prayer whose primary aim is "delight"; that is, the very experience of merging within the divine naught. In this, he differed from the Kabbalists, for whom the striving for *dvekut* and the hopes to influence the Upper Worlds were closely bound to each other. As an alternative channel to the prayers accompanied by *kavvanot* that are to influence the Upper Worlds, the Besht employed his ascents of the soul. These gave him the opportunity to affect the fate of the public as a whole through direct intercession in the heavenly court.

As said, this new path on the essence of *dvekut* and the means for achieving it was conveyed by the Besht to his peers as well. Who, then, were the targets of the Besht's pioneering efforts in divine worship? It will be recalled that we have rejected the view according to which the Besht sought to convey his teachings about *dvekut* to the broad public. We found, instead, that although the Besht indeed took an interest in teaching his method to others, this applied only to the few found fit for such. These are the same few individuals whom the scholarly literature tends to designate as members of the Besht's circle. That circle comprised, as I have said, several rings of people who were distinct both in the times of their affiliation with the Besht and in the nature of the relations they formed with him. Some of these people could be considered colleagues of an equal footing with the Besht, while others viewed him as their rabbi and master. In either case, one can list two prominent features shared by these people: virtually all were Hasidim of the old type, and all at one stage or another formed a personal and intimate bond with the Besht.

From the Besht's point of view, the existence of the circle had decisive significance. The Besht revealed his powers, when these began to appear, to a few members of the circle, expecting that they would recognize his spiritual exaltedness. A further essential function filled by certain members of the circle was their promotion of the Besht's public fame, on the basis of their own direct contact with him and the experiences that ensued from this contact. Above all, these were the people to whom the Besht taught his manner of divine worship and it was from this circle that those who adopted this manner emerged and worked to convey it to others. In sum, the mutual relations between the Besht and the members of the circle were paramount in all that concerns the influence of the Besht on his contemporaries and through them on subsequent generations. Although, clearly, this circle is not to be identified with the movement of Hasidism, still, in retrospect one may affirm that the Besht's circle was a kind of kernel from which the Hasidic movement was destined to grow.

This last assertion returns us to the question with which we began. May one consider the Besht as having been decisive for the initiation of the Hasidic movement? Can one regard him as the person who set in motion the process that was later to generate the emergence of Hasidism as a movement?

It seems to me that the conclusions of this summary lead to a reply in the affirmative. Such a positive response may be summarized through several key assertions:

1. The path paved by the Besht on the nature of *dvekut* and how it is to be achieved came to be the main route followed by the Hasidic movement in its first generations.

2. A few associates and students of the Besht were the people who worked to spread the Hasidic way in the 1760s and 1770s. I refer to figures such as R. Menahem Mendel of Peremyshlyan, R. Yehiel Michal of Zloczow, R. Dov Ber the *maggid* of Mezerich, R. Yaakov Yosef of Polonne, and others.

3. In contrast to the Hasidim of the old type, who tended to be reclusive, the Besht presented a model of a mystic who was deeply involved in the affairs of the public, working within it and on its behalf. In effect, the Besht had created a new model of public leader. This model was characterized by a combination of three features: a *baal* shem who is empowered to relieve individual suffering; a leader who applies his endowment of unusual powers to the spiritual and material welfare of the public; and a mystic who paves new paths in divine worship that others are to

follow. This model of leadership was to have decisive formative effects on the Hasidic leadership for generations.

4. One of the most important new aspects of the model of leadership advanced by the Besht was the absence of scholarliness as a requirement for spiritual authority. The Besht was not a "scholar" in the traditional sense; that is, someone with demonstrable mastery of the Talmud. He had no pretensions of being able to issue Halachic edicts or offer novel Talmudic interpretations.[5] The Besht drew his authority from the intense mystical experiences he underwent and from his ability to act on behalf of the Jewish people in the Upper Worlds. In this respect too the Besht's set a precedent that was to be followed for generations. From his time forward, scholarliness was no longer considered to be a necessary prerequisite among Hasidim for public leadership.

5. Despite the numerous and complex links between Hasidism and its antecedents (namely, the living and literary heritage of the Kabbalists and the Kabbalah), Hasidism is to be considered a pathbreaking movement. This was true not only of its social and organizational aspects, but also of its form of spirituality and the ideas it advanced. Within traditional society, no such breakthrough could have occured had there not been a person or persons who lent their authority to its achievement. Thus, the function the Besht filled in the launching of Hasidism is not confined to his formation of a new religious ethos and promulgation of it to others, nor even solely to his provision of a new model of spiritual leadership. The Besht also served as a source of inspiration and authority for these innovations. It stands to reason that his authority was based upon the elements of the miraculous in his person: on his skills in magic, his exceptional endowment of powers, his ascents of the soul, his ecstatic prayers, and his mystical experiences. In short, it was the Besht's charisma that gave authorization and sanction to the new way of Hasidism.

These are the main conclusions prompted by this book. To them, one may add the testimony of the relevant parties—the Hasidim—themselves.

From the first generations of the Hasidic movement up to the present day, the Hasidim have constantly spoken of the Besht as the father and progenitor of Hasidism. A characteristic expression of this attitude may be found in the statements of R. Meshulam Feibush Heller, author of *Yosher Divrei Emet.*

R. Meshulam belongs to what is usually termed the "third generation" of Hasidism. He himself was not a Hasidic leader, but his book, the first part of which was written in 1777, is considered to reflect properly the prevailing modes of thought among Hasidim during the 1760s and 1770s; that is, during the period of the Hasidic movement's coalescence. In the course of presenting the Hasidic approach to divine worship, R. Meshulam notes that his teachers in Hasidism were R. Dov Ber the *maggid* of Mezerich, R. Menahem Mendel of Peremyshlyan, and R. Yehiel Michal of Zloczow. He is thus referring to the figures who were active in promoting the Hasidic way during the 1760s and 1770s. And here is how R. Meshulam describes these teachers: "The learned of the era, men of marvels possessed of the Holy Spirit, whom my eyes beheld and not a stranger's; like an angel of God is their fear and awe, and all had drunk at the same fountain, namely the divine R. Israel Baal Shem Tov of blessed and righteous memory."[6] These statements give a clear and unequivocal expression of the perspective that names the Besht as the person who initiated the new spiritual approach of Hasidism.

Should someone seek to argue that in such matters the testimony of Hasidim themselves is unreliable—for the "true founders" of Hasidism, the Hasidic leaders, used the Besht as someone to whom they could attribute the spiritual innovations which they themselves advanced, and for the sake of securing their own authority—we should ask in return: Why, then, was it the Besht who was specifically chosen for this task? Why not, for instance, draw upon the authority and prestige of so mystical and charismatic a figure as the *maggid* of Mezerich? The conclusion one is forced to is, the Besht was seized upon precisely because of the genuine connection these Hasidim had to his character and to his spiritual path.

Accordingly, for all that concerns the function the Besht filled in the development of Hasidism at its outset, there is considerable correspondence between the contents of Hasidic tradition and the implications of critical historical reconstruction.

MAGIC AND MIRACLE WORKERS
IN THE LITERATURE OF THE HASKALAH

The Haskalah movement, following the lead of its parent, the European Enlightenment, declared all-out war on "superstition."[1] Motivated by the desire to reform Judaism and Jewish society according to the dictates of reason, the maskilim aspired to uproot superstition and to eradicate behavior patterns they considered mere vestiges of ignorance and illusion. One of their prime targets was the belief in magic in all its manifestations.

This chapter will discuss the position of the Haskalah movement regarding magic and magicians (*baalei shem*), as revealed in the Haskalah literature of nineteenth-century eastern Europe. Haskalah authors, as we know, considered magic and Hasidism to be two sides of the same coin and fought both with equal ferocity: I discuss the significance of this juxtaposition below. First, however, I shall examine some pertinent excerpts from the literature and try to determine its influence on the way magic and *baalei shem* have been seen in the historiography of Hasidism. Finally, I shall address the question, What does Haskalah literature's attitude to magic and *baalei shem* tell us of the inner world of the Haskalah?

I

An early critic of magic and *baalei shem*, anticipating Haskalah literature by a few decades, was Solomon Maimon (1753–1800), who wrote the following in his memoirs:

> A well-known kabbalist, R. Yoel Baal Shem, earned much fame at the time by virtue of a few successful healings, achieved with the help of his medicinal knowledge and illusory trickery; he claimed, however, to have done all this through practical kabbalah and the power of the Ineffable Name. This gained him much renown in Poland.[2]

Maimon returns several times to the assertion that the *baalei shem* employed "conventional medications" and that their so-called magical powers were mere illusions. His view represents the position of a devout rationalist, deeply troubled that *baalei shem* successfully gained people's confidence. It was important, he believed, that his readers should have no doubt as to the real reason for the magicians" successes.

The equation of magic with the Hasidic movement is a central motif in nineteenth-century Haskalah satire.[3] There is no more typical representative of the trend than Yoseph Perl (1773–1839). As early as 1819, in the preface to his book

Megaleh Temirin, he describes a wonderful experience that befell the "anthologizer and editor." Portrayed by Perl as a typical Hasid, this person relates the following tale:

> When I journeyed from the Holy Community of Miedzybóz to the Holy Community of Zwaniecz and went astray by night . . . exhausted by the journey, I fainted away and fell upon a certain stone. There came an old man and woke me, and I was terrified of this old man. . . . I asked him, Who are you? and he said, I am the guardian posted by the Besht to watch over the writings of R. Adam, which he enclosed in this stone. And since the Besht commanded me to stand here on guard, until some person should stray from the path in the dark . . . and give him one of the said writings, I am therefore awakening you and am full of joy that the time has come. . . . And I began to weep before him and implore him to give me all the writings, but he said that he was not permitted to do so. And forthwith he chanted a spell, and a small crack formed in the stone. . . . A piece of paper emerged through the crack, and the guard took the paper and the stone immediately closed. The guard then took that paper and told me that, by the power of what was written thereon, I would be able to become invisible—that is, provided I kept it in my pocket, but specifically in my right pocket, for if I were to keep it in my left pocket the writing would be useless.[4]

Perl's anti-Hasidic satire was based on the book *Shivhei Habesht* (1814), in this particular case on the stories about Rabbi Adam Baal Shem. These stories purported to reveal the source of the Baal Shem Tov's knowledge as a *baal shem:* the "writings" that Rabbi Adam gave the Besht contained esoteric magical lore. It is also related in *Shivhei Habesht* that the Besht sealed up Rabbi Adam's "writings" in a stone on a nearby mountain.[5] The blurred borderlines between legend and reality exemplified in the above excerpt are a typical feature of Hasidism as described by Perl. The magical elements in the Besht's person and biography, which the maskil sees as nothing but delusion or hallucination, are perfectly real for the Hasid.

The Hasid's uncritical acceptance of the legend about the Besht is just one side of the coin. The other is the Hasidic conviction that even the contemporary leaders of Hasidism were capable of performing miracles like those attributed to the Besht. Indeed, one of Perl's characters, Rabbi Zelig Letitshiber, says: "And now all respond in unison and exclaim with awe . . . that the tsadikim can do everything their heart desires, and that they compel the Lord, praise be to Him, to do everything they wish, and that they perform wondrous deeds."[6] The letters that make up Perl's book are full of stories of Hasidim and their wives who appeal to the tsadik and avail themselves of his miraculous powers. While doing his best to demonstrate the boorish naiveté of the rank-and-file Hasidim, Perl spares no effort to expose the avarice of their leaders, the zaddikim. To that end he repeatedly returns to the subject of the redemption money (*pidyon*) that the Hasidim bring their leaders when they come to them for help.[7]

Underlying Perl's satire is the assumption that no one—at least, among his enlightened readers—doubts the ridiculous and contemptible nature of magic in general and of the belief in the magical powers of the Hasidic leaders in particular. Hence the mere description of various instances of this belief among the Hasidim should suffice to provoke derision and revulsion. Nevertheless, Perl did not make magic the focus of his critique of Hasidism merely because he considered it a weak point where the enemy was most vulnerable to attack. He was in fact convinced that belief in the miracles performed by the Besht or the contemporary tsadikim was a major factor in the steady growth and spread of Hasidism. It was therefore imperative to challenge such beliefs.[8]

While Perl's strong point was the indirect barb of parody, another Galician maskil preferred to mount a direct frontal attack. Judah Leib Mieses (1798–1831) indeed devoted a large part of his *Kinat Ha'emet* (1828) to a fierce assault on superstitious beliefs in demons and sorcery. Relying on the views of some of the greatest Jewish sages in the past, particularly Maimonides, Mieses argued that "pure" Judaism rejected such beliefs, which were not only baseless but also at times dangerous. Many foolish practices, deleterious to the moral fiber of the Jewish people, were the outcome of such superstitions.

Mieses considered Hasidism a misfortune that had befallen the Jewish people because of their belief in demons and sorcery, "In so far as only people who believe in demons and sorcery . . . might ascribe any sanctity to the leaders and heads of this sect." Like Perl and other maskilim, Mieses also argued that belief in the Hasidic leaders' magical powers was basic to the existence of the despised movement. It was only a natural conclusion that those who wished "for the eradication of this sect . . . from the Jewish people" must tackle the popular belief in demons and sorcery.[9]

Like most maskilim of this time, Mieses was convinced that these obscurantist beliefs were the outgrowths of ignorance and folly. People of learning and wisdom would never tolerate them. In an attempt to illustrate this important principle, Mieses cited no less an example than the Besht himself.

> There was once a person, of little knowledge, named Israel son of Eliezer, known among the masses as Baal Shem. His ancestors had been from the poorest and basest of the people living in a certain village in Poland (the home of darkness and ignorance), and therefore they could not afford to hire a teacher for him, to tutor him in his youth. . . . And even later, when the boy grew up, he did not mix with the wise of heart, nor did his feet cross their threshold, for his heart was void of sense and his mind quite incapable of understanding scholarly things. Therefore, even as an adult, he was ignorant, bereft of words of learning and knowledge, not understanding any passage of the Talmud, how much less so of the Bible.[10]

Thus the Besht's biography was presented as proof that poverty, ignorance, and stupidity went hand in hand to mold his character as *baal shem*. Where, then, did

the Besht obtain the knowledge he needed to become a *baal shem?* Mieses's explanation is also no credit to the founder of Hasidism: the Besht learned from the
non-Jewish peasants among whom he lived how to pick medicinal herbs and how
to use them. He took up sorcery after realizing that herbal healing would not earn
him the fame he wanted. The model that he chose to emulate was that of the non-
Jewish sorcerer.[11] In sum, the two main factors that shaped the Besht's career were
poverty and ignorance on the one hand, and the non-Jewish subculture on the
other. No wonder, therefore, that conclusions could be drawn from the person of
the Besht as to the nature of his followers.

Views like those of Perl and Mieses were so deeply entrenched among the Galician maskilim that their colleagues and fellow writers in Italy embraced them
too.[12] A typical example is a letter written by Samuel David Luzzatto (1800–1865)
to his maskil friend Samuel Leib Goldenberg. The occasion for the correspondence
was a rumor that the Hasidic leader Rabbi Israel of Ruzhin (1797–1850) had settled
in Galicia. This news inspired Luzzatto to set out his view of Hasidic beliefs in the
tsadik's supernatural powers. His account begins as follows:

> I know not whether to laugh or to weep at the rumor that you have conveyed,
> my friend, concerning that man named Israel, bearing the same name as his
> master Israel Baal Shem Tov, who has led the children of Israel astray this past
> generation in your country; that same Baal Shem Tov who received books of
> secrets and mysteries from R. Adam, who moved the king's palace through the
> power of Names and brought it to another city, that same Besht who moves
> mountains from their place and brings them near one another . . . that same
> Besht who found the frog in the desert in which was embodied a Jewish soul
> who had neglected [the commandment of] washing the hands, and redeemed
> that soul, which had already spent five centuries in the body of a frog; that
> same Besht who performs wonders and miracles too numerous for the mouth
> to tell or the ear to hear.[13]

Like his colleagues of the Galician Haskalah, Samuel David Luzzatto was familiar with Dov Ber of Linces's *Shivhei Habesht* and took advantage of his familiarity
to ridicule the Hasidim. The reference to some of the miracles ascribed to the Besht
in the book reinforces the idea that belief in his magical powers (and those of the
other leaders of Hasidism) was a cornerstone of Hasidic life. Like Perl, Luzzatto
also thought this so contemptible and repulsive a belief that merely describing it
would lend his words an overtone of irony and arouse an appropriate reaction in
the reader.

Samuel David Luzzatto was so ensnared by Haskalah preconceptions that he
unhesitatingly ascribed to Israel of Ruzhin the same predilections as the popular
figure of the Besht. Had he taken the trouble to check his facts, he would have
found that Rabbi Israel dissociated himself from the performance of miracles.[14]
Luzzatto, however, together with the maskilim as a whole, automatically identified
the Hasidic leaders with the *baalei shem*, believing that he needed no supporting

proof. Not content merely to ridicule the superstitions of the Hasidim, he took issue with them directly. If the Hasidim should respond to his criticisms, he mused, by asking, "Why judge the tsadikim differently from biblical and talmudic figures who had also experienced wonders?" one should reply:

> How are their eyes besmeared, and they see not, their minds, and they cannot think, that they cannot distinguish between the holy and the profane, between the impure and the pure? Were the saints of old like these pretenders to sanctity? . . . Did they entreat the Lord on behalf of their brethren for their own personal gain? When they prayed for their companions, were they showered with gold and silver?[15]

Clearly Luzzatto, like his Galician colleagues, entertained no doubts: the primary basis for the Hasidic leaders' pretensions to supernatural powers such as the ability to heal their followers and to render material help of various kinds was simply their desire to enrich themselves.

The literary assault of the Galician maskilim on Hasidism, with its focus on ludicrous beliefs in the supernatural, was also taken up by representatives of the Russian Haskalah. Thus, Isaac Baer Levinsohn (1788–1860) wrote his satirical work *Emek refa'im* (1830) in the form of a confession by a supposed miracle worker or Hasidic tsadik. This character makes a clean breast of his misdeeds, admitting that all the "wonders" he has performed were fraudulent. Levinsohn does not omit to mention that the wonder-worker's success in misleading the public was due to the nature of his audience:

> I therefore elected to settle in a very small town, where there were neither scholars nor scribes, neither wealthy men nor merchants, but people who were so poor that they were forever preoccupied with making a living and did not understand even the ways of the world, let alone deceit and subterfuge. They were sincere believers in every lie and deception and vanity, consulted soothsayers and sorcerers, believed old crones and their magic spells.[16]

Thus Levinsohn shared the view of the Galician maskilim that poverty and ignorance were the soil that nurtured the belief in the miraculous powers of the *baalei shem.* Another important motif in the Haskalah attack on magic and its manifestations in Hasidism was the extreme contrast between the magicians on the one hand and legitimate medicine on the other. For example, Levinsohn's wonder-worker declares, "I would prove to them at all times that they should not believe in any physician or doctor at all, just come to me and give me their pidyonot that I should pray for them."[17]

The contrast between magic and conventional medicine in *Aviezer,* received much prominence in the autobiography of the Lithuanian maskil Mordecai Aaron Guenzburg (1795–1846). Guenzburg renders a lively account of his contemporaries' superstitious beliefs. He himself fell victim to superstition when, having married at an early age, he discovered that he was sexually impotent. His mother-in-law, convinced that he had been bewitched, forced her young son-in-law to drink a "remedy" concocted by an old witch to counteract the spell that had been cast on him. As a result, he fell ill with a fever and a bad cough. Nevertheless, relates Guenzburg, "my mother-in-law would not agree to consult a doctor, only old women, by whose flame I had already been burned."[18]

Guenzburg was cured of his ills by an elderly physician with many decades of medical experience. Needless to say, unlike the old crones with their nostrums, the old man summoned up his experience and medical knowledge, and in addition "took no money for his fee, for he was a very wealthy man, and practiced medicine for nothing but the love of humanity." Moreover, he was also a scholar, well versed in languages, and in fact encouraged the young Guenzburg to set out on the path of Haskalah.[19] Throughout, Guenzburg contrasts the grotesqueries of magic and witchcraft with their respectable, useful counterpart: conventional medicine based on science. Living in Lithuania, he aimed his criticism not at Hasidism but at traditional Lithuanian Jewish society, which he thought was unduly influenced by superstitions and witch doctors. His own consultation of a proper doctor was considered exceptional and frowned upon by Lithuanian society.[20]

Some echoes of Haskalah literature's anti-Hasidic campaign are discernible in the works of Mendele Mokher Seforim (1835–1917), particularly in his *Ha'avot vehabanim* (1868), one of whose major characters is a Hasidic tsadik who claims to be a wonder-worker and to heal all his followers' ills.[21] Mendele's picture of magic and magicians is painted with colors not used by his predecessors.[22] Nevertheless, despite some moderation in his polemical tone, Mendele does make his contribution to the image prevalent in Haskalah literature of the ignorant masses steeped in magical beliefs. Moreover, he reveals the non-Jewish roots of the magical practices common among Jews.[23] This equation of *baalei shem* with gentile magicians was not Mendele's innovation. Nevertheless, he characteristically placed the equation in a striking literary mould. The following excerpt, in which a woman is searching for her husband who has disappeared, is a case in point.

> If you will hearken to me and heed my advice, said Hannah, I advise you to consult a gypsy woman, a witch. . . . Last year a woman came to me grieving, clad in sackcloth for the husband of her youth, who had abandoned her some years before, and she had consulted *baalei shem* and wonder-workers, to no avail. Not one of them passed through the village but she gave him money for redemption of the soul—but there was no salvation. And she came to the gypsy woman and implored her to heal her sorrow and bring her husband back. So she went out with her at evening with magic spells. . . . She placed a pot full of bones and the innards of unclean creatures on a fire, and made spells and cakes. . . . Then she said to the woman: Look into the pot. . . . All of a sudden she began to tremble, like a woman in travail, and screamed out with a loud voice. Fear not—said the witch—for what have you seen? Said the woman: I saw my husband rising from the ground. . . . Said the gypsy: May I not live to see redemption if you do not see your husband this very night! . . .

> And it came to pass, scarcely had the woman lain down in her bed . . . but lo!
> her beloved was knocking at the door. . . . And she rose to let in her beloved,
> who rushed into the house helter-skelter, riding on a rake, holding a broom
> in his hand![24]

The butt of the ridicule in the passage is surely the *baalei shem* and those who believe in them. Not only is there no real difference between the magical practices of the *baalei shem* and those of a gypsy witch, the witch is in fact more powerful. This comparison, almost an equation, between the magical arts of the Jewish *baalei shem* and the gentiles contradicts the common belief among Jews that the former derive their abilities from the Kabbalah.

Of course, these excerpts from Haskalah literature do not exhaust that literature's attitude to magic in general and its Hasidic manifestations in particular. Nevertheless, even these few passages are sufficiently representative. The Haskalah position may thus be summarized as follows:

1. Magic of all kinds is based on illusion and deception; it has no place in a society founded on reason and science.

2. Magical beliefs and practices are characteristic of the popular, ignorant classes.

3. There is no real difference between the magic of the *baalei shem* and that of their non-Jewish neighbors.

4. Magic is central to the Hasidic movement. The masses of Hasidim are steeped in superstition and their leaders are deluding them for their own personal interests.

II

As we know, the Haskalah was unable to stem the tide of Hasidism, despite the war it waged against the movement through literature and other means. Haskalah literature may nevertheless be credited with some success: its constant emphasis on magic and *baalei shem* significantly affected the perceptions of the historians of Hasidism.[25] Traces of this influence were visible in historical literature and in the minds of educated people until quite recently. A few examples will illustrate this. One historian who applied a rational criterion to the evaluation of Hasidism was Heinrich Graetz (1817–1891). He chose to define and characterize the movement by presenting it as the polar opposite of the Haskalah, aptly expressing the self-perception of the Haskalah and its relationship with Hasidism:

> It seems remarkable that, at the time when Mendelssohn declared rational
> thought to be the essence of Judaism, and founded, as it were, a widely
> extended order of enlightened men, another banner was unfurled, whose
> adherents announced the grossest superstition to be the fundamental principle of Judaism, and formed an order of wonder-seeking confederates.[26]

The "wonders" of which Graetz was speaking were those that Hasidism attributed to its founder and its leaders. Graetz thus accepted the thesis that the essence of Hasidism was belief in the tsadik's magical powers. Echoes of what we have read in Haskalah literature may also be heard in his account of the life of the Baal Shem Tov. For example, Graetz wrote that the Besht had learned his magical lore "probably from the peasant women who gathered herbs on the mountain-tops and on the edges of the river. As they did not trust the healing power of nature, but added conjurations and invocations to good and evil spirits, Israel also accustomed himself to this method of cure."[27] Nevertheless, historical perspective and a desire for objectivity rid Graetz of certain Haskalah misconceptions concerning the Besht and the new movement. For example, he did not repeat the canard that the Besht used magical remedies to make money. He was also more restrained in his discussion of the Besht's ecstatic prayer and mystical experiences.[28] For all that, one cannot help sensing the continuity between Haskalah literature and Graetz's account of Hasidism.

It was Eliezer Tsevi Zweifel (1815–1888) who first broke with the Haskalah's traditional hostility to Hasidism. In his *Shalom al yisra'el* (1868), Zweifel described Hasidism as a legitimate phenomenon, alongside the Talmud and Kabbalah. Moreover, he argued, Hasidism was—or, at least at its inception had been—a religious revival movement.[29] But even Zweifel, who revealed both the spiritual-ideological and the social virtues of Hasidism, maintained the negative Haskalah position vis-à-vis magic. This position is particularly striking in view of his efforts to defend the Besht against the accusation of being a *baal shem*:

> It is an error of those who think and write "Besht" meaning wonder-worker and one who activates segulot and medicines by Holy Names. (1) For it is known that the Besht did not generally use Names save in prayers. (2) How could the Besht refer to himself and sign his name as a wonder-worker? (3) What point would there be to add the word tov [good]—is there a wonder-worker who is anything but good?[30]

Zweifel was trying to smooth over the magical elements in the Besht's character, both by arguing that the Besht had almost never used "Names" and by denying the magical content of the epithet Baal Shem Tov. It is hard to say whether Zweifel was sincere or whether he was dissembling when he wrote, "How could the Besht refer to himself . . . as a wonder-worker?" Whatever the case may be, the very formulation of the question, as well as the other arguments adduced, clearly imply that Zweifel was faithful to the traditional distaste of the Haskalah for anything to do with magic. Like other maskilim, previous and contemporary, he viewed healing through Holy Names and *segulot* as contemptible and repellent. It was inconceivable, therefore, that this could have been the occupation of the founder of a religious revival movement.

Some subsequent writers took a similar approach. While casting Hasidism in a positive light, they felt it necessary to belittle the prominence of the magical element in the figure of the Besht. One of these was Samuel Abba Horodezky

(1871–1957), who tried to portray Hasidism on the basis of his own familiarity with the movement's literature. Despite his rather detached point of view, he evinced some sympathy for the movement and its leaders. Unlike Zweifel, Horodezky was fully aware that the Besht was a "genuine" *baal shem,* who actually used "Names." Nevertheless, he saw fit to differentiate between the Besht and other practitioners of the art: "Hasidism knows how to elevate the Besht above the level of previous *baalei shem.* Although they too healed the sick with spells and charms and *segulot,* the Besht, in contrast, could detect sicknesses before they occurred and fended them off with his remedies." At this point Horodezky refers to two cases described in *Shivhei Habesht,* in both of which the Besht called upon his ability to foretell the future in order to help the invalid.[31] Another sign of the Besht's superiority over other *baalei shem* is that "the Besht objected to consulting sorcerers and magicians, as was the popular custom in those days. He himself sometimes ordered a doctor to be summoned."[32] These distinctions between the Besht and other *baalei shem* illustrates how difficult it was for Horodezky to break the Haskalah's shackles of contempt for magic and magicians.

If this was the case with such authors as Zweifel and Horodezky, whose object was to defend Hasidism, it was all the more so with a scholar and thinker like Saul Israel Hurwitz (1861–1927) who, in an essay entitled "Hasidism and Haskalah" (1923),[33] wrote a reply in the spirit of Haskalah to those who had begun to speak favorably of Hasidism. He was thinking of authors such as Y. L. Peretz and Micha Josef Berdyczewski and scholars like Samuel Horodezky, whose neohasidic romanticism, as he saw it, angered him. In his essay, he tried to draw up a balance sheet, comparing the good and evil that each of the two movements had caused the Jewish people. His point of departure in this comparative survey is that of a nationalist maskil. For him, the Haskalah movement had brought the Jews out of the darkness of the ghetto and paved the way for the emergence of Jewish nationalism. Hasidism, by contrast, had tried to block any positive step and was therefore a typical Diaspora phenomenon.

Among the many faults that Hurwitz attributed to Hasidism was, naturally, its association with magic. The accusation was linked mainly to the Besht:

> It would seem that the gentile environment in which the Besht had grown up and lived influenced him to a considerable degree and obscured his spiritual nature. It was from that Haydamak-Wallachian environment that the Besht took his melodies, the *nigunim* . . . and, especially, the melancholy melodies of the peasant maids (together with whom he had picked medicinal herbs in the Carpathians). . . . From that very same environment he also derived a good many strange tendencies and superstitions. . . . He also liked to jest and curse with coarse expressions, like a bloodletting, spell-chanting sorcerer, a familiar type among the peasants. . . . Such was the Besht. This Besht, they say, left "people" behind after him. It is easy to guess just who those "people" were who had come to learn Torah from this sorcerer and *baal shem* . . . a few backward people, remnants of the Frankists, an ignorant, coarse riffraff, con-

temptible and vulgar, lickers of leftovers, believers in miracles and familiar spirits and all kinds of superstitions.[34]

In other words, neither the distance in time nor the nationalist viewpoint had weakened Hurwitz's animosity toward Hasidism. Moreover, his attitude to the Besht and to his magical practices could have come from any essay by a Galician maskil of the first half of the nineteenth century.

It was Simon Dubnow (1860–1941) who laid the foundations for the critical historical treatment of Hasidism. His influence on the scholarly study of the movement in the last few generations is inestimable. He was no less important in shaping the image of Hasidism held by the educated public. When one examines Dubnow's position in regard to magic and *baalei shem*, it turns out that he was well rooted in the Haskalah literature of the nineteenth century and the writings of the authors who followed its lead. Describing the background of the Besht's activities as the founder of Hasidism, Dubnow wrote:

> At that time the wonder-working kabbalists known as *baalei shem*—that is, those who worked wonders by combinations of Holy Names—were quite popular. They would wander around the cities and villages, healing all sorts of diseases and ills by means of spells, charms, and other *segulot*. . . . As the masses believed that mental disorders were caused by a *dybbuk* or evil spirit entering a person's body, some of the *baalei shem* were experts in that area and knew how to expel the *dybbuk* from the invalid's body.[35]

To help his readers understand the cultural environment of the *baalei shem*'s actions, Dubnow related a story about demons who had allegedly occupied a Jewish home in Poznan toward the end of the seventeenth century. The story illustrated, he claimed, "to what degree the belief in demons and spirits was widespread at the time." Moreover, he asserted, such stories not only showed the kind of ideas that had become popular; the very telling of the stories had a negative influence, for "they were passed around by word of mouth, inspired religious hallucinations and spread superstitious beliefs among the people."[36]

These passages clearly demonstrate Dubnow's view that the *baalei shem* constituted a typical folk phenomenon. Evidence of their popular, not to say vulgar, nature was their particular popularity among the masses and the fact that their activities were based on "hallucinations" and "superstitious beliefs." Dubnow's sympathy for the Haskalah position is also obvious in his description of the *baalei shem* as intruding in matters that properly belonged to the medical profession: "At a time when learned physicians were rare and in fact non-existent in the smaller towns and villages, the *baalei shem* took the doctors' place as healers of physical and mental sickness among the people, who were steeped in hallucinations and superstitious beliefs."[37] Not content with having reiterated for his readers that the activities of the *baalei shem* relied on popular superstition, Dubnow also exposed the scoundrels' base motives: "The *baalei shem* exerted considerable spiritual influence on the masses, who believed in their remedies and "miracles." Many exploited such superstitions for their own good, exacting payment."[38]

In general, Dubnow's negative attitude to magic and *baalei shem* derived from a historiographical tradition deeply entrenched in Haskalah literature and ideology. He may nevertheless be counted among those scholars who were resolved to demonstrate the positive elements of Hasidism. He maintained that Hasidism constituted a challenge to the fossilized Judaism of the rabbinic establishment. How could one reconcile the fact that the Besht was a *baal shem* on the one hand, and the founder of a movement that played a positive role in Jewish history on the other? Dubnow found his solution ready-made in the writings of Zweifel, Horodezky, and their colleagues. Like his predecessors, Dubnow made a distinction between the Besht and other *baalei shem;* more precisely, he distinguished between the corrupt, fraudulent *baalei shem* and "the best of them," one of whom was the Besht. While he had also started out as a *baal shem,* he ultimately abandoned that vocation and focused his efforts on "revealing a new Torah." Moreover, the rumors that had spread about his miracles prepared people's minds for his teachings. And as he was not content to heal the body but also cared for the soul and became a religious and ethical guide for all those who sought his help, the masses sensed that this was no ordinary *baal shem,* but a *good,* benevolent *baal shem,* a guide and an educator. Hence the epithet Baal Shem Tov [the good *baal shem*] (and its abbreviated form, the Besht), which became the permanent nickname of the creator of Hasidism.[39]

Dubnow's assertion concerning the transformation in the Besht's career, as well as his explanation of the origin of the nickname Baal Shem Tov, were sharply criticized by Gershom Scholem, who essentially offered three objections:

1. Of the *baalei shem* known to us, almost none made any attempt to expound religious beliefs and ideas.

2. The nickname Baal Shem Tov was not new; neither was it applied solely to the Besht.

3. We do not know of any proven transformation in the Besht's career; on the contrary, he continued to practice his magical arts all his life, and was even proud of them.[40]

Scholem's objections to the attempt to remove the magical sting from the Besht's personality were not confined to Dubnow. Among the other authors who provoked Scholem's criticism was Martin Buber, who claimed that the charms the Besht gave to those requesting his aid were not magic spells; rather, they served as a kind of symbol linking the helper to those being helped. Scholem firmly rejected this suggestion too, citing incontrovertible proof that the Besht gave out charms and in this respect was no different from any other *baal shem.*[41]

III

What can one learn about the inner world of the Haskalah movement from the treatment of magic and *baalei shem* in Haskalah literature? Before answering this question, we must consider why the Haskalah aimed its attack on magic and its practitioners specifically at Hasidism; obviously, the belief that demonic powers could determine the fate of human beings and that magic could be used as protection against such powers was not confined to Hasidism. It will be remembered that Mordecai Aaron Guenzburg consulted a witch to combat the spell that had made him impotent and Guenzburg lived in Lithuania, stronghold of the mitnagedim. His case was by no means exceptional; there is copious evidence that magic was commonly used throughout traditional Jewish society in eastern Europe, including among the learned scholars of Lithuania. Here are some examples:

1. R. Nahman Reuben of Samorgon, a Lithuanian rabbi who studied in his youth at the Volozhin yeshiva, related that Isaac, the son of Hayim of Volozhin, wrote charms to heal two yeshiva students of epilepsy.[42]

2. R. Yosef Sundel of Salant (1786–1866), one of R. Hayim of Volozhin's closest disciples, who exerted a profound influence on R. Israel Salanter (1810–1883, the founder of the *musar* movement) and was later consulted on Halachic matters by the *perushim*[43] of Jerusalem, possessed a manuscript list of "Spells and Remedies." Among other things, these spells were supposed to help barren women, women in childbirth, epileptics, and other unfortunates. We may assume that R. Yosef Sundel actually used these charms.[44]

3. Lithuanian scholars and rabbis were involved on several occasions in exorcizing a dybbuk. According to traditions passed on by the disciples of R. Hayim of Volozhin, the Vilna Gaon himself was involved in two such cases.[45] Among the manuscripts of Samuel of Kelmy is a letter rendering a detailed account of an exorcism performed by the rabbi of Deliatitz in 1844.[46] Two other accounts of the exorcism of dybbukim in Lithuania at the end of the nineteenth and beginning of the twentieth centuries are cited by Gedaliah Nigal.[47] In one case the exorcism was performed by R. Moshe Hakohen of Stotzin. In the second case the presiding rabbi was R. Elhanan Wasserman, then a student at the Hafets Hayim's yeshiva in Radin and later a yeshiva principal in his own right.

These examples are surely sufficient to disprove the prevailing conception, resulting from the influence of Haskalah literature, that the practice of magic was specific to Hasidism; the truth was quite different. We are therefore faced again with the question of why Haskalah literature persisted in this misrepresentation of the facts. The question becomes even more acute if we observe that Hasidism may in fact have mitigated the influence of magic. Wherever Hasidism gained ascendancy, the zaddikim inherited the function of the *baalei shem* in the sense that they became the new address for requests for help in material matters. At the same time, not all the tsadikim thought of themselves as wonder-workers.[48] Even those who considered themselves successors of the Besht as wonder-workers frequently exercised their powers through prayer rather than through charms and spells. On the other hand, it is a reasonable assumption that, in areas where Hasidism made no headway, people continued to consult *baalei shem* of the old type, who unabashedly used the paraphernalia of magic.

The motives of the Haskalah movement's opposition to Hasidism were no doubt deep-seated and more varied than the mere objection to magical elements. For the maskilim, Hasidism was the most extreme manifestation of the multiple deficiencies of traditional life, which they strove to "mend" and change. In addition, they perceived the spread and upsurge of Hasidism as a threat to the future of Jewish society. That being so, nothing was easier for the maskilim than to seize on the magical elements in Hasidism in order to attack it. It had always been the contention of east European maskilim that the opposition to the Haskalah came from an obscurantist movement of the ignorant masses.[49] The prominence they ascribed to the role of magic in Hasidism enabled them to prove decisively that these were the Haskalah movement's most bitter enemies. No wonder, then, that Haskalah authors portrayed magic as a central motif in Hasidism, ignoring the spiritual elements that played such an important role in it.

The treatment of the magical arts in Haskalah literature has an additional and more profound significance. Indeed, beyond the desire to combat the "enemy," the literary war against Hasidism was crucial in shaping the Haskalah leaders' self-image. This idea has been stated with admirable clarity by Shmuel Werses:

> Indeed, Hasidism inadvertently contributed to the strengthening and coalescence of Haskalah literature. . . . The slogans and self-awareness of the Haskalah were consolidated and more clearly formulated through its polemical portrayal of Hasidism; moreover, the existence and success of the Hasidic movement sometimes lent motivation and meaning to the objectives of the Haskalah.[50]

This penetrating observation is also relevant to the present analysis. Haskalah literature, by ridiculing magic and *baalei shem* and by identifying the phenomenon with Hasidism, which provided the Haskalah movement with both an adversary and a kind of reverse mirror-image, was better able to express its own inner truth—its image of itself—as having transcended the superstition of the magical arts. This was no trivial matter: after all, the writers of the Haskalah movement had been reared and educated in an environment where magic, in all its manifestations, played a crucial role.

APPENDIX II

THE BESHT'S EPISTLE

Written in the [week of] Trumah Torah portion, 5512, here in the community of Raszkow.

This is the letter given by Rabbi Israel Besht of Blessed and Righteous Memory to our Rabbi the author our teacher (etc.) Yaakov Yosef Hacohen to be passed to his brother-in-law Rabbi Gershon Kotover who was in the Holy Land and because of a delay which came from the Blessed Lord he did not travel to the Land of Israel and it remained in his hands so as to benefit our nation the people of Israel.

So as not to put out blank pages I have written out a great story from R. Israel Baal Shem.

The Sacred Epistle

To my beloved, my brother-in-law, and my friend dearly cherished as my own soul and heart, he being the Rabbinic wonder, the Hasid, famous in Torah and piety, his honor our teacher Avraham Gershon, may his candle shine and peace be to all that is his, and to his chaste wife Mrs. Bluma and all her offspring, may they all be granted the blessing of life, Amen Selah.

To my beloved, my brother-in-law, and my friend dearly cherished as my own soul and heart, he being the Rabbinic wonder, the Hasid, famous in Torah and piety, his honor our teacher Avraham Gershon, may his candle shine and peace be to all that is his. And to his chaste wife Mrs. Bluma and all her offspring, may they all be granted the blessing of life, Amen Selah.

The imprimateur of his holy hand I received at the Lukov fair in the year 5510,

The imprimateur of his holy hand I received at the Lukov fair in the year 5510, that which you sent with the emissary who left Jerusalem and which was written in the essence of brevity; there it is said that you had already written at length to each and every one employing someone who was traveling to Egypt, yet those letters written at length did not reach me and I was greatly pained by this that I have not seen the figure of your holy hand which you wrote out in detail, and no doubt this is owing to the deteriorated conditions in the countries (by our sins) as the plague has spread to every country and even has reached nearby regions, the community of Mohilev and the districts of Walachia and Kedar, and there it is also said that those innovations and secrets about which I had written to you via the scribe the Rabbi and *Mokhiah* of the Polonne community did not reach you and I was greatly pained by this as well for surely you would have been greatly pleased to have received them and although at the present I have forgotten certain parts yet some of the details which I can recollect I will write about quite briefly.

For on Rosh Hashana of the year 5507 I took an oath for an ascent of the soul as you know and I beheld amazing things in a vision

that which you sent with the emissary who left Jerusalem and which was written in the essence of brevity; there it is said that you had already written at length to each and every one employing someone who was traveling to Egypt, yet those letters written at length did not reach me and I was greatly pained by this that I have not seen the figure of your holy hand which you wrote out in detail, and no doubt this is owing to the deteriorated conditions in the countries (by our sins) as the plague has spread to every country and even has reached nearby regions, the holy community of Mohilev and the districts of Walachia and Kedar, and there it is also said that those innovations and secrets about which I had written to you via the scribe the Rabbi and *Mokhiah* of the Polonne community did not reach you and I was greatly pained by this as well for surely you would have been greatly pleased to have received them and although at the present I have forgotten certain parts yet some of the details which I can recollect I will write about quite briefly.

For on Rosh Hashana of the year 5507 I took an oath for an ascent of the soul as you know and I beheld amazing things in a vision such as

Surely it will be a wonder to you and gladden your soul for it is amazing to me as well, the vision which God showed me in the ascendancies, wonderful things as you know happen when souls ascend, as is known, and I beheld wonders such as I had not seen since I acquired reason and that which I beheld and learned in the ascent of the soul it is impossible to relate and to speak of even face to face. Yet when I returned to the lower Garden of Eden and beheld many souls of the living and of the dead, both familiar and unfamiliar to me, immeasurable and innumerable, running to and fro to rise from world to world via the pillar familiar to those who know mysteries, with such great and vast joy

I had not seen since I acquired reason and that which I beheld and learned in the ascent of the soul it is impossible to relate and to speak of even face to face. Yet when I returned to the lower Garden of Eden and beheld many souls of the living and of the dead, both familiar and unfamiliar to me, immeasurable and innumerable, running to and fro to rise from world to world via the pillar familiar to those who know mysteries, with such great and vast joy that the mouth does not suffice to relate and the physical ear is too heavy to hear, and there were also many wicked ones who repented and were absolved of their sins, as the hour of favor was then great; I myself was quite surprised at how many had their repentance accepted, some of whom you knew as well, and amongst them too there was extreme happiness and they too ascended in the said ascendancies; and everyone together asked of me and beseeched me (to the point of embarrassment) saying: Your honorable Torah eminence, the Lord has granted you the extra intelligence to discover and comprehend these matters; you shall ascend together with us and be our helper and provider; and owing to the great joy I saw amongst them I decided to

that the mouth does not suffice to relate and the physical ear is too heavy to hear, and there were also many wicked ones who repented and were absolved of their sins, as the hour of favor was then great; I myself was quite surprised at how many had their repentance accepted, some of whom you knew as well, and amongst them too there was extreme happiness and they too ascended in the said ascendancies; and everyone together asked of me and beseeched me (to the point of embarrassment) saying: Your honorable Torah eminence, the Lord has granted you the extra intelligence to discover and comprehend these matters; you shall ascend together with us and be our helper and provider and support; and owing to the great joy I saw amongst them I decided to rise along with them; and I asked the reason of the happiness and what was this day of days that had not been since the days of the ancients and what was this happiness about and they had no answer to give nor could even my Rabbi who you know of who was always by my side [give an answer]. I saw also all the ministers of the nations arriving in submission, like slaves before thier masters, before the Archangel Michael; he showered many that Samael rose to give evil counsel with great delight as never before and he worked his work, issuing decrees of forced conversion upon several souls who would be killed by strange deaths and I was horrified and literally risked my life and asked my teacher and rabbi to go with me for it is a great danger to go and ascend to the Upper Worlds for from the day I stood on my own I had not ascended by such great ascents and I rose step after step until I entered the palace of the Messiah where the Messiah studies Torah together with all the Tannaites and the Righteous Ones and also with the Seven Shepherds and there I beheld a very great happiness and I did not know what this happiness was all for and I was convinced the happiness was (God forbid) on account of my demise from the present world and I was later informed that I was not yet deceased as they like it up there when I perform *yihudim* below by means of their holy Torah and what the rejoicing meant I do not know to this day. And I inquired of the Messiah, when will Sir be coming, and he replied, once your Torah has spread through all the world etc.

rise along with them; and I beheld in a vision that Samael rose to give evil counsel with great delight as never before and he worked his work, issuing decrees of forced conversion upon several souls who would be killed by strange deaths and I was horrified and literally risked my life and asked my teacher and Rabbi to go with me for it is a great danger to go and ascend to the Upper Worlds for from the day I stood on my own I had not ascended by such great ascents and I rose step after step until I entered the palace of the Messiah where the Messiah studies Torah together with all the Tannaites and the Righteous Ones and also with the Seven Shepherds and there I beheld a very great happiness and I did not know what this happiness was all for and I was convinced the happiness was (God forbid) on account of my demise from the present world and I was later informed that I was not yet deceased as they like it up there when I perform *yihudim* below by means of their holy Torah and what the rejoicing meant I do not know to this day. And I inquired of the Messiah, when will Sir be coming, and he replied, by this you shall know: once your learning becomes

fine gifts on the *Tsadikim,* so that they might stand and bear the gladness and rejoicing that was just like at the giving of the Torah and which can't be grasped in materiality and I was frightened and shocked by this sight as I said to myself perhaps this was on my account and the time had come (God forbid) to depart from this world and perhaps for this sake it would be proper to do so and a hint is sufficient for the wise and I grieved for myself and my friends that my soul had deceased in the diaspora until I arrived and rose to the actual palace of the Messiah King and I actually saw face to face what I had not seen thus far from the day I [acquired] reason and they revealed to me that this was not on my account and they also revealed to me wonderful and awesome things in the profundities of Torah that I had not seen or heard and that no ear had heard of for some years and it occurred to me and I decided to ask him if it was perhaps because of preparations for his coming that there was this goodness and happiness and rejoicing and when will Sir be coming and the answer from His Eminence was that this could not be revealed but by this you shall know: once your learning becomes

publicly known and is re-
vealed in the world and your
fountains have overflowed
beyond what I have taught
you and what you have
achieved, and others too are
able to perform *yihudim* and
ascents just as you can, then
all the *Qlipot* shall terminate
and it will be a time of favor
and salvation; and I worried
about this and it greatly
pained me on account of the
length of time this was liable
to take; yet while I was there I
learned three charms and
three holy names which are
easily learned and explained,
so I calmed down and
thought that perhaps by this
means my colleagues too
would be able to come to the
level and rank that I have,
that is, would be able to have
ascents of the soul and to
learn and perceive as I have,
yet I was not given permission my whole life long to reveal this and I asked on your
behalf to teach it to you and
was not at all permitted and I
was sworn fast to this. Yet this
I shall inform you; and let the
Blessed Lord assist you, and
may your paths be in God's
presence and lose not sight of
them especially when in the
Holy Land. While you are
praying or studying, in each
and every utterance and issuance from your lips intend
to make a unification of it,
for in each and every letter

publicly known and is
revealed in the world and
your fountains have spread
overflowed what I have
taught you and what you
have achieved, and others too
are able to perform *yihudim*
and ascents just as you can,
then all the *Qlipot* shall terminate and it will be a time
of favor and salvation; and I
worried about this and it
greatly pained me on account
of the long time it would take
before this became possible;
yet while I was there I learned
three charms and three holy
names which are easily
learned and explained, so I
calmed down and thought
that perhaps by this means
my colleagues too would be
able to come to the level and
rank that I have, that is,
would be able to have ascents
of the soul and to learn and
perceive as I have, yet I was
not given permission my
whole life long to reveal this
and I asked on your behalf to
teach it to you and was not
permitted to at all and I was
fast forsworn from this. Yet
this I shall inform you; and
let the Blessed Lord assist
you, and may your paths be
God's presence, and lose not
sight of them especially when
in the Holy Land. While you
are praying or studying, in
each and every utterance and
issuance from your lips
understand how to make a

there are worlds and souls
and divinity which rise and
commune and bind to each
other and afterward the letters commune and unify
thoroughly and form a word
and are truly unified with
Godliness and you will
include your soul with them
at each and every level of the
above and all the worlds will
unify as one and rise and
make unaccountable joy and
delight; if you can conceive of
the joy of bride and groom in
smallness and materiality, so
much the more it is in this
Upper Level; and surely God
will be aiding you, and in all
you turn to you will succeed
and prevail; provide to the
wise and he will make wise;
and so pray for me with this
intention that I shall be
graced to share in the endowment of God while alive, and
for my offspring in the
Diaspora.

I prayed there why has God
done thus and wherefore the
great wrath owing to which
several souls of Israel have
been handed to Samael for
execution and several of them
for conversion and then for
execution and they permitted
me to directly inquire it of
Samael himself and I asked
Samael what was the point of
this and what he thought of
the fact that they were being
converted and afterward
being killed, and he

unification of it, for in each
and every letter there are
worlds and souls and divinity
which rise and commune and
bind each other to Godliness
and afterward the letters
commune and unify thor-
oughly and form a word and
are completely unified with
Godliness and you will
include your soul with them
at each and every level of the
above and all the worlds will
unify as one and rise and
make unaccountable joy and
delight; if you can conceive of
the joy of bride and groom in
smallness and materiality,
how much more so it is in
this Upper Level; and surely
God will be aiding you, and
in all you turn to you will
succeed and prevail; provide
to the wise and he will make
wise; and so pray for me with
this intention that I shall be
graced to share in the endowment of God while alive, and
for my offspring in the
Diaspora.

And I also beheld, after be-
holding the said ministers of
the nations, I beheld Samael
among them as well, and he
came as a slave, vanquished
and compliant before the
archangel and before all the
righteous ones etc. and the
fury of the Lord of Hosts was
arrested in my heart like a
fierce blaze for the fact that
there had not been Godly
vengeance returned to his

replied that his intentions are for a heavenly cause for if they were allowed to stay alive after converting then when there was some future edict then they would not sanctify God's name but would instead convert so as to save themselves therefore his method of operation was to have those who convert be killed afterward so that no son of Israel would convert and would instead sanctify the Name of God and so it was by our sins later on that in the community of Zaslav there was a libel against several souls and two of them converted and were afterward put to death. And the rest sanctified the Name of Heaven in a great sanctity and died by strange deaths and afterward when there were libels in the community of Szepetowka and the holy community of Dunajow they did not convert having seen what took place in the holy community of Zaslav but rather all of them gave over their lives to sanctify the Lord and sanctified the Heavenly Name and withstood the test and thanks to it our Messiah will come and take his vengeance and redeem his land and his people.

replied that his intentions are for a heavenly cause and so it was by our sins later on that in the community of Zaslav there was a libel against several souls and two of them converted and were afterward put to death and the rest sanctified the Name of Heaven in a great sanctity and died by strange deaths and afterward when there were libels in the holy community of Szepetowka and the holy community of Dunajow they did not convert having seen what took place in the holy community of Zaslav but rather all of them gave over their lives to sanctify the Lord and sanctified the Heavenly Name and withstood the test and thanks to it our Messiah will come and take his vengeance and redeem his land and his people.

tormentors for the martyrs etc., and I could not resist from asking him, you have killed in body why did you need to kill in soul, tricking them to convert, and he answered with great meekness before the said great Minister, this I did by the counsel and permission of the great and awesome minister Gabriel for the sake of All of Israel, so that in the several future decrees wherein several Jews would be tempted to convert, it would do them no good; and I was greatly pained by the evil of this report, and I prayed before God I from here and you from there [do the same], and this vision I had while awake and not in a dream, in a vision and not as a riddle, and up on Mount Sinai a church I saw there was abolished.

And on the Rosh Hashana of the year 5510 I made an ascent of the soul as is known and beheld a great evil counsel, in which Samael was nearly given permission to lay waste countries and communities entirely and I risked my life and prayed, let us fall by the hand of God and please not at the hand of man and they permitted me to have this be exchanged for a great pestilence and a plague the likes of which had not been known in all of Poland and the rest of the countries near us and so it was that the weakness expanded greatly and immeasurably, as did the plague in the remaining countries and I arranged with my fraternity to have [*ketoret*] recited at dawn prayers so as to nullify the said edicts and it was revealed to me in a night vision: It was you yourself who chose this, let us fall by the hand of God etc., and how is it you want to nullify it now, for "an accuser cannot etc. [become a defender]" and from then on I did not recite the *ketoret* and did not pray on this matter except on Hoshana Raba when I went to the synagogue together with the whole congregation and took several oaths owing to the terror and once I said the *ketoret* so that the plague would not spread to our environs and in this

And on the Rosh Hashana of the year 5510 I made an ascent of the soul as is known and beheld a great evil counsel, in which Samael was nearly given permission to lay waste countries and communities entirely and I risked my life and prayed, let us fall by the hand of God and please not at the hand of man and they permitted me to have this be exchanged for a great pestilence and a plague the likes of which had not been known in all of Poland and the rest of the countries near us and so it was that the weakness expanded greatly and immeasurably, as did the plague in the remaining countries and I arranged with my fraternity to have *ketoret* recited at dawn prayers so as to nullify the said edicts. And it was revealed to me in a night vision: It was you yourself who chose this, let us fall by the hand of God and so on, and why do you want to nullify it now, for "an accuser cannot etc. [become a defender]" and from then on I did not recite the *ketoret* and did not pray on this matter except on Hoshana Raba when I went to the synagogue together with the whole congregation and took several oaths owing to the terror and once I said the *ketoret* so that the plague would not be spread to our environs and in

we succeeded by the grace of God and I would gladly say much more and wander on at length but on account of the tears I have in recalling your departure from me I cannot speak yet I ask of you to review the words of morals I told you several times and to always have them present in mind and to think of them and be scrupulous with them surely you will find in each and every maxim all sorts of delicacies for it is no empty matter what I told you for the Lord knows that I have not despaired of voyaging to the Land of Israel if the Lord so desires it so as to be together with you yet the times do not permit this.	this we succeeded by the grace of God. And I would gladly say much more and wander on at length but on account of the tears I have in recalling your departure from me I cannot speak yet I ask of you to review the words of morals I told you several times and to always have them in mind and to think of them and be scrupulous with them surely you will find in each and every maxim all sorts of delicacies for it is no empty matter what I told you for the Lord knows that I have not despaired of voyaging to the Land of Israel if the Lord so desires it so as to be together with you yet the times do not permit this.
Also do not be upset that I have not sent you funds on account of the treacherous times we have had in our country with the plague and hunger and the several infants who depend on me from our family to support and feed them besides the rest of the Jewish poor and the money has run out now we are left only with our bodies and God willing when the Lord enlarges etc. then to be sure etc.	Also do not be upset that I have not sent you funds on account of the treacherous times we have had here with the plague and hunger and the several infants who depend on me from our family to support and feed them besides the rest of the Jewish poor and the money has run out now we are left only with our bodies and God willing when the Lord enlarges etc. then to be sure etc.
Also my grandson the young groom, the important and honorable Ephrayim is a great prodigy in the essence of study surely if the time permits it would be proper	Also my grandson the young groom, the important and honorable Ephrayim is a great prodigy in the essence of study surely if the time permits it would be proper

FRENKEL-BAUMINGER VERSION	KORETZ VERSION	MANUSCRIPT VERSION
for you to come here yourself to see and be seen with him face to face and to rejoice in our gladness as you promised me.	for you to come here yourself to see and be seen with him face to face and to rejoice in our gladness as you promised me.	
I would also like very much to ask of you on behalf of the famous Rabbi the Hasid our Master Yosef Katz a servant of the Lord, to bring him near with both hands and all sorts of favors as his deeds are welcome before God and all his deeds are for a heavenly cause and also to write on his behalf to the wealthy people to encourage them to keep him well provided for and adequately maintained, for surely you will take satisfaction if he is there with you nearby. So wrote your loving brother-in-law who hopes to see you face to face and prays for a long life for you and your wife and children and seeks after your welfare daily and at night as well for a good long life *Amen Selah.*	I would also like very much to ask of you on behalf of the famous Rabbi the Hasid our Master Yosef Katz a servant of the Lord, to bring him near with both hands and all sorts of favors as his deeds are welcome before God and all his deeds are for a heavenly cause and also to write on his behalf to the wealthy people to encourage them to keep him well provided for and adequately maintained, for surely you will take satisfaction if he is there with you nearby. So wrote your loving brother-in-law who hopes to see you face to face and prays for a long life for you and your wife and children and seeks after your welfare daily and at night as well for a good long life *Amen Selah.*	

THE VERSIONS OF THE BESHT'S EPISTLE

The epistle sent by the Besht to his brother-in-law, R. Gershon of Kotov is available to us in three versions. The epistle was first printed as an appendix to *Ben Porat Yosef* by R. Yaakov Yosef of Polonne, a book published in Koretz in the year 1781. The connection between the Besht's Epistle and R. Yaakov Yosef is made explicit in the initial lines added by the publisher:

> This is the letter given by Rabbi Israel Besht of Blessed and Righteous Memory to our Rabbi the author Our Teacher (etc.) Yaakov Yosef Hacohen to be passed to his brother-in-law Rabbi Gershon Kotover who was in the Holy Land and because of a delay which came from the Blessed Lord he did not travel to the land of Israel and it remained in his hands so as to benefit our nation the people of Israel.

And indeed, at the end of the letter the Besht asks his brother-in-law to extend assistance to Rabbi Yaakov Yosef upon his arrival in the land of Israel.[1]

Another version of the Epistle was printed by Rabbi David Fraenkel in his book *Michtavim Mehabesht Zal Vetalmidav*, which was published in Lvov in 1923. This version was reprinted, on the basis of a transcription from the original manuscript, by Mordechai Shraga Bauminger in the year 1972.[2] Bauminger corrected certain mistakes in the Fraenkel printing and added some introductory lines, in which he described the various incarnations of the letter from the time it had been, as it seems, in the possession of R. Israel the *maggid* of Kozhenits and until it reached him. Relying on the opinions of experts in handwriting analysis, Bauminger affirmed that the Epistle was written down by R. Yehiel Michal b. R. Baruch, the Besht's son-in-law.

If we compare these two versions of the Besht's Epistle we find that certain passages found in the Koretz version are lacking from the version printed by Bauminger. Conversely, certain sentences present in the Bauminger version are lacking from the Koretz version. These differences have caused scholars to question the veracity of *each* of the two versions. Gershom Scholem mentions this issue in two small footnotes. In one of them, he asserts that the "authenticity of the letter is evident from its contents." In the second footnote Scholem advances the conjecture that the differences in the versions are due to "revisions to the original letter made by the Besht himself."[3] It would thus appear that Scholem regarded both of these versions as authentic. Rubinstein pointed out numerous difficulties that challenge the authenticity of the version published by Bauminger. He came to the conclusion that the Koretz edition was original but that the Bauminger one was fraudulent.[4] Bauminger responded to Rubinstein's arguments one by one. Among other things, he rejected the charge of fraudulence by arguing that it would not make sense for a forger to delete passages from the original text he is copying. Bauminger explained the presence of the passages found in the Koretz version yet lacking from the manuscript version that he had transcribed by the conjecture that the Besht gave R. Yaakov Yosef a second letter or a supplement to the original letter.[5]

Meanwhile, Yehoshua Mondshine discovered a third version of the Besht's Epistle. This version was included in a Hasidic manuscript dating to 1766.[6] At first it appears as though this third version only compounds the difficulty: it contains passages not found in either of the other versions, while at the same time it includes passages that appear in the Koretz version yet are missing from the Bauminger version. A further feature of this version is its lack of introductory and closing passages. The transcriber seems to have deleted these passages in the belief that the letter's chief importance lay in the passages describing the ascents of the soul. Yet as it turns out, Mondshine himself put forward a persuasive explanation to account for the three versions.[7] According to Mondshine's account, the Besht wrote two distinct letters; one of them is represented by the manuscript version from the year 1766 and the other by the Bauminger version. The Koretz version, for its part, combines passages from both of these letters.

To be more precise: in the opening passage of the Bauminger version, the Besht expresses his regret that a previous letter he had sent to his brother-in-law, a letter that contains "innovations" and "secrets," did not arrive at its destination. He therefore wrote an additional letter, in which he repeats what he had said in the first epistle. According to Mondshine's account, the version appearing in the manuscript from 1766 is the first letter the Besht wrote; in it he describes the ascent of the soul that he had experienced on Rosh Hashana of 1747. The second letter the Besht wrote is the one we have as the Bauminger version. In this letter, the Besht again describes the ascent of the soul from 1747. And indeed, a comparison of the two versions shows that the writer refers to the same events, though with a difference of emphasis and language, as would be expected of a person who describes powerfully emotional events in accounts at two different times. And as the Bauminger version represents the later letter, it also contains a description of a later event; namely, the Besht's ascent of the soul from the year 1750. The person who brought the Ben Porat Yosef version to press had these two versions in front of him, and he saw fit to complete the supposedly missing sections in the earlier letter. Indeed, the Koretz version is identical to the Bauminger one, except that it has passages added out of the manuscript version that are "missing" from the Bauminger version.

In his book on the Besht, Moshe Rosman devotes an extensive discussion to the question of the versions of the Besht's Epistle. In essence, Rosman rejects the solution proposed by Mondshine and offers a solution of his own.[8] I shall review the main points of Rosman's perspective, and shall state the considerations that have led me to prefer the solution proffered by Mondshine.

The fact that the transcriber of the manuscript from 1776 merely noted the title "the Sacred Epistle," and did not see fit to add details about the author of the letter, strikes Rosman as indicating that the intended reader of the manuscript was meant to know that the "Sacred Epistle" was the letter of the Besht. From this, Rosman infers that between the time the Besht wrote the letter and until it came to be included in the 1776 manuscript, it had been copied over several times and had even become familiar to many people, who heard it in oral form. Rosman further observes that the transcriber of this manuscript did not bother to copy out fully the will of R. Aharon Hagadol of Karlin, that was incorporated in the same manuscript. Likewise he did not bother to copy out the sections that open and close the Besht's Epistle. From these facts, Rosman infers that there is no reason to suppose, as does Mondshine, that the manuscript version is a copy that survived from an earlier form of the letter; instead, it "was probably reproducing a version of the already famous 1752 letter that he had seen or heard in one or more forms circulating among the Hasidim."[9]

This far-reaching conclusion is perplexing. It stands to reason that after repeated transcriptions of a letter slight variations would be expected, the result of errors made by the copiers. Yet the Bauminger version and the manuscript version of the Besht's Epistle differ quite substantially. That is why Rosman uses the word "reproducing"; he evidently attributes a more radical intervention in the letter on the part of the transcribers.

The main evidence on which Rosman bases this conclusion is the fact that a certain passage contained in the book *Tsava'at Haribash* appears also in the Bauminger and Koretz versions of the Besht's Epistle. *Tsava'at Haribash* consists of a collection of practices attributed to the Besht. Despite being attributed to the Besht, they mostly originate from the school of the *maggid* of Mezerich.[10] And as the *maggid* passed away in 1772, whereas the manuscript version is from 1776 and the Koretz version from 1881, Rosman concluded that these two versions of the Besht's Epistle had been influenced by the sayings of the *maggid*, which had spread among the Hasidim in written and oral form. In other words: one of the transcribers of the Besht's Epistle planted a saying of the *maggid* in it and mistakenly attributed it to the Besht. That this implanted passage is not included in the Bauminger version is a sign, according to Rosman, that that version is the most authentic form of the original letter. As to the two other versions, Rosman goes on to argue, the fact that they include additional material not present in the original letter of the Besht's should not astonish us. For as Dinur, Scholem, Piekarz, Gries, and Haran have already shown, Hasidic editors and printers of Hasidic texts were not always scrupulous in their attributions or in the material they cited.[11]

It seems to me that this sweeping conclusion, which is based on the statements of scholars dealing with quite different types of Hasidic writings, does not help us to elucidate the problem before us; the cases are not analogous. If Piekarz showed, for example, that certain sermons that R. Yaakov Yosef attributed to the Besht also appear in reference to other figures—contemporaries of the Besht or later persons—

this tells us something about the flow of ideas and influences between various figures.[12] From here to the introduction of extraneous material into the letter of the Besht is quite a large step. Likewise, Gries's conclusions about the evolution and process of formation of the Conduct Literature tells us nothing at all about the extent of the authenticity of versions of the Besht's Epistle.[13] The same applies to the other scholars mentioned here.

Raayah Haran is the only scholar whose study pertains to our subject. In an effort to explain the significance of differences in versions of letters written by R. Menahem Mendel of Vitebsk to his Hasidim, Haran reached the conclusion that the original letters had later additions incorporated into them. Now, to anyone relying on Haran's conclusions as a source of inference for other cases, the dictum of the Sages applies: "Your guarantor needs a guarantor":[14] indeed, Haran's determinations have been roundly refuted by Yehoshua Mondshine.[15]

In any event, the evidence Rosman puts forward ought to be evaluated on its own merits. How are we to understand the fact that a passage found in *Tsava'at Haribash* appears also in two of the versions of the Besht's Epistle? Did the transcribers actually extract a passage from *Tsava'at Haribash* and place it within the Besht's Epistle? Perhaps the opposite is the case, and the editors of *Tsava'at Haribash* are the ones who took a passage from the Besht's Epistle and incorporated it in a book attributed to him! So as to be able to respond to this question, we need to compare the two versions. Following is the version of the passage as it appears in the Besht's Epistle to R. Gershon of Kotov:

> Yet this I shall inform you; and let the Blessed Lord assist you, and may your paths be in God's presence, and lose not sight of them especially when in the Holy Land. While you are praying or studying, in each and every utterance and issuance from your lips understand how to make a unification of it, for in each and every letter there are worlds and souls and divinity which rise and commune and bind each other to Godliness and afterward the letters commune and unify thoroughly and form a word and are completely unified with Godliness and you will include your soul with them at each and every level of the above and all the worlds will unify as one and rise and make unaccountable joy and delight; if you can conceive of the joy of bride and groom in smallness and materiality, how much more so it is in this Upper Level; and surely God will be aiding you, and in all you turn to you will succeed and prevail; provide to the wise and he will make wise; and so pray for me with this intention. . . .[16]

And here is the passage as it appears in *Tsava'at Haribash:*

> for in each letter there are worlds and souls and divinity, and they rise and commune and bind with each other, with Godliness, and afterward the letters unify and commune and a word is formed, and true unifications are made with Godliness. And one must include one's soul with each and every level [of the above], and then all the worlds will unify as one and rise and unaccountable joy and delight will be made.[17]

If we compare the two versions of this passage, there is no difficulty in determining that the original version is the Besht's Epistle and that it is the one that was copied into *Tsava'at Haribash*. This conclusion follows from the passage's content, context, and language. In terms of the content, the passage provides guidance on how to employ *kavvanah* in study and prayer. The stress is on the inherent mystical potential that the letters of the Torah and the prayer hold within them. Cognizance of the presence of divinity in these letters is presented as a point of departure and a basis for mystical union of the soul with Godliness. This idea is cited numerous times in Yaakov Yosef's writings as being that of the Besht, and there is no reason to doubt that attribution. Quite naturally, then, just as the Besht spoke of matters of this nature to his close student Yaakov Yosef, he would likewise have included them in a letter to his friend and brother-in-law, R. Gershon.

Let us next consider the context of this passage in the Besht's Epistle. Recall that the Besht was disappointed by the Messiah's reply to his question, "When will Sir be coming?" as the possibility that many others will come to know what he had learned from the Messiah struck him as unlikely. He tried to console himself with the thought that he could teach his "men of virtue"—that is, his associates—three holy names. Yet he was not given permission to do so. He asked that at the least he be allowed to reveal these names to his brother-in-law R. Gershon: "And I asked on your behalf to teach it to you and was not permitted to at all and I was fast forsworn from this." It is in this context that the Besht goes on to write to his brother-in-law the lines cited above. We find that the guidance as to how mystical union with the divinity may be obtained is offered as a sort of compensation for those three holy names that the Besht was not permitted to reveal to his brother-in-law. The connection with the Besht's Epistle is thus entirely natural and appropriate to its place in the narrative sequence.

As to language, the text in the Besht's Epistle is formulated in a personal tone. Among other things, the Besht refers to the fact that R. Gershon is away in the land of Israel. He even asks R. Gershon to make use of the proffered prayer *kavvanot* while praying on his behalf from there. Now it would have been quite natural for editors of *Tsava'at Haribash* to have taken the personal counsel they found in the Besht's Epistle, stripped the personal elements from it, and included it in their book as a general instruction. Conversely, it would have made no sense for the transcribers of the Besht's Epistle to take a general instruction from *Tsava'at Hebesht*, reformulate it as if it were a piece of personal guidance the Besht offered his brother-in-law, and incorporate it within the letter, while revising the entire context to make everything fit together. This would have been forgery in its most serious form; and we have no reason to suppose that any one of the Besht's Hasidim was interested in or capable of forgery of this kind.

So much for the issue of the passage from *Tsava'at Haribash*. Some additional arguments of Rosman follow. If we suppose that both the Koretz version and the manuscript version are faithful representations of the Besht's Epistle, as Mondshine proposed, we would be forced to conclude that the transcriber of the

Bauminger version deleted, or that the Besht forgot, the two most interesting passages in the Epistle; namely, the section describing the fate of the souls in the Upper Worlds and the passage where the Besht explains how Redemption is to be brought about. Rosman asks, What makes more sense? That the passages relating to the foundations of Hasidic faith and doctrine were deleted from the original letter, or that they were added once these foundations were clarified?[18]

Later, Rosman clarifies his thoughts as to how the revisions in the Besht's Epistle would have been made: Avraham Dov Orbach of Chmielnik, who brought the book *Ben Porat Yosef* to press, was R. Yaakov Yosef's son-in-law and a student of both the Besht and the *Maggid*. It is nearly certain that he conceived of Hasidism, as it had developed by the 1780s, as a single fabric whose different strands were interwoven to achieve a harmonious perfection. It should not surprise us, continues Rosman, that either he or earlier transcribers sharing such a perspective would have made amendments to the Besht's Epistle, omitting what they deemed worthless and adding what they considered important and authentic. In sum, the Besht's Epistle evolved by a process of reiterated transcriptions in the course of which extraneous materials came to be incorporated in it. This process came to an end when the letter was published in *Ben Porat Yosef*, a text that achieved wide circulation.[19]

Rosman's proposed reconstruction presumes that the transcribers and the publisher regarded the Besht's Epistle as a document whose purpose was to present the essentials of the Hasidic creed to the public. This perspective as to the Epistle's purpose accords well with the thought of scholars such as Dubnow and Ben-Zion Dinur, who indeed drew upon the Epistle to learn about the Hasidic stance toward Messianism. It will be recalled that Tishbi rejected the perspective according to which the Besht's Epistle is an expression of Hasidic doctrine.[20] Yet here Rosman continues to maintain this view, and even attributes it to the transcribers and the publisher. There is no doubt that the Hasidim who transcribed and read the Besht's Epistle considered it to be a document of utmost importance. After all, a letter in which the Besht describes ascents of the soul that he himself experienced is no minor matter. Yet from this to the conclusion that they viewed this document as a sort of summary of Hasidic doctrine, from its inception up to the 1780s, and that they therefore saw fit to incorporate later sources from the *maggid's* school within it, is quite a large step. Were these people so naive as to be unable to distinguish between detailed descriptions of ascents of the soul and writings stating the doctrines and practices of the school of the *maggid*?

Rosman, it will be recalled, raised the problem, Why does the Bauminger version lack the "most interesting" passages from the Besht's Epistle, those that deal with the fate of souls in the Upper Worlds and the topic of Redemption? According to Mondshine's reconstruction, the Bauminger version reflects the second letter the Besht wrote, once he realized that the first letter, the one reflected by the manuscript version dating to 1776, did not reach its destination. A considerable gap in time separates the writing of the first letter from the writing of the second; the later letter is signed and dated 1752 while the first was written before 1750. It thus comes as no surprise that there are certain matters discussed in the first letter that the Besht would not have seen fit to repeat in the second. Moreover, in the interim the Besht had experienced an additional ascent of the soul, which he likewise describes in his second letter. Comparison of the description of the first ascent of the soul in the two versions reveals variations in texture and emphasis of just the sort one would expect when so unsettling an event is described in two distinct periods.

Rosman posed the further problem: How is it possible that the lost letter, represented according to Mondshine's reconstruction by the 1776 manuscript, was not in the Besht's possession, so that he was forced to reconstruct it from memory? I fail to understand this difficulty. The fact that the Besht was forced to write his brother-in-law a second time, because the first letter had not reached its destination, is not an issue that has been called into doubt: the Besht himself explicitly states this in his second letter. It is not inconceivable, then, that the Besht did not himself retain a copy of the first letter, or was unable to locate a copy of a letter he had written some two years earlier. Yet a copy of this letter was retained by the Polonne *mokhiah,* who wrote it out at the Besht's dictation;[21] it is this copy that reached us by means of the manuscript version from 1776.

In sum, it seems to me that Mondshine's reconstruction presents a convincing explanation of the differences between the versions of the Besht's Epistle. The possibility that the manuscript version represents the first letter the Besht sent to his brother-in-law, while the Bauminger version represents the second letter, is quite plausible, both in view of the content and in view of the language of the two versions. Likewise plausible is Mondshine's proposal that the version of the letter published in *Ben Porat Yosef* is an amalgam of these two versions. Consequently, I am convinced that a historian is permitted to treat both versions of the Besht's Epistle as authentic sources, which can and indeed ought to be relied upon in a reconstruction of the figure of the Besht.

NOTES

Introduction (pp. 1–6)

1. See Immanuel Etkes, "The Study of Hasidism: Past Trends and New Directions"; in *Hasidism Reappraised*, ed. Ada Rapoport-Albert, (London, 1996), pp. 447–464.

2. See appendix III.

3. See Moshe Rosman, "Miedzybóz and Rabbi Israel Baal Shem Tov," in *Essential Papers on Hasidism*, ed. G. D. Hundert (New York, 1991).

4. See Immanuel Etkes, "The Historical Besht, Reconstruction or Deconstruction?" *Polin: Studies in Polish Jewry* 12 (1999): 298–306.

Chapter One: Magic and *Baalei Shem* in the Days of the Baal Shem Tov (pp. 7–45)

1. See Shimon Dubnow, *Toldot Hahasidut* [History of Hasidism] (Tel Aviv, 1930–31) pp. 30–31, 74; Joseph Weiss, "Beginnings of Hassidism," *Zion* 16 (1951): 53–55 (Weiss asserts, *inter alia*, that R. Yaakov Yosef forged a Midrashic text as a way of supporting the case for the *baalei shem*. This charge was disproved by Haim Liberman; see *Ohel Rahel* [Rachel's tent], (New York, 1980), 1: 3–5.) See also Joseph Weiss, *Studies in Eastern European Jewish Mysticism* (Oxford, 1985), pp. 12–14. It appears that Ben Zion Dinur too could not shake free of his disapproval of the *baalei shem*: in his comprehensive and detailed article, "The Beginnings of Hasidism" Dinur ignores the Besht's occupation; Dinur, Ben Zion, "The Beginnings of Hasidism and its Social and Messianic Foundations," in: *Bemifneh Hadorot, Mehkarim Veiyunim Bereshitam Shel Hazmanim Hahadashim Betoldot Israel* [At the change of generations: studies and research on the beginings of the Modern Era in Jewish history] (Jerusalem, 1955), pp. 83–227. For Dinur, the Besht's essential significance is that he paved a new path toward Redemption; from this perspective, to delve into his *metier* as a *baal shem* would be to demean him and the subject is best avoided.

2. For a discussion of the origins of this conception in nineteenth-century Haskalah literature, see appendix I.

3. On Haskalic satire and the role it played in the battle against Hasidism, see Shmuel Werses, "Hasidism as Viewed In Haskalah Literature—From the Debates of the Galicean Maskilim," in *Megamot Vetzurot Besifrut Hahaskalah* [Trends and forms in Haskalah literature] (Jerusalem, 1990), pp. 91–109. For a detailed discussion of the attitude of Haskalah literature toward magic and its identification with Hasidism, see appendix I.

4. See op. cit., for examples.

5. Gershom Scholem, "The Historical Figure of R. Israel Baal Shem Tov," in his *Dvarim Bego* (Tel Aviv, 1975), pp. 292–293.

6. Mendel Piekarz, in *The Beginning of Hasidism* [The beginning of Hasidism—ideological trends in Derush and Musar literature] (Jerusalem, 1978), pp. 136–137, seems to have been the first to comment on the distortion in the reputation of the *baalei shem*. One may now also see Rosman, *Founder of Hasidism: A Quest for the Historical Ba'al Shem Tov* (Berkeley, 1996), pp. 11–26. The conclusions Rosman reaches as to the status of the

baalei shem in the society in which the Besht lived and acted are similar to those suggested in this chapter.

7. For a discussion of the evolution of the concept of magic in the two strands of Kabbalist thought, from the end of the fifteenth century through the eighteeenth century, see Moshe Idel, "Jewish Magic from the Renaissance Period to Early Hasidism," in *Religion, Science and Magic*, ed. J. Neusner, E. S. Frerichs, and P. V. M. Flesher (New York, 1989), pp. 82–117.

8. For a general survey of magic in Western culture, see Richard Cavendish, *A History of Magic* (London, 1990). On the development of magic in Christian Europe in the early Middle Ages, see Valerie I. J. Flint, *The Rise of Magic in Early Medieval Europe* (Princeton, 1991). On the place of magic in Christian culture in the early modern era, see Keith Thomas, *Religion and the Decline of Magic* (London, 1971). On magic in medieval Jewish society, see Joshua Trachtenberg, *Jewish Magic and Superstition* (New York, 1970). On amulets in Hebrew, see Theodore Schrire, *Hebrew Amulets* (London, 1966).

9. On books of charms in the eighteenth century, see Hagit Matras, *Hebrew Charm Books: Contents and Origins (Based On Books Printed in Europe During the 18th Century)* (Ph.D. diss., Hebrew University, 1997).

10. Repellent or attractive lights.

11. *Menahot Yaakov Solet*, by R. Yaakov b. R. Moshe Katz of Yanov (Willhelmsdorf, 1731), p. 31b.

12. *Toldot Adam* (Zolkiew, 1720), sec. 80.

13. Op. cit., sec. 86. Details about R. Eliyahu of Chelm appear below.

14. See ibid, secs. 39, 43, 49, 50, 80, and others.

15. Op. cit., sec. 38; see as well secs. 20, 27, 28, 35, and others.

16. Op cit., secs. 1–15.

17. Op cit., secs. 16, 17, 33, 45–48, and others.

18. *Mifalot Elokim* [God's deeds] (Zolkiew, 1725), sec. 59.

19. Zvi Hirsch Kaidanover, *Sefer Kav Hayashar* [The book of righteous measure], (Jerusalem, 1982), chap. 69.

20. Ibid. For a detailed discussion of this story, see Sara Zfatman, *Nisuei Adam Ve'sheda* [The marriage of a mortal man and a she-demon] (Jerusalem, 1987), pp. 82–102. Zfatman takes a comparative literature approach, stating among other things: "We have before us a tale of an extremely persuasive authenticity" (op cit., p. 98).

21. Kav Hayashar, ibid.

22. Mifalot Elokim, secs. 60, 62, 69, 70.

23. Op. cit., secs. 81–91.

24. Op. cit., secs. 82–83.

25. *Shem Tov Katan*, by R. Binyamin Binush of Krotoszyn (Saltzbach, 1706), 24A.

26. *Mifalot Elokim*, secs. 68, 71, 72; *Toldot Adam*, sec. 30; *Menahot Yaakov Solet*, 38A.

27. *Zevach Pesach*, by R. Yaakov Pesach (Zolkiew, 1722), compiler's introduction.

28. An edition of R. Pinchas Katzenelbogen's *Yesh Manhilin* was published in Jerusalem in 1986. The editor, Yitzhak Dov Feld, transcribed the original manuscript from the Bodleian Library in Oxford University, adding a foreword and index.

29. *Yesh Manhilin*, editor's foreword, pp. 14–25.

30. Ibid, author's introduction, p. 69.

31. Ibid., p. 87.

32. Ibid., pp. 88–89. The passage cited is from *Sefer Hasidim*, as composed by Rabenu Yehuda Hehasid, sources, notations, and commentary by Reuven Margaliot (Jerusalem, 1957), sec. 469.

33. *Yesh Manhilin*, p. 89.

34. Op. cit., p. 92.

35. Op. cit., p. 93.

36. Ibid.

37. On R. Zvi Hirsch Kaidanover and his book, see Yeshayahu Shachar, *Bikoret Hahevra Vehanhagat Hatzibur Besafrut Hamussar Vehadrush Bepolin Bameah ha 18* [Criticism of society and leadership in the Musar and Drush literature in 18th Century Poland] (Jerusalem, 1992), pp. 3–6.

38. *Yesh Manhilin*, pp. 93–95.

39. Op. cit., pp. 95–96.

40. Op. cit., pp. 96–97.

41. Op. cit., p. 97.

42. (Kushta, 1515).

43. *Yesh Manhilin*, pp. 97–99.

44. Op. cit., pp. 107–108.

45. Ibid.

46. Op. cit., pp. 100–101.

47. Op. cit., pp. 101–102.

48. The charms books to which R. Pinchas refers in his book proper are *Toldot Adam* by R. Moshe Galina, and *Amtahat Binyamin* by R. Binyamin of Krotoszyn (Willlemhersch, 1716). The charms books are mentioned also in the list of books that R. Pinchas included in his will (pp. 41–51). The texts are *Sefer Zchira* and *Menahot Yaakov Solet*.

49. *Yesh Manhilin*, p. 176.

50. See note 37 to this chapter.

51. *Yesh Manhilin*, pp. 175–176.

52. Gedalyah Nigal's *Magic, Mysticism And Hasidism* (New Jersey and London, 1994), contains a chapter on the *baalei shem*. Nigal in this chapter assembles important data that sheds light on this issue; nonetheless, Nigal's focus is literary and not historical. Moshe Hillel's *Baalei Shem* (Jerusalem, 1993), is a curious amalgam of facts and legends that makes it difficult to regard as contributing to a critical study of the topic.

53. J. D. Eisenstein, ed., *Ozar Yisrael, Encyclopedia of All Matters Concerning Jews and Judaism* vol. 3 (in Hebrew) (New York, 1951), p. 137.

54. Op cit., p. 138. *Sefer Toldot Adam*, which I shall discuss below, is based in part on a manuscipt attributed to R. Eliyahu of Luanez.

55. *Ozar Yisrael*, p. 139.

56. Gedalyah Nigal, "On R. Naftali Katz of Poznan," *Sinai* 92 (1983): 91–92.

57. Gedalyah Nigal, *A Ba'al Shem Condemned To Life Sentence—the Tragedy of R. Hirsch Fraenkel* (Ramat Gan, 1993).

58. Nigal, *Magic, Mysticism And Hasidism*, pp. 13–23.

59. *Ozar Yisrael*, pp. 138–139. See also Richard I Cohen, *Jewish Icons, Art and Society in Modern Europe* (Berkeley, 1998), pp. 137–140.

60. In the introduction to his *Amtahat Binyamin*, which he wrote in 1716, the author includes the phrase: "my days are gone through accumulation of years." It seems very likely that a man who expresses himself thus in the beginning of the eighteenth century is about fifty years old. It follows that R. Binyamin Binush would have been born sometime between 1660 and 1670. R. Binyamin is last noted in the literature as alive in *Yesh Manhilin*, p. 95; the author relates that R. Binyamin Binush visited him in the year 1720. As we do not find R. Binyamin mentioned later, one may gather that he passed away in the 1730s.

61. *Sefer Shem Tov Katan*; *Sefer Amtahat Binyamin*.

62. *Yesh Manhilin*, p. 95.

63. *Shem Tov Katan*, p. 7b.

64. Op. cit., p. 8a.

65. Ze'ev Gries, *Safrut Hahanhagot, Toldoteha Umekoma Behayei Hasidei Rabbi Yisrael Baal Shem Tov* [Conduct literature, its history and place in the life of the Beshtian Hasidim] (Jerusalem, 1989), pp. 96–97.

66. Author's preface, *Amtahat Binyamin*.

67. On his date of birth see *Ozar Yisrael*, p. 137. Several sources shed light on his date of death. In the *haskamah* to *Hilchot Olam*, by R. Meir b. R. Moshe Meizelisch, (Saltzbach 1756), R. Yoel is described using terms referring to the deceased. And R. Pinchas Katzenelbogen, author of *Yesh Manhilin*, wrote in 1758 that R. Yoel had passed away two or three years earlier (*Yesh Manhilin*, p. 89).

68. Details on R. Yoel the first are given above.

69. The ratifications to *Mifalot Elokim*.

70. The compiler's preface to *Mifalot Elokim*; and see below, the quotation from *Yesh Manhilin*.

71. Solomon Maimon, *Hayei Shlomo Maimon* (Tel Aviv, 1953), p. 137.

72. *Yesh Manhilin*, p. 89.

73. On Rabbi Israel Zamosc and his book *Nezach Israel* (Frankfurt Dauder, 1741), see Israel Zinberg, *A History of Jewish Literature*, vol. 6. (New York, 1975); Rafael Mahler, *Divrei Yemei Israel—Dorot Ahronim* [Jewish history—the Modern Period], (Merhavia, 1962), 4: 26–30; Immanuel Etkes, "On the Question of Harbingers of the Haskalah in Eastern Europe," *Tarbiz* 57 (1988): 95–114.

74. The ratification was written in the month of Ellul, 1737.

75. Preface to *Netzah Israel*, (Frankfurt Dauder, 1741).

76. *Tavnit Habayit*, by R. Mordechai b. R. Meir of Lublin (Frankfurt Dauder, 1747). R. Yoel's ratification is dated 1748.

77. *Hilchot Olam*, by R. Meir b. R. Moshe Meislisch, (Soltzbach, 1756).

78. Evidently, close relations were sustained between R. Yoel and R. Yaakov Pesach. This speculation is supported by R. Yaakov Pesach's testimony as told to *Toldot Adam*, which is cited below.

79. *Menahot Yaakov Solet*, 40A, 50A.

80. The printing of books of charms was thought to be a promising commercial venture: when R. Shlomo ben Hayim of Jerusalem, author of the compilation of charms published within *Menahot Yaakov Solet*, gave the compilation as a gift to R. Yaakov b. R. Moshe Katz in gratitude for saving his life, the latter incorporated the charms collection within *Menahot Yaakov Solet* so as to increase sales of his book. See *Menahot Yaakov Solet*, 29b.

81. (Koretz, 1784), attributed to the "students of Nachmanides." The book discloses "secrets" concerning the influence of the *mitzvot* and prayers in the upper heavens; it likewise deals with Holy Names.

82. (Amsterdam, 1648). The book deals with the names of the holy and their influence in the heavens.

83. Compare the introduction by R. Shlomo ben Hayim to the charms section in *Menahot Yaakov Solet*, 30a–b.

84. *Toldot Adam*, sec. 171.

85. *Mifalot Elokim*, sec. 352.

86. *Yesh Manhilin*, p. 108.

87. See, for example, the story on R. Eliyahu Baal Shem, cited in the first part of this chapter.

88. *Yesh Manhilin*, p. 96.

89. Examination of the catalogues of the National and University Library in Jerusalem reveals that in the course of the sixteenth century three charms books were published; in the course of the seventeenth century fourteen charms books were published; whereas from the beginning of the eighteenth century through to 1760 (the year of the Besht's death), thirty- six books of charms were published. On the editions and circulation of particular charms books published in the eighteenth century, see Hagit Matras, *Hebrew Charm Books*, p. 128 passim.

90. We learn of the efforts of maskilim to stifle the *baalei shem* and the popular healers, and to have them replaced with scientifically trained healers, from compositions and publications of medical texts from the end of the eighteenth century. The two famous cases are the book by Moshe Markuse, *Ezer Israel* (Paricek, 1790), and Menahem Mendel Lefin's *Refuot Haam* (Zlokiew, 1795). For more on Lefin's book, see Yosef Klausner, *Historia Shel Hasifrut Haivrit Hahadasha* (Jerusalem, 1952), 1:226–230. For a close treatment of Markuse's text, with a comparison to that of Lefin, see Chone Shmeruk, *Yiddish Literature in Poland—Historical Studies and Perspectives* (Jerusalem, 1981), pp. 184–203.

91. Jewish doctors with university diplomas were rare in Poland in the eighteeenth-century, yet the few that did exist mainly served the royal court and the high aristocracy. The "expert doctors" mentioned in the charms books were, evidently, popular healers, who worked on the basis of accumulated knowledge passed from master to apprentice. On Jewish doctors in eighteenth-century Poland, see David E. Fishman, *Russia's First Modern Jews: The Jews of Shklov* (New York, 1995).

92. See Ze'ev Gries, "The Transcription and Printing of Books of Kabbalah as a Study Method," *Mahanayim* 6 (1994): 204–211.

Chapter Two: Isreal Baal Shem (pp. 46–78)

1. See "A Letter by the Besht to R. Moshe of Kotov", cited at the end of *Buzina Dinehora* (attributed to R. Baruch of Miedzybóz, 1880; no location listed, unpaginated)); and "A Letter

by the Besht to R. Gershon of Kotov," in *Shivhei Habesht,* ed. Yehoshua Mondshine, facsimile of a unique manuscript, with introduction, variant versions, and appendices (Jerusalem, 1982), p. 237.

2. *Shivhei Habesht,* (In praise of the Baal Shem Tov), with introduction and annotations by Avraham Rubinstein (Jerusalem, 1991), pp. 74–75

3. That is, a heavenly voice. See for example Tractate Brachot 18a.

4. *Shivhei Habesht,* p. 187. On the identity of R. Yosef see ibid., note 2 by Rubinstein.

5. Op. cit., p. 175.

6. Op. cit., pp. 198–200, 213–214, 229–230.

7. See also ibid., 136–138, 229–230.

8. Op. cit., p. 227. The location referred to is Winnica in Podolia.

9. Op. cit., p. 32.

10. Op. cit., p. 29.

11. See op. cit., pp. 227–229. For another instance of the Besht prognosticating for one of his associates, see op. cit., pp. 277–278.

12. Op. cit., pp. 269, 272–275; for a detailed treatment of this tale, see chapter 6 of this book.

13. On the doctrine of reincarnation from the beginnings of the Kabbalah and through Hasidism, see Gershom Scholem, *Elements of the Kabbalah and Its Symbolism* (Jerusalem, 1976), pp. 308–357. On reincarnation of souls in the Hasidic tale, see Nigal, *Magic, Mysticism, and Hasidism,* pp. 51–66.

14. *Shivhei Habesht,* p. 154.

15. Dubnow, *Toldot Hahasidut,* p. 484.

16. *Shivhei Habesht,* pp. 178–180, 189–191, 304.

17. Op. cit., pp. 154–155.

18. Cf. the story about a demon who attempted to injure the Besht, op. cit., pp. 168–169.

19. Op. cit., pp. 232–234. The passage is from p. 234.

20. Op. cit., pp. 175–176.

21. Op. cit., p. 162.

22. Testimonials from sixteenth- and seventeenth-century England about prayer formulae possessing magical healing powers may be found in Keith Thomas, *Religion and the Decline of Magic.*

23. The topic of the Besht's ecstatic prayer will be treated in chapter 4.

24. *Shivhei Habesht,* p. 175.

25. On the extreme spiritual effort required for ecstatic prayer, see chapter 4.

26. *Shivhei Habesht,* p. 169; see also ibid., p. 127.

27. Gedalyah Nigal, ed., *Gedolim Maasei Tsadikim, Hasidic Tales,* by Yaakov Margaliot, critical edition with introduction and notes (Jerusalem, 1991) pp. 17–18.

28. Yehoshua Mondshine, "The Prayerbook of Our Rabbi the Baal Shem Tov," *Kovetz Siftei Tsadikim—Measaf Letorat Hahasidut, Pirsum Genazeha Veheker Toldoteha* [An anthology of the doctrine of Hasidism, its archival documents and scholarship] (Kislev, 1995), pp. 72–100.

29. *Shivhei Habesht,* pp. 67–68.

30. Op. cit., pp. 68–69. The image of the Angel of Death dancing after someone as a representation of his imminent death, derives from the Zohar. See Tishbi, *Mishnat Hazohar*, 1: p. 9. Ze'ev Gries points this out in "Between Literature and History: Preface to a Discussion and Examination of *Shivhei Habesht*," Tura 3 (1994):166–169.

31. *Shivhei Habesht*, pp. 267–270. This topic will be dealt with extensively in chapter 6.

32. Op. cit., pp. 177–178, 239–240.

33. See earlier, this chapter.

34. *Shivhei Habesht*, pp. 119–123.

35. The letter was printed at the end of *Buzina Dinehora*.

36. *Shivhei Habesht*, pp. 103–105.

37. Op. cit., pp. 261–262.

38. Ya'acov Barnai, ed., *Igrot Hasidim Me'eretz Israel* [Hasidic letters from Eretz-Israel: from the second part of the eighteenth century and the first part of the nineteenth century] (Jerusalem, 1980), p. 39. Barnai's estimate is that the letter dates to 1748.

39. Attributed to R. Leib of Letitchev, who had been R. Ephrayim's *melamed* when he was a boy, at the end of *Buzina Dinehora*. And compare R. Ephrayim's dreams, cited at the end of *Degel Mahene Ephrayim*, by R. Ephrayim of Sadilkov (Jerusalem, 1994).

40. Mircea Eliade, *Shamanism, Archaic Techniques of Ecstasy* (Princeton, 1972), pp. 110–144.

41. A detailed discussion of R. Adam Baal Shem appears later in this chapter.

42. *Shivhei Habesht*, pp. 61–64.

43. This phenomenon will be treated at length in chapter 5.

44. The Besht was evidently influenced by the *Hekhalot* literature: the picture of the upper worlds reflected in his account of his ascent of the soul is typical of this literature.

45. *Shivhei Habesht*, pp. 61–67.

46. Op. cit., p. 67.

47. Op. cit., p. 253.

48. For more details, see chapter 1.

49. Ibid.

50. *Shivhei Habesht*, pp, 74–75.

51. Cf. ibid., 214–215.

52. *Tsofnat Paaneach*, by R. Yaakov Yosef of Polonne, ed. Gedalyah Nigal (Jerusalem, 1989), p. 85.

53. The compiler of *Shivhei Habesht* cites what he heard directly from R. Yaakov Yosef of Polonne about the Besht's prophetic abilities: "And I heard regarding the Besht that by listening to someone at study he could tell what his fate would be at year's end"; I cite a story illustrating this capacity below (*Shivhei Habesht*, pp. 223–224). Several of the tales about the Besht derive from the Besht himself. This point has already been noted by Khone Shmeruk and Gedalyah Nigal. See Khone Shmeruk, *Yiddish Literature: Aspects of Its History* (Tel Aviv, 1978), p. 203; Gedalyah Nigal, "New Light on the Hasidic Tale and its Sources," in *Hasidism Reappraised*, ed. Ada Rapoport-Albert (London, 1996), pp. 345–353.

54. Barnai, *Igrot Hasidim Me'eretz Israel*, pp. 39–40.

55. Cf. *Shivhei Habesht*, pp. 255–256.

56. Op. cit., pp. 81–83, 213–214, 226–227; Nigal, *Gedolim Maasei Tsadikim*, pp. 18–20.

57. *Shivhei Habesht*, pp. 224.

58. Op. cit., p. 226.

59. Yosef Weiss regards this tale as giving evidence of the inferior status of the *baalei shem* in the days of the Besht. Further, Weiss interprets a passage from a sermon by R. Yaakov Yosef of Polonne as an attempt to alter the negative attitude toward *baalei shem;* Weiss, "Beginnings of Hassidism," p. 54. Hayim Liberman disagreed with the interpretation Weiss gave to R. Yaakov Yosef's statements and showed it to be founded on an error; Hayim Liberman, "How is Hasidism Studied in Israel?" in *Ohel Rachel,* [Rachel's Tent], by Hayim Liberman, (New York, 1980), 1: 3–4. Mendel Piekarz challenged Weiss's conclusions as well, and even cites refuting evidence; Piekarz, *The Beginning of Hasidism*, p. 136. Avraham Rubinstein challenged Piekarz's evidence in an effort to defend Weiss; Avraham Rubinstein, "The Revelation of the Besht in the *Shivhei Ha-Besht*," *Alei Sefer* 6–7 (1979): 184–186. Rubinstein's stance on this matter does not seem to me to be correct, both because of the anachronistic nature of the story in question and because of the findings about the status of the *baalei shem* discussed in chapter 1.

60. The reference of course is to Hasidim of the old kind. A detailed discussion of the nature of these Hasidim is given in chapter 5.

61. The Besht arrived at Miedzybóz in 1740. He had earned fame as a *baal shem* several years earlier. According to a reconstruction proposed by Adam Teller (see chapter 6), the Besht received his invitation from the leaseholders of Sluck in 1733.

62. *Shivhei Habesht*, pp. 188–189.

63. Ibid.

64. Op. cit., p. 269.

65. Op. cit., pp. 187–188.

66. Op. cit., pp. 120–121.

67. Op. cit., p. 74.

68. Op. cit., pp. 73–74.

69. Compare also the story on p. 229.

70. Op. cit., p. 74.

71. An additional story from this group appears on pp. 188–189.

72. Op. cit., p. 122.

73. This interpretation follows Rubinstein, ibid., note 33.

74. Op. cit., p. 232.

75. Op. cit., pp. 258–259.

76. Op. cit., pp. 257–258.

77. Op. cit., p. 257.

78. Recall that *Toldot Adam* was published in 1720, and *Mifalot Elokim* in 1725. These books were discussed in detail in chapter 1.

79. *Shivhei Habesht*, pp. 41–46.

80. If the main function of the story about the son of R. Adam is to link R. Adam to the Besht, the tale at the same time reflects the "recluse" motif in the Besht's biography. The

account of the encounter between the two figures and the relationship they forged creates an especially ironic effect. In this respect this story is similar to the other tales about the Besht's "recluse" period.

81. Gershom Scholem, "The Sabbatean Prophet R. Heschil Tsoref—R. Adam Baal Shem," *Zion* 6 (1941): 89–93.

82. Khone Shmeruk, "Tales About R. Adam Baal Shem in the Versions of Shivhei Ha' Besht," *Zion* 28 (1963): 86–105. A revised version of this article may be found in Shmeruk's *Yiddish Literature in Poland—Historical Studies and Perspectives* (Jerusalem, 1981), pp. 146–199.

83. Gershom Scholem, *Studies and Texts Concerning the History of Sabbetianism and Its Metamorphoses* (Jerusalem, 1974), p. 91.

84. Joseph Dan, *The Hasidic Story—Its History and Development* (Jerusalem, 1975), p. 82; Avraham Rubinstein, "The Mentor of R. Israel Ba'al Shem-Tov and the Sources of His Knowledge," *Tarbiz* 48 (1979): 156.

85. Mondshine, *Shivhei Habesht*, pp. 58–65. On this topic see also Gershom Scholem, "More on R. Adam Baal Shem," in his *Studies and Texts Concerning the History of Sabbetianism and Its Metamorphoses* (Jerusalem, 1974), pp. 596–597. Yehuda Liebes, the book's editor, added a bibliographic appendix that surveys the scholarship on the R. Adam issue; see ibid., pp. 597–599.

86. *Shivhei Habesht*, p. 59.

87. Gries, "Between Literature and History," p. 162.

88. Op. cit., p. 163.

89. Peter Scheffer, *Synopsis of the Hekhalot Literature* (Tübingen, 1981), pp. 673–678.

90. Dan, *The Hasidic Story*, pp. 80–83.

91. The Yiddish version is cited by Rubinstein, *Shivhei Habesht*, p. 59 n. 47. In the Hebrew printing of *Shivhei Habesht*, R. Adam is mentioned without the designation *baal shem*. See Mondshine, *Shivhei Habesht*, p. 144; *Shivhei Habesht*, p. 41 n. 7.

92. Op. cit., p. 59.

93. One should note that the R. Adam stories appear in the first part of *Shivhei Habesht*, the part edited by the publisher, whereas the section dealing with the fate of the writings is in the main part of the book, which was edited by the compiler.

94. *Shivhei Habesht*, p. 235.

95. Op. cit., p. 101.

96. Op. cit., p. 107.

97. Op. cit., pp. 299–300.

98. Op. cit., pp. 96–98.

99. See also op. cit., p. 69. In the next chapter we shall see that the "redemption" of souls of sinners was one of the main tasks the Besht took upon himself. Cf. op. cit., p. 172, where it is related that R. Gershon boasted that he saw the spirit of a holy man and the Besht reprimanded him: "You are fooling yourself." Later in the tale it turns out that R. Gershon had indeed "seen" this!

100. On R. Gershon's powers, see chapter 5. For a conversation held by the Polonne *Mokhiah* with a spirit of the deceased, see *Shivhei Habesht*, pp. 189–191.

Chapter Three: A Leader of the Jewish People (pp. 79–112)

1. Barnai, *Igrot Hasidim Me'eretz Israel*, pp. 33–45.

2. Mordechai Shraga Bauminger, "Letters of Our Rabbi Israel Baal Shem Tov and his Son-in-Law R. Yehiel Michal to Rabbi Avraham Gershon of Kotov," *Sinai* 71 (1972): 248–269. This text will henceforth be referred to as the Bauminger version.

3. This version will henceforth be referred to as the manuscript version. The three versions were printed side by side in Mondshine's *Shivhei Habesht*; they are reproduced in translation in appendix II.

4. On the debate among scholars on this point, see appendix III.

5. Mondshine, *Shivhei Habesht*, p. 234.

6. Ibid.

7. Ibid., p. 235.

8. Dubnow, *Toldot Hahasidut*, p. 62.

9. Dinur, "The Beginnings of Hasidism," pp. 182–183. Dinur devoted considerable efforts to a reconstruction of the "doctrine of redemption," which he attributed to Hasidism. See op. cit., pp. 207–227. A fundamentally different stance was taken by Gershom Scholem, who held that Hasidism neutralized the inherent Messianism in the ARI's Kabbalah. See Gershom Scholem, "The Neutralization of the Messianic Element in Early Hasidism," in *The Messianic Idea in Judaism* (New York, 1971), pp. 176–202. Dinur's proposed reconstruction of the Hasidic "Doctrine of Redemption" was rejected by Scholem with the assertion that "a conjunction of quotations, crossword-puzzle fashion, from Hasidic literature does not amount to a program that would have been foremost in the mind of any Hasid." See Scholem, "The Historical Figure of R. Israel Baal Shem Tov," p. 290.

10. Isaiah Tishbi, "The Messianic Idea and Messianic Trends in the Growth of Hasidism," *Zion* 32 (1967): 1–45.

11. Op. cit., p. 31.

12. Op. cit., p. 32.

13. Op. cit., p. 45.

14. Avraham Rubinstein, "The Besht's Epistle to R. Gershon of Kotov," *Sinai* 67 (1970): 120–138.

15. Op. cit., p. 134.

16. Barnai, *Igrot Hasidim Me'eretz Israel*, pp. 39–40.

17. Mondshine, *Shivhei Habesht*, Bauminger version, p. 237.

18. Dinur, in "The Beginnings of Hasidism," pp. 192–206, asserted that the failure of the Besht's trip to the land of Israel was a factor in the formation of his Messianic mission.

19. Hasidim sought to immigrate to the land of Israel in part because of a desire for spiritual elevation and proximity to God. The very settling in the land of Israel was the fulfillment of a *mitzvah*. In addition, only someone living in the land of Israel could satisfy the commandments associated with the Holy Land. In the land of Israel prayer has a greater effect, an effect that is further augmented if the prayers are recited at holy sites or over tombs of the righteous. A characteristic statement of the thought of someone deciding to emigrate to the land of Israel is given by R. Elazer of Amsterdam: "And I said to myself, when shall I act for my house and worship the Lord in awe and love without any distraction in the world.

I was awakened by the heavens: Why sleepest thou: Arise, call to your Lord in the Holy Land. And I resolved in my mind to travel from here to there via the sea"; cited in Israel Bartal, "The 'Aliyah' of R. Elazar Rokeah (1740)," in *Exile in the Homeland: Essays* (Jerusalem, 1994), p. 25.

20. Mondshine, *Shivhei Habesht*, pp. 234–235. On the subject of Samael, see Ephrayim A. Urbach, *The Sages: Their Concepts and Beliefs* (Jerusalem, 1979), pp. 146–154.

21. Mondshine, *Shivhei Habesht*, p. 234. About the Angel Michael, see Reuven Margaliot, *Malachei Elyon* (Jerusalem, 1945), pp. 108–117.

22. Mondshine, *Shivhei Habesht*, p. 236.

23. The Angel Gabriel is the one who allowed Samael to turn to evil deeds, as Gabriel is the lefthand mate of Michael, who takes the side of courage and judgment. See Margaliot, *Malachei Elyion*, pp. 21–44.

24. Mondshine, *Shivhei Habesht*, pp. 236–237.

25. On the blood-libels in Poland in the eighteenth century, see Semen Marcovitch Dubnow, *History of the Jews in Russia and Poland* (Philadelphia, 1916), 1: 172–180; and Rosman, *Founder of Hasidism*, pp. 55.

26. Mondshine, *Shivhei Habesht*, p. 237.

27. On the subject of the Heidemak rebellion and its consequences for the the the Jews of Poland see Dubnow (note 25), p. 180 passim; Rosman, *Founder of Hasidism*, pp. 54–55.

28. The ARI used to recite the *Pitum Haktoret* during outbreaks of plague, as it had the power of overwhelming the *qlipot*. The ARI considered it especially important that the *Pitum Haktoret* be recited by ten God-fearing men. See *Sefer Hakavannot*, by R. Isaac Luria (Jerusalem, 1984) (facsimile edition of Koretz printing), pp. 21a-b. Compare *Journey To A Nineteenth-Century Shtetl*, ed. David Assaf (Wayne State University Press, 2002), p. 350 n. 7.

29. *Shivhei Habesht*, pp. 91–94.

30. For various examples of the relation between ecstasy and ascents of the soul, see Joan Myrddin Lewis, *Ecstatic Religion: A Study of Shamanism and Spirit Possession* (London and New York, 1989).

31. On *pilpul* and *hilukim* (sophistry and disputation) and its place in Ashkenazi yeshivas at the end of the Middle Ages, see Mordechai Broyer, "The Emergence of *Pilpul* and *Hilukim* in the Ashkenazy Yehivas," in *Sefer Hazikaron Larav Yehiel Yaakov Weinberg* (Jerusalem, 1970), pp. 241–255; Hayim Zalman Dimitrovsky, "On the Pilpulistic Method," in *Salo Wittmayer Baron Jubilee Volume* (Hebrew Section)(Jerusalem, 1974), pp. 111–181; Dov Rappel, *The Debate Over the Pilpul* (Jerusalem, 1979); Elchanan Reiner, "The *Yeshivas* of Poland and Ashkenaz During the Sixteenth and Seventeenth Centuries—Historical Developments," in *Studies in Jewish Culture in Honor of Chone Shmeruk,* ed. Israel Bartal, Ezra Mendelsohn, and Chava Turniansky (Jerusalem, 1993), pp. 9–80.

32. The identification of the Besht's teacher with the biblical figure of Ahia Hashiloni first appears in *Toldot Yaakov Yosef*, by R. Yaakov Yosef of Polonne, (Koretz, 1780), Balak, p. 156a. The Besht's teacher is mentioned elsewhere in the writings of Yaakov Yosef of Polonne and in *Shivhei Habesht*. It appears from these references that Ahia Hashiloni helped the Besht fulfil his mission in the Upper Worlds, came to his aid in times of crisis, and guided him in

his mystical life. For a detailed discussion, see Gedalyah Nigal, "The Rabbi and Teacher of Israel Baal Shem Tov," *Sinai* 71 (1972): 150–159. The subject of the Besht's teacher was addressed also by Yehuda Liebes in his article "The Messiah of the Zohar—the Messianic Figure of R. Shimon Bar Yohai," in *Haraayon Hameshihi Beyisrael: An Anthology Dedicated to Gershom Scholem on his Eightieth Birthday* (Jerusalem, 1982), p. 113. Liebes maintains that the fact that Ahia Hashiloni was the Besht's teacher indicates that the Besht "saw himself as patterned on R. Shimon Bar Yohai." This assertion is based upon the associations between Ahia Hashiloni and R. Shimon Bar Yohai made in the Midrash and in the Zohar.

33. See Avraham Yaari, "The Burning of the Talmud in Kamenets Podolesk" *Sinai* 42 (1958): 294–306; Meir Balaban, *Letoldot Hatnuah Hafrankit* [History of the Frankist movement] (Tel Aviv, 1934), pp. 181–185.

34. *Shivhei Habesht*, p. 94.

35. Op. cit., p. 95.

36. On the mystical experiences of the Chariot Descenders, see Rachel Elior, "The Concept of God in Hekhalot Mysticism," *Binah* 2 (1989): 97–129; Joseph Dan, "The Entrance To the Sixth Gate," *Jerusalem Studies in Jewish Thought* 6 (1987): 197–220; *The Ancient Jewish Mysticism* (Tel Aviv, 1989), pp. 59–69. For a general discussion of the phenomenon of ascents of the soul, see Moshe Idel, *Kabbalah: New Perspectives* (New Haven, 1988), pp. 88–96. About the Besht's ascents of the soul in relation to previous stages of Jewish mysticism, see Naftali Loewenthal, *Communicating the Infinite* (Chicago, 1990,),pp. 6–10.

37. Benayahu, *Toldot Haari*, p. 155.

38. Ibid.

39. *Shivhei Habesht*, pp. 124–125.

40. Op. cit., pp. 210–211.

41. Op. cit., p. 212.

42. For more on this blood-libel, see Hayim Bar Dayan, "The Pavolitch Blood Libel and Zhitomir Trial," *Eder Hayakar, Divrei Safrut Vemehkar Mukdashim le S.A. Horodezky* [literature and scholarship dedicated to S. A. Horodezky] (Tel Aviv, 1947), pp. 131–144.

43. *Shivhei Habesht*, p. 245.

44. Op. cit., p. 266.

45. Op. cit., p. 237. For cases of sight from afar serving to deliver individuals from robbery, see op. cit., pp. 153–154; Nigal, *Gedolim Maasei Tsadikim*, pp. 20–21.

46. *Shivhei Habesht*, pp. 240–241. For further instances of defending the public from edicts and persecutions, see *Shivhei Habesht*, pp. 106–107, 298.

47. See Solomon Maimon, *Hayei Shlomo Maimon*, pp. 76–78; Khone Shmeruk, "The Hasidic Movement and the 'Arendars,'" *Zion* 35 (1970): 182–192. A thorough and comprehensive treatment of the topic of leaseholding may be found in Murray Jay Rosman, *The Lord's Jews* (Cambridge, 1990), pp. 110–142.

48. *Shivhei Habesht*, pp. 257–259. See also Nigal, *Gedolim Maasei Tsadikim*, p. 21.

49. The letter was published by Mordechai Shraga Bauminger (see note 2).

50. *Zion* 20 (1955): 47–72.

51. Op. cit., p. 49.

52. Op. cit., p. 50.

53. Something of this kind is related, for instance, about R. David Furkes. See *Shivhei Habesht*, p. 247; and cf. Shmeruk (note 50), pp. 58–59. Shmeruk proposes a further cause for the strict examination of the *shekhita* knife by the Hasidim and the pious: the belief in the reincarnation of the souls of sinners in the bodies of animals. According to this belief, slaughtering an animal by the Halachah is a necessary condition for the redemption of any soul reincarnated as that animal.

54. *Shivhei Habesht*, pp. 267–268.

55. Cf. Nigal, *Gedolim Maasei Tsadikim*, pp. 19–20.

56. *Shivhei Habesht*, pp. 307–308.

57. Op. cit., p. 247.

58. Op. cit., pp. 138–139.

59. Op. cit., p. 60.

60. Op. cit., pp. 71–73.

61. Recall that the Besht healed the rabbi of Sdeh Lavan. See chapter 2 and *Shivhei Habesht*, pp. 73–75.

62. *Shivhei Habesht*, pp. 215–216.

63. See Babylonian Talmud, Tractate Rosh Hashanah 27a; Tractate Yoma 39a; Maimonidies, *Mishneh Torah*, Hilchot Arachin Veharamin, chap. 8, Halachah 13.

64. See Nigal, *Gedolim Maasei Tsadikim*, p. 14.

65. See Shmeruk, *"The Hasidic Movement and the 'Arendars,'"* pp. 182–192.

66. *Shivhei Habesht*, pp. 165–166.

67. Op. cit., pp. 158–159.

68. Nigal, *Gedolim Maasei Tsadikim*, p. 23.

69. *Sefer Hasidim*, Yehuda Wistinesky edition (Berlin, 1891), secs. 5–6.

70. The collection of stories "Gedolim Maasei Tsadikim" was first published in *Kvutsat Yaakov*, by R. Avraham Yaakov b. R. Israel of Sadigora (Berditchev, 1896); yet the book was completed thirteen years earlier (see Nigal, *Gedolim Maasei Tsadikim*, p. 8).

71. See the tale cited above about the ascent of the soul that occurred when the Besht passed in front of the ark during the Neilah service of Yom Kippur.

72. *Shivhei Habesht*, pp. 235–236.

73. For more on this topic, see chapter 4.

74. A tradition of the Habad Hasidim attributes to the Besht statements about the superiority of the simple man who worships his Lord in an innocent faith. See *Keter Shem Tov* (New York: Otzar Hasidim Press, 1987), pp. 214–216.

75. A thorough discussion of the topic of chastisement and reprovers in the early days of Hasidism may be found in Piekarz, *Biyemei Tsmihat Hahasidut*, (The beginning of hasidism), pp. 96–172.

76. *Toldot Yaakov Yosef*, Kdoshim, p. 94a.

77. See R. Shlomo of Lucek's introduction to *Maggid Devarav Leyaakov*, by R. Dov Ber of Mezerich, critical edition based on manuscripts with an introduction, commentary, notes, and indexes by Rivka Schatz-Uffenheimer (Jerusalem, 1976), p. 2.

78. *Shivhei Habesht*, p. 32. What is meant is that the Besht is a "spark" of the soul of R. Shimon Bar Yohai. R. Yekil is mentioned as the one who read out the poetic prayers to the

Besht as the latter passed in front of the ark on Yom Kippur in the Miedzybóz Beit Midrash. See *Shivhei Habesht*, p. 92.

Chapter Four: The Besht as Mystic and Pioneer in Divine Worship (pp. 113–151)

1. On the relation between Hasidism as a way of life and Hasidic doctrine, cf. Buber, *Bepardes Hahasidut* [In the Orchard of Hasidism] (Jerusalem, 1979), pp. 22–23.

2. Gershom Scholem, "Devekut, or Communion with God," in *The Messianic Idea in Judaism* (New York, 1971), pp. 203–206.

3. Op. cit., pp. 208–210.

4. Op. cit., pp. 208–210. It would seem that the sole innovation having to do with *dvekut* that Scholem ascribes to the Besht is the technique of achieving *dvekut* via the letters of the prayers. Yet instead of analyzing the relevance of this innovation for the Besht's mysticism, Scholem uses it to support his perspective on the change that Hasidism made in the "place" of *dvekut* (see op. cit., p. 212).

5. Isaiah Tishbi, "The Influence of Rabbi Moses Hayyim Luzzatto in Hasidic Teaching," *Zion* 43 (1978): 201–234, 214–215; Ada Rapoport-Albert, "God and the Tsadik as Two Focal Points of Hasidic Worship," *History of Religion* 18 (1979): 303–307; Gedalyah Nigal, ed., *Ketonet Pasim*, by R. Yaakov Yosef of Polonne, (Ramat Gan, 1985), introduction, p. 21; Immanuel Etkes, "Hasidism as a Movement—The First Stage," *Hasidism: Continuity or Innovation*, ed. Bezalel Safran (Cambridge, Mass., 1988), pp. 1–26; Ada Rapoport-Albert, "Hasidism After 1772: Structural Continuity and Change," in *Hasidism Reappraised*, ed. Ada Rapoport-Albert (London, 1996), p.85; Mendel Piekarz, *Between Ideology and Reality: Humility, Ayin, Self-Negation and Devekut in the Hasidic Thought* (Jerusalem, 1994), pp. 160–161. A different stance was recently taken by Rachel Elior. She shares Scholem's position according to which Hasidism made *dvekut* something any Jew could attain. In her opinion, the stance of Hasidism on this issue stemmed from the radical interpretation given to the Kabbalist principle "no site is clear of him." See Rachel Elior, *Hasidic Thought—Mystical Origins and Kabbalistic Foundations* (Tel Aviv, 1999), pp. 21–22, 55, 57 passim.

6. Weiss, "Beginnings of Hassidism," pp. 60–61.

7. Op. cit., pp. 46–47.

8. Op. cit., pp. 47–49.

9. *Toldot Yaakov Yosef*, p. 186b.

10. Evidence supporting the claim that the Besht's concept of *dvekut* was identical to that of members of the circle is provided by Weiss in "Beginnings of Hassidism," p. 64.

11. On the Besht's innovations on the topic of "elevating straying thoughts" see Weiss, op. cit., pp. 88–103. This topic will be treated in detail later in this chapter.

12. For a critical review of certain aspects of Weiss's article, see Piekarz, *The Beginning of Hasidism*, pp. 22–25, 96–98, passim.

13. Mendel Piekarz, *Between Ideology and Reality*, p. 150–178.

14. Op. cit., p. 153.

15. Op. cit., pp. 163–168.

16. See op. cit., pp. 10–11; 150–178; passim.

17. Tishbi and Dan, *Hasidism—Doctrine and Literature.*

18. Schatz-Uffenheimer, *Hasidism as Mysticism.*

19. Moshe Idel, *Hasidism: Between Ecstasy and Magic* (New York, 1995).

20. *Tarbiz* 65 (1996): 671–709. See also Nigal's criticism of this article; Gedalyah Nigal, "The Figure of the Besht and his Philosophy," *Sinai* 120 (1997): 150–160.

21. As this book went to press, Rachel Elior's *Hasidic Thought* was published. This book contains discussions about what was unique about the Besht that I am unable to address here.

22. See the following writings by Mordechai Pachter: "The Theory of Devekut in the Writings of the Sages of Safed in the Sixteenth Century," *Jerusalem Studies in Jewish Thought* 1, 3 (1982): 51–121; *Homiletic and Ethical Literature of the Sages of Safed in the 16th Century* (Ph.D. diss., Hebrew University, 1976), pp. 480–487; "The Life and Personality of R. Elazar Azcari According To His Mystical Diary," *Shalem* 3 (1981): 127–148; *Milei De-Shmaya by Rabbi Elazar Azcari* [Heavenly words, by R. Elazar Azcari] (Haifa, 1991); *From Safed's Hidden Treasures, Studies and Texts Concerning the History of Safed and Its Sages in the 16th Century* (Jerusalem, 1994). An interesting attempt to clarify the link between *dvekut* and insanity in early Hasidism may be found in Tzvi Mark's "*Dibbuk* and *Devekut* in *In Praise of the Baal Shem Tov:* Notes On the Phenomenology of Madness in Early Hasidism," in *Within Hasidic Circles—Studies in Hasidism in Memory of Mordecai Wilensky,* ed. Immanuel Etkes, David Assaf, Israel Bartal, and Elchanan Reiner (Jerusalem, 1999), pp. 247–286.

23. Pachter, "The Theory of Dvekut," pp. 58–60, 69–71, 74, 82–83, 89, 105–106, 111.

24. Op. cit, pp. 79, 88–89.

25. Although Pachter employs the term *ecstasy* in characterizing Azikri's experience (ibid., 89; and "Life and Personality," p. 136), nonetheless, the broad picture suggested by Azikri's diary is one of continual awareness of the presence of God. This experience, while it contains a clear strain of mysticism, lacks the element of the break from normal consciousness that characterizes mystical ecstasy in the stronger sense of the term.

26. Pachter, "The Theory of Dvekut," p. 79.

27. Op. cit., pp. 60, 79–80, 84–85, 87–88, 90–91.

28. The conception of *dvekut* as a continuous focus of thought on God appears also in the highly influential book *Shnei Luhot Habrit,* by R. Yeshayah Horowitz. See Piekarz, *The Beginning of Hasidism,* p. 24.

29. *Toldot Yaakov Yosef,* p. 113d.

30. *Hanhagot Yesharot,* facsimile edition, in *Sfarim Kdoshim Mitalmidei Baal Shem Tov* [Sacred texts by students of the Baal Shem Tov] (New York, 1993), 91: 3.

31. *Shivhei Habesht,* p. 205.

32. Op. cit., pp. 64, 103–104, 126.

33. This discussion is based on the following works: Evelyn Underhill, *Mysticism* (London, 1945), pp. 358–379; Friedrich Heiler, *Prayer* (New York, 1958), pp. 135–171; Marghanita Laski, *Ecstasy* (Los Angeles, 1990). On the religious significance of ecstasy in ancient cultures and its links to the phenomenon of prophecy, see Joshua Abraham Heschel, *The Prophets* (New York, 1962), pp. 324–366.

34. *Shivhei Habesht,* pp. 85–86.

35. Ibid.

36. Op. cit., pp. 86–87.

37. Op. cit., p. 92.

38. Op. cit., pp. 66–67.

39. For more on the Besht's tendency to shake while praying, see op. cit., p. 311

40. *Likutim Yekarim*, by R. Dov Ber of Mezerich (Jerusalem, 1974), p. 55a–b.

41. The external manifestations of ecstatic prayer became the butt of ridicule for the opponents of Hasidism. See for example Wilensky, *Hasidim Umitnagdim* [Hasidim and Mitnagedim: A study of the controversy between them in the years 1772–1815], 1 (Jerusalem, 1970), pp. 39–41, 59–60, passim.

42. *Degel Mahaneh Ephrayim*, Yitro, p. 101.

43. See *Likutim Yekarim*, sec. 33, p. 6a.

44. Op. cit., sec. 24, p. 5b.

45. *Keter Shem Tov*, p. 16a.

46. On *kavvanah* in the Kabbalah, see Tishbi, *Mishnat Hazohar*, 2, p. 268 passim; Gershom Scholem, *Kabbalah* (Jerusalem, 1974), pp. 32–33, 44–45, and many others; use his index for "Kavvanah" and "Kavvanot." On Kavvanah in the Lurianic Kabbalah see Idem, *Major Trends in Jewish Mysticism* (New York, 1941), pp. 273–280.

47. Joseph Weiss, "The Kavvanoth of Prayer in Early Hasidism," *Studies in Eastern European Jewish Mysticism* (Oxford, 1985), pp. 95–125; Schatz-Uffenheimer, *Hasidism as Mysticism: Quietistic Elements*, pp. 215–241.

48. Weiss relies upon statements cited in *Tsava'at HaRibash*, Kohet edition (New York, 1991), sec. 118 p. 21a.

49. *Keter Shem Tov*, sec. 129, pp. 16b, 17a; sec. 88, p. 12b; see also sec. 27, p. 5a.

50. Op. cit., sec. 16, p. 4a.

51. Yehuda Liebes believes that there is an affinity between the erotic aspects of Hasidic prayer and Sabbatean antinomian rituals; Yehuda Liebes, *On Sabbateanism and Its Kabbalah: Collected Essays* (Jerusalem, 1995), pp. 98–99. It seems to me that the differences between these phenomena are greater than the similarities.

52. See Laski, *Ecstasy*, pp. 57–66.

53. *Keter Shem Tov*, 121, p. 16a.

54. *Tsava'at HaRibash*, sec. 35, p. 6a. Cf. op. cit., 42, 6b.

55. Cf. *Keter Shem Tov*, 34, p. 6a; 110, p. 15a.

56. Op. cit., 77, p. 10a.

57. *Toldot Yaakov Yosef*, p. 146c.

58. Cf. *Keter Shem Tov*, 25, p. 5a.

59. Op. cit., 37, p. 6a; 77, p. 10a.

60. *Degel Mahane Ephrayim*, Yitro, pp. 99–100.

61. This sentence is in Yiddish in the original text.

62. The Passover Hagaddah is alluded to here: " 'And we were taken from Egypt by the Lord'—not by an angel, not by a Seraph and not by an emissary, but by the Holy One Blessed Be He by his Majestic Self."

63. *Degel Mahaneh Ephrayim*, p. 257.

64. *Keter Shem Tov,* 51, p. 8a.

65. Op. cit., 66, p. 9a.

66. Op. cit., 51, p. 8a. Cf. ibid., 66, p. 9a; 85, p. 12a.

67. See Tishbi and Dan, *Hasidism—Doctrine and Literature,* p. 775; Schatz-Uffenheimer, *Hasidism as Mysticism: Quietistic Elements,* chap. 8, pp. 189–203; Rachel Elior, "The Affinity Between the Kabbalah and Hasidism—Continuity and Change" (in Hebrew), presented at the Ninth World Congress on Jewish Studies, division 3 (Jerusalem, 1986), pp. 107–114.

68. Op. cit., p. 109.

69. On the tendency of mystics to translate their experiences into theosophisms of this kind, see Heiler, pp. 146–147.

70. *Keter Shem Tov,* 30, p. 5b. See also op. cit., 55, p. 8a–b.

71. Op cit., 51, p. 8a.

72. See Tishbi, *Mishnat Hazohar,* 1, pp. 285–359, and *The Doctrine of Evil and the "Kelippah" in Lurianic Kabbalism* (Jerusalem, 1960); Gershom Scholem, *Kabbalah* (Jerusalem, 1974), Chapter 6, pp. 122–128.

73. *Keter Shem Tov,* 26, p. 5a.

74. Ibid.

75. Op. cit., 106, p. 14a. Cf. ibid., 20, p. 4b.

76. Tishbi and Dan, *Hasidism—Doctrine and Literature,* p. 773.

77. On the powers of the Other Side, see note 72. On Kabbalist *mussar* literature, see Joseph Dan, *Safrut Hamussar Vehadrush* (Jerusalem, 1975), pp. 202–229; Pachter, *Safrut Hadrush Vehamussar Shel Hachmei Zfat.* A more detailed treatment of the moral ethos of the Safed Kabbalists will be given in chapter 5.

78. *Keter Shem Tov,* 115, p. 15b. See also ibid., 134, p. 17b.

79. See for example *Keter Shem Tov,* 58, p. 8b. In his well-known essay "On Joy in Hasidism," *Zion* 16 (1951): 30–43, Azriel Shohet drew attention to the literary sources that anticipated the Besht's restriction of asceticism and emphasis on the supremacy of joy in divine worship. As a marginal point, Shohet suggests how the Besht nevertheless differed from his predecessors. To Shohet's explanation one should add: the contribution of the Besht on this issue was not limited to the fact that his rejection of self-mortification was much more decisive and unequivocal than his predecessors, but in his articulation and transmission of a religious ethos that opposed asceticism and presented alternatives to it.

80. *Shivhei Habesht,* p. 105.

81. *Toldot Yaakov Yosef,* p. 137a–b.

82. *Shivhei Hebesht,* p. 125. And cf. ibid., pp. 304–305.

83. A succinct review of the idea of worship through corporeality may be found in Tishbi, "The Influence of Rabbi Moses Hayyim Luzzatto in Hasidic Teaching," pp. 207–210; see the bibliographic references there, note 15.

84. *Toldot Yaakov Yosef,* p. 23a.

85. Scholem, *Devekut, or Communion with God,* p. 205.

86. Weiss, "Beginnings of Hassidism," p. 65.

87. *Mesilat Yesharim,* by Moshe Hayim Luzzato, Eshkol edition, (Jerusalem, 1964), pp. 126–127.

88. On this topic I am in agreement with Buber, who sees "worship through corporeality" as involving the broad context of ordinary life and not as linked specifically to *dvekut*. Nevertheless, I find it hard to agree to his interpretation of the *content* of "worship through corporeality"; namely, that someone worshiping God in this manner intends "to have it be the essence and content of each and every action" (Buber, note 1 above, pp. 66–67). And see Scholem's sharp critique of Buber on this point: Gershom Scholem, "Martin Buber's Hasidism: A Critique," *Commentary*, 32 (1961), p. 311.

89. *Tsofnat Paaneach*, pp. 408–409.

90. See Eliahu Hacohen, ed., *Midrash Talpiyot* (Warsaw, 1875), p. 220a.

91. *Toldot Yaakov Yosef*, p. 39a.

92. See Tishbi, "The Influence of Rabbi Moses Hayyim Luzzatto"; Schatz-Uffenheimer, *Hasidism as Mysticism*, pp. 56–58.

93. See Immanuel Etkes, "Rabbi Hayyim of Volozhim's Response to Hasidism," in *The Gaon of Vilna—The Man and His Image* (Berkeley, 2002), pp. 189–191.

94. On the topic of straying thoughts in Hasidism, see Isaiah Tishbi and Joseph Dan, "Hasidism—Doctrine and Literature," *Encyclopaedia Hebraica* (Jerusalem and Tel Aviv, 1965), 17:784–786; Weiss, "Beginnings of Hassidism," pp. 88–103; Piekarz, *The Beginning of Hasidism*, p. 269–279.

95. *Keter Shem Tov*, p. 39, 6b.

96. Ibid.

97. The text is evidently corrupted and should be "the place." The MS reads: "And when I came to my home and in my home it was very hot."

98. *Shivhei Habesht*, p. 205.

99. *Degel Mahaneh Ephrayim*, p. 177.

100. *Keter Shem Tov*, 112, p. 15a. See also op. cit., 99, p. 13b.

101. See, for example, Schatz-Uffenheimer, *Hasidism as Mysticism*, p. 179 passim.

102. Weiss, "Beginnings of Hassidism," p. 91.

103. In the framework of his efforts to prove the Besht's connction to the circle of *maggidim*, Weiss clamed that the Besht's innovations on the subject of straying thoughts are associated with ideas the *maggidim* held about public leadership. More specifically: in his opinion there is a considerable affinity between the idea of the "descent of the Zaddik," (that is, the moral descent of the leader for the sake of elevating the souls of sinners) and the idea of elevating straying thoughts (op. cit., pp. 80–81). This association seems to me tenuous: The former case concerns a mission assigned to a leader whereas the latter has to do with a private individual who seeks to use prayer to attain to the hights of mystical experience; the former involves a deliberate "descent," whereas in the latter case the stray thought "descends" involuntarily on one's consciousness. Furthermore, nowhere in any of the traditions attributed to the Besht regarding straying thoughts does the issue of the "descent of the *Zaddik*" appear. On this point see also Piekarz's critique, in *The Beginning of Hasidism*, pp. 276–279.

104. An instructive discussion on this topic is given in Moshe Idel's *Hasidism: Between Ecstasy and Magic*, pp. 149–170. Idel brings to light source materials in the Kabbalah of Abulafia and Cordovero that may have inspired the Besht here and that can potentially help us to understand his conceptions. Nevertheless, Idel points out differences between the

Kabbalist materials, which discuss techniques of a magical nature, and the Hasidic texts, where the mystical tendency prevails.

105. See Gershom Scholem, "The Meaning of the Torah in Jewish Mysticism," in his *On the Kabbalah and Its Symbolism* (New York, 1965), pp.32–86.

106. *Igeret Aliyat Haneshama Lehabesht* [The ascent of the soul epistle by the Besht], in *Sefer Shivhei Habaal Shem Tov* (a facsimile of a unique manuscript, variant versions, and appendices), by Yehoshua Mondshine (Jerusalem, 1982), pp. 235–236.

107. *Keter Shem Tov,* 44, p. 7a.

108. Op. cit., 56, p. 8b.

109. *Likutim Yekarim,* 4a.

110. See above, note 104.

111. *Maggid Devarav Leyaakov,* by R. Dov Ber of Mezerich, critical edition based on manuscripts with an introduction, commentary, notes, and indexes by Rivka Schatz-Uffenheimer (Jerusalem, 1976), pp. 85–86; see her interpretation of this passage. Although what is cited is attributed to the *maggid,* it is nevertheless likely that for the most part they reflect the mode of prayer that the *maggid* learned from the Besht, even if there is a certain amount of innovative development to them.

112. Cf: *Keter Shem Tov,* 166, p. 21b.

113. *Likutim Yekarim,* p. 10a.

114. The Besht's perspective that one may attain *dvekut* through communication with the Devine Presence that is inside the letters of the Torah and the prayers, had substantial implications for the status of Torah study in early Hasidism. On this topic see Joseph Weiss, *Studies in Eastern European Jewish Mysticism* (Oxford, 1985), pp. 56–68; Immanuel Etkes, *The Beginning of the Hasidic Movement* (Tel Aviv, 1998), pp. 89–99.

115. *Toldot Yaakov Yosef,* p. 20a.

Chapter Five: The Besht and His Circle (pp. 152–202)

1. See chap. 4, note 5.

2. See under "Hasid," *Haencyclopedia Hamikrait* (Jerusalem, 1965), 3: 224–225; Louis Jacobs, "The Concept of Hasid in Biblical and Rabbinic Literature," *Journal of Jewish Studies* 8 (1957): 143–154.

3. Ibid. For a comparison of the concepts of *Zaddik* and *Hasid* in rabbinic literature, see Gershom Scholem, *Elements of the Kabbalah and its Symbolism* (Jerusalem, 1976), pp. 213–216.

4. For a selection of studies about the Hasidim of Ashkenaz, see Ivan G. Marcus, ed., *The Religious and Social Ideas of the Jewish Pietists in Medieval Germany* (Jerusalem, 1986); see also its bibliography, pp. 279–281. About the influence of the Hasidim of Ashkenaz on the concept of repentance as held by the sages of Poland in the sixteenth and seventeenth centuries, see Jacob Elbaum, *Repentance and Self-Flagellation in the Writings of the Sages of Germany and Poland, 1348–1648* (Jerusalem, 1992), chaps. 3–4, pp. 37–53.

5. On the lifestyles of the Hasidim of Safed in the sixteenth century, see Solomon Shechter, *Studies in Judaism* (Philadelphia, 1908); Refael Werblowsky, *Joseph Karo, Lawyer and Mystic* (Philadelphia, 1980), chapter 4, David Tamar, *Studies in the History of the Jewish People in Eretz Israel and Italy* (Jerusalem, 1973), pp. 95–100.

6. Benayahu, *Toldot Haari*, p. 5; see also p. 6.

7. Op. cit., pp. 5–6.

8. Op. cit, p. 17b; cf. *Shivhei Rabbi Hayim Vital* (Ashdod, 1988), p. 19a.

9. Regulations of the Hasidic fraternities in Safed are reproduced in Shechter, *Studies in Judaism*, pp. 292–301; and Tolidano, *Otzar Genazim*, pp. 48–51.

10. See, for example, Shechter, *Studies in Judaism*, p. 292, sec. 1; ibid., sec 10.

11. See, for example, Shechter, op. cit., p. 294, secs. 31, 36; Tolidano, *Otzar Genazim*, p. 48, sec. 5.

12. Shechter, op. cit., p. 292, sec. 5. Cf. Tolidano, op. cit., p. 49, sec. 9.

13. Cf. Tolidano, p. 49, sec. 2; cf. Shechter, op. cit., p. 297.

14. Shechter, op cit., p. 294, sec. 1.

15. A characteristic expression of this line of thought may be found in the following regulation: "Nightly he should sit on the ground and lament the Destruction and intend to weep also for his sins which lengthen the End for Redemption; Shechter, ibid., p. 293, sec. 2.

16. Op. cit., p. 294, sec. 3; p. 295, sec. 9; p. 297, sec. 28; p. 299, sec. 1, etc.

17. Benayahu, *Toldot Haari*, p. 316. Liebes, *Hamashiah Shel Hazohar*, p. 158, notes how the stress on the virtue of love among students of R. Simon Bar Yokhai served as a model that inspired the ARI's students.

18. See Shechter, *Studies in Judaism*, p. 293, sec. 14. Cf. ibid., sec 15. See also Tolidano, *Otzar Gnazim*, p. 48, sec. 4.

19. An example is the Confederation Document of the ARI's students, dated Safed 1575, which runs as follows: "We the undersigned have taken upon ourselves to be in one society to worship the Blessed Lord and to engage in his Torah day and night, in all that we are instructed by our teacher the Rabbi the Wise the Perfect the Divine [. . .] Hayim Vital, we shall study with him in the true wisdom and shall be faithful in spirit and keep all he tells us secret and shall not burden him by excessive entreaties to reveal to us that which he does not wish to reveal and we shall not reveal to others any secret of all we have heard from his mouth in the way of truth . . . . And this resolution is undertaken with a severe oath by the Blessed Lord with the agreement of our teacher the above-mentioned Rabbi R. Hayim may his candle shine and the duration of this resolution is from today till ten years from now"; quoted in the version published by Zeev Rabinowitcz, "Manuscripts From the Archive in Stolin," *Zion* 5 (1940): 125–126. A more or less identical version of the Confederation Document was published by Baruch David Hacohen in *Birchat Haaretz* (Jerusalem, 1904), p. 61. On the authenticity of this document, its meaning, and the identities of its signatories, see Gershom Scholem, "A Document By the Disciples of Isaac Luria," *Zion* 5 (1940): 133–160. The document expresses its signers' recognition of the status of R. Hayim Vital as the supreme authority in all that concerns the ARI's teachings. He was expected to reveal to the members of the group the secrets he heard from the ARI, and he was qualified to interpret even what the members of the group heard from the ARI directly. In addition the group was bound by the commitment not to reveal to others what their master had revealed to them. What one clearly notices is that the formal and strict form of organization that this group took was linked to its attributes and purposes; that is, to the revelation of Torah secrets and the need to keep them secret.

20. Dinur, "The Beginnings of Hasidism," p. 159.

21. Ibid., pp. 163–170. Although there is no doubt about these three attributes, it is hard to endorse the remaining attributes Dinur proposed, as he bases his claims on a combination of passages written in different times and places.

22. *Hayei Shlomo Maimon* (Tel Aviv, 1953). In the original German, the book was first published in Berlin in 1792–93.

23. Op. cit., pp. 120–122, 132–133.

24. For more on Pinchas Katzenelbogen and his book *Yesh Manhilin,* see chapter 1.

25. *Yesh Manhilin,* p. 85.

26. *Shivhei Habesht,* pp. 64, 103–105, 126.

27. The sources for the subject of Yaakov Yosef's conflict with the Shargorod community will be noted below. On the place of the Third Sabbath Meal in Hasidic life see Weiss, *A Circle of Pneumatics in Pre-Hasidism,* pp. 31–34.

28 . Yaakov Hisdai, "Servant of God in the Era of the Fathers of Hasidism" *Zion,* 47 (1982): 253–292; see esp. 258–264.

29. Israel Halpern, "Communes for Torah and Commandments and the Expanding Hasidic Movement," in his *Yehudim Veyahadut Bemizrah Eropa* (Jerusalem, 1969), p. 317.

30. Hisdai (see note 28), p. 261.

31. Wilensky, *Hasidim Umitnagdim,* 1: 47–48.

32. Elchanan Reiner, "Wealth, Social Position and the Study of Torah: The Status of the Kloiz in Eastern European Jewish Society in the Early Modern Period," *Zion* 58 (1993): 287–328.

33. Op. cit., p. 288.

34. Op. cit., pp. 320–322.

35. Weiss, *A Circle of Pneumatics in Pre-Hasidism.*

36. *Shivhei Habesht,* p. 181; Weiss, "Beginnings of Hassidism," p. 60.

37. *Shivhei Habesht,* pp. 264–266.

38. Op. cit., pp. 64–65.

39. Ibid.

40. Scholem, "The Two First Testimonies."

41. (Frankfurt an der Oder, 1751). For more on R. Shlomo of Chelm, see Israel Zinberg, *A History of Jewish Literature* vol. vi, (New York, 1975) 7: 241–243; Raphael Mahler, *Jewish History—the Modern Period* (Merhavia, 1962), 4:25–27; Immanuel Etkes, "Immanent Factors and External Influences in the Development of the Haskalah Movement in Russia," in *Toward Modernity: The European Model,* ed. Jacob Katz (New York, 1978), pp. 16–17.

42. *Merkevet Hamishneh,* by R. Shlomo of Chelm (Frankfurt An Der Oder, 1751), p. 1a.

43. Op. cit.

44. (Zolkiew, 1746).

45. *Mishmeret Hakodesh,* by R. Moshe b. R. Yaakov of Stanov (Zolkiew, 1746), 1:2a.

46. Op. cit., p. 2d.

47. Op. cit., p. 2c.

48. Op. cit.

49. Confirmation of this hypothesis is provided by the accounts of the Kotov Hasidic fraternity. See *Shivhei Habesht*, p. 265.

50. Scholem, "The Two First Testimonies"; the text is cited on p. 232, sect. 8, and discussed on p. 236.

51. See Hayim Liberman, "How is Hasidism Studied in Israel?" pp. 38–49. Scholem was not persuaded by Liberman's criticism and repeatedly argued that R. Moshe of Satanow's statements hinted at the Besht. See Gershom Scholem, "The Historical Figure of the Besht," p. 300, and his response to Liberman, ibid., note 20. See also Liberman's response to Scholem's remarks, *Ohel Rachel*, pp. 46–49. An examination of the texts and Liberman's arguments leaves no doubt in my mind that Scholem was mistaken on this point. See also Piekarz's comments in *The Beginning of Hasidism*, pp. 131–136, which add evidence supporting Liberman's stance.

52. Scholem, "The Two First Testimonies," p. 236.

53. Op. cit., p. 238. The characterization of these Hasidim as commoners appears in Scholem's statements several times.

54. On this issue I am in agreement with what Hisdai has long since written; see "Servant of God," pp. 257–258, 260–261.

55. *Shivhei Habesht*, pp. 48–51, 64.

56. Ibid., pp. 75–76.

57. For further examples see op. cit., pp. 54–56, 64–65, 79–81, etc.

58. The reference is to stories included in the part of *Shivhei Habesht* revised by the "printer," R. Israel Yaffe (pp. 35–59). In this section the fictional element is particularly noticeable.

59. Cf. Scholem, "The Historical Figure of the Besht," p. 315 passim.

60. *Shivhei Habesht*, p. 49.

61. Biographical data about R. Gershon of Kotov is quite scarce. An attempt to present a comprehensive picture, to the extent possible, may be found in Abraham J. Heschel's article, "Rabbi Gershon Kutover: His Life and Immigration to the Land of Isreal," in *The Circle of the Baal Shem Tov: Studies in Hasidism*, ed. by Samuel H. Dresner (Chicago, 1985), pp. 44–122. A short discussion of R. Gershon and his immigration to the land of Israel may be found in Israel Halpern's *The Hasidic Immigration to Palestine During the Eighteenth Century* (Jerusalem and Tel-Aviv, 1946), pp. 11, 13–16. For an account that fills out the picture, see Yaakov Barnai, "Notes on the Immigration of R. Abraham Gershon Kutower to Eretz-Israel," *Zion* 42 (1977): 110–119.

62. See Rubinstein's remarks, *Shivhei Habesht*, p. 48, n. 6.

63. Heschel, *R. Gershon Kutover*, pp. 45, 52–56.

64. Barnai, *Igrot Hasidim Me'eretz Israel*, p. 37. Further confirmation is given by the remarks of R. Meir, the rabbi of Konstantin, who describes him using the designation *muflag* (prodigy), which usually is applied to someone who is decidedly a *Talmid Hacham*. See R. Hayim Cohen Rapoport, *Mayim Hayim* (Zhitomir, 1857), 1, sec. 27, p. 50.

65. *Shivhei Habesht*, pp. 97, 113; and see Heschel, *R. Gershon Kutover*, p. 18.

66. Cited by Heschel, *R. Gershon Kutover*, p. 46.

67. Opening lines of the Besht's Epistle, Bauminger version, in Mondshine, *Shivhei Habesht*, p. 233.

68. Halpern, *The Hasidic Immigration To Palestine,* p. 13 n. 15; Heschel, *R. Gershon Kutover,* pp. 23–24.

69. *Shivhei Habesht,* p. 184.

70. Halpern, *The Hasidic Immigration To Palestine,* p. 15. Rubinstein, *Shivhei Habesht,* p. 48 n. 7, notes that R. Gershon's gravestone on the Mount of Olives is located among the tombs of the Kabbalists of *Beit El.*

71. *Shivhei Habesht,* pp. 96–98.

72. Op. cit., pp. 172–173. See ibid., note 2, for Rubinstein's explanation.

73. R. Gershon had no doubt that the Prophet Elijah revealed himself to him and even saved his life. See *Shivhei Habesht,* pp. 111–113, and note 31 on p. 113.

74. *Shivhei Habesht,* p. 184.

75. Op. cit., pp. 114–115; and compare ibid., p. 66. For additional tales dealing with R. Gershon's magical powers, see ibid., pp. 111, 118–119.

76. Heschel, *R. Gershon Kutover,* p. 73. Halpern, *The Hasidic Immigration to Palestine,* pp. 15–16, rightly rejects all sorts of attempts to link R. Gershon's immigration to the Hasidic movement that originated in the Besht.

77. R. Gershon arrived in the land of Israel in the month of Sivan, 1747. He first settled in Hebron and six years later relocated to Jerusalem, where he died in the year 1761. See Barnai (note 61). Heschel, in *R. Gershon Kutover,* p. 90 passim, attempted to show that R. Gershon's 1747 immigration was not his first. Scholem, however, entirely rejects this hypothesis. See Gershom Scholem, "Two Letters from the Land of Israel from the years 1760–1764," *Tarbiz* 25 (1956): 429–430, n. 4. The two letters that R. Gershon wrote, the first evidently dating to 1748 and the second to 1757, were published by Barnai, *Igrot Hasidim Me'eretz Israel,* pp. 33–45. The passages cited from the Besht's Epistle use the versions found in Mondshine, *Shivhei Habesht,* pp. 233–237. See appendix II.

78. R. Gershon writes to his student as follows: "My beloved, son of my sister, my friend and favorite student Mr. Zvi Hirsch may his candle shine, my humble request is that you carry on in studies so that the labors I labored with you shall not have been in vain heaven forbid. And you know that I labored and toiled, that I did not come to the holy community of Miedzybóz except on your account and thank goodness I raised you in the way of the Torah" Barnai, *Igrot Hasidim Me'eretz Israel,* p. 41. A tradition that originated in R. Gershon's grandson tells that he reached Miedzybóz in 1742 and remained there for about three years. During that period he was a regular member of the Behst's household (Heschel, *R. Gershon Kutover,* p. 59) It thus appears that when he settled down in Miedzybóz, where he had moved in 1740, the Besht invited his brother-in-law to join him so as to serve as the Talmud instructor for his son. Zvi Hirsch was then apparently a boy of thirteen or fourteen.

79. *Besht's Epistle,* p. 237.

80. Barnai, *Igrot Hasidim Me'eretz Israel,* pp. 39–40.

81. *Besht's Epistle,* the manuscript version, pp. 235–236. Cited in full and discussed in chapter 4.

82. Ibid., p. 237.

83. Rubinstein, "A Possibly New Fragment of *Shivhei Ha-Besht,*" p. 182.

84. *Shivhei Habesht,* pp. 58–59.

85. So asserts Rubinstein, ibid., note 39; it is he who is correct and not those who interpret matters as referring to the sages of the Brod Kloyz.

86. For more about him, see the article by Abraham Joshua Heschel, "R. Nahman of Kosów: Companion of the Baal Shem," in his *The Circle of the Baal Shem Tov*, pp. 113–117.

87. *Shivhei Habesht*, pp. 64–65.

88. Ibid., p. 55.

89. Heschel, "R. Nahman of Kosów," p. 116–117.

90. The Besht's letter to R. Moshe of Kotov was printed as an appendix to the book *Buzina Kadisha*, by R. Baruch of Miedzybóz. For a discussion of this letter, see Moshe Rosman, "The Besht's Letters: Towards a New Assessment," in *Studies in Hasidism, Jerusalem Studies in Jewish Thought*, no. 15, ed. David Assaf, Joseph Dan, and Immanuel Etkes (Jerusalem 1999), pp. 12–14.

91. Heschel, "R. Nahman of Kosów," (in Hebrew), *Sefer Hayovel Lichvod Zvi Wolfson* (Jerusalem, 1965), p. 113.

92. *Shivhei Habesht*, pp. 100, 264.

93. Op. cit., pp. 100, 201.

94. Op. cit., pp. 59, 184–185, 235, 298–299.

95. Op. cit., pp. 232–234.

96. Op. cit., pp. 101, 206–209, 259.

97. See note 86.

98. *Shivhei Habesht*, p. 180. See also p. 181.

99. Op. cit., p. 180.

100. Weiss, "Beginnings of Hasidism," p. 60.

101. *Shivhei Habesht*, p. 291.

102. *Toldot Yaakov Yosef*, 127, p. 4

103. *Shivhei Habesht*, p. 99. The words "As he was not yet a Hasid" are an interpretive addition by the compiler.

104. Op. cit., p. 86.

105. Op. cit., p. 100.

106. Op. cit., pp. 100–101.

107. Thus, for example, says Shmuel Abba Horodezky, *Hahasidut Vehahasidim* [Hasidism and Hasidim] (Berlin, 1928), 1: 106; Dubnow, *Toldot Hahasidut*, p. 94. I also made this mistake in my article, "Hasidism as a Movement."

108. This point has already been made by Yaakov Hisdai, *The Emergence of Hassidim and Mitnagdim in the Light of the Homiletic Literature*, (Ph.D. diss., Hebrew University, 1984), pp. 147–153. A similar interpretation was given by Rosman, *Founder of Hasidism*, pp. 33–34.

109. *Toldot Yaakov Yosef*, 123a.

110. Mendel Piekarz recently discussed the confrontation between R. Yaakov Yosef and the Shargorod community in "The Impetus For Early Anti-Hasidic Polemics," in *Within Hasidic Circles—Studies in Hasidism in Memory of Mordecai Wilensky*, ed. Immanuel Etkes, David Assaf, Israel Bartal, and Elchanan Reiner, (Jerusalem, 1999), pp. 9–12.

111. See the remarks at the beginning of this chapter on the use of the concept "servant of God."

112. *Besht's Epistle*, Bauminger version, p. 237.

113. *Shivhei Habesht*, p. 105. On the authenticity of this letter, see Rosman, *Founder of Hasidism*, p. 115.

114. This matter was discussed in chapter 4.

115. *Shivhei Habesht*, p. 106.

116. Op. cit., p. 128. On the subject of Matatron, see: Margaliot, *Malachei Elyon*, pp. 73–108. Another version of the story of how the *maggid* affiliated himself with the Besht is contained in *Keter Shem Tov*; it is cited by Rubinstein, *Shivhei Habesht*, appendix 13, p. 345. It has a clearly fictional form. Nevertheless, the two versions have a common core: The test that the Besht applies to the *maggid*, the *maggid*'s failure and the revelation of the Besht. It is thus possible that the version that appears in *Keter Shem Tov* is a later legendary development of the version contained in *Shivhei Habesht*.

117. The noises and lightening suggest, of course, the events at Mount Sinai. See Numbers 19:16. This was also what the compiler of *Shivhei Habesht* understood: "it seemed to me that this was the reception of the Torah," ibid.

118. *Shivhei Habesht*, pp. 86–87.

119. See *Maggid Devarav Leyaakov*. The passages cited are from pp. 2–3.

120. "Eliezer" is a corruption of "Elazar." This corruption also occurs in the letter of the Jews of Safed to the *Vaad Arba Artzot*. See comments by Rubinstein, *Shivhei Habesht*, p. 130 n. 3. On R. Elazar's immigration to the land of Israel see chapter 6.

121. *Shivhei Habesht*, p. 239.

122. *Shivhei Habesht*, p. 205. The manuscript version reads: And when I came to my home in my home it was very hot.

123. The Besht's doctrine of "straying thoughts" was discussed in chapter 4. On the shift that occurred in R. Nahman of Horodenka's stance as regards self-mortifications, apparently at the influence of the Besht, one may learn from a tale about him, attributed to R. Yaakov Yosef: "And [R. Nahman] told what he had dreamt while in the land of Israel and he worried whether he had to leave the country for reasons he kept private etc. until he saw in a dream that someone reported that there were several doctors giving medication using a bitter potion yet the doctor is best whose medicine is a drink sweeter than honey. And the same applies here, that fasting and self-mortifications and perpetual study makes melancholy grow and makes people think they are not living up to divine standards . . . and that is medicine by bitter waters, which gives no cure . . . by means of a potion sweeter than honey is mercy aroused in the world." See the end of *Toldot Yaakov Yosef*, in the section "And these are the things I heard from my Master."

124. At the beginning of this chapter, I mentioned the practice of the Kabbalists to put on their phylacteries during the afternoon service.

125. *Shivhei Habesht*, pp. 217–218.

126. Op. cit., pp. 216–217.

127. Op. cit., pp. 200–201.

128. In chapter 3, I noted that the Besht interpreted the great rejoicing that greeted him in the Upper Worlds as a reaction to his impending demise. Was R. Nahman of Horodenka aware of the Besht's Epistle? Or did he perhaps hear from the Besht directly about his experiences in the ascent of the soul described in the letter?

129. *Shivhei Habesht*, p. 201.

130. Rubinstein, *Shivhei Habesht*, p. 201 n. 1; Haya Stiman-Katz, *Early Hassidic Immigration To Eretz-Israel* (Jerusalem, 1986), pp. 24–27.

131. *Shivhei Habesht*, pp. 202–204.

132. Op. cit., p. 205.

133. The person who discovered this testimony and discussed it is Avraham Rubinstein; see Rubinstein, "A Possibly New Fragment of *Shivhei Ha-Besht*," pp. 174–191. The document itself appears on p. 191. We do not know exactly when the author of these reports was a guest in the home of Menahem Mendel; obviously this was before he left for the land of Israel. Accordingly, it would seem that the testimony can be dated to the 1750s or 1760s. Yehoshua Mondshine doubted the authenticity of this document and claimed that it was forged by Yosef Perl; see Yehoshua Mondshine, "Is it Indeed One of the Praises of the Besht?" *Tarbiz* 51 (1982): 673–677. Rubinstein dismissed Mondshine's doubts of the authenticity of the document; see op. cit., pp. 677–680. I am inclined to accept the document as authentic.

134. Rubinstein, ibid., persuasively argues that the expression *laasok beasakim* (to deal with affairs) in this context refers to activities as a miracle worker.

135. An anecdote that is also contained in the same report of the family member adds to the portrait of R. Menahem Mendel as a Hasid: When R. Menahem Mendel made his way to the land of Israel he spent time with his relatives in the town of Tchikanoki, on the banks of the Dneister. His uncle, who lived in that town, gave him a gift of some funds for traveling expenses. One day R. Menahem Mendel went to bathe in a *mikvah* that was near the river. While doing so he heard cries that came from across the river. These were the cries of a Jew being taken prisoner by a Muslim because of a debt (the river then was the border between Poland and Turkey). R. Menahem Mendel did not hesitate, forded the river, and paid the ransom with the money his uncle had given him. The latter was quite upset at this, but another relative gave R. Menahem Mendel two hundred zlotyes for traveling expenses.

136. R. Menahem Mendel was born in the year 1728; see *Shivhei Habesht*, p. 204, where it is noted that in 1764 he was thirty-six years old. Cf. Rubinstein, "A Possibly New Fragment of Shivhei Ha-Besht," p. 182.

137. Rubinstein, op. cit.

138. Meshulam Feivush Heller, *Yosher Divrei Emet*, in *Likutim Yekarim* (Jerusalem, 1974), p. 110a.

139. *Shivhei Habesht*, p. 238. Rubinstein is precise about the language of the tale and relies also on the Yiddish version to draw the conclusion that *Shivhei Habesht*'s compiler did not hear these matters from R. Yehiel Michal directly, but that instead, as a resident of Lince he heard them from someone who had heard it from R. Yehiel Michal (ibid., note 2). As to R. Zeev, for whose son's wedding R. Yehiel Michal had come to Lince, Rubinstein makes it clear (ibid., note 5) that the person spoken of was R. Zvi Zeev of Zbaraz, the son of R. Yehiel Michal.

140. Abraham Joshua Heschel, "Rabbi Pinchas of Korzec," in his *The Circle of the Baal Shem Tov*, pp. 1–43.

141. Heschel, op. cit., pp. 15–17. On the visit R. Pinchas paid to the Besht's home on the Shavuot holiday prior to the Besht's death, see Shivhei Habesht, pp. 308–309.

142. *Shivhei Habesht*, pp. 87–88.

143. Op. cit., pp. 182–183.

144. For further mention of R. David Furkes in *Shivhei Habesht*, see op. cit., pp. 247–248, 277–279, 304. See also Nigal, *Gedolim Maasei Tsadikim*, p. 22.

145. *Shivhei Habesht*, pp. 243–245.

146. Op. cit., pp. 85–86.

147. Op. cit., p. 92.

148. See also op. cit., p. 261.

149. As will be recalled, R. Moshe passed away in 1738. We do not know the exact date of R. Nahman of Kosov's death. Heschel, however, estimates that this occurred before 1746; see Heschel, *R. Nahman of Kosów*, p. 122. We have no information about ties between R. Nahman and the Besht after the latter moved to Miedzybóz. *Shivhei Habesht*, p. 217, tells that a R. Nahman and R. Yaakov Yosef traveled together to see the Besht. Heschel, ibid., p. 119, mistakenly believed the reference was to R. Nahman of Kosov, whereas in fact it was to R. Nahman of Horodenka.

150. *Besht's Epistle*, Bauminger version, p. 237.

151. Ibid., manuscript version, p. 235. In the Koretz version the term *bnei gili* (colleagues) appears instead of *anshei segula* (men of virtue).

152. Responsa *Mayim Hayim*, 1, sec. 27, p. 50.

153. A suggestion of this may be found in the Besht's signature on the letter sent to R. Meir in the name of "Israel Baal Shem of Tluste." It would therefore seem that in the first years of his residence in Miedzybóz the Besht continued to call himself by the name of the town he had come from and where he had first earned fame as a *baal shem*. A further indication of the date of the responsum is the mention of R. Gershon as someone who was by the Besht's side. Recall that R. Gershon emigrated to the land of Israel in the year 1747. For a discussion of this evidence about the Besht and his group, see Moshe Rosman, "The Besht's Letters: Towards a New Assessment" pp. 1–14, and *Founder of Hasidism*, pp. 127–128.

154. *Shivhei Habesht*, pp. 101, 125, 210, 219, 280, 309.

155. Ibid., p. 224.

156. See Rosman, *Founder of Hasidism*, pp. 165–170.

157. Barnai, *Igeret Hasidim Me'eretz Israel*, p. 40. Recall that the Besht's Epistle to R. Gershon mentions that the Besht and members of his group used to pray the morning service at dawn. It appears that this is the same minyan R. Gershon is referring to.

158. *Keter Shem Tov*, 224, p. 129b. On the Besht's *havura*, see Haviva Pedia, "On the Development of the Social-Religious-Economic Pattern in Hasidism: Ransom-payment, Fraternity and Immigration to the Land of Israel," in *Dat Vekalkalah Yahasei Gomlin* [Mutual relations in religion and economics], ed. Menahem Ben Sasson (Jerusalem, 1995), p. 327.

159. See chapter 3.

160. The two Margaliot brothers are an illustration of this. In the collection of tales titled *Gedolim Maasei Tsadikim*, Nigal edition, they are described as being very close to the Besht, yet in *Shivhei Habesht* they appear to be mentioned only once.

161. R. David's testament and biographical particulars about him are cited in Rubinstein, *Shivhei Habesht*, pp. 119–120 n. 4.

162. Cf. Pedia (note 158), pp. 353–354.

163. *Shivhei Habesht,* pp. 101, 106.

164. See, for example, op. cit., pp. 201–202.

Chapter Six: The Historicity of *Shivhei Habesht* (pp. 203–248)

1. For treatments of *Shivhei Habesht,* see Dan, *The Hasidic Story,* pp. 64–131; Gedalyah Nigal, *The Hasidic Tale,* pp. 23–37; Mondshine, *Shivhei Habesht,* introduction, pp. 5–70; Rosman, "The History of a Historical Source: On the Editing of *Shivhei Ha-Besht,*" *Zion* 58, (1993): 175–214. For a survey of how scholars have viewed the historicity of *Shivhei Habesht,* see: Rapoport-Albert, *Hagiography with Footnotes.*

2. See appendix I.

3. Dubnow, *Toldot Hahasidut,* p. 41.

4. Op. cit., pp. 41–42.

5. Ibid.

6. Op. cit., pp. 43–46.

7. Op. cit., p. 48.

8. Yitzhak Shiffer, "R. Israel Baal Shem Tov and His Figure in Early Hasidic Literature," *Hadoar,* 39 (1959–60), pp. 525–532.

9. On this issue see Rappaport-Albert, *Hagiography with Footnotes,* pp. 119–120.

10. Schiffer relies here on the memoirs of Solomon Maimon, which associated the beginnings of Hasidism with R. Yoel Baal Shem; see *Hayei Shlomo Maimon,* pp. 137–138. Schiffer asserted that it was impossible that Maimon could have been mistaken about this.

11. Schiffer, op. cit., p. 525.

12. A similar position was taken a few years earlier by Aharon Zeev Eshkoli. On this subject see Scholem, "The Historical Figure of R. Israel Baal Shem Tov," pp. 287–289; Rapoport-Albert, *Hagiography with Footnotes,* pp. 120–121.

13. Israel Zinberg, *A History of Jewish Literature,* 9: 27–61.

14. See for example his remarks there on p. 33.

15. Op. cit., p. 28.

16. Op. cit., p. 34.

17. Op. cit., pp. 52–53.

18. Op. cit., p. 53.

19. Scholem, "The Historical Figure of the Besht," pp. 287–324.

20. Scholem noted the principle which guided him in this regard; see ibid., p. 307.

21. Op. cit., pp. 307–308.

22. Op. cit., pp. 291–293.

23. Op. cit., pp. 293–294. Scholem declined here to discuss the Besht's perspectives on *dvekut* in detail, presumably because he had previously dealt with this topic in his article "Devekut, or Communion with God."

24. Op. cit., p. 295.

25. Op. cit., pp. 295–296.

26. Buber anticipated Scholem on this point, though he did not express himself in so detailed or forceful a manner. See Martin Buber, "The Beginnings of Hasidism," *Moznayim* 11 (1940–41): 201.

27. Dan, *The Hasidic Story*, pp. 88–89.

28. Op. cit., pp. 89–90.

29. Op. cit., p. 89.

30. Weiss, *A Circle of Pneumatics in Pre-Hasidism*.

31. The reference is to the son of R. Yaakov Yosef of Polonne. However, the print edition of this story contains corruptions and the manuscript version is superior here: "The father of the Polonne community rabbi arrived from the Land of Israel. [R. Yaakov Yosef] asked his father: What is this R. Elazar doing?"; Mondshine, *Shivhei Habesht*, p. 171.

32. In the MS: "How do you know, as no man arrived before me from the Land of Israel"; Mondshine, *Shivhei Habesht*, ibid.

33. In the MS: "On that very same *motzaei shabbat*"; Mondshine, ibid.

34. *Shivhei Habesht*, pp. 129–132. Later in the story it turns out that the reference is to *Hemdat Yamim*. For more on this book see Avraham Yaari, *Taalumat Sefer, Sefer "Hemdat Yamim," Mi Hibro Umeh Haytah Midat Hashpaato* [Mystery of a book: Hemdat Yamim— who composed it and how influential was it] (Jerusalem, 1954): 134–136; Gershom Scholem, "And the Mystery Remains," *Bhinot* 8 (1955): 79–95.

35. Bartal, "The 'Aliyah' of R. Elazar Rokeah (1740)," pp. 23–40.

36. Op. cit., p. 27.

37. Ibid.

38. Op. cit., p. 23.

39. Op. cit., p. 27.

40. Op. cit., p. 30.

41. Op. cit., p. 28.

42. *Shivhei Habesht*, pp. 129–130.

43. This assertion is based on a letter sent by R. Gershon of Kotov to the Besht and on things written by R. Yaakov Yosef of Polonne. See chapter 2.

44. Jacob Barnai, "Some Clarifications on the land of Israel's Stories of 'In Praise of the Baal Shem Tov,'" *Revue des Etudes Juives* 146 (1987): 367–380.

45. *Shivhei Habesht*, pp. 267–275.

46. Adam Teller, "The Sluck Tradition Concerning the Early Days of the Besht," in *Studies in Hasidism*, Jerusalem Studies in Jewish Thought no. 15, ed. David Assaf, Joseph Dan, and Immanuel Etkes (Jerusalem, 1999), pp. 15–24.

47. Israel Halpern, "The Wozczylo Revolt and Its Jewish Aspect," *Zion* 22 (1957): 56–67; reprinted in *Eastern European Jewry Historical Studies* (Jerusalem, 1968), pp. 277–288.

48. Solomon Maimon, *Hayei Shlomo Maimon*, p. 54.

49. The reference is to a magic ritual meant to purify the house of demons. It follows that also according to the version of R. David of Makov, the leaseholders summoned the Besht because they had built a new house and were afraid to move into it on account of the possible infiltration of demons.

50. This is cited by Halpern, op. cit., p. 58. The full text of the letter by R. David of Makov may be found in Wilensky, *Hasidim Umitnagdim*, 2:241–242.

51. Halpern, op. cit., pp. 60–62. From this point on Halpern concentrates on various aspects of the revolt and makes no further appeal to the story in *Shivhei Habesht*.

52. Dan, *The Hasidic Story*, pp. 110–118.

53. Op. cit., p. 114.

54. Op. cit., p. 118. Dan bases his assessment of the tale's veracity on an analysis of its content as well.

55. Teller (see, note 46), pp. 23–31.

56. Op. cit., pp. 32–35.

57. Op. cit., p. 36.

58. Op. cit., p. 37.

59. Ibid.

60. Op. cit., pp. 37–38.

61. A bibliography of the scholarship on *Shivhei Habesht* is provided by Mondshine, *Shivhei Habesht*, pp. 69–70.

62. *Shivhei Habesht*, p. 35.

63. Op. cit., p. 59.

64. Mondshine, *Shivhei Habesht*, introduction, pp. 5–70.

65. Moshe Rosman, "The History of a Historical Source: On the Editing of *Shivhei Ha-Besht*," *Zion* 58, (1993): 175–214.

66. On this point Rosman drew on Hayim Liberman's research. See op. cit., p. 188 no. 44.

67. Op. cit., pp. 188–192.

68. This edition was described by Israel Zinberg, *A History of Jewish Literature* (Vilna, 1936), 7:205, 318–321.

69. Chone Shmeruk, "Tales About R. Adam Baal Shem in the Versions of Shivkhei Ha' Besht," *Zion* 28 (1963): 86–105; also published in *Yiddish Literature in Poland—Historical Studies*, pp. 119–146.

70. The existence of such copies was attested to by the son of the compiler, R. Dov Ber of Lince, in an appendix he added to the compiler's preface in the Berditchev edition of 1815.

71. Avraham Yaari, "Two Basic Recensions of *Shivhe-Ha-Besht*," *Kirjath Sepher* 39 (1964): 249–272, 394–407, 552–562.

72. Op. cit., p. 252.

73. Op. cit., p. 260.

74. Op. cit., p. 262.

75. See also Avraham Rubinstein, "The Revelation of the Besht in the *Shivhei Ha-Besht*," *Alei Sefer* 6–7 (1979): 157–186. In this article Rubinstein examines the "revelation" of the Besht tales on the basis of a comparison between the Hebrew and Yiddish versions.

76. Mondshine, *Shivhei Habesht*, introduction, pp. 22–47.

77. Op. cit., pp. 24–25.

78. Liberman had a very hard time understanding a certain story in *Shivhei Habesht* and was able to resolve all his difficulties once he looked at the story in the manuscript version. See Mondshine, op. cit., pp. 5–6.

79. Op. cit., pp. 5–18.

80. Elchanan Reiner, "In Praise of the Ba'al Shem Tov: Transmission, Editing, Printing," *Proceedings of the Eleventh World Congress of Jewish Studies* (Jerusalem, 1994), Division c, 2:145–152.

81. Op. cit., pp. 145–146.

82. Op. cit., pp. 146–147.

83. Op. cit., p. 149.

84. Op. cit., pp. 150–151.

85. Op. cit., p. 146.

86. The author's preface to the Berditchev printing, cited by Rubinstein, *Shivhei Habesht*, p. 323.

87. Op. cit., pp. 85–94.

88. Op. cit., pp. 180–182.

89. See, for example, the set of tales about R. Gershon of Kotov (pp. 111–119) and the set of tales from which one can learn fear of God (pp. 157–159). In the beginning of one of these stories the author explicitly states the reasoning that guided him when he included this story in his book: "Although this tale is not from the Besht, in spite of it I am writing it as from this tale one can learn fear of God"; ibid.

90. Rosman, *Founder of Hasidism*, pp. 143–155.

91. Op. cit., pp. 143–147.

92. Op. cit., pp. 149–150.

93. Op. cit., pp. 148–150. As a further instance of a story that is unreliable despite the authentic historical details it contains, Rosman notes the story about the cold reception that R. Zeev Kotses and R. David Furkes gave to the Besht when he moved to Miedzybóz; *Shivhei Habesht*, pp. 224–226. Rosman lists several items in this story that he considers authentic. Later he shows that from the picture that emerges on the basis of external sources, there are no grounds to believe that the Besht encountered any opposition when he first settled in Miedzybóz; op. cit., pp. 150–153.

94. Op. cit., p. 153.

95. Ibid.

96. Op. cit., p. 154–155.

97. See *Shivhei Habesht*, pp. 36–39, 41–46. And compare Dan, *The Hasidic Story*, pp. 79–83. For a detailed discussion of the R. Adam tales, see chapter 2.

98. See Immanuel Etkes, "Rabbi Shneur Zalman of Lyady as a Hassidic Leader," *Zion*, 50 (1985): 321–354.

99. The "revelation" tale that the printer includes is cited without a source; it does not contain names of identifiable figures and does not make reference to an actual context in which the events supposedly took place. In addition, it conspicuously follows a literary pattern and tries to cause the reader to derive the intended moral in the most impressive manner possible. Such is evident in the accentuation of the ironic tension in the disparity between the "secret" and revealed sides of the Besht. The Besht, of course, was aware of his exaltedness and his mission, and so are the readers (whereas the guest to whom the Besht will later reveal himself is deceived by the Besht's pretenses and takes him for a rude village ignoramus). In this ironic context, as the tale progresses various aspects of the Besht's personality are exposed, astonishing the guest and hinting to the reader about what is about to take place. The story reaches its dramatic climax when the Besht tells his guest "Torah secrets which no ear has ever heard." At the Besht's command, the stunned guest rushes to tell what

he had seen and heard to the Hasidic fraternity in the nearby town; these latter anoint the Besht as their leader. For a comparison of the Besht's "revelation" tale as quoted by the printer to the revelation story cited by the compiler, see Immanuel Etkes, "From Esoteric Circle To Mass Movement: The Emergence of Early Hasidism," in *Polin, the Jews of Eastern Europe: History and Culture*, units 9–10 (The Open University, Tel Aviv, 1991), pp. 23–28.

100. This is the number obtained in the division of the text in the English translation. By Rubinstein's division there are seventeen stories.

101. This was pointed out by Weiss, "Beginnings of Hassidism," p. 53.

102. A permutation of *hinerflet*, meaning deep sleep or seeming death. The reference is evidently to the phenomenon today known as clinical death (I am indebted to Professor Chava Turniansky for this clarification).

103. The compiler's preface according to the Berditchev printing; *Shivhei Habesht*, pp. 322–324.

104. Ibid.

105. In the manuscript he is called "Hertz."

106. *Shivhei Habesht*, pp. 119–120. The print edition is corrupt and the citation here is from the manuscript. See op. cit., p. 120 n. 7. See also ibid., p. 257.

107. Op. cit., p. 94; see also p. 90.

108. Op. cit., p. 156.

109. Op. cit., pp. 215, 261.

110. The R. Gershon mentioned here is R. Gershon of Kotov; the story refers to his voyage by sea to the land of Israel.

111. *Shivhei Habesht*, p. 111.

112. The discovery of the dybbuk's identity is often a stage in the exorcism process. See Gedalyah Nigal, "*Dybbuk*": *Tales in Jewish Literature* (Jerusalem, 1994), pp. 81, 86.

113. *Shivhei Habesht*, p. 65.

114. Op. cit., p. 242.

115. The rabbis are R. Yaakov Yosef of Polonne, R. Gedalyah of Lince, R. Yaakov of Smela, R. Falk Hacohen of Titchelnic, and R. Meir Margaliot. The *maggids* are Leib of Ladizen, R. Yoel of Nemirov, R. David of Tulchin, and R. Shmeril of Wierzchowka. The Hasidic Zaddik is R. Manehem Nahum of Chernobyl.

116. See *Shivhei Habesht*, p. 60.

117. See ibid., pp. 245–247. The family tradition about the close connection between the Besht and R. Meir Margaliot as a youth was preserved in the collection of tales *Gedolim Maasei Tsadikim*. See Nigal, *Gedolim Maasei Tsadikim*, introduction, pp. 7–10.

118. See *Shivhei Habesht*, pp. 227–228. As to R. Moshe Harbater, the tale refers to a prophecy made by the Besht at the time he was circumcised; presumably he heard of this from his parents.

119. See *Shivhei Habesht*, pp. 129–132. In the beginning of the story the author notes that R. Yoel was a regular guest in the home of R. Yaakov Yosef in Shargorod; immediately following it is the story about what the Besht said when he spent the Sabbath in Shargorod. Likewise, the way the story is told suggests that R. Yoel heard it directly from the Besht.

120. Op. cit., p. 191.

121. About this R. David and the amounts of money he bequeathed to a few of the Besht's associates, see chapter 5.

122. *Shivhei Habesht*, p. 121.

123. Op. cit., pp. 85–86.

124. Op. cit., pp. 177–178.

125. Op. cit., pp. 90–91, 91–94, 96–98, 169–171. R. Yosef is designated as "the Besht's leader of prayers" evidently because he used to read out to him from books such as *Ein Yaakov*. The Besht preferred not to read from books but to have them read out to him. See also ibid., pp. 85–86.

126. Op. cit., pp. 129–130.

127. Op. cit., pp. 108, 110–111, 218.

128. Op. cit., p. 238.

129. Op. cit., pp. 114–119.

130. Op. cit., pp. 86–87.

131. Op. cit., pp. 87–88.

132. Op. cit., p. 205.

133. R. Yehuda Leib brought the book by R. Gedalyah of Lince to press. See the preface to *Teshuot Hen* (Berditchev 1816). In the preface, R. Yehuda Leib gives particulars about the communities in which R. Gedalyah served on the rabbinate prior to serving as the rabbi of Lince.

134. See Yitzhak Alfasi, *Hayahid Bedorot* [Unique in generations] (Tel Aviv and Bnei Brak, 1997), p. 351.

135. See R. Yehuda Leib's preface to *Teshuot Hen*, in which R. Gedalyah is described as "one who licked honey from the body of the lion of the group, the rabbi the *Mokhiah* author of *Kol Arieh*." In the body of the book, R. Gedalyah cites at length from the sermons he heard from the *mokhiah*.

136. *Shivhei Habesht*, pp. 85–88.

137. Op. cit., pp. 36–39.

138. Dan, *The Hasidic Story*, pp. 68–74.

139. Op. cit., p. 71.

140. *Shivhei Habesht*, pp. 133–134.

141. Dan, *The Hasidic Story*, p. 73.

142. Op. cit., p. 74.

143. Nigal, *The Hasidic Tale*, pp. 25–27.

144. See Dan Ben-Amos and Jerome R. Mintz, In *Praise of the Baal Shem Tov* (Bloomington, 1970), pp. 290–305.

145. Cf. the use recently made of *Shivhei Habesht* by Haviva Pedia; see chapter 5 note 158.

Conclusion (pp. 249–258)

1. See, for instance, *Shivhei Habesht*, pp. 99, 268.

2. Dinur, "The Beginnings of Hasidism," p. 192 passim.

3. *Ben Porat Yosef*, by R. Yaakov Yosef of Polonne, facsimile edition (New York, 1954), 77b.

4. *Shivhei Habesht*, p. 106.

5. See *Shivhei Habesht*, pp. 215–216, 243–245; Scholem, "The Historical Figure of R. Israel Baal Shem Tov," pp. 315–321; Joseph Weiss, "Study of the Torah in Israel Baal Shem's Doctrine," *Essays Presented To Chief Rabbi Israel Brodie On the Occasion of His Seventieth Birthday*, ed. H. J. Zimmels, J. Rabbinowitz, and I. Finestein (Hebrew Volume) (London, 1967), pp. 151–170. The Besht's "unscholarliness" bothered the Hasidim in subsequent generations and some of the leaders of Hasidism tried to "dismiss" the fact in various ways. See Avraham Nathan Bernata, *Gedulat Rabenu Israel Baal Shem Tov* (Shamloya, 1941), p. 5.

6. Meshulam Feibush Heller, *Yosher Divrei Emet*, in *Sefer Likutim Yekarim* (Jerusalem, 1974), p. 110a.

Appendix I. Magic and Miracle Workers in the Literature of the Haskalah (pp. 259–271)

1. On the European Enlightenment's war against superstition in general and the belief in sorcery in particular, see Paul Hazard, *The European Mind, 1686–1715* (Harmondsworth, Eng., 1964), pp. 185–212.

2. Solomon Maimon, *Hayei Shlomo Maimon*, p. 137.

3. On Haskalah satire and its role in the struggle against Hasidism, see Shmuel Werses, "Hasidism in the Eyes of Haskalah Literature: From the Polemic of Galician Maskilim," in *Trends and Forms in Haskalah Literature* (in Hebrew), (Jerusalem, 1990), pp. 91–109.

4. Yoseph Perl, *Megaleh Tamirin* [Revealer of Secrets] (Vienna, 1819), introduction, p. 1a.

5. *Shivhei Habesht*, 41–46, 59. On the stories of Rabbi Adam in *Shivhei Habesht* and their sources and purpose, see Chone Shmeruk, "The Stories about R. Adam Baal Shem and their Formulations in the Versions of the Book *Shivhei Habesht*" (in Hebrew) *Zion* 28 (1963): 86–105; Joseph Dan, *The Hasidic Story* (in Hebrew) (Jerusalem, 1975), pp. 79–83.

6. *Megaleh Temirin*, letter I, p. 3a.

7. Ibid, 5b, 11, 13b, 33a–b, and passim.

8. Ibid., e.g., letter 76, p. 29.

9. *Kinat Haemmet* [Zeal for truth] by Yehuda Leib Meizis (Vienna, 1828), pp. 6–8. On Meizis and his book, see Yehuda Friedlander, *Hebrew Satire in Europe*, vol. 3: *The Nineteenth Century* (in Hebrew) (Ramat Gan, 1994).

10. *Kinat ha'emet*, p. 22.

11. Ibid., p. 23.

12. Werses, "Hasidism in the Eyes of Haskalah Literature," p. 93.

13. *Kerem hemed*, 2 (1836), letter 24, pp. 149–150. *Kerem hemed* was an annual publication of the Galician Haskalah from 1833 to 1856.)

14. See David Assaf, *The Regal Way: The Life and Times of Rabbi Israel of Ruzhin* (Stanford, 2002), 261–264.

15. *Kerem hemed*, letter 24.

16. Isaac Ber Lewinsohn, *Yalkut Ribal* (Warsaw, 1878), p. 121.

17. Ibid., p. 125. Cf. Levinsohn's condemnation of the use of Holy Names for magical purposes in the guise of "practical kabbalah" in his *Beit yehudah* [The house of Judah] (Vilna, 1858), pp. 130–133.

18. Mordecai Aaron Guenzburg, *Azi'ezer* (Vilna, 1860), pp. 94–98.

19. Ibid., p. 124.

20. East European maskilim, eager to displace the *baalei shem* and popular healers and enhance the prestige of scientific medicine and its practitioners, also wrote and published medical literature. The two best-known examples are Moses Markuze, *Ezer yisra'el* [The help of Israel] (Paritzk, 1790), and Menahem Mendel Lefin, *Refu'at ha'am* [Book of popular healing] (Zolkiew, 1794). For Lefin's book, see Joseph Klausner, *History of Modern Hebrew Literature* (in Hebrew), 6 vols. (Jerusalem, 1952–54), 1:226–230. A detailed discussion of Markuze's volume, including a comparison with Lefin's work, may be found in Chone Shmeruk, *Yiddish Literature in Poland: Historical Research and Insights* (in Hebrew) (Jerusalem, 1981), pp. 184–203.

21. *Ha'avot vehabanim* [Fathers and sons], in *Mendeleh Mocher Sepharim*, collected writings (in Hebrew) (Tel Aviv, 1952), pp. 28–31.

22. As Shmuel Werses writes, "However, unlike his predecessors and his contemporaries, [Mendele] does not intend to expose the deceptions of *baalei shem* and swindlers, and he does not concentrate on harsh accusations hurled at the leaders of the Hasidic movement, who claim to be wonder-workers—except for his description of the false *tsadik* and his cronies in *Fathers and Sons*. His primary emphasis lies not on the practitioners of magic themselves . . . but mainly on the people who appeal to magic. . . . These acts of healing and wonders worked by magical arts are not seen here as exceptional, unusual cases . . . but portrayed as a common phenomenon in the life of the popular, uneducated classes." Werses, "The World of Folklore in Mendele's Works" (in Hebrew) *Dapim lemehkar basifrut* 9 (1994): 8.

23. Ibid., 12. Cf. Israel Bartal, "Gentiles and Gentile Society in Hebrew and Yiddish Literature in Eastern Europe, 1856–1914" (in Hebrew) (Ph.D. diss., Hebrew University, 1981), 95.

24. *Complete Works*, 24.

25. The influence of Haskalah literature on the historiography of Hasidism in areas other than those discussed here has been pointed out by Israel Bartal in his article "From Distorted Reflection to Historical Fact: Haskalah Literature and the Study of the Hasidic Movement" (in Hebrew) *Mada'ei hayahadut* 32 (1992): 7–17.

26. Heinrich Graetz, *History of the Jews* (Philadelphia, 1956), pp. 374–375.

27. Ibid., p. 376.

28. Ibid., pp. 375–378.

29. Avraham Rubinstein, introduction to *Shalom al Israel*, by Eliezer Tzvi Hacohen Zveiwfel, 1–2, Zhitomir 1868–1869 (Jerusalem, 1973), 1:13–21; on this point see also Shmuel Feiner, "The Turning-Point in the Evaluation of Hasidism: Eliezer Zweifel and the Moderate Haskalah in Russia" (in Hebrew) *Zion* 5 (1986): 167–210.

30. Zweifel, *Shalom al yisra'el*, 2:20.

31. Shmuel Abba Horodezky, Hahasidut Vehahasidim [Hasidism and Hasidim], 12.

32. Ibid., p. 13.

33. The article was published in Hebrew in *He'atid*, bk. 2, 2nd ed., pp. 29–99.

34. Ibid., pp. 36–37.

35. *A History of Hasidism* (in Hebrew) (1931; Tel Aviv, 1960), p. 30.

36. Ibid. pp. 30–31.

37. *A History of Hasidism*, p. 47.

38. Ibid.

39. Ibid., pp. 47–48.

40. Scholem, "The Historical Figure of R. Israel Baal Shem Tov."

41. Ibid., pp. 297–279.

42. Yizhak Yudelow, "The Book *Helkat re 'uven*" (in Hebrew), *Alei sefer* 114 (1987): 139–140.

43. *Perushim* (separatists) was the name given to the disciples of the Vilna Gaon in Erets Yisra'el.

44. Eliezer Rivlin, *The Tsadik Rabbi Joseph Sundel of Salant and His Masters* (in Hebrew) (Jerusalem, 1927), pp. 65–68.

45. Asher Hakohen Ashkenazi, *Keter rosh: Orehot hayim* [The crown of the head: ways of life] (Warsaw, 1914), p. 75, secs. 6, 8.

46. National and Hebrew University Library, Jerusalem, MS 8° 3287. Deliatitz (Polish: Dolatycze) is a small town some thirty kilometers northeast of Novogrudok.

47. *Dybbuk Stories* (in Hebrew) (Jerusalem, 1983), pp. 186–196.

48. See Immanuel Etkes, "R. Shneur Zalman of Lyady as a Hasidic Leader" (in Hebrew) *Zion* 50 (1985): 323–331.

49. See Isaac Baer Levinsohn, *Te'udah beyisra'el* [Testimony in Israel] (Vilna and Horodno, 1828), introduction, pp. 2–3.

50. See Werses, "Hasidism in the Eyes of Haskalah Literature," 91.

Appendix III. The Versions of the Besht's Epistle (pp. 282–288)

1. See the Besht's Epistle, Koretz edition, p. 281.

2. Mordechai Shraga Bauminger, "Letters of Our Rabbi Israel Baal Shem Tov and his Son-in-Law R. Yehiel Michal to Rabbi Avraham Gershon of Kotov," *Sinai* 71 (1972): 248–269.

3. See Scholem, "The Historical Figure of Rabbi Israel Baal Shem Tov," pp. 309–310, nn. 33, 34.

4. Avraham Rubinstein, "On a Manuscript of the Besht's Epistle to R. Gershon of Kotov," *Sinai* 62 (1973): pp. 189–202.

5. Mordechai Shraga Bauminger, "More on the Letters of the Besht and his Son-in-law to R. Avraham Gershon of Kotov," *Sinai*, 72 (1973): pp. 270–282.

6. Yehoshua Mondshine, "An Early Version of the 'Ascent of the Soul Epistle' by the Besht," *Migdal Oz*, ed. Yehoshua Mondshine (Kfar Habad, 1980), pp. 119–126.

7. Mondshine, *Shivhei Habesht*, pp. 229–231.

8. Rosman, *Founder of Hasidism*, pp. 97–113.

9. Op. cit., pp. 102–103.

10. See Zeev Gries, *Conduct Literature, Its History and Place in the Life of Beshtian Hasidism* (Jerusalem, 1989), pp. 149–181.

11. Rosman, *Founder of Hasidism*, pp. 103–104.

12. Piekarz, *The Beginning of Hasidism*, pp. 16 passim.

13. Gries, op. cit, p. 106 passim.

14. Tractate *Sukkah* 26a.

15. Raayah Haran, "The Authenticity of Letters By Hasidim in Eretz Israel," *Cathedra* 55 (1990): pp. 22–58; Yehoshua Mondshine, "The Authenticity of Hasidic Letters," *Cathedra* 63 (1992): pp. 65–97; 64 (1992): 79–97; Raayah Haran, "A Rejoinder To Criticism," *Cathedra* 64 (1992): pp. 98–102.

16. The Besht's Epistle, ibid.

17. *Tzavaaat Haribash*, sec. 75, p. 23.

18. Rosman, *Founder of Hasidism*, p. 104.

19. Op. cit., pp. 104–105.

20. See chapter 3.

21. See the Besht's Epistle, Bauminger version.

BIBLIOGRAPHY

Primary Sources

Amtahat Binyamin. By R. Binyamin Binush of Krotoszyn. Willhemhersch, 1716.

Aviezer. By Mordecai Aharon Guenzburg. Vilna, 1864.

Beit Yehuda. By Isaac Baer Levinsohn. Vilna, 1858.

Ben Porat Yosef. By R. Yaakov Yosef of Polonne. Facsimile edition. New York, 1954.

Birchat Haaretz. By Baruch David Hacohen, Jerusalem, 1904.

Butzina Dinehora. By R. Baruch of Miedzyódz. 1880.

Degel Mahaneh Ephraim. By R. Ephraim of Sadilkov. Jerusalem, 1994.

Ezer Israel. By Moses Markuze. Paricek, 1790.

Gedolim Maasei Tsadikim, Hasidic Tales. By Yaakov Margaliot. Critical edition with introduction and notes by Gedalyah Nigal. Jerusalem, 1991.

Gedulat Rabenu Israel Baal Shem Tov. By Avraham Nathan Bernata. Shamloya, 1941.

Hanhagot Yesharot. Facsimile edition within *Sfarim Kdoshim Mitalmidei haBaal Shem Tov.* New York, 1993.

Hasidim Umitnagdim [Hasidim and Mitnagdim: A study of the controversy between them in the years 1772–1815], edited by Mordechai Wilensky, vol. 1–2, Jerusalem, 1970.

Hayei Shlomo Maimon. By Solomon Maimon. Tel Aviv, 1953.

Hilchot Olam. By R. Meir (b. R. Moshe Meizelisch). Saltzbach, 1756.

Igeret Aliyat Haneshama Lehabesht [The ascent of the soul epistle by the Besht]. In *Sefer Shivhei Habaal Shem Tov* (a facsimile of a unique manuscript, variant versions and appendices), by Yehoshua Mondshine. Jerusalem, 1982.

Igeret Habesht le R. Moshe Mekotov [The Besht's letter to R. Moshe of Kotov]. Appended in *Sefer Butzina Dinehora.* 1880.

Igrot Hasidim Me'eretz Israel [Hasidic letters from Eretz-Israel: From the second part of the eighteenth century and the first part of the nineteenth century]. Edited by Ya'acov Barnai. Jerusalem, 1980.

Kav Hayashar. By R. Tzvi Hirsch Kaidanover. Jerusalem, 1982.

Keter Rosh—Orhot Hayim. By Asher ben Zvi Hirsch Hacohen Ashkenazi. Warsaw, 1914.

Keter Shem Tov. New York: Otzar Hasidim Press, 1987.

Ketonet Pasim. By R. Yaakov Yosef of Polonne. Edited by Gedalyah Nigal. Jerusalem, 1985.

Kinat Haemmet. By Judah Leib Miesis. Vienna, 1828.

Kvutzat Yaakov. By R. Avraham Yaakov (b. R. Israel of Sadigora). Berditchev, 1896.

Likutim Yekarim. By R. Dov Ber of Mezerich. Jerusalem, 1974.

Ma Sheraiti [Memoirs of Yehezkel Kotick]. Edited by David Assaf. Tel Aviv, 1999. (Also published as Y. Kotik, *Journey To A Nineteenth-Century Shtetl*, ed. David Assaf [Detroit, Mich.: Wayne State University Press, 2002]).

Maggid Devarav Le-ya'akov. By R. Dov Ber of Mezerich, critical edition based on manuscripts with an introduction, commentary, notes, and indexes by Rivka Schatz-Uffenheimer. Jerusalem, 1976.

Mayim Hayim. Responsa by R. Hayim Cohen Rapoport. Zhitomir, 1857.

Megaleh Temirin. By Yosef Perl. Vienna, 1819.

Menahot Yaakov Solet. By R. Yaakov (b. R. Moshe Katz of Yanov). Willhelmsdorf, 1731.

Mendele Mokher Seforim. Collected writings. Tel Aviv, 1954.

Merkevet Hamishneh. By R. Shlomo of Chelm. Frankfurt An Der Oder, 1751.

Mesilat Yesharim. By Moshe Hayim Luzzato. Eshkol edition. Jerusalem, 1964.

Midrash Talpiyot. Edited by Eliyahu Hacohen. Warsaw, 1875.

Mifalot Elokim. Zolkiew, 1725.

Mishmeret Hakodesh. By R. Moshe (b. R. Yaakov of Satanov). Zolkiew, 1746.

Netzah Israel. By R. Israel of Zamosc. Frankfurt An Der Oder, 1741.

Otzar Gnazim. Collected letters from ancient manuscripts on the history of the Land of Israel, with introduction and comments by Yaakov Moshe Tolidano. Jerusalem, 1960.

Refuot Haam. By Menahem Mendel Lefin. Zolkiew, 1795.

Sefer Hakavannot. By R. Isaac Luria. Jerusalem, 1984 (facsimile edition of Koretz printing).

Sefer Hasidim. As composed by Rabenu Yehuda Hehasid. Sources, notations, and commentary by Reuven Margaliot. Jerusalem, 1957.

Sefer Hasidim. Yehuda Wistinesky edition. Berlin, 1891.

Shalom al Israel. By Eliezer Tzvi Hacohen Zweifel, vol. 1–2. Zhitomir, 1868–69.

Shem Tov Katan. By R. Binyamin Binush of Krotoszyn. Saltzbach, 1706.

Shivhei Habesht. Berditchev, 1815.

Shivhei Habesht. Kapost, 1814.

Shivhei Habesht [In praise of the Baal Shem Tov]. With introduction and annotations by Avraham Rubinstein. Jerusalem, 1991.

Shivhei Habesht. Facsimile of a unique manuscript, with introduction, variant versions, and appendices, ed. Yehoshua Mondshine. Jerusalem, 1982.

Shivhei Rabbi Hayim Vital. Ashdod, 1988.

Tavnit Habayit. By R. Mordechai (b. R. Meir of Lublin). Frankfurt An Der Oder, 1747.

Teshuot Khen. By R. Gedalyah of Lince, Berditchev, 1816.

Teudah Beyisrael. By Isaac Baer Levinsohn. Vilna and Horodna, 1828.

Toldot Adam Vehochmat Haparzuf Vesirtutei Yadayim. Zolkiew, 1720.

Toldot Yaakov Yosef. By R. Yaakov Yosef of Polonne. Koretz, 1780.

Tsava'at haRibash. Kohet edition. New York, 1991.

Tsofnat Paaneach. By R. Yaakov Yosef of Polonne. Edited by Gedalyah Nigal. Jerusalem, 1989.

Yalkut Ribal. By Isaac Baer Levinsohn. Warsaw, 1878.

Yesh Manhilin. By R. Pinchas Katzenelbogen. Jerusalem, 1986.

Yosher Divrei Emet. By R. Meshulam Feivush Heller. In *Sefer Likutim Yekarim.* Jerusalem, 1974.

Zevach Pesach. By R. Yaakov Pesach. Zolkiew, 1722.

Secondary Sources (Hebrew)

Alfasi, Yitzhak. *Hayahid Bedorot* [Unique in generations]. Tel Aviv and Bnei Brak, 1997.

Balaban, Meir. *Letoldot Hatnuah Hafrankit* [History of the Frankist movement]. Tel Aviv, 1934.

Bar Dayan, Hayim. "The Pavolitch Blood Libel and Zhitomir." In *Eder Hayakar: Divrei Safrut Vemehkar Mukdashim le S.A. Horodezky* [Literature and scholarship dedicated to S. A. Horodezky], pp. 131–144. Tel Aviv, 1947.

Barnai, Ya'acov, "Notes on the Immigration of R. Abraham Gershon Kutower to Eretz-Israel." *Zion* 42 (1977): 110–119.

Bartal, Israel, "The 'Aliyah' of R. Elazar Rokeah (1740)." In *Galut Baaretz* [Exile in the Homeland]. pp. 23–40. Jerusalem, 1994. Also published in *Studies in the History of Dutch Jewry*, ed. Jozeph Michman, 4: 7–25. Jerusalem, 1985.

———. "Haskalah Literature and the Study of the Hasidic Movement," *Jewish Studies* 32 (1992) (Hebrew Section): 7–17.

———. Halo Yehudim Besafrut Ivrit Veyiddish Bemizrah Eropa Bein Hashanim 1856–1914 [Non-Jews and gentile society in East-European Hebrew and Yiddish literature, 1854–1914]. Ph.D. diss., Hebrew University, 1980.

Bauminger, Mordechai Shraga. "Letters of Our Rabbi Israel Baal Shem Tov and his Son-in-Law R. Yehiel Michal to Rabbi Avraham Gershon of Kotov," *Sinai* 71 (1972): 248–269.

———. "More on the Correspondence of the Besht and his Son-in-Law to Rabbi Avraham Gershon of Kotov," *Sinai* 72 (1973): pp. 270–282.

Benayahu, Meir. *Hadat Vehahayim* [The Toledoth Ha-Ari and Luria's "Manner of Life" (Hanhagoth)]. Jerusalem, 1967.

Broyer, Mordechai. "The Emergence of *Pilpul* and *Hilukim* in the Ashkenazi Yeshivas." In *Sefer Hazikaron Larav Yehiel Yaakov Weinberg* [Book in memory of Rabbi Yehiel Yaakov Weinberg], pp. 241–255. Jerusalem, 1970.

Buber, Martin. "The Beginnings of Hasidism." *Moznayim* 11 (1940–41): 200–214.

———. *Bepardes Hahasidut* [In the orchard of Hasidism]. Jerusalem, 1979.

Dan, Joseph. *Hamistika Haivrit Hakeduma* [The ancient Jewish mysticism]. Tel Aviv, 1989.

———. *Hasippur Hahasidi* [The Hasidic story: Its history and development]. Jerusalem, 1975.

———. "The Entrance To the Sixth Gate." *Jerusalem Studies in Jewish Thought* 6 (1987): 197–220.

———. *Sifrut Hamussar Vehadrush* [Hebrew ethical and homiletical literature]. Jerusalem, 1975.

Dimitrovsky, Chaim Zalman. "On the Pilpulistic Method." In *Salo Wittmayer Baron Jubilee Volume* (Hebrew Section), pp. 111–181. Jerusalem, 1974.

Dinur, Ben Zion. "The Beginnings of Hasidism and its Social and Messianic Foundations." In *Bemifneh Hadorot: Mehkarim Veiyunim Bereshitam Shel Hazmanim Hahadashim Betoldot Israel* [At the change of generations: Studies and research on the beginnings of the modern era in Jewish history], pp. 83–227. Jerusalem, 1955.

Dubnow, Shimon. *Toldot Hahasidut* [History of Hasidism]. Tel Aviv, 1930–1931.

Eisenstein, J. D., ed. *Ozar Yisrael* [Encyclopedia of all matters concerning Jews and Judaism]. New York, 1951.

Elbaum, Jacob. *Tshuvat Halev Vekabbalat Yissurim: Iyunnim Beshitot Hatshuva Shel Hachmei Ashkenaz Vepolin* [Repentance and self-flagellation in the writings of the sages of Germany and Poland, 1348–1648]. Jerusalem, 1992.

Elior, Rachel. *Herut Al Haluhot: Hamahshava Hahasidit, Mekoroteha Hamistiyim Veyesodoteha Hakabbaliyim* [Hasidic thought: Mystical origins and kabbalistic foundations]. Tel Aviv, 1999.

———. "Kabbalah and Hasidism: Continuation or Change?" *Proceedings of the Ninth World Congress of Jewish Studies,* Division C, pp. 107–114. Jerusalem, 1986.

———. "R. Joseph Karo and R. Israel Baal Shem Tov: Mystical Metamorphosis, Kabbalistic Inspiration and Spiritual Internalisation." *Tarbiz* 65 (1996): 671–709.

Etkes, Immanuel. *Tenuat Hahasidut Bereshita* [The beginning of the Hasidic movement]. Tel Aviv, 1998.

——— [as Emanuel E.]. *Mehavura Letnuah: Tenuat Hahasidut Bereshita* [From esoteric circle to mass movement: The emergence of early Hasidism]. In *Polin* (Unit 9–10). The Open University, Tel Aviv, 1991.

———, ed. *Hadat Vehahayim: Tnuat Hahaskalah Hayehudit Bemizrah Eropa* [The East European Jewish Enlightenment], pp. 25–44. Jerusalem, 1993.

———. "Rabbi Shneur Zalman of Lyady as a Hasidic Leader." *Zion* 50 (1985): 321–354.

Feiner, Shmuel. "The Turning Point in the Evaluation of *Hasidism*: Eliezer Zweifel and the Moderate *Haskalah* in Russia." *Zion* 51 (1986): 167–210. Also published in the *East European Jewish Enlightenment*, ed. Immanuel Etkes, pp. 336–379. Jerusalem, 1993.

Friedlander, Yehuda. *Bemisterei Hasatira* [Hebrew satire in Europe in the nineteenth century]. Vol. 3. Ramat Gan, 1994.

Gries, Ze'ev. "Between Literature and History: Preface to a Discussion and Examination of *Shivhei Habesht,*" *Tura* 3 (1994): 166–169.

———. *Safrut Hahanhagot: Toldoteha Umekoma Behayei Hasidei R. Israel Baal Shem Tov* [Conduct literature, its history and place in the life of Beshtian Hasidism]. Jerusalem, 1989.

———. "The Transcription and Printing of Books of Kabbalah as a Study Method." *Mahanayim* 6 (1994): 204–211.

Halpern, Israel. "Associations for the Study of Torah and for Good Deeds and the Spread of the Hasidic Movement," *Yehudim Veyahadut Bemizrah Eropa* [Eastern European Jewry: Historical studies], pp. 313–332. Jerusalem, 1968.

———. *Haaliyot Harishonot Shel Hahasidim Leeretz Israel* [The Hasidic immigration to Palestine during the eighteenth century]. Jerusalem and Tel-Aviv, 1946.

———. "The Wozczylo Revolt and Its Jewish Aspect." *Zion* 22 (1957): 56–67.

Haran, Raya, "The Authenticity of Letters by Hasidim in Eretz Israel." *Cathedra* 55 (1990): 22–58.

———. "A Rejoinder to Criticism." *Cathedra* 64 (1992): 98–102.

Hillel, Moshe. *Baalei Shem.* Jerusalem, 1993.

Hisdai, Ya'akov. Reshit Darkam Shel Hahasidim Vehamitnagdim Leor Safrut Hadrush [The emergence of Hasidim and Mitnagdim in the light of the homiletic literature]. Ph.D. diss., Hebrew University, 1984.

———. "Eved Ha-Shem" (Servant of the Lord) in Early Hasidism." *Zion* 47 (1982): 253–292.

Horodetzky, Shmuel Abba. *Hahasidut Vehahasidim* [Hasidism and Hasidim]. Berlin, 1923.

Horowitz, Shmuel Yosef. "Hasidism and the Haskalah." In *He'atid,* book 2, 2nd ed., pp. 29–99. Berlin and Vienna, 1923.

Klauzner, Joseph. *Historia Shel Hasafrut Haivrit Hahadasha* [A history of modern Hebrew literature]. Vol. 1. Jerusalem, 1952.

Lieberman, Hayim. "How is Hasidism Studied in Israel?" In *Ohel Rachel* [Rachel's tent], 1:1–49, New York, 1980.

Liebes, Yehuda. *Sod Haemuna Hashabtait* [On Sabbateanism and its Kabbalah] *(Collected Essays).* Jerusalem, 1995.

Mahler, Raphael. *Divrei Yemei Yisrael: Dorot Aharonim* [History of the Jewish people in modern times]. Merhavia, 1962.

Marcus, Ivan G., ed. *Dat Vehevra Bemishnatam Shel Hasidei Ashkenaz* [The religious and social ideas of the Jewish pietists in medieval Germany]. Jerusalem, 1986.

Margaliot, Reuven. *Malachei Elyon* [Heavenly angels]. Jerusalem, 1945.

Mark, Tzvi. "*Dibbuk* and *Devekut* in *In Praise of the Baal Shem Tov:* Notes on the Phenomenology of Madness in Early Hasidism." In *Within Hasidic Circles: Studies in Hasidism in Memory of Mordecai Wilensky,* ed. Immanuel Etkes, David Assaf, Israel Bartal, and Elchanan Reiner, pp. 247–286. Jerusalem, 1999.

Matras, Hagit. Sifrei Segulot Verefuot Beivrit: Techanim Umekorot [Hebrew charm books: Contents and origins (based on books printed in Europe during the 18th century)]. Ph.D. diss., Hebrew University, 1997.

Mondshine, Yehoshua. "The Authenticity of Hasidic Letters." *Cathedra* 63 (1992): 65–97; 64 (1992): 79–97.

―――. "An Early Version of the 'Ascent of the Soul Epistle' by the Besht." In *Migdal Oz,* ed. Yehoshua Mondshine, pp. 119–126. Kfar Habad, 1980.

―――. "The Siddur of the Baal Shem Tov." In *Kovetz Siftei Zaddikim: Measef Letorat Hahasidut, Pirsum Genazeha Veheker Toldoteha* [An anthology of the doctrine of Hasidism, its archival documents and scholarship], pp. 72–100. Kislev, 1995.

Nigal, Gedalyah. *Baal Shem Lemaasar Olam* [A Ba'al Shem condemned to life sentence: The tragedy of R. Hirsch Fraenkel]. Ramat Gan, 1993.

―――. *Sipurei Dybbuk Besafrut Israel* [Dybbuk tales in Jewish literature]. Jerusalem, 1994.

―――. "The Figure of the Besht and His Philosophy." *Sinai* 120 (1997): 150–160.

―――. *Hasiporet Hahasidit: Toldoteha Venoseha* [The Hasidic tale: Its history and topics]. Jerusalem, 1981.

―――. "On R. Naftali Katz of Poznan." *Sinai* 92 (1983): 91–94.

―――. "A Primary Source for the Literature of Hasidic Tales: On *Keter Shem Tov* and its Sources." *Sinai* 79 (1976): pp. 132–146.

―――. "The Rabbi and Teacher of Israel Baal Shem Tov." *Sinai* 71 (1972): pp. 150–159.

Pachter, Mordechai. *Mitzfunot Zefat: Mehkarim Umekorot Letoldot Zefat Vehachameha Bameah ha-16* [From Safed's hidden treasures: Studies and texts concerning the history of Safed and its sages in the 16th century]. Jerusalem, 1994.

―――. *Safrut Hadrush Vehamussar Shel Hachmei Zefat Bameah ha-16: Maarechet Raayonoteha Haikarim* [Homiletic and ethical literature of Safed in the 16th century]. Ph.D. diss., Hebrew University, 1976.

―――. "Milei Deshmayah le-R. Elazar Azcari" [The Life and Personality of R. Elazar Azcari According to His Mystical Diary]. *Shalem* 3 (1981): 127–148.

―――, ed. *Milei DeShmaya le-Rabbi Elazar Azcari* [Heavenly words, by R. Elazar Azcari]. Haifa, 1991.

―――. "The Theory of Devekut in the Writings of the Sages of Safed in the Sixteenth Century." *Jerusalem Studies in Jewish Thought* 1, no. 3 (1982): pp. 51–121.

Pedia, Haviva. "On the Development of the Social-Religious-Economic Pattern in Hasidism: Ransom-payment, Fraternity and Immigration to the Land of Israel." In *Dat Vekalkalah Yahasei Gomlin* [Mutual relations in religion and economics]. ed. Menahem Ben Sasson, pp. 311–373. Jerusalem, 1995.

Piekarz, Mendel. *Biyemei Tzmihat Hahasidut: Megamot Raayoniyot Besifrei Drush Umussar* [The beginning of Hasidism: Ideological trends in Derush and Musar literature]. Jerusalem, 1978.

―――. *Bein Ideologiya Limetziut: Anava, Ayin, Bitul Mimetziut Vedevekut Bemahshavtam Shel Rashei Hahasidut* [Between ideology and reality: Humility, ayin, self-negation and devekut in the Hasidic thought]. Jerusalem, 1994.

———. "The Impetus For Early Anti-Hasidic Polemics." In *Within Hasidic Circles: Studies in Hasidism in Memory of Mordecai Wilensky*, ed. Immanuel Etkes, David Assaf, Israel Bartal, and Elchanan Reiner, pp. 3–20. Jerusalem, 1999.

Rabinowitcz, W. "Manuscripts From an Archive in Stolin." *Zion* 5 (1940): 125–132, 244–247.

Rappel, Dov. *Havikuach al Hapilpul* [The debate over pilpul]. Jerusalem, 1979.

Reiner, Elchanan. "In Praise of the Baal Shem Tov: Transmission, Editing, Printing." *Proceedings of the Eleventh World Congress of Jewish Studies*, Division C, 2:145–152. Jerusalem, 1994.

———. "Wealth, Social Position and the Study of Torah: The Status of the Kloiz in Eastern European Jewish Society in the Early Modern Period." *Zion* 58 (1993): 287–328.

———. "The *Yeshivas* of Poland and Ashkenaz During the Sixteenth and Seventeenth Centuries: Historical Developments." In *Keminhag Ashkenaz Upolin: Sefer Yovel le-Chone Shmeruk* [Studies in Jewish culture in honor of Chone Shmeruk], ed. Israel Bartal, Ezra Mendelsohn, and Chava Turniansky, pp. 9–80. Jerusalem, 1993.

Rivlin, Eliezer. *Hazaddik R. Yosef Zundel Misalant Verabotav.* [The *Zaddik* R. Yosef Zundel of Salant and his rabbis]. Jerusalem, 1927.

Rosman, Moshe., "The Besht's Letters: Towards a New Assessment." In *Studies in Hasidism, Jerusalem Studies in Jewish Thought*, no. 15, ed. David Assaf, Joseph Dan, and Immanuel Etkes, pp. 1–14. Jerusalem, 1999.

———. "The History of a Historical Source: On the Editing of *Shivhei Ha-Besht*." *Zion* 58, (1993): 175–214.

Rubinstein, Avraham, "The Besht's Epistle to R. Gershon of Kotov." *Sinai* 67 (1970): 120–138.

———. A Manuscript Version of the Besht's Epistle to R. Gershon of Kotov." *Sinai* 72 (1973): 189–202.

———. "The Mentor of R. Israel Ba'al Shem-Tov and the Sources of His Knowledge." *Tarbiz* 48 (1979): 146–158.

———. "A Possibly New Fragment of *Shivhei Ha-Besht*." *Tarbiz* 35 (1966): 174–191.

———. "The Revelation Stories of the Besht in the *Shivhei Ha-Besht*." *Alei Sefer* 6–7 (1979): 157–186.

Scholem, Gershom. "And the Mystery Remains." *Bhinot* 8 (1955): 79–95.

———. "Chapters in Sabbatian Research." *Zion* 6 (1941): 85–100.

———. "A Document by the Disciples of Isaac Luria." *Zion*, 5 (1940), pp. 133–160.

———. *Hakabbalah Vesmaleha* [Elements of the Kabbalah and its symbolism]. Jerusalem, 1976.

———. "The Historical Figure of R. Israel Baal Shem Tov." In his *Dvarim Bego*, pp. 287–324. Tel Aviv, 1975.

———. "More About Rabbi Adam Baal Shem." *Zion* 7 (1941–1942): 28.

———. "The Sabbatean Prophet R. Heschil Tsoref: R. Adam Baal Shem." *Zion* 6 (1941): 85–100.

———. *Mehkarim Umekorot Letoldot Hashabtaut Vegilguleha* [Studies and texts concerning the history of Sabbetianism and its metamorphoses]. Jerusalem, 1974.

———. "The Two First Testimonies on the Relations between Hasidic Groups and Baal-Shem-Tov." *Tarbiz* 20 (1950): 228–240.

———. "Two Letters From Palestine: 1760–1764." *Tarbiz* 25 (1955): 429–440.

Shachar, Yeshayahu. *Bikoret Hahevra Vehanhagat Hatzibur Besafrut Hamussar Vehadrush Bepolin Bameah ha-18* [Criticism of society and leadership in the Musar and Drush literature in 18th-century Poland]. Jerusalem, 1992.

Sheffer, Peter. *Synopsis Lesafrut Hahekhalot* [Synopsis of Hekhalot literature]. Tübingen, 1981.

Shiffer, Yitzhak. "R. Israel Baal Shem Tov and His Figure in Early Hasidic Literature." *Hadoar* 39 (1959–60): 525–532.

Shmeruk Chone. "The Hasidic Movement and the 'Arendars.'" *Zion* 35 (1970): 182–192.

———. "The Social Significance of the Hasidic Shekhita." *Zion* 20 (1955): 47–72.

———. "Tales About R. Adam Baal Shem in the Versions of Shivkhei Ha Besht." *Zion* 28 (1963): 86–105.

——— [as Khone Shmeruk]. *Safrut Yiddish: Prakin Letoldoteha* [Yiddish literature: Aspects of its history]. Tel Aviv, 1978.

———. *Safrut Yiddish Bepolin* [Yiddish literature in Poland: Historical studies and perspectives]. Jerusalem, 1981.

Shochat, Azriel. "On Joy in Hasidism." *Zion* 16 (1951): 30–43.

Stiman-Katz, Haya. *Reshitan Shel Aliyot Hahasidim* [Early Hasidic immigration to Eretz-Israel]. Jerusalem, 1986.

Tamar, David. *Mehkarim Betoldot Hayehudim Beeretz Israel Ubeitaliya* [Studies in the history of the Jewish people in Eretz Israel and Italy]. Jerusalem, 1973.

Teller, Adam. "The Sluck Tradition Concerning the Early Days of the Besht." *Studies in Hasidism, Jerusalem Studies in Jewish Thought*, no. 15, ed. David Assaf, Joseph Dan, and Immanuel Etkes, pp. 15–38. Jerusalem, 1999.

Tishbi, Isaiah. *Torat Hara Vehaklipa Bekabbalat ha-Ari* [The doctrine of evil and the kelippah in Lurianic Kabbalism]. Jerusalem, 1960.

———. "The Influence of Rabbi Moses Hayyim Luzzatto in Hasidic Teaching." *Zion* 43 (1978): 201–234.

———. "The Messianic Idea and Messianic Trends in the Growth of Hasidism." *Zion* 32 (1967): 1–45.

———. *Mishnat Hazohar* [The wisdom of the Zohar: Texts from the *Book of Splendour*]. 2 vols. Jerusalem, 1949–1961.

———, and J. Dan. "Hasidism: Doctrine and Literature." *Encyclopaedia Hebraica*, 17: 769–822. Jerusalem and Tel Aviv, 1965.

Weiss, Joseph, "Beginnings of Hasidism." *Zion* 16 (1951): 46–105.

———. "Study of the Torah in Israel Baal Shem's Doctrine." *Essays Presented to Chief Rabbi Israel Brodie on the Occasion of His Seventieth Birthday,* ed. H. J. Zimmels, J. Rabbinowitz, and I. Finestein [Hebrew Volume], pp. 151–170. London, 1967.

Werses, Shmuel, "Folklore in the Work of Mendele." *Dappim: Research in Literature* 9 (1994): 7–27.

———. "Hasidism as Viewed in Haskalah Literature: From the Debates of the Galicean Maskilim." In *Megamot Vetzurot Besafrut Hahaskalah* [Trends and forms in Haskalah literature], 91–109. Jerusalem, 1990.

——— [as Verses, Shmuel]. "Magical and Demonological Phenomena as Treated Satirically by Maskilim of Galicia," *Jerusalem Studies in Jewish Folklore* 17 (1995): 33–62.

Yaari, Avraham. "The Burning of the Talmud in Kamenets Podolsk" *Sinai* 42 (1958): 294–306.

———. *Taalumat Sefer: Sefer "Hemdat Yamim," Mi Hibro Umeh Haytah Midat Hashpaato,* [Mystery of a book: *Hemdat Yamim,* who composed it and how influential was it]. Jerusalem, 1954.

———. "Two Basic Recensions of *Shivhe-Hai-Besht.*" *Kirjath Sepher* 39 (1964): 249–272, 394–407, 552–562.

Yudelov, Yitzchak. "The Book *Chelkat Reuven.*" *Alei Sefer* 14 (1987): 139–142.

Zfatman, Sara. *Nisuei Adam Vesheda* [The marriage of a mortal man and a she-demon]. Jerusalem, 1987.

Zweifel, Eliezer Zvi Hacohen. Introduction to *Shalom al Israel,* ed. Avraham Rubinstein. 1: 7–34. Jerusalem, 1973.

Secondary Sources (English)

Assaf, David. *"The Regal Way": The Life and Times of Rabbi Israel of Ruzhin.* Stanford, Calif., 2002.

Barnai, Jacob. "Some Clarifications on the Land of Israel's Stories of *In Praise of the Baal Shem Tov.*" *Revue des Etudes Juives* 146 (1987): 367–380.

Ben-Amos, Dan, and Jerome R. Mintz. *In Praise of the Baal Shem Tov.* Bloomington, Ind., 1970.

Buber, Martin. *Hasidism.* New York, 1948.

Cavendish, Richard. *A History of Magic.* London, 1990.

Cohen, Richard I. *Jewish Icons: Art and Society in Modern Europe.* University of California Press, Los Angeles, 1998.

Dubnow, Semen Marcovich. *History of the Jews in Russia and Poland.* Philadelphia, 1916.

Eliade, Mircea. *Shamanism: Archaic Techniques of Ecstasy.* Princeton, N.J., 1972.

Elior, Rachel. "The Concept of God in Hekhalot Mysticism." *Binah* 2 (1989): 97–129.

Etkes, Immanuel. *The Gaon of Vilna: The Man and His Image.* Berkeley and Los Angeles, Calif., 2002.

———. "Hasidism as a Movement: The First Stage." In *Hasidism: Continuity or Innovation,* ed. Bezalel Safran, 1–26. Cambridge, Mass., 1988.

———. "The Historical Besht: Reconstruction or Deconstruction?" *Polin* 12 (1999): 297–306.

———. "Immanent Factors and External Influences in the Development of the Haskalah Movement in Russia." In *Toward Modernity: The European Jewish Model,* ed. Jacob Katz, 13–32. New York, 1987.

———. "The Study of Hasidism: Past Trends and New Directions." In *Hasidism Reappraised,* ed. Ada Rappoport-Albert, 447–464. London, 1996.

Fishman, David E. *Russia's First Modern Jews: The Jews of Shklov.* New York, 1995.

Flint, Valerie I. J. *The Rise of Magic in Early Medieval Europe.* Princeton, 1991.

Graetz, Heinrich. *History of the Jews.* Philadelphia, 1967.

Hazard, Paul. *The European Mind, 1680–1715.* Harmondsworth, England, 1964.

Heiler, Frederick. *Prayer.* New York, 1958.

Heschel, Joshua Abraham. *The Prophets.* New York, 1962.

Idel, Moshe. *Hasidism: Between Ecstasy and Magic.* New York, 1995.

———. "Jewish Magic from the Renaissance Period to Early Hasidism." In *Religion, Science, and Magic,* ed. J. Neusner, E. S. Frerichs, and P. V. M. Flesher, pp. 82–117. New York and Oxford, 1989.

———. *Kabbalah: New Perspectives.* New Haven, 1998.

Jacobs, Louis. "The Concept of Hasid in Biblical and Rabbinic Literature." *Journal of Jewish Studies* 8 (1957): 143–154.

Laski, Marghatina. *Ecstasy.* Los Angeles, Calif., 1990.

Lewis, Ioan Myrddin. *Ecstatic Religion: A Study of Shamanism and Spirit Possession.* London, 1989.

Loewenthal, Naftali. *Communicating the Infinite.* Chicago, 1990.

Nigal, Gedalyah. *Magic, Mysticism and Hasidism: The Supernatural in Jewish Thought.* London, 1994.

———. "New Light on the Hasidic Tale and its Sources." In *Hasidism Reappraised,* ed. Ada Rappoport-Albert, pp. 345–353. London, 1996.

Rapoport-Albert, Ada. "God and the Tsadik as Two Focal Points of Hasidic Worship." *History of Religion* 18 (1979): 296–325.

———. "Hagiography with Footnotes: Edifying Tales and the Writing of History in Hasidism." In *Essays in Jewish Historiography,* pp. 119–159. *History and Theory,* no. 27. Atlanta, 1991.

———. "Hasidism After 1772: Structural Continuity and Change." In *Hasidism Reappraised,* ed. Ada Rappoport-Albert, pp. 76–141. London, 1996.

Rosman, Moshe. *Founder of Hasidism: A Quest for the Historical Ba'al Shem Tov.* Berkeley, Calif., 1996.

———. "Miedzybóz and Rabbi Israel Baal Shem Tov." In *Essential Papers on Hasidism,* ed. Gershon D. Hundert, pp. 209–225, New York, 1991.

Rosman, Murray Jay. *The Lord's Jews.* Cambridge, 1990.

Schatz-Uffenheimer, Rivka. *Hasidism as Mysticism: Quietistic Elements in 18th Century Hasidic Thought.* Jerusalem, 1993.

Schechter, Solomon. *Studies in Judaism.* Philadelphia, 1908.

Scholem, Gershom. "Devekut, or Communion With God." In his *The Messianic Idea in Judaism,* pp. 203–227. New York, 1971.

———. *Kabbalah.* Jerusalem, 1974.

———. *Major Trends in Jewish Mysticism.* New York, 1941.

———. "Martin Buber's Hasidism: A Critique." *Commentary* 32 (1961): 305–316.

———. "The Meaning of the Torah in Jewish Mysticism." In his *On the Kabbalah and Its Symbolism,* pp. 32–86. New York, 1965.

———. "The Neutralization of the Messianic Element in Early Hasidism." In his *The Messianic Idea in Judaism,* pp. 176–202. New York, 1971.

Schrire, Theodore. *Hebrew Amulets.* London, 1966.

Thomas, Keith. *Religion and the Decline of Magic.* London, 1971.

Trachtenberg, Joshua. *Jewish Magic and Superstition.* New York, 1970.

Underhill, Evelyn. *Mysticism.* London, 1945.

Urbach, Ephrayim E. *The Sages: Their Concepts and Beliefs.* Jerusalem, 1979.

Weiss, Joseph. "A Circle of Pneumatics in Pre-Hasidism." In his *Studies in Eastern European Jewish Mysticism,* pp. 27–42. Oxford, 1985.

———. "The Kavvanoth of Prayer in Early Hasidism." In his *Studies in Eastern European Jewish Mysticism,* pp. 95–125. Oxford, 1985.

———. "Torah Study in Early Hasidism." In his *Studies in Eastern European Jewish Mysticism,* pp. 56–68. Oxford, 1985.

Werblowsky, Zwi R. J. *Joseph Karo, Lawyer and Mystic.* Philadelphia, 1980.

Zinberg, Israel. *A History of Jewish Literature.* Vol. 7. Cincinnati, Ohio, 1975.

INDEX